ROYCE'S MATURE PHILOSOPHY OF RELIGION

Royce's Mature Philosophy of Religion

Frank M. Oppenheim

UNIVERSITY OF NOTRE DAME PRESS
Notre Dame, Indiana

B
945
.R64
O657
1987

Copyright © 1987 by
University of Notre Dame Press
Notre Dame, Indiana 46556
All Rights Reserved

Manufactured in the United States of America

Library of Congress Cataloging-in-Publication Data

Oppenheim, Frank M., 1925–
   Royce's mature philosophy of religion.

   Includes index.
   1. Royce, Josiah, 1855–1916 – Contributions in
philosophy of religion. 2. Royce, Josiah, 1855–1916.
Problem of Christianity. I. Title.
B945.R640657   1987   200'.1   87-12458
ISBN 0-268-01633-X

Contents

Foreword	vii
Preface	xi
Chronology	xvii

I. ROYCE BECOMES AN INTERPRETER OF PROBLEMATIC CHRISTIANITY

1. Growing through Philosophy, Pain, and Prayer	3
2. Developing a Mature Philosophy of Religion	20
3. Creating a Pure Logic and Methodology	43
4. A General Science of Order, System Σ	54
5. Genesis of Σ and Its Application	72

II. ROYCE EXPLORES THE HUMAN INTERESTS THAT PRODUCE RELIGIOUS EXPERIENCES

6. The Seven Sources of Elementary Religious Experience	91
7. The Most Basic Structure of Elementary Religious Experience	106
8. The Social Form of Complex Religious Experience	122
9. Orientation to *The Problem of Christianity*	144
10. Overview of *The Problem of Christianity*	160

III. ROYCE DEVELOPS HIS MATURE METHOD

11. Introduction to Royce's Method	173
12. Empirico-Historical Method: First Stage	183
13. Empirico-Historical Method: Second and Third Stages	205
14. An Instance of the Second Stage: Royce Muses on the Idea of Community	219

15. Metaphysical Method	231
16. Underlying General Method: Interpretive Musement	264

IV. ROYCE'S MUSEMENT ENLIVENS HIS DOCTRINE

17. Loyalty: Center of Christianity and of Human Interests	283
18. Simplification for the Greater Unity of Christians	292

V. TOWARDS A CRITICAL APPRECIATION OF ROYCE

19. Evaluation of Strengths and Weaknesses	309
20. Contribution to Method for Philosophy of Religion	324
21. The "Christian" Future of the Universe	335
Epilogue	345
Abbreviations and Short Titles	347
Notes	349
Appendix	389
Index of Names	395
Index of Topics	397

Foreword

In an article in *Harvard Magazine's* March/April issue of 1978 Dorothy Rieber Joralemon gives a delightful quote of her father, Charles Henry Rieber: "All that will be remembered of Harvard, five hundred years from now, will be that Josiah Royce once taught there." Presently, it almost looks as if the opposite were true; namely, that anything but Royce is remembered at and about Harvard. But Frank Oppenheim's study gives every reason to assume that the present forgetting is merely a temporary lapse of memory and that the small man from Cambridge's Irving Street was, in fact, not only a great philosophical mind but also a momentous prophet whose importance rests on a penetrating insight and foresight which are bound to find recognition again, and a lasting one for that matter.

The biographical approach, with which the present work starts, is part of a penetrating acknowledgment of the need for historical appreciation. This corresponds with Royce's own interest in the historical dimensions of thought. It is not only Royce's own self-understanding which is reflected here but also the entire intellectual experience of "that man from California." The consistency of Royce's approach in *The Problem of Christianity* with his previous work has been called into question many a time since the appearance of that monumental work. A major contribution of Oppenheim's analysis to Royce scholarship is the proof that Royce's intellectual and spiritual development are interrelated. The comprehensive combination of philosophical and of theological reflection in the *Problem,* therefore, is no longer a surprise.

By testing major concepts of the *Problem* against the life and thought of Royce, Oppenheim proves that they have grown naturally and consistently with the philosopher. It is shown that Royce's own life verifies his conviction that there is meaning in history, a radical unity, in fact, of meaning and of truth, and that religious experience and the interpretation thereof are major expressions of that unity.

We learn, moreover, that the *Problem* is consciously and closely related to contemporary history, especially to the situations of philosophy, of religion, and, in particular, of Christianity. The discussion of the thoughts of two of his philosopher friends, William James and Charles Peirce, is prominent in the two volumes of the *Problem*. Although concurring with

James' emphasis on unique individuals, Royce sharply scored the individualistic doctrine of James because it affirmed that the human person need not be attached to, or concerned about, the life and interests of communities. By contrast, Peirce's notion of interpretation and, specifically, of the community of interpretation, became of focal importance in Royce's second volume.

Oppenheim stresses that Royce's approach is a social one. He argues strongly that this anti-individualistic stance is that of a leader of the twentieth century who uncovers a universal pedagogy and reveals the momentum of history at work. Oppenheim quite rightly points out that Royce appreciatively grasped this pedagogy and momentum, not through a solitary insight, but through communication among minded people. It happens among and with a dialoguing community, that is, a community of interpretation.

One of the most helpful observations of Oppenheim is that the strong interest in method, which Royce had demonstrated in his earlier works, is not lost in the *Problem* but culminates there, as the composition and style of the *Problem* prove. The deceptively simple and general language at the start, for instance, is very consciously not definite, and so it protests against an ever increasing, overstated, and, in most cases, premature preoccupation with linguistic precision, which kills the integral life of the subject matter at hand before it is even recognized, let alone appreciated. This avoidance of complexity in the beginning of the *Problem* is but the first indication of a continuous and methodical self-limitation which increases the focus of perception and the precision of the presentation.

Royce's interest in method coincided with his interest in logic, which culminated in his essay, "The Principles of Logic," published in 1912. The reader and interpreter of Royce is bewildered by the close temporal proximity of this major study on logic and the lectures on the "Problem of Christianity" because there appears little or no relationship or correspondence between either work. Royce seems intent on hiding his "other" interest in each case from the respective audience. But Oppenheim shows in an ingenious way how the two approaches and answers of Royce correspond and complement each other. The relational and functional character of Royce's logic is shown, demonstrating its relationship to and importance for the concepts of interpretation and community. The Royce reader learns also of the intrinsically logical dimensions of the structure of questions, arguments, and propositions in the *Problem*. Thus Oppenheim makes a strong case for understanding Royce as a major contributor to the vexing as well as vital debate about the relationship of praxis and theory. Although not immediately addressed, it should be observed, too, that the student of the later Wittgenstein might benefit from this particular part of Oppenheim's discussion of Royce.

Oppenheim advises his readers that Royce moves away from the tendency of turning method into abstraction and that, instead, he develops a method which is concrete—not just subject-related but life-related. The biblical scholar is happy to note that in this enterprise interpretation is not an abstract postulate but that Royce includes an actual and a very comprehensive interpretation of Scriptures, both imaginative and stimulating. Royce's anticipation of much later insights of professional biblical scholarship is truly remarkable and proves his prophetic instinct. Royce's unique contribution to hermeneutics, i.e., to the theory of the art of understanding, sketched by Oppenheim, has yet to be recognized by the established representatives of that discipline. The particular communal experience of Pauline Christianity becomes for Royce a valuable hermeneutical model. In it he can demonstrate that interpretation and understanding happen in a historical context and that such particular interpretive musement is representative for universal human experience. In so doing, Royce, according to Oppenheim, presents a new metaphysics of the universe. In the *Problem,* then, Royce sensed and stressed the corporate and historical dynamisms at work within the interpretation process more concretely and skillfully than Bultmann or Heidegger have done. For these reasons, in his mature work, Royce considerably surpassed Bultmann as an interpreter of the New Testament.

Oppenheim's description of Royce as a pathfinding pilgrim of Christianity provides us with a stimulating picture of a constructive social critic. In the universal crisis of world society today he presents another option besides the chaos of individualism and the cemetery of totalitarianism, — that of the community of interpretation, the concept of Charles Peirce as sharpened and as comprehensively applied by Josiah Royce. I am certain that the reader will leave Oppenheim's study as enriched as I did. I am grateful for the new perspectives I received from my friend Frank for the reading of Royce. They will greatly enhance my own scholarship in a field other than philosophy.

                            Dieter Georgi
                            Frothingham Professor of Biblical Studies
                            Harvard University

Preface

Josiah Royce described his last major work, during its composition, as follows:

> My lectures on "The Problem of Christianity,". . . will be a definite effort to interpret the essence of Christianity in the light of some of its leading ideas, as these gradually developed in apostolic and post apostolic churches, and as these same ideas are with us (as developing, and not as finished ideas) today, not only in the Church but in the world.[1]

This quotation integrates many complex facets, organizing compactly most of the main ideas of his *Problem of Christianity:* will to interpret, essence, ideas and their development, communities, time, Church, and the processing universe. The quotation illustrates a rhetoric requiring wide parameters and reveals a mind "trying to control a bursting complexity of thought."[2] Most significantly, since this statement in a letter to a friend is marked by closeness of personal touch, breadth of range, and the coherence of a unified synoptic view, it expresses the insight of a far-seeing sage.[3]

The present study aims to bring the American philosopher Josiah Royce (1855-1916) out of the shadows that often cover his final decade. More specifically, it aims to discover and to present accurately the method and doctrine of the mature Royce (1912-1916) in his late philosophy of religion. Still more precisely, it aims carefully to search out from Royce's *The Problem of Christianity* his principal and subordinate methods and accurately to identify his human and "Christian" doctrines as rooted in experience. Through these methods and doctrines, Royce refined from communal religious experiences a core of reasonable affirmations which he called the "sword of the spirit." He predicted that, from the human side, this doctrine would vivify religion and keep it in touch with the basic ethico-religious needs of humankind, even amid the deep cultural changes that he foresaw would become ever more rapid.

Royce's *Problem of Christianity* was a suffering sage's gift that climaxed his forty-year experience of the philosophy of religion and his reflections on it. This work constitutes our principal source. Careful attention must also be given to the developmental context which Royce drew upon when he wrote the *Problem.* In this context some of the most noteworthy influences are his "Principles of Logic" (1910) and his experientially based *Sources of Religious Insight* (1912).

The present work does not provide an intellectual biography of Royce. For that, one need only consult John Clendenning's second significant contribution to Roycean studies, *The Life and Thought of Josiah Royce*.[4] Rather, I imitate the steps that one takes when coming to know a person empathetically yet realistically. Only with such knowledge can one be fair and accurate in one's appreciative understanding of an author's central ideas and ways. And only by having won such an understanding may one finally venture an evaluation.

Accordingly, we can better understand the mature Royce as a philosopher of religion if we first assemble the relevant parts of his background (part one). These included incidents in his life pertinent to his religious philosophy, preduring themes in his decades-long research into the philosophy of religion, the relation of his "Principles of Logic" to the *Problem,* and his initial options for directing the course of the latter work.

The needed background must also include a summary of the method and doctrine which Royce presented in his late "philosophy of religion in general" (part two). He approached this topic from an experiential and developmental perspective in his *Sources of Religious Insight,* drafted in 1911. Of this work, written just a year before the *Problem,* he said, "It contains the whole sense of me in a brief compass."[5] In this work he utilized his four previous decades of reflection on the philosophy of religion. He thus equipped himself in the *Sources* with the "principles" he was to use in the forthcoming application of his philosophy of religion to Christianity. Moreover, his experiential method in the *Sources* called for a parallel approach in the *Problem.*

Once this background has been erected, my central intent focuses on the *Problem* itself. First and foremost, I bring to center stage Royce's philosophical method (part three). I start with the distinctive methods he tailored for the two Parts of the *Problem.* I then search for his general method which permeates and unifies the whole work. Then, in part four, I examine his chief doctrines, especially that of genuine loyalty and of the simplification of certain traditional problems. These four parts of the present work supply the reader with enough evidence to evaluate the mature Royce's method and doctrine in the *Problem* in part five. The task in this evaluation may be formulated as a call to appraise Royce's final pair of imperatives: 1) Theoretically, *believe in* the Universal Community, its Spirit, the triadic mode of interpretive knowing, the universal doctrine of signs, and the "Christian" doctrine of life; and 2) Practically, through one's ordinary daily choices wherein one embodies the foregoing theoretical belief, *acknowledge* the Interpreter-Spirit's saving presence in the Universal Community.

I close by showing how Josiah Royce, as a twentieth-century John the Baptist, points to the Interpreter-Spirit of the Universal Community. The Spirit calls each person to engage in loyal, even atoning, deeds. The Spirit invites each person along a time-tested, yet further refined and newly formulated, ethico-religious path that leads to the "Christian" upbuilding and development of humankind's Great Community.

My intent in the present work is to witness that the mature Royce identified and carried out, in a generally successful way, both a new and fully human method of philosophizing and a Christian metaphysics of community. Several reasons lead me to offer this witness. In the history of American philosophy, a variety of factors has led to a frequent misrepresentation of Royce.

Pragmatism and the New Realism won center stage after 1907, in part by stereotyping Royce as a romantic mystic, an unoriginal mouthpiece of German idealism, a non-developing advocate of a detached Absolute, and an Hegelian holder of a "block universe." Royce's image was further distorted by caricaturing his physical features or rhetorical style. Amid Americans' preoccupations with World War I and their problems and projects following that war, Royce's claim went largely unnoticed that his late "Peircean insight" had worked as great a transformation of his philosophy as had his initial "religious insight." Instead, the mood of the post–World War I years fixed upon Royce labels like "Germanic" and "Hegelian" without taking into account either Royce's direct disclaimers[6] or his post-1912 developments. Meanwhile, over in France, Gabriel Marcel had accurately discerned that the Royce of *The Problem of Christianity* had finally found *the medium and method* which fit his deepest self and that this 1912 transformation of Royce's philosophy was needed not only to communicate his basic message successfully but even to have it "essentially understood."[7] However, as the American philosophic temper became increasingly desacralized from 1920 to 1960, Marcel's discovery drew scant attention and the "straw man" Royce, the "religious philosopher irrelevant to American reality," became increasingly dominant.[8] As an overall result, then, if Royce has not been simply discarded, he has usually been consigned to oblivion—benign or otherwise.

What place, then, does the present study have amid the fresh scholarship that is rejuvenating the history of classical American philosophy? Critical editions of the entire works of Charles S. Peirce, William James, George Santayana, and John Dewey are well under way.[9] Only recently has a definitive edition of Royce's works taken embryonic form. Until the fruit of this Royce edition is published, we have a helpful interim tool in John J.

McDermott's edition of *The Basic Writings of Josiah Royce* (2 vols.), which also includes the editor's well-balanced introduction and Ignas Skrupskelis' scholarly bibliography. The careful research of John Clendenning has provided what is likely the most significant recent support for Roycean studies, first in his *The Letters of Josiah Royce* (1970) and recently in his *Life and Thought of Josiah Royce* (1985). The recent histories of American philosophy by Flower-Murphey and Bruce Kuklick advanced Roycean studies by presenting a more sensitive and accurate reading of Royce. In the present study the interpretations of Royce usually concur with those of Flower-Murphey and Kuklick. Yet I here emphasize that the mature Royce's personal and communal rationality is historically experiential, interpretively insightful, realistically affective, religiously evaluative, and steadfastly loyal. However, all these major studies, even when complemented by the unmentioned dozens of recent Roycean articles, cannot in ensemble grasp adequately that mind of Royce, "trying to control a bursting complexity of thought."

How, then, does the present work aim to contribute to Roycean studies? To borrow one of Royce's resolute phrases, I trust it will "lead to a fairer understanding" of that man from California. Counterbalancing the present work's lengthy treatment of the way Royce's late logic relates to the *Problem,* my main emphasis is on the mature Royce's concern for communal life in the unity of the spirit, for that genuine freedom and individuality which arise only in community. This emphasis aims at a better balanced portrait of Royce. By his own acknowledgment,[10] Community and Spirit became the governing ideas of his mature years. Both lie beyond the grasp of the conceptual analytic method of most modern logic. Already in 1892 Royce had tried to indicate this difference by calling for a shift from the "world of description" to the "world of appreciation."[11] The latter is the communal life of minded beings who share their freely appropriated common values. Only in the latter world can there arise the mature Royce's "insight," namely, an appreciative knowledge characterized by "breadth of range, coherence and unity of view, and closeness of personal touch." For the mature Royce, then, the only way to enter insightfully into communal life is through the intent of an interpreter to eventually unify two or more minded beings by the inventive or creative discovery of a "third" idea that mediates them. Of course, this "interpretive musement" of Royce has its own logic—of the unfamiliar "pathfinder" kind. But equally important ingredients in his progressive serial insights are loyal love of community, sensitivity to human frailty, and participation in a suffering servant role—all meant to reconcile human selves within a "unity in the spirit."

Helping me produce this work has been a large "community of the loyal." I am grateful to all its members. But I am so specially indebted to several groups within this vast community that I should offer public thanks to Professors Peter Bertocci, John Clendenning, the late James Collins, Leonard Eslick, Robert Evans, Max Fisch, Peter Fuss, Dieter Georgi, Richard Hocking, John McDermott, Ignas Scrupskelis, and John E. Smith for offering ideas, suggestions, and healthy criticisms; to John Brooks, John Fitzgerald, and David Van Vactor for stylistic recommendations; to my fellow Jesuits, particularly Joseph Appleyard, Walter Bado, Joseph Bracken, Richard Deters, Daniel Flaherty, Robert Harvanek, Michael Perko, Daniel Price, the late Thomas Savage, Robert Schmidt, Murel Vogel, and Bernard Wuellner, as well as to the Jesuit Communities at LaFarge House, Schott Residence, Espinal Community, and especially to the John C. Murray Writers Group and the Chicago Province of the Society of Jesus.

I would also like to express publicly my gratitude to countless library staff members, archivists, and reference librarians at Harvard, Berkeley, Xavier, and other Roycean deposits for efficient service and courtesies far beyond the call of duty, to Nancy Hacker for preserving Royce family records; and to Eunice Staples, Helen Cecilia Swift, and others for their dedicated secretarial services. I am most indebted and grateful, however, to David J. Hassel, S.J., who supported, encouraged, and inspired this entire work, and who, during my brief African mission, midwifed the manuscript into yet another of its drafts. More than any other person, he has made this book possible. Yet to none of these benefactors can the responsibility for any remaining inadequacies and errors be attributed because these are my own doing.

What efforts I have invested in this work will be amply repaid if the readers should somehow experience with Royce a growing conviction that "religious problems, . . . of all human interests, deserve our best efforts and our utmost loyalty."[12]

Xavier University
Cincinnati, Ohio

Chronology

1855	Josiah Royce born in the mining town of Grass Valley, California (November 20).
1866	The Royce family moves to San Francisco where Josiah enters Lincoln Grammar School and later Boys' High School in 1869.
1875	Receives B.A. degree from the University of California; spends the next school year in Germany and the following two in Baltimore at the Johns Hopkins University completing his doctoral studies in philosophy.
1878	Returns to Berkeley as lecturer in the English Department of the University of California.
1880	Marries Katharine Head; their son Christopher is born 18 months later.
1882	Joins the faculty of Harvard University as an instructor in philosophy; he brings his young family to Cambridge, Massachusetts.
1883	Gains his "religious insight" into the actuality of an all-knowing Absolute; published in *The Religious Aspect of Philosophy* (1885).
1888	Suffers a nervous breakdown; his health voyage to Australia so enriches his religious insight that hereafter he appreciates the all-Knower as also absolute Experience and Will.
1892	Appointed professor of the history of philosophy at Harvard; publishes *The Spirit of Modern Philosophy*.
1896	Discovers his ultimate ethical insight into "the individual," whom he defines pragmatically as "the object of exclusive interest" — published in his supplementary essay to *The Conception of God*.
1899–1900	Royce presents the Gifford Lectures at the University of Aberdeen, published in two volumes as *The World and the Individual* (1899–1901).
1902	Urged by Peirce, Royce starts his fourteen years of in-depth study of logic.

1905	Extending the work of British logician A. B. Kempe, Royce publishes "The Relation of the Principles of Logic to the Foundations of Geometry."
1908	*Philosophy of Loyalty* published; its conclusion leads him both to wonder what is vital in Christianity and to investigate the Christian religion directly as a philosopher.
1910	Creates "The Principles of Logic"; son Christopher and Wm. James die.
1911	Delivers the Bross Lectures, his experientially based general philosophy of religion; published as *The Sources of Religious Insight* (1912).
1912	After suffering a stroke, he reads Christian theologians and scrutinizes Peirce's intellectual development. He reaches his insight into Peirce's theory of signs and method of interpretation. Thus prepared, Royce employs a new philosophical medium, method, and message with depth and ease when drafting his lectures on Christianity.
1913	Delivers the complete set of these lectures to the Hibbert Foundation, Manchester College, Oxford University; published as *The Problem of Christianity*.
1914	During a lecture at Berkeley, he narrates how his Peircean insight dawned.
1916	Royce dies in Cambridge, Massachusetts (September 14).

PART ONE

Royce Becomes an Interpreter of Problematic Christianity

1. Growing through Philosophy, Pain, and Prayer

The temperament of a person is what determines his or her philosophy. Both William James and Josiah Royce held this view, but Royce refined it by identifying more accurately the radical determinant of one's philosophy: the "*essential* temperament."[1] By this he meant one's carefully cultivated temperament, one's historically purified set of values. By "essential temperament," then, Royce meant neither that uniqueness of a child's promising potential—such as he had in Grass Valley—nor the instinctual bearing of an adolescent's undisciplined urges—such as he felt rising up in rebellion while at Boys' High School in San Francisco.

Since the present work considers Royce's late philosophy of religion, it needs to identify his own essential temperament as the control point of his philosophy. What values and insights survived and intensified in his mind after his lengthy scrutiny of the positions of philosophers through the centuries, and, especially, after fifty years of life had tested him? Surely his late testimony that "these two ideas, the Community and the Spirit," had grown in vitality in his mature mind reveals critically important foci in this thinker's essential temperament.[2] Yet the whole set of cultivated values, choices, habits, and ideas which emerged through Royce's "more insistent self-criticism" were part of the essential temperament which he recognized as the root of his philosophy.

He often tried to get in touch with this historically refined core of his philosophical self-identity for he frequently reconsidered the highpoints of his own philosophical growth. Recognizing that the possibility of factual human error requires the actuality of an infinite all-Knower, he had come to his "religious insight" of 1883. He regarded it as definitive of that basic philosophical orientation which he maintained during the rest of his life.[3] Looking back on his earlier years from 1875 to 1882, he described himself in that period as a "decidedly skeptical critical empiricist."[4] So we may call this his "pre-formed" period and the years from 1883 to his death in 1916 his "formed" period. During his career at Harvard—the thirty-three years of his formed period—Royce steadily drew upon his 1883 religious insight, the root of his ever constant yet always developing philosophy of religious idealism. From 1883 to 1916 the most varied theoretical and practical problems challenged his mind and heart. Royce recognized that through them his intellectual development showed momentous advances even while always intensifying his radical philosophical self-identity, first formed in 1883.

During his formed period, he broke through to his two remaining maximal insights: individuality in 1896 and interpretation in 1912. The decisive influence of these insights is my basis for subdividing his formed period into the early Harvard Royce (1883-1895), the middle Royce (1896-1911), and the mature Royce (1912-1916). In 1912, when Royce succeeded in grasping at a hitherto unknown depth the "simplest ideas" and method of Charles Sanders Peirce, the resultant understanding transformed Royce's philosophical mind, inspired his mature philosophy of religion, and culminated in his masterpiece, *The Problem of Christianity*.[5]

Leading up to this, many movements in America—historical, political, cultural, academic, familial, and personal—had impinged on Royce's life. To identify these influences, we first scan the main events *of religious moment* in the life of this philosopher of religion.[6] Then, since he was undergoing an unplanned but mysterious schooling through his experiences of interpretation, evil, and salvation, we next probe to find how these lessons of life affected his mature philosophy of religion. Finally, since he held that religion lies in our union with God, we focus on his own personal rapport with the divine—specifically on his prayer-life. The evidence thus advanced to highlight Royce's genuine religious life needs to be viewed in the fuller context of both the vital tension disciplining his mature philosophy of religion and the ultimately unfathomable mystery of the unique person Royce was.

THE EVENTFUL GROWTH OF ROYCE'S RELIGIOUS LIFE AND THOUGHT

Many years of reflective life disposed Plato and Goethe for their masterful achievements in the *Republic* and *Faust*. Similarly, from the cradle to his endowed chair at Harvard, a rich accumulation of reflective experiences prepared Royce to write *The Problem of Christianity*. During his boyhood years at Grass Valley, California,[7] powerful faith experiences operated within him even before religious problems first drove him to philosophy.[8]

His father, Josiah Royce, Senior, had for decades been a steadfast Baptist who observed the Sabbath and so regularly read the Bible as to quote it easily. Around 1857, the senior Royce became a member of Grass Valley's new "Christian Church." The boy's mother, Sarah Eleanor Bayliss

Royce, was educated in the evangelical atmosphere of Phipps Union Female Seminary at Albion, New York. Because of the father's frequent absences, she became the Royce household's economic, intellectual, and religious mainstay. This courageous frontier woman held the Bible as her treasure, wanted total immersion at baptism, and mystically experienced the divine presence. As Disciples of Christ, the parents profoundly influenced their three daughters and only surviving son by their example and teaching. An alert, sensitive boy, the young Josiah enjoyed both the frequent reading of the Bible in his home and his family's singing of traditional evangelical hymns.[9] His first independent reading was from the Apocalypse. This experience sharpened his desire to read more and more, even as it lured him to rereadings of the whole Bible, especially of St. Paul.

The boy encountered several frontier preachers with narrow teachings and some Sunday School teachers who required rigid observances. The folk who gathered at organized church services behaved with severe formality. All this gradually disaffected Josiah from such religion and fueled the flames for future revolt. However, neither at Grass Valley nor during his early years in San Francisco and the Bay Area (1866-1872) did he rule out organized religion completely. As a teenager he was occasionally seen beside his mother and sister Ruth attending services in an Oakland church.

At a group worship-service before the boy's birth, his mother had discovered how this kind of organized religion "works" and can produce an "intensity of earnestness" in the people worshiping together there.[10] So, too, at these church-goings in his early teens, Josiah noticed the powerful influences of communal religious experience. Reflecting later on the way those early California churches formed men during troubled times, he came to appreciate these organizations for their socially conservative forces.[11] Because of such mixed experiences, "the problem of Christianity" was already taking shape within his religious consciousness.

Meanwhile, from 1866 to 1869, another organized group had persistently pressured him. The thundering herd of nearly a thousand lads at Lincoln Grammar School in San Francisco had disciplined this boy—quaint, countrified, independent—into at least minimal cooperation with their demands and preferences.[12] This training rubbed raw his sense of inner dignity and taught him to cover the sore with reluctant compliance. He thus became conscious of the way in which social antagonism starts and intensifies the infection of rebellious, alienated individuality. He never forgot this experience of what he later called the meaning of original sin.[13]

As a teenager, Royce felt tension and conflict, not only at church services and school, but within his own personal loyalties to religion and science. As he witnessed the argument mounting between science and the literal tenets of religious leaders, he began to lean towards science and away from the detailed traditions of his religious upbringing, personified by his dear but didactic mother. He intensified his search into the real life of religion, even as his agnosticism and his disbelief in traditional formulas and routines grew. Feeling compelled to "accept the modern theory of evolution as the real truth of nature,"[14] he could not reconcile it with the dogmatic claims of local preachers.

One day, probably in the early 1870s, his inner struggle finally came to a climax. During his reflective encounters with death, he had for years fought to keep up his hope for individual immortality.[15] Now he honestly faced the truth that through death evolution irresistibly sloughs off each living organism, including his own. To adjust fully to this fact, truth-seeking Josiah uttered such a mighty "No" to his own will for life that he fell into the opposite extreme of viewing as vain any hope for personal immortality of a limited kind. Never did he forget the impact of that decision. He afterwards recounted:

> I remember the failing at heart when I first had to throw overboard my little old creed. . . . Once having doubted, we can never quite go back to that early creed; but something of its spirit we regain when we come to see once more the worth of faith as faith, the moral and intellectual importance of a mind at peace with itself.[16]

After graduating from the University of California in 1875, Royce encountered a still sharper test of the Christianity he had known. He left Sarah Eleanor's home with its deeply Christian biblical and mystical "school" and briefly entered several universities in Germany with their "attitudes of critical indifference or of philosophical hostility towards traditional Christian faith."[17] His experience of these diametrically opposed attitudes towards Christianity impressed him deeply and would energize his search for a *via media* between these two antithetical attitudes for thirty-seven years until his discovery came in *The Problem of Christianity*.[18]

Near the close of his year in Germany, twenty-year-old Josiah accepted a fellowship in that bold experiment of exclusively graduate study and research which was the Johns Hopkins University. Later he described his two years in Baltimore (1876–1878) as when it was "bliss . . . to be alive" and "very Heaven."[19] Part of that bliss came in the summer of 1877 when Royce researched his dissertation in Boston and, more significantly, renewed there his friendship with William James—a friendship initiated on his way to Germany but now cultivated and soon destined to become, beyond his family circle, the closest and deepest intellectual and personal bond of his life.

Having won his doctorate at the Hopkins but not an opportunity to teach philosophy there, Royce reluctantly returned to Berkeley to instruct undergraduates in English composition and literature. Amid the then philosophical wasteland at the University of California, Royce discovered in Edward Rowland Sill, the chairman of his English department, an intimate friend, a wise counselor, and a courageous spirit with a unique type of ethico-religious stamina.

In 1880 Josiah married Katharine Head. After four years at Berkeley, he took her and their first son, Christopher, to Harvard on the risky offer of a one-year position. There, in early 1883, he further studied what we mean by error and what conditions make our meaning of error possible.[20] The investigation drastically changed his attitude toward religion.

When publishing his argument, Royce wrote that every possible error

> implies a judgment whose intended object is beyond itself, and is also the object of the corresponding true judgment. But two judgments cannot have the same object save as they are both present to one thought. . . . Only as present to an including thought are they either true or false.[21]

Furthermore, unless the "including thought" which constitutes finite judgments as false or as true is an infinite knower of *all* possible judgments, all meaning collapses into total relativity. But this latter assertion is self-contradictory. For our starting point was that erroneous human judgments are not merely possible, they are actual. Now such human judgments can be actual only if an infinite Constitutor of finite error and truth actually knows such judgments are erroneous. So, he *is* actual.

This religious insight generated a profound intellectual conversion in Royce. For the rest of his life, it established his basic philosophical orientation and gained for him rich intellectual, moral, and religious potentials.[22] Still the insight contained no implication that he should seek membership in any visible religious body. In fact, he soon frankly confessed that he neither had, nor desired to have, any such connection.[23] Moreover, he and his wife, Katharine, a former Episcopalian, decided that any children of theirs would be educated without attendance at church or denominational schools.[24]

Personally, Royce transcended his childhood view of God as distant by coming to regard him in 1885 as divine Father, intimate and immanent.[25] Philosophically, from the conception of God as all-Knower (*logos*) —published in his first major writing, *The Religious Aspect of Philosophy* (1885)—Royce developed by 1888 an enriched notion of God as also Life, Will, and Experience.[26]

In 1893, while preparing his review of Edward Caird's Gifford Lectures, *The Evolution of Religion,* Royce encountered five themes in the philosophy of religion which he would critically reinterpret twenty years later in the *Problem*.²⁷ These were: (1) Religion is the belief that unity somehow exists above all the distinctions and puzzles of philosophy and life. (2) Philosophy is an attempt by perplexed man, in his longing for knowledge, to interpret our problematic situation. (3) Within the idea of development, one spiritual principle is at work. (4) The proper object of religious philosophy has now evolved into the possibility of "something like a rational proof of a creed." (5) As a third or most evolved kind of religion, Christianity has the problematic task of consistently combining the grains of truth from the pantheistic and from the ethico-monotheistic notions of the divine. The fifth thesis foreshadowed the clarification of his theory that the Western conception of God is composed of three traits: Greek unchangingness, Hebrew moral will, and Oriental negative theology.²⁸ Until his death, he continued to refine this theory.²⁹ He even deepened it to embrace a fourth trait, beauty.³⁰

Called to deliver the Gifford Lectures on Natural Religion in 1899–1900, he invested all his mental resources to create his middle-period masterpiece, *The World and the Individual*. Of the three paths here open to him for his inquiry into reality and its divine dimension, he chose the most difficult: a critical examination of the fundamental intentionality of human reason.³¹ To integrate his research along this path he employed the first three themes from his review of Caird.

William James's *Varieties of Religious Experience* (1902) genuinely inspired Royce at first.³² Yet he soon saw that James, by focusing one-sidedly on solitary and extraordinary religious experiences, had left unexamined all shared and ordinary religious experiences.³³

Royce saw another imbalance in two other colleagues in Harvard's philosophy department.³⁴ He noticed George Santayana and Dickinson S. Miller defining religious consciousness by relationship to symbolic terms. True, thought Royce, our personal relations with the Eternal could not be definite without religious symbols, but these must pass a more rigorous test than our ordinary symbols. A religious symbol must "suggest to me some very deep meaning in life and in the universe . . . with peculiar authority." Our religious symbols easily lose their suggestive power in our culturally changing world which at first puzzles and eventually frustrates us. When we thus lose this effective symbolism, where shall we go to restore our languishing religious life? Unless we *already* are vitally related to *something more* than a simple symbol, we cannot turn some particular object into a revered religious symbol.³⁵ Indeed, we cannot even have religious consciousness.

During his final decade (1907–1916), Royce developed his philosophic religion of loyalty and applied it to Christianity.³⁶ In 1908 C. S. Peirce's "A Neglected Argument for the Reality of God"³⁷ deeply interested Royce and later influenced him more and more.[38] In it he found a mode of thought which Peirce called "Musement"—that is, the mind's "Pure Play without any breach of continuity," obedient to no rule except the law of liberty, without any purpose except recreation.[39] Interested in Peirce's openness to beauty in his "Neglected Argument," Royce allowed fuller scope to an aesthetic component within his own religious "musement."[40] In this way, that side of him which loved Browning and poetic interpretation played its role in Royce's philosophy of religion.[41]

In 1910, by instituting long-term researches into the sources of religious insight, he began to investigate thoroughly humankind's sensitivity to the Spirit. He shared with a Yale audience his conviction that a fundamental prerequisite must be present if

> any source of religious insight whatever is to be recognized as genuine. The witness of the spirit must be, at least in its deepest essence, an internal witness. Religious insight cannot exist unless the spirit itself bears internal witness, unless something—call it faith, or the inner workings of divine grace, or reason, or intuition, or what you will—has first adapted us to know religious truth when we meet it, to recall the true sound of the divine voice when and if we ever externally hear it.[42]

In Royce's doctrine of Spirit he interwove two themes—the activity of the Spirit and human persons' sensitivity to this activity. This idea of the Spirit was rapidly integrating Royce's thought as another focus as vital and important as that of Community.[43]

Partly because belief in the Holy Spirit was a distinctive aspect of the Christian religion, Royce began about 1909 to concentrate upon Christianity as his special topic. His intent grew into a major investigation of his mature period and culminated in *The Problem of Christianity* (1913). This late work showed that he had recently undergone a transformation of thought, especially in his philosophy of the Christian religion, even though the five themes of his 1893 review of Caird were clearly discernible under this critical re-interpretation of them. Soon Royce told the public how his recent discovery of the import of Peirce's intellectual development for theory of knowledge had transformed his own philosophy.[44]

Precisely where, when, and how this "insight into Peirce" gradually took place still remains partly obscure. Royce had already in 1910 created his "Principles of Logic" in which he found "a programme of a future possible Logic, . . . a programme [that] has a place in a fairly extensive plan."[45] During the "enforced leisure" of his 1912 leave of absence, he eventually broke through to grasp how Peirce had, through four decades, developed his way of freely pondering his "simplest notions." Something of the inner results of this breakthrough showed itself already in the late summer of 1912, when Royce, on the rear deck of a fruit steamer plying its West Indian route, often sat alone, simply musing. There, as Caribbean breezes soothed his brow, his mind mused over the mysteries of reality in a new way that was peaceful, penetrating, and Peircean.[46] Throughout his life the Christian reality—with its history and hopes, its strengths and weaknesses—had held his attention and had increasingly absorbed it during his final decade. It was now leading him to see that the destiny of the whole human race is tied inseparably with the outcome of Christianity. So with utmost loyalty he chose to become a sympathetic, yet insistently reasonable, interpreter of Christianity for by 1912 he had come to appreciate it "as a central, as an intensely interesting, life-problem of humanity."[47]

In sum, from 1875 to 1900 Royce had nourished, disciplined, and refined his interest in the philosophy of religion so that he fathered a growing family of interrelated, often profound, studies of religion. This genetic line began with his significant collegiate essay, "The Holy Grail," continued through his penetrating address of 1896, "The Problem of Job," and included his closing Gifford Lecture of 1900, "The Union of God and Man."[48]

The line of development continued in his 1902 Dudleian Lecture on Natural Religion and went beyond his 1908 "creed of the Absolute Religion" to his distinctive analysis of elementary religious experience in *The Sources of Religious Insight*.[49] Although generally overlooked, this work evoked Royce's appraisal, "It contains the whole sense of me in a brief compass."[50] Applying the principles discovered in the *Sources* to the particular case of Christianity, he created the most philosophically significant work of his life, *The Problem of Christianity* (1913). In overview, then, Royce's more than forty years of investigating humankind's religious life make it strikingly evident how intense and sincere he had meant that opening statement in his first major work, "The religious problems, . . . of all human interests, deserve our best efforts and our utmost loyalty."[51]

THE MYSTERIOUS SCHOOLING OF ROYCE

Through the experiences, encounters, and insights just surveyed Royce grew in religious life and thought. Beneath these more cerebral developments, deep-running streams were moving and directing this growth. From them we select three currents underlying his personal experiences—those that trained him as an interpreter, those that challenged him to face up to the problem of evil, and those that called him to purify his conception of God.

Living Within Communities of Interpretation

Royce's boyhood homes in Grass Valley and nearby Avon Farm were the scenes of his early encounters with a community of interpretation. His family's frequent reading of the Bible was a delight to the alert, inquisitive lad. Undoubtedly he asked questions and received interpretations from parents and sisters. Informally they schooled him how to draw meaning from Scripture.[52] After his sister Ruth trained young Josiah in dialectics, he could bring the power of logic to bear on the biblical utterances that arose among these Disciples of Christ. Soon he could notice how his mother's or sisters' use of history or science or dogma to interpret the Bible really produced different kinds of language within his family's Community of Interpretation.[53] The same held true when, from these three diverse viewpoints, they offered interpretations of the world or of themselves.

The clashes between evolutionists and Christian apologists forced Royce as a young collegian to scrutinize the earliest historical developments of the Christian people. Delving into Milman's six volume *History of Latin Christianity,*[54] Royce was concerned enough to copy by hand the most significant portion of Milman's chronology of the first four Christian centuries.[55] In three neat columns, Josiah arranged the "Bishops of Rome, Emperors, and Remarkable Events" from 42 to 134 A.D. He carefully footnoted the source relied upon: "according to" Jerome, or Rufinus, or Tertullian, and so on.

Spread there before his eyes, his chronological map showed the passage of Christianity's first five centuries just as clearly as the fossils of his professor Joseph LeConte portrayed physical evolution. Royce's chronology of events outlined that intriguing process whereby the early Christian community, after its master's death, had encountered Paul, held its first council, been persecuted, received Paul's various letters, recorded oral traditions, been deprived first of Peter and Paul, then of John and Ignatius, eventually met the texts of the Johannine school and of the Acts of the Apostles and of the Catholic Epistles, begun sifting these from other writings in a development towards an accepted New Testament, and meanwhile adjusted to living the Christian life in such varied places as Jerusalem, Antioch, Cyrene, Ephesus, and Rome with their so diverse cultures and problems, opinions and developments. As these early Christians met new situations, they had serially formed and developed further interpretations of their own Christian life, organization, founder, and hope. They always believed that they were being guided in these interpretations by the Spirit of the risen founder. For Royce, how strikingly this approach to Christianity by the critical, historical, scholarly Milman contrasted with the approach taken by that wholehearted, sacrificing, practical pioneer Sarah

Eleanor Royce! Later Josiah felt the same basic contrast during his graduate studies, not only when examining published criticisms of Christianity but also when conversing with university people in Germany and at the Hopkins.[56]

During his twenties his continued reading of the philosophical giants further refined his skills as an interpreter. For instance, at the Hopkins, when investigating Spinoza's way of defending religious liberty, Royce revealed his own method of interpreting Scripture.[57] More than a decade later, while reading a poetic utterance of Schelling, Royce recognized something in it with which he so closely identified that he wanted it to come alive in English, at least for himself. In the following first lines of Royce's eleven page translation, the reader can perhaps detect how skillfully Royce interpreted Schelling, even as he may have unveiled within the guarded confines of his personal notebook something of his inner religious life around 1889:

> Therefore do I all creeds forsake
> No faith of old shall my fealty take
> I visit no church to hear them preach
> No long confession shall they me teach
> Save one that already possesses my will
> Glows in my verse and inspires me still
> Daily my heart with its joy doth thrill;
> Eternally showing new forms,
> And I knowing this faith so clear
> This truth so near
> This poem undying
> Must witness its truth beyond denying.
> So that I can nothing hold nor conceive
> Save what it counsels me to believe,
> Nor aught as certain or right maintain
> Save what it shows to my eyes so plain.[58]

The inner light of Royce's 1883 religious insight had so possessed and vitalized him that it operated as a norm for all his beliefs and actions. In fact, it had rendered organized religion at its best something derivative from both "this truth so near" and the shared witness found in a community of interpretation.

Royce's 1912 apoplexy rendered him physically quiet enough for a new and penetrating rereading of Peirce's writings. After detecting Peirce's unique way of musing interpretively over a few simple ideas, Royce reencountered Paul's command that Christians pray for the power to interpret. In the "spiritual gift" of interpretation Royce found the taproot of his whole life — that is, of everything to be done in philosophy and religion.[59]

Among the hidden underlying currents affecting Royce's mental growth was that deep process sponsored by the various communities of interpretation to which he belonged—his family, schoolmates, readings, efforts at translation, and discussions with students and colleagues both before and during his Harvard years. Through the decades these communities schooled him into being an ever more sensitive and faithful interpreter.[60] He would need such a power of interpretation when meeting the pains, heartbreaks, and reverses of his life.

Being Disciplined by Pain and Evil

As a child in Grass Valley, young Josiah encountered harsh realities. For instance, in a lonely place not far from his home, he found a miner's grave which drew him into deep religious meditation.[61] He was wounded within by his father's long absences, especially since they were linked with his family's stark poverty. Nor did preying creditors and war-inflated food prices lessen the pinch of pain for his family. The "thundering herd" at Lincoln Grammar School in San Francisco displayed no mercy as they insensitively disciplined this awkward lad.[62] Having dreamt that one of his few school friends was lost at sea, Royce took his heartbreak to religious meditation.[63] When typhoid fever struck him in his grade-school days, he was quarantined to a solitary coal shed where he lay "on some straw on the bare ground with nothing but an old quilt for bedding."[64]

These early experiences were already training Royce to more than a mere stoic endurance of pain. His courageous pioneer mother taught her son to see a religious dimension in sufferings. This learning was strongly reinforced at Berkeley by Edward Rowland Sill, the poet of its English department. Sill confronted Josiah one day with the challenging message that we do not know whether our deeds are truly good "until we feel the tusks" of the swinelike, irrational, chance events that attack those deeds.[65] Sill's remark opened Royce's eyes to the fact that hidden within suffering lies a unique potential for insight.

Criticizing Royce's 1895 "Conception of God" address, G. H. Howison sharply scored Royce's tendency to consign finite individuals to unreality. To make amends, Royce pushed his mind in 1896 to create a new "American theory of individuality"—that only through an ethical concept and choice can any individual be known genuinely.[66]

If attacks and sufferings occasioned his growth in religious insight before 1907, they intensified and accelerated it during his final decade. He was then touched by several painful experiences and by a series of deaths among dear ones. In these wounds he felt, like his biblical hero Job, that "the hand of God was upon him."[67] First of all, with disappointment he noticed how many Americans were uncritically accepting a crass pragmatism and crude neo-realism while turning away from his own more complex and balanced doctrine. Then, in late 1910, within the span of a few weeks, he lost both his closest friend, William James, and his first-born son, Christopher. Hardly more than a year later, apoplexy struck him and he discovered his bodily strength so diminished that he had to give up his cherished hope of completing a masterwork in logic. Soon he learned that his admired Peirce had died before completing his own projected synthesis of logic. Later, in early 1915, Royce experienced the pathetic death of his only granddaughter, the infant "Petsy." By then, another kind of death had infected Western civilization as the world's leading nations plunged deeper into World War I. This unprecedented tragedy agonized Royce whose whole life was committed to further realizing the Great Community of humankind. This conflict also turned to bitterness Royce's decades-long friendship with Hugo Münsterberg who increasingly became Harvard's outspoken protagonist for Germany's cause.

So in his late life Royce had more than ample opportunity to penetrate what he called "the religious mission of sorrow."[68] When a series of historic events drew Americans closer to compelled entry into World War I, Royce, purified by personal hardships, rose up as an energetic prophet. With flaming oratory he confronted Americans in their conscience. Did they not see that by clinging to neutrality they invited the Teutons to further atrocities? Was not the most pressing need of the day American action fully committed to save the world community from such barbarities? By his public stand in 1915-1916, Royce may most fittingly have fulfilled his role as prophet and as philosopher of religion. In a time of extreme crisis, this sage called his fellow Americans to a more steadfast service of the Great Community.[69]

Experiencing a Saving Influence

Though plunged in sorrow at times, Royce was unswervingly convinced that, as the poet Gerard Manley Hopkins put it, "There lives the dearest freshness deep down things."[70] Royce found a medicinal power in nature. He was sure that persons' basic potentials—their sensitiveness, docility, and initiative—tended to their true good.[71] During his desert years of 1876-1882 he had often cried out of the depths of his arid agnosticism until he was freed by his religious insight of 1883. After his 1888 breakdown from overwork, he had experienced a healing power permeating his whole person during his sailing trip for recovery in the South Pacific. He was saved from the superficiality of his partly prepared 1895 address to the Union at Berkeley by the call of Howison and the philosophical community for better service of the truth. His atoning response was revealed in his Supplementary Essay of 1896-1897.

As he entered the final decade of his life, he found more and more that *loyalty* was the unique pathway for receiving the saving influences of the community. For example, in 1908, when his disagreement with his closest friend and colleague had become very acute, he waited in humble trust for more light from the saving community so that this precious friendship might be even deepened. Speaking of William James, Royce then wrote:

> If he and I do not see truth in the same light at present, we still do well, I think, as friends, each to speak his mind as we walk by the way, and then to wait until some other light shines for our eyes. I suppose that so to do is loyalty.[72]

Finally, in his *Problem of Christianity,* he intimated his knowledge of several persons who were mediating salvation to the community by serving as genuine atoners.[73]

In all these experiences of a saving influence Royce was being further schooled in the doctrine that the only way the morally detached individual is saved is through the community and often only through its atoning servants. Royce saw that the human self's growth in rational moral awareness occurs only through the social conflicts which widen the original moral split in every self. Reacting to social situations and pressure, each child develops through many a thrust in the dark—thus growing simultaneously both as a depersonalized collectivist and as a rebel individualist, just as Royce had done at Lincoln Grammar School.

To save a person from this inner alienation, each self must have within itself at least the potential to recognize the "touch" of the salvation process and to respond to it.[74] So Royce, despite his unsparing realism in describing human tendencies to moral blindness and selfishness, neither regarded a person's conduct as universally depraved nor considered his nature as totally corrupt.[75] Even more significantly, he saw the Spirit of the saving community at work amid humankind.[76]

This deliverance through transformation, along with the two other processes—of interpretive communities and of potentially educative sufferings—created that "mysterious school" in which Royce's essential temperament was purified and developed. At a still deeper level, if the all-Knower lived, contact with him would occur in Royce's prayerful communion.

ROYCE'S PERSONAL PRAYER-STATE

His closest friend, William James, found religion lay in "making proper connection with the higher powers."[77] Did Royce regard opening himself to communication with the Holy One as a suitable way of making this connection properly? More specifically, did Royce take part in sacramental liturgies? Did he "listen to the Word of God"? Did he engage in private prayer? These questions open the door to our third and deepest level of studying Royce's personal life insofar as it affected his drafting of the *Problem*. The present inquiry into Royce's ways of seeking union with the divine may at first blush seem strained to those less familiar with such exercises than Royce was. Yet if his converse with the divine was as habitual and deep as the evidence suggests, his "personal prayer-state" had to affect his "essential temperament." What such communion led him to value most highly had to alter radically his core personality at least as much as his mother's almost four years of being pregnant had affected her essential temperament — not to mention what her own decades of prayer-life did to it.

Royce found the many Christian communities fenced off from each other by jealous jurisdictional claims and the preference to exercise power rather than to promote the reconciliation of all peoples with God. This tragic sickness contorted the Christian People of God into a disjointed body. As this tragedy has maimed millions of Christians, so it maimed Josiah Royce. He, too, was cut off from the Christian community's faith-filled celebration of the Lord's Supper, according to the intent of Christ: "Do this in memory of me." Royce did not experience frequent, full, active and conscious participation in this Supper. This form of spiritual malnutrition was intensified by his elitist choice of those with whom he would worship rather than assembling with the *hoi polloi* the way Jesus did with publicans and prostitutes.

In lieu of sacramental liturgies with ordinary people, however, Royce at least occasionally attended the "Sunday morning seminars" at the home of Richard and Ella Cabot, 291 Marlborough.[78] With the Hockings and other friends of the Cabots they gathered for mutual support and friendly discourse. Experiencing a shared religious life more basic than orthodox conformism, these "loyalists" confirmed Royce in that ecumenical conviction he later published:

> For, after all, it is more important that we should together recognize in religion our own common personal needs and life-interests than that we should agree about our formulas.[79]

As an adult Royce rarely attended services in the Episcopal Church. When he did, he found himself not supported or strengthened but stifled by his fellow worshippers. They repeated the same begging prayers eternally and their routine confession of sin left him with a deep sense of changelessness and of solemn melancholy.[80]

Victimized with millions of other Christians by routinized noncelebrations, he would agree with William James that the religious experience of a church is often "conventional" and consequently lacks depth and wholeheartedness. Yet he would not hold, as James did, that church experience *must* be this way.[81] Royce's lack of experience in vibrant celebrations of the Word and of the Eucharist may account in part for Royce's taciturnity about Jesus and for his seeming lack of personal devotion to him. He had been deprived of personal entry into the vital drama of liturgically renewing the covenant with the Risen Lord and his People.

Secondly, Royce's "listening to the Word of God" deserves close scrutiny. His family's reading of the Bible so impressed him as a preschooler that more than fifty years later he easily recalled how he had then reached out curiously to the large print New Testament on the living room table to do his first reading by himself — in the Apocalypse![82] From 1875 to about 1906, his encounters with radical, often exaggerated biblical criticism and his own scholarship made Royce too wary and reserved for a simple listening to "God's Word." During his final decade, however, his boyhood immersion in the sounding biblical word reasserted itself to overcome the reserve of his middle years. In 1913, for instance, he acknowledged that he was now reading the Scriptures as simply and as much like a child as he could.[83] During his final decade, then, he seems to have accepted the Bible as the nourishing norm of life for the Christian community and for himself.

No American philosopher I know from the "classical" or later periods has been so saturated with the Bible as Royce or has in his philosophical writings drawn from the Bible so heavily for quotation, reference, imagery, and allusion. Yet the scriptural atmosphere Royce mediates is remarkably free from fundamentalism and sectarianism. This echoing of evangelical Christianity in the United States is a minor but distinctively Roycean contribution to American philosophy that prides itself on its pluralistic roots.

Finally, when turning to Royce's prayer, we come to a most delicate point. For while he always opposed superstition — that "leaning upon the intervention of such spiritual agencies as the old mythologies conceived"[84] — he nevertheless recognized the apostle Paul's directive to "pray that one may interpret" as indispensable for both philosophy and religion.[85] Presently available evidence indicates that Royce's prayer, while sometimes of the begging type, usually was a communing with the divine Spirit, a shared living with "the higher powers." What are some empirical clues supporting such statements?

The wise practices he learned in the school of his deeply religious mother certainly included earnest prayer and devout reading of the Bible with its Psalms as well as communal religious prayer-experiences at home and in Sunday worshipping. In 1879, when Berkeley's young instructor Royce composed his "Meditation before the Gate," he expressed a tone of reverent union with the "World-Spirit."[86] As we saw, Royce's fundamental "religious insight" of 1883 exerted its vital influence throughout his life of philosophizing. In fact, it is difficult to find any Roycean writing—even his pure logic—not permeated with a sense of the "Divine Whole." With a sense of honesty more acute than in most people, Royce actually published some of his prayers—for instance, when he entered into colloquy with the "all-Knowing One,"[87] or pleaded for mercy with Sill's prayer, "O Lord, be merciful to me a fool!"[88]

His forty-year investigation of mysticism at times led him from theory about mysticism into personal practice, otherwise his neighbors would hardly have called him "the mystic of Irving Street."[89] When the mature Royce described the "plain man [who] . . . knows what is meant by saying, 'Out of the depths have I cried,'" he seems to presuppose a practical, rather than a merely theoretical, acquaintance with this type of experience.[90] When he went on to insist that the saving light cannot come to him unless he cries "out of the depths" in union with the community's saving influence, and when he then stressed that the essence of Christianity is this triad of the whole saving community's shared religious experience, the lost individual's cry for rescue, and the Spirit's liberating light,[91] Josiah Royce apparently revealed his own deepest religious experience. He concurred with his beloved Paul, who also witnessed "God has sent his Spirit into *our* hearts, whereby *we* cry 'Abba,' Father."[92] At least after the Peircean insight of his final years, Royce enjoyed entering into a musement that, following only the law of liberty, eventually delighted in the reality of God.[93] Sometimes, too, he would simply commune with the spirits of his beloved departed selves in his well-known cult of the dead.[94] At other times, as Royce's attendant during his final weeks witnessed, Royce would sit for long silent periods of active attention and musing.[95] Thus, usually, Josiah's "communing with the divine" was a simple living in the presence of the Spirit and a loyal committing of himself to his felt will. Such communing seems to have been the mainstay of his religious life.

These evidences, then, indicate that at the heart of Royce's personal religious life there was a continuing prayer-life—primarily, a prayer of communing, yet including some prayer of begging.

To summarize, one can note that Royce's published philosophy of religion will naturally rise out of this type of personal prayer-life, out of his grappling with the problems of evil and salvation, and out of his life in an evangelical family, in professional academe, and in his inmost personal philosophizing. In other words, from the inexpressible personal mystery of Josiah Royce will issue an expressed and logically unified system of choices, feelings, and ideas. In all the chapters that follow, we attempt to explore this ultimate paradox. The delicacy of such an attempt, however, demands that we first carefully survey the immediate philosophical context in which Royce lived as he approached his masterpiece, *The Problem of Christianity*. We turn, then, to the development of his philosophy of religion, especially during the years shortly preceding his writing of the *Problem*.

Royce's mother, Sarah Eleanor
Bayliss Royce, ca. 1867
Courtesy of Nancy Hacker

Young Josiah Royce, ca. 1872–
1875, possibly while attending
the University of California
Courtesy of Nancy Hacker

Josiah Royce in Gottingen, Germany, during the summer of 1876 *Courtesy of Nancy Hacker*

Josiah Royce (seated) and John Dewey at Thomas Davidson's Summer School for Cultural Sciences at Glenmore, New York, ca. 1893 *Permission by Daniel S. Robinson; detail from photograph reserved in the Hoose Library of Philosophy, at the University of Southern California, Los Angeles*

2. Developing a Mature Philosophy of Religion

Royce's *Problem of Christianity* is a simple yet subtle work. His usually simple terms, his easy flowing style, and his almost familiar tone tend to lull the ordinary reader into the dreamy feeling that the *Problem* is merely a set of religious reflections by a gentle philosopher turned pious in his old age. But such a misreading forgets Royce's forewarning that in this work his "views . . . need to be carefully considered" (1:ix).[1]

To facilitate such careful consideration, we need to study Royce's growth in both philosophy of religion and in his late logic—both pure and applied. The present chapter focuses upon his development in philosophy of religion with three goals: to scan how his method in philosophy of religion grew to maturity during forty years; to examine more carefully the five final years of that growth which flowered in the *Problem;* and to familiarize ourselves with Royce's usage of some central terms which he later reemployed in the *Problem*.

FOUR DECADES OF FAMILIARIZATION WITH METHOD IN THE PHILOSOPHY OF RELIGION (1872-1913)

In the course of his forty years of studying the philosophy of religion, Royce first employed different patterns of procedure one by one. Gradually, after sifting these, he integrated many of these patterns into his mature method. At each stage of his intellectual development he was only partially aware of the full implication of his latest advance. Thus his mature method in philosophy of religion came about through trial and error almost as much as it did through his careful forethought and reflection. Much like leafing through a picture-album, the following rapid survey seeks to catch significant moments in the development which led to Royce's final method.

Written during his high school days, the first of his compositions on religious philosophy reveals pietism in control of his method, just as a later high school essay shows agnosticism in charge.[2] A few years later at Berkeley, for his significant article "The Holy Grail," he chose a far more analytic procedure to examine just how religious symbols are constructed and function. Then in his bachelor's thesis, Royce investigated Aeschylus' art in choosing such rhetoric as would suit his Greek audience when relating them to the "divine." Already Royce was examining the art of an "interpreter of the community." Adopting a positivistic descriptive method for this study, he sharply limited himself to produce a result that resembles a careful phenomenology of the religious responses of a group when stimulated by a mediating genius.

To attract attention to his first major publication, *The Religious Aspect of Philosophy,* Harvard instructor Royce spiced his presentation with a wide-swinging, stimulating dialectic—a technique he later criticized in himself. Yet in this 1885 work, his method of philosophizing might accurately be called "intentionality-analysis." In treating moral insight, he concentrated on people's basic and ineradicable co-intending of a harmony among all selves and sought the conditions making this co-intending possible. Then, when treating the conditions required for the possibility of actual error, he identified both the co-intentions required if an error in judgment were to be actual and the impossibility of such co-intentions unless an absolute Knower of all truth and error really exists.

Within the following decade Royce expanded from an exclusive emphasis on knowledge in the Absolute to an equally distributed emphasis on its experience and will, as well as knowledge.[3] His method in philosophy of religion began to expand proportionately, just as implicitly it began to express the life of a community of selves. In his 1897 response to G. H. Howison's pointed criticisms,[4] Royce did more than draw some careful distinctions. He found that other kinds of meaning—affective, volitive, elective—also called for elucidation in one's "conception of God." For this conception he created his own "American theory of individuality,"[5] not only by comparing Aquinas' and Scotus' doctrines on individuation but also by drawing upon the biblical theme of God's selective love of each human person in this his chosen universe.[6]

For his Gifford Lectures (1899–1900), published as *The World and the Individual,* Royce deliberated over his choice of a method.[7] He discerned three paths leading to the goal established for this lecture series: one leading through Nature to God, another moving through subjective consciousness, and a third investigating the intentionality within one's meaning of Being. Royce chose the third path, even though the most difficult, because he trusted that in this way he could eventually best raise the question, "What is Being?" and thus could discover what light metaphysics might throw upon religion.

Soon his major insight into individuality (1896), as deepened by his

Gifford Lectures, led him to choose life-problems and logic as the two chief foci for the rest of his philosophical career. Around this pair of mutually enriching interests and topics, Royce's maturing energies spiraled steadily down into the deep reality of community. The contemporary life-problems that demanded some of his attention were racism, provincialism, excessive idealism, and the vital link between physical training and moral development. But fundamental questions in ethics and religion presented him with far more demanding life-problems because they raised issues of universal transcultural values. For example, Royce felt the challenge of identifying that fundamental decision which makes ethical life genuine. Furthermore, did such a decision require a moral conversion? If so, was such a conversion possible without religious implications? Or again, alerted by the results of logical modes of denial, he wondered whether the fact that certain ethical judgments are necessarily reaffirmed when one tries to deny them actually reveals some constant eternal norm operating amid the swirling currents of relativity? If so, does this ethical constant have a bearing upon the divine and call for a religious response?

One result of Royce's interest in these passing and permanent life-problems during his final decade was that it injected a healthy pragmatism into his method. Having decided to grapple earnestly with radical human problems, he found that somewhat paradoxically these problems, rather than burdening and fatiguing him, nourished and freshened his mind. If he followed genuine loyalty when making his choices as a philosopher, he found a light of wisdom guiding each such choice (2:388). This light revealed the right way to act because it led him, through community, towards humankind's supreme good.

One intensely interesting life-problem to which his researches in loyalty drew him was Christianity. Because several critical happenings touched him during his studies of Christianity between 1908 and 1913, his method in philosophy of religion showed rapid maturation. In 1908 he proposed a new theory of truth[8] and two years later had developed enough logical skill to create "The Principles of Logic."[9] Then in 1911, as he admitted at the close of his "Error and Truth" article,[10] felt tensions in his theory of knowledge made him confess how inadequate a base is offered by a mere subject-object framework. Within a year, however, perhaps his most significant late discovery occurred, his "insight into Peirce," which rescued his theory of knowing from a subject-object (dyadic) basis to a sign-sender, sign-interpreter, and sign-receiver (or triadic) basis. This growth enabled him to detect and express a radically novel interpretation of Christianity.

Meanwhile, in preparation for his *Problem of Christianity,* Royce had carefully researched the human sources of religious insight.[11] The foundation of these sources was people's common religious awareness of their need for salvation. Hence he interpreted humankind's common religious experiences as expressions of this universal need of salvation. Methodically, then, he had to draw constantly upon the materials of these common religious experiences. This empiricism marked the maturation of his method in philosophy of religion.

Despite his stroke in early 1912, Royce felt that for the *Problem* he had a religious topic and a methodic plan perfectly suited to his potentials both as a person and as a philosopher.[12] He followed the apostle Paul's advice to pray for the gift of interpretation (2:221) and put into practice Peirce's way of pondering a few simple ideas.

Two years later he confessed that he had discovered this mature philosophical method by a close comparison-contrast of the different stages of development in C. S. Peirce's decades-long method of reflection.[13] Accordingly, I construct the phrase "interpretive musement" to indicate the mature Royce's overall method of philosophizing about the Christian religion. The phrase credits Peirce fittingly yet emphasizes the uniqueness of Royce's mature method, which, while resembling Peirce's musing and interpretation in general and sharing its playfulness is anything but pure play. It is as breathtakingly simple in its long range purpose as it is amazingly complex in its organization and highly sophisticated in its actual operation.

Intellectually transformed by his insight into Peirce, the Royce of 1912 found that when he now attempted to articulate his most recent phase of experience and thinking, he was in possession of a unique and distinctive method of synthesizing them. The more he used his interpretive musement to keep in touch with his empirical bases, the more the ideas of Community and of Spirit showed themselves alive, well, and increasingly dominant.[14] He also recognized how different his new method was from the one he had used in 1900.

In *The World and the Individual* his fundamental question had been "What do we mean by Being in general?"[15] Now in the *Problem* how did this question relate to his central metaphysical concern? In both works the metaphysician Royce was searching for our ultimate meaning of Reality but in 1912 he no longer relied mainly on conceptions of Being, but on interpretations of Life—life both within and without community. In the *Problem* Royce approached his metaphysical inquiry by testing whether the meaning internal to the Christian doctrine of life consistently directs humankind into the fullness of reality, into a unity of shared conscious life available to all minded beings. To do such testing, Royce moved from experienced facts (the psychological bases of persons' fundamental spiritual interests), through ethical and religious values and truth-validation, to life in the unity of the Beloved Community. These steps towards greater generalization *and* more concrete interpretation resembled the path of his earlier four steps in his 1900 work. For then, always seeking to conceive our ultimate meaning of Being more accurately, he had moved from extreme realism, through mysticism and critical rationalism, to absolute individualism.

Again, in both works Royce's starting point was our human intentionality towards Reality, but in the *Problem* he no longer viewed Reality primarily through a conception of "Being in general." Rather, giving primacy to interpretive knowing, he approached Reality as a processing community of minded individuals and gained "close personal touch" with it. A detailed and serial view shows that in the *Problem* Royce first scrutinized the real foundations which the Christian ideas have in persons' basic spiritual needs. Then, convinced that people cannot intend a basis of facts without adopting some volitional attitude towards it — that is, they cannot avoid somehow valuing or disvaluing Reality — he next pushed beyond an apparently value-free encounter with Reality. He began to study the fact that the Christian doctrine of life leads people to a loyal love of the universe. This love is their fundamental ethico-religious valuation of Reality, the only basic valuation that is self-reinstating when one tries to deny it. Since this loyal commitment to the universe (as both fact and valuation) needed a multifaceted critique of its truth, Royce next engaged in an elaborate truth-test of the Christian doctrine of life in the concluding half of the *Problem*. He grounded this test upon humankind's shared appraisals of their real spiritual interests and of the values involved therein. This led him, through true interpretation, to the final recognition that the fullness of life for human beings ultimately means taking part in a universal Community of Interpretation.

In the *Problem,* then, Royce employed a more human, experiential, and genuinely loyal style of philosophizing than he did in *The World and the Individual.* The judgment resulting from the *Problem* is that the intentionality common to the ethico-religious life of humankind is so purified by these facts of experience, values, and true judgments that people *can* be lifted to a *genuine* participation in the universal community's real life in the Spirit.

Accordingly, one does well to regard *The Problem of Christianity* as more than the chief exemplar of Royce's mature philosophy of religion. For the *Problem* records how he submitted his experience to interpretive musement during the actual composition of that work.[16] Even more, the overall method and subordinate methods through which he designed and composed the *Problem* are what best reveal Royce's fully mature mind, spirit, and religious style.

COMPARISON AND CONTRAST OF ROYCE'S
FOUR LATE WORKS IN THE PHILOSOPHY OF RELIGION

Royce built the *Problem* upon his loyalty studies of the previous five years (1:ix), yet he thought a person could understand the book without any previous reading of his 1908 *Loyalty,* his 1911 *Essays,* or his 1912 *Sources* (1:viii).[17] Nevertheless, he provided a caution. If someone found himself totally at variance with the interpretation of Christianity advanced in the *Problem,* Royce advised that:

> he should not finally condemn my book without taking the trouble to compare its principal theses with those which my various preliminary studies of "loyalty," and of the religion of loyalty, contain. (1:viii)

Such a comparison is our first task.

In Royce's investigations of loyalty he sought a philosophy of life that would provide sound ideals for personal guidance.[18] He also sought to draw the vitality of his religion of loyalty from a "complete spiritual reaction of the entire man."[19] In other words, Royce's ideally loyal person was to have reached mature spirituality by integrating faith and works.[20] "Right belief" in such a person would fill her or him with the truth necessary both for instilling an inner peace of blessedness and for generating strong steady motives towards good deeds — deeds that would also meet society's external requirements. In this way loyalty was to make Royce's ideal person both moral and religious.

A researcher can notice how Royce's ethical and religious views on loyalty develop from 1908 to 1912. But if a reader of the *Problem* were unfamiliar with these earlier investigations, he might easily think that the *Problem's* focus on *communal* religious experience was unbalanced and inadequate. So, to understand the *Problem* as fairly as possible, we first need to see in outline how Royce's researches into religious experience in general and into individual religious experience developed and diverged in *Loyalty, Essays,*[21] *Sources,* and the *Problem.*

Clear parallels in doctrine and attitude link *Loyalty, Essays, Sources,* and the *Problem.* To trace out these parallels and also to see the differences of these works helps one appreciate how Royce's method in the *Problem* employed comparisons and contrasts. In 1913 he articulated his new developments more distinctly, thanks to his previous researches into religious experience, yet the basic ingredients of such experience remained the same in his eyes.[22] He knew that most people felt the need for a life that made ultimate sense — or, in religious terms, that they felt the need to be saved. They sensed a supreme good beyond their own power to secure, yet were aware of a superhuman saving presence. Already in 1900 he had interpreted the heart of such religious experiences as their Internal Meaning.[23] About a decade later he found functioning within that heart "the spirit of the community" — the spirit that moved at the centers of the individual self and of the human brotherhood.

Then, too, in his mature works, Royce repeatedly emphasized the fact that emotion, imagination, and symbols play central roles within individual and communal religious consciousness.[24] In both he found the following rich emotions: weakness approaching despair, grief penetrated with hope of a future life, occasional intimations of the divine presence amid a sense of profound peace and reverence, and, even more importantly, loyal love for persons and for the community itself along with the reciprocated supportive love one receives from both these levels. Moreover, as affective, a personal religious response requires the use of imaginative symbols. For during its efforts to respond personally and creatively to what transcends the human, the human self remains embodied and needs to imagine embodied signs. So Royce stressed the need for those symbols which the Scriptures, tradition, doctrinal formulas, and religious practices supply, though he never regarded them as fully adequate to the truth.[25]

To counterbalance the roles of affection and imaginative symbols in religious life, Royce increasingly emphasized the role of true belief — that is, the creedal aspect of religious life. In his 1908 *Loyalty* he eventually synthesized the "creed of the Absolute Religion" from five factual theses.[26] In his 1913 *Problem* he immediately began with a remarkably similar but simplified creed, the "Christian doctrine of life," synthesized from his three "essential Christian ideas" (1:44, 52).

In another striking parallel, Royce's published works of 1908-1913 rise out of his doctrine of the "two levels of reality." Gradually he had explicated the radical need in his philosophy for two levels; "man the individual" and "man the community."[27] He had hinted at this doctrine in *Loyalty*,[28] laid its foundations in his 1910 "Principles of Logic,"[29] and clearly sketched it in *Essays*.[30] In the *Sources* he hinted that the doctrine was at work.[31] Finally, in the *Problem* he described the two levels more completely and indicated how all his mature philosophy flowed from this doctrine (1:404-406). These late works witness that between these two levels of reality vital transactions occur, of which the most significant is the community's offer of ongoing salvation and the individual's rejection or acceptance of this gift.

Royce's 1908-1913 research reveals these three doctrinal parallels. Do they also reveal that Royce maintained a constant attitude on how to deal with the inexhaustible data of religious experience? Was he also open to new facts entering religious experience? Do his 1913 researches show this attitude as much as or more than his earlier inquiries do?

As a first response, Royce's attitude towards investigating religious experiences remained "methodologically positivistic."[32] Shunning ontological and dogmatic interpretations, he viewed the human self as constituted by deeds (or ageric) and interactional. He believed that researches into the presence or absence of religious life in the human self have adequate materials on hand in the self's religious needs, ideals, values, choices, lifeplan, and process of self-identification. There is no need to suppose an underlying monadic substance since that would only double one's trouble. The experientially verifiable factors constitute a methodologically autonomous structure. This supplies researchers with enough evidence to initiate helpful questions and to test whether their interpretations about the human self's religious life are fitting or not.

In his "methodological positivism," then, Royce refrained from metaphysical and creedal assertions about the human self. He restricted himself to those religious facts discoverable in common human experience. These facts did not have to be perceptible by the five senses to be really experienced.[33] This limitation is evident in many loci of *Loyalty* and the *Problem*,[34] and most evident in the *Sources*.

Furthermore, Royce's methodological positivism kept him open during his mature inquiries for additional pertinent data. He often refrained from completely settling a question because he did not want to foreclose on data possibly forthcoming. For example, Buddhism, Islam, and other "higher" positive religions retreat and advance in their histories. Sensitive to new processes at work in these world religions, Royce only tentatively evaluated them.

Again, in the United States, the widespread use of the Bible, public profession of creeds in church, and sincere concern about salvation are facts that mark the distinctive way in which a majority of Americans experience "the religious quality" in their lives. Although in *A Common Faith* a later John Dewey would scarcely attend to these conspicuous facts of American Christianity, Royce reached out to embrace these data as facts required for adequate inquiry into religious experience.

Or again, Royce's 1911 search into the givens of ordinary religious life resulted in his neat spectrum of seven different sources of religious insight. Yet his methodological self-limitation kept him tentative enough to avoid regarding his list as complete. Responding to still further data, he came to regard both beauty and the cult of the dead as additional sources of religious insight.[35]

Finally, his openness also enabled Royce to recognize in the growing assembly of scientific facts the suggestion that there may be need to generalize evolutionary theory—even breathtakingly—so as to cover the entire realms of metaphysics and religion. He viewed the evolutionary sciences as dynamic signs, which taken together point to the coming of the Beloved Community (2:408-418).

Royce's late works on religious experience also reveal noteworthy differences—especially through their diverse emphases. For example, he stressed the ethical aspect of religion in *Loyalty*. He emphasized the contemporary relevance of Christianity in his essay, "What is Vital in Christianity?" In the *Sources* his concern was the perennial and complementary founts of religious insight. Finally, in the *Problem* his stress was on the objective form of the highest good: transformation into a genuinely loyal member of the saving Community.

Different topics, too, characterized these works. In *Loyalty* he treated the unseverable bond between ethics and religion, but in the *Sources* he sought "the great common features and origins of the religious consciousness."[36] Then presupposing these doctrines, he concentrated in the *Problem* on the cognitive consistency of certain beliefs at work in our universe.

MEANINGS OF SOME CENTRAL TERMS IN ROYCE

For adequate orientation to the *Problem* we must also examine the meanings of certain basic Roycean terms because these noticeably predetermined how he moved in the *Problem*. Since he experienced concern in choosing his title, "The Problem of Christianity" (1:3, 9), his selected terms "Christianity" and "Problem," and their implicit terms, "community" and "experience," merit clarification. Moreover, since Royce based the *Problem* on human religious experiences (1:ix), we also need to clarify what he meant in 1912 by "human person" and "religion." Finally, because Royce viewed human religious experience as involving a felt divine presence in which communication occurs (1:398), we need to know his late meaning for "revelation." To start with, then, we need to notice Royce's usage of a pair of paired terms: Christianity and community, problem and experience. Then we can turn to examine in greater detail a triad of terms basic to the mature Royce: the human person, religion, and revelation.

Other basic terms guided his approach to the *Problem*. They, too, can be arranged in triads—for example: time, interpretation, and process; or sin, salvation, and grace; or Spirit, doctrine, and hope. Royce thought these latter terms just as essential to his meaning of religious experience as were the seven terms we first highlighted. Why, then, select the above-mentioned paired pair and first triad of terms? Royce's example (1:35-36) —he himself chose for his purposes three "most essential ideas of Christianity," knowing that these were interrelated enough with Christianity's other basic ideas to illuminate them. Similarly, our first seven terms are so central to Royce's mature thought that they will knit closely together the many other basic ideas of the *Problem*. The entire assembly forms the vibrant tapestry of Royce's mind when he tried to portray the intricate problem of Christianity.

Regarding Christianity, Royce insisted on avoiding a simplistic concentration on either the master or his believers. Rather, Christianity is inescapably a *Community with two foci:* the risen master's Spirit *and* the believing Community which interprets it (1:22-35). Though not satisfied with a purely spiritual Christianity, Royce did not view it as essentially a visible institution (1:115). Nor did he simply identify it with the Christian community (1:xviii-xx). Rather, for him it was *most* essentially the single shared belief that the redeeming Spirit is saving humankind by its presence in the Church (2:428-429). In Royce's understanding of history, Christianity is the elevating, yet accident-prone, religion of loyalty which is centered around this single shared belief. Thus, much like Karl Rahner's "anonymous Christians," anyone of any time or place who has committed himself through genuine loyalty to some Beloved Community (that is, to a not merely natural, but a grace-transformed community open to serve the universe of *all* minded beings)—any such person is a member of Christianity. For Royce, this religion of graced loyalty has been sending its roots both more and less deeply into different people's individual lives, communities, and cultures as these developed both up and down the sharp escarpments and along the tranquil plains of the past two millennia and of all human millennia.

Since Christianity is a community, and since the idea of community is one Royce identified as central to his life and work, we need to notice his technical way of defining community and the various kinds of communities he referred to. In the *Problem* he wanted community to mean something more precise than a social group that seems to behave as a unity (2:57), so he defined it technically, according to its members' shared memories and hopes, as follows:

> Now when many contemporary and distinct individual selves so interpret, each his own personal life, that each says of an individual past or of a determinate future event or deed: "That belongs to my life;" "That occurred, or will occur, to me," then these many selves may be defined as hereby constituting, in a perfectly definite and objective, but also in a highly significant, sense, a community. (2:49-50)

For Royce, then, a community is "one conscious spiritual whole of life" (2:406), formed when "the interests of a self lead it to accept any part or item of the same past or the same future which another self accepts as its own" (2:51–52).

Roycean communities are distinguished and graded on the bases of genuine loyalty, scope, and logical form. A *"natural* community" consists of members attached to each other through a common cause yet somehow closed to all other human selves who are thus made into outsiders. Many families, tribes, and nations are not only primarily self-interested but also exclusive towards the interests of outsider selves and groups. At times, when Royce put less emphasis on the commitment to a common cause in the members of these natural communities and more upon their exclusivism, alienation, and hostility, he highlighted how base and divisive such communities are in their captivity to sin by calling them "communities of hate" (1:168, 183).

By contrast, a *"genuine* community" is one in which a living, conscious union of love and loyalty binds members to each other and to their community and it to them. In it the members have been transformed from being "lost individuals" into such whole-hearted servants of the community that they are opened to a universal loyalty towards all minded beings and to the growth of this genuine (universal) loyalty in everyone. Such a favored or graced community is the "ideal community," or, when viewed as united to the Spirit of the universal community, an instance of a "Beloved Community."

Three selves or more is the basis for variously sized communities. Insofar as each present self makes ideal extensions to its remembered past and expected future, it reveals the pattern of community within each living human person. From this limit instance, communities range through conjugal selves united in their cause, then through familial, tribal, and national communities, up to that union of all *human* selves of all times, which Royce calls the "*Great* Community," and even more inclusively to that union of all selves whatever (minded and physical) which constitute the "*universal* community." When the universal community is viewed as loved and directed by its Spirit, it is called the "Universal *Beloved* Community" or extensively "the Realm of Grace" (1:172). Here the Spirit loves each member with the gift or "grace" of true (or universal) loyalty while all its members appreciate their shared life of communication and cooperation for the further birth and development of true loyalty in all minded selves.

Finally, a *"Community of Interpretation"* is Royce's technical term (2:211) for any community whose members are diversely yet complementarily animated by the "Will to interpret," open and loyal to the interpretive process that creates novel signs, and differentiated by their roles which are determined by that distinctive, triadic, logical form of sign-sender, sign-interpreter, and sign-receiver. This form is the indispensable basis for any genuine community life.

In Royce's title, the term "Problem" is understood appreciatively, not descriptively. That is, a problem like Christianity is not suited for the descriptive methods of the positive sciences. Rather, with this kind of problem, one enters into a reality to ponder its paradoxical features with appreciation and understanding while tentatively probing its mystery with respect and wisdom (1:11-13). The latter is an appreciative understanding of the problem.

After his 1912 Peircean insight, Royce's meaning of "experience" became enriched. Without downplaying the need for percepts, concepts, and their blendings as materials feeding experience, Royce came into more sure touch with a unique new level in human experience. Sign-theory transformed his earlier subject-object articulation of human experience. He now viewed experience as the process of interpreting signs. In the *Problem* he wrote:

> Our experience, as it comes to us, is a realm of Signs. . . . You can never exhaustively find out what they [the facts of experience] are by resorting either to perception or to conception. . . . For a fact of experience, as you actually view that fact, is first an event belonging to an order of time,—an event preceded by an infinite series of facts whose meaning it summarizes, and leading to an infinite series of coming events, into whose meaning it is yet to enter. . . . Past time we regard as real, because we view our memories as signs which need and possess their interpretations. Our expectations are interpreted to our future selves by our present deeds. Therefore we regard our expectations as signs of a future. (2:289-290)

Royce continued by showing that for a person who could *only* unite percepts and concepts, "past time and future time would be as meaningless as the signpost would be to the wayfarer who could not read, and who found nobody to interpret to him its meaning" (2:289-290). Here his final words reveal the parallel between social experience and temporal experience. Our past selves are linked by memory-signs to our present interpreting self just as our future selves are linked by expectation-signs to our present interpreting self. This temporal process of interpretation also marks all human social experience because the latter is also mediate, serial, and moving. My genuine social experience goes beyond percepts and concepts of you to encounter you through a close, personal touch that is mediated by that series of living signs through which you manifest or hide your deeper self, interact with me or abstain, as you decide. Similarly, at the higher level of community experience, the socio-temporal process of sign-interpretation is what Royce means by experience (2:60–69).

At both levels, the interpretive processes circulate around signs. With Peirce, Royce defined a sign as an "object of interpretation" (2:282). Some most frequently used kinds of signs are general ideas, leading ideas, "thirds," and "betweens." The general idea is a vague sign, enjoying much indeterminacy and calling recipient minds to enjoy their freedom. The leading idea is less indeterminate, orients the procedure of a community of investigators, yet is almost as dominant as the general idea. As interpretation proceeds, there emerge "third ideas," or a kind of "thirds" called "betweens" whose function is to bring hitherto divergent minds into unity by completing one phase of the interpretive process and by thus inviting them to begin a further phase.

It becomes clear, then, that Royce's much earlier descriptions of human experience—found, for instance, in his writings of 1885 and 1900—have been startlingly surpassed by the descriptions occurring in the *Problem*. In few areas of Royce's 1912 thought is Peirce's presence more felt than in the mature Royce's meaning of experience.

Although the Roycean meanings—"Christianity," "community," "problem," and "experience"—connote some mystery, when the Roycean terms "human person," "religion," and "revelation" are mentioned, mystery immediately surfaces. This triad of terms, then, calls for more thorough treatment.

The Human Person

The living subject who experiences Christianity as a problem that involves religion, revelation, and even salvation is the human person. What did the mature Royce mean by the term "human person"?[37] Through ongoing interpretation Royce came to an intimate knowledge of the individual human person as an embodied minded being whose inmost life is *as* uniquely individual and eternal *as* it is inescapably temporal and social. With the living inflow of a significant past and the sign-expectations of the future, the human person is itself a process of interpretation that lives by communication with other minded beings in community.[38] Royce viewed human nature as "the very nature of the processes of growth themselves" (1:57–58). If the human person happened to be an educated civilized self, inculturated within the rapidly changing twentieth century, he received the title "modern man" (1:14–19). Thus, for Royce, human nature was neither a static essence nor some inert particle moved only externally. For him, the idea of the human person was neither some collage of reenforcing images of various perceived persons nor some set of abstract conceptual characteristics.

Physical, biological, and psychological accounts of the human person are interesting, validated, and enriching. Primarily, however, they are descriptions in the objective mode. Such was the middle Royce's insightful yet mechanical symbol of the human self as a "dynamo of ideas."[39] Only in his final years did he come to regard the human person as an embodied "minded being" who, according to his or her inmost creativity, receives and sends purposive ideas through psychic and organic structures in the hope of communicating and cooperating with others within a universal and communal historical process of interpretation. A more accurate appreciation of the meaning of the human person is seen in Royce's phenomenological, metaphysical, and ethical approaches to the human person.

Phenomenologically, Royce arrived at his fundamental view of the human subject by following a pathway of increasing interiority.[40] When one penetrates his different layers of consciousness, he experiences different degrees of psychic "warmth." These degrees mark out Royce's pathway of increasing interiority. One experiences, for instance, the more passive reception of perceptions as "colder" than one's feeling of active familiarity when one responds by habit according to one's desires. Again, one's passive perception is "colder" than the felt sense of making an intellectual discovery. As "colder," perceptions reveal themselves as less intimate to the human self than the "warmer" ongoing conscious life of inner habits. Accordingly, Royce situated sensitiveness at the outer ring of consciousness and active docility in an intermediate ring. Finally, at the inmost core of the human self he situated the psyche's creative initiative for from it arises the person's unique *élan* to seek the new, to turn attention elsewhere, to be authentically in touch with one's truest self.

Metaphysically, Royce sometimes spoke of the human person as a "human self," sometimes as a "minded being." In still other contexts he referred to him as "man the individual" and "man the community." These usages need to be clarified.

The mature Royce viewed minded beings (or minds) as the highest kind of selves. He employed the wider term "self" to refer universally to every reality from the smallest material particle to the infinite all-Knower, since he viewed each reality as a self-reflective order, whether finite or not. He wrote,

> A self is, by its very essence, a being with a past. . . . no mere datum, but is in its essence a life which is interpreted, and which interprets itself. (2:40, 61)

As a creative agency, the self must have some ideal interpretation of itself. Otherwise it cannot search for its fullest individuality as it further interprets its own life through self-identifying serial activities.[41] The term "minded being," rather than indicating something directly perceptible or conceivable, points to a sign-sending subject who calls for interpretation. Minded being is an intelligent will that not only has the nature of a unique self but also has the nature of a community, so that

> whether through or apart from an organism it expresses its purposes to other minds . . . and is in essence a mode of self-expression which progressively makes itself known either to its fellows or to minds above or below its own grade.[42]

Ethically, Royce's term "human self" conveys clear moral significance. That meaning which constitutes the self, which unites its series of choice, and which provides the basis for its process of self-identification and its sense of self-identity is either "open" or "not open" to dedicated activity on behalf of the community. This difference in basic self-constitutive meanings led Royce to distinguish between "man the mere individual" and "man the loyal individual." The former is the morally detached individual whose own self-interest is his supreme value. The latter has been transformed through the advent of loyalty into a self wholeheartedly dedicated to the universalistic cause of a genuine community.[43]

Moral deadness (or impotence to integrate knowledge, will, love, and deed) is a mark of "man the mere individual." This last term can refer to a morally isolated individual human self or to the whole human race viewed as a morally impotent mass of such individuals.[44] Essentially, man the mere individual cannot move towards the goal of human life because only through the saving influence of the whole human community can he become empowered to dedicate himself in loyalty to a genuine community and spell out his dedication in the loyal deeds that progressively save him.

Royce's term "man the community" needs careful handling. His intent is often missed because people mistake it for a mere collectivity of human individuals. Rather, by "man the community," Royce meant the invisible community of humankind's shared spiritual interests, ideals, and hopes and of its shared processes of communication and cooperation. It is Royce's deeper "second level" of humankind's existence and consciousness — even if this second level is not exclusively human but is "in its inmost nature, a divine community" (1:39). Coming to his own critically important description of "man the community," Royce took exceptional care to clear away all the debris of misleading interpretations before defining this term positively. Our two excerpts concern first the reality and then the way we come to the saving idea of it.

> Man the community is the source of salvation. And by man the community I mean, *not* the collective biological entity called the human race, and not the merely natural community which gives to us, as social animals, our ordinary moral training. Nor by man the community do I mean the series of misadventures and tragedies whereof the merely external history of what is

called humanity consists. By man the community I mean man in the sense in which Paul conceived Christ's beloved and universal Church to be a community,—man viewed as one conscious spiritual whole of life. And I say that this conscious spiritual community is the sole possessor of the means of grace, and is the essential source of the salvation of the individual. . . .
   The saving idea of man the community comes to us through two kinds of perfectly human experience. . . . the failure both of our natural self-will and of our mere morality to save us . . . [and] the experience of the meaning of loyalty. . . . [This experience] justly seems to be a revelation of something not ourselves which is worthy to be our guide and salvation. (1:405–408)

Lines more Roycean and more deserving of meditation are difficult to find.

In sum, Royce viewed the human person phenomenologically as an historical process whose chosen plan of life gives unity and self-identity. Metaphysically, the human person is an embodied minded being interacting in community. Ethically Royce saw the human person as a living reality called to transmute its individualistic self-identity by devoting oneself to the cause of some genuine community (1:15–20). Since the mature Royce habitually viewed the contemporary human person as essentially both a unique individual and a community member destined and called to ever deeper community through present-day cultural matrices, the human person is radically a two-leveled reality. Persons remain in their roots mysteries never fully to be comprehended by finite minded beings. In the end, then, they can be "fairly understood" only if interpreted through at least a pair of approaches: one as unique individual, the other as community; one as real interpreter, the other as sign to be interpreted communally.[45]

Royce acknowledged that his meaning of "modern man" assumes that the human person is undergoing a coherent process of education through cultural evolution, is called to teach what one has learned from the past, and is able to read the lesson of history's educational process (1:17–18). More than all other human dimensions, the fact that through the ages all human persons are undergoing an educational process (which in its inmost message is the same for all) accounts for the unity of the human race "as one conscious spiritual whole of life" (1:406). The one life that energizes this "conscious spiritual whole" "is no mere flow and strife of opinions, but includes a growth in genuine insight" (1:18–19). This dynamic spiritual life of billions of human participants is "man the community" and its interest is the "cause" which calls all to genuine loyalty.

Religion

We make our way towards Royce's meaning of "religion" by first finding what he meant by "religious experience." He knew it was viewed at different levels and he wanted to delve into it more deeply than four groups of his contemporaries wanted to.[46] First, Jamesian enthusiasts considered religious experience a random game of hide-and-seek with subliminal forces. They thought that religious experience lay in feverish agitation. Secondly, pure action-oriented utilitarians felt that it was poor strategy to ask probingly whether religious experiences were really genuine. In our actual world of morose restless doubters, it seemed shrewder to give full recognition to the occurrence of religious experiences. This tactic supplies a fitting antidote to that scepticism which paralyzes action. Thirdly, fundamentalist readers of Scripture saw "no hope except in holding fast by a literal acceptance of tradition."[47] In such tenacity alone, they claimed, lay saving religious experiences. Finally, romantics imagined religious experience as some idyllic return to the lifestyle achieved by the first followers of some great leader like Jesus or Buddha.

Royce considered these four views essentially trivial and to be shunned. Instead, he held that however varied and mysterious religious experiences are, when genuine they have a living bond at their heart: they put the person having the experience into a "practical relation to a spiritual world" which serves supremely as the "cause" that genuine loyalty seeks.[48] Or, putting the essence of religions from the other side, Royce portrayed it as "a spiritual world's . . . close and comforting touch with our most intense personal concerns."[49]

Besides the need to penetrate beneath surface perceptions of religious experience, Royce knew the need of seeing its development. He surveyed the religious experience of various peoples, ranging from primitives to the most sophisticated humanitarian servants of his world. Throughout this range, he discerned that religion, as the basic living bond of the human self with a superhuman other, undergoes transformations during the following four stages of humanity's developing religious consciousness.

In its first steps, primitive religious consciousness emphasizes group ritual practices. But when civilization rises, religious consciousness stresses sincere creedal profession by the individual even more than external conformity in group actions.[50] A third and higher stage appears when, through the presence of transforming grace, there occurs "an experience of the highest realities of human life and of the universe," such that the person reacts in an integrated faith and practice.[51] This gracious conversion shows itself in a love of *all* human selves without exclusion *and* of "something superhuman." But when a thinker attempts to specify "precisely what this vital feature of the higher religion is," then the forces of twentieth-century individualism, doubts, and Christian disunity keep him from reaching a clear exact formulation.[52] Finally, however, this development reaches its fourth and final stage, the religion of loyalty. This occurs when the previous universal love of individuals is transfigured by the distinctive life of genuine loyalty towards communities *as such.*

In this highest flowering of religious consciousness, loyalty is the wholehearted dedication of oneself to a community as such and to that kind of "cause" which unites many loyal selves into "one conscious spiritual whole of life" (1:406). To preserve and increase a community's "spiritual whole of life" insofar as it promotes that of the universal community is the fundamental intent of this religious community (1:68). By adopting its distinctive "cause" as one's own, one becomes a genuinely loyal member, and allows this "cause" to function as an indispensable factor in genuine self-identification (2:89, 187).

Viewing genuine loyalty from various perspectives lets one understand why Royce found the highest stage of religious consciousness in his "religion of loyalty." Viewed in its specificity, genuine loyalty does not relate a person directly to other individuals as such, but rather, it relates a person directly to the Community *as* a community and to God *as* the all-Knowing Community of Interpretation (2:11, 219). Viewed in its mutuality, loyalty means that the higher reality (true community in any of its genuine forms) lovingly supports each of its members while each member wholeheartedly serves the community in and through orderly service to all human selves and their supporting communities. Viewed in its practical thrust, loyalty moves the members of its community to commit themselves intensely towards first discovering the fittest ways of dealing with world problems and then cooperating so fully in the practical execution of the resultant plans that members constantly advance the coming of the Great Community (1:171-172, 190-191; 2:98).

Royce limited himself to interpret religious experience "from the human side only" — that is, from the side of common religious needs and interest of human nature (1:35, 122) or of "only the universally human significance of the ideal [of community]" (2:12). He wanted to "restrict our answer to human objects, and deliberately avoid theology" (1:374-375; 304-305). He chose *not* to view religious experience "from the divine side." That is, he *avoided* considering it in the light of three perspectives: (1) of the activity of some supposed divine object; (2) of the divinely given insights communicated through the gift of Faith to members of a community (claiming a special revelation about God's covenantal intervention in their group, about his intent in so doing, and about his inner life); and (3) of the subsequently constructed dogmas, doctrines, and theologies that try to articulate such a Faith.

Next, by comparing and contrasting a pair of Royce's refined descriptions, we can better grasp his mature meaning of "religion." Royce saw that simple people experience religion as a lived reality; they know it deeply without comprehending it fully or articulating it adequately. He felt that attempts to define the richness of this "deep popular mind" would result in impoverishment.[53] His growing conviction was that emotion, fitting symbolic images, and aesthetic guidance are as necessary and vital to religion as are its beliefs and commitments.[54] Royce tried to portray religion by including feelings, commitment to action, imagination, and symbols in his description. In this he followed the lead of C. S. Peirce.[55] Furthermore, in 1912, when Royce was shifting from his earlier dyadic mode of knowing to a Peircean triadic manner of interpretive knowing, he recognized how awkward it was to treat religion as if it were a subject related to an object. Even when he used a personal term to describe the object, he shortly expanded it to include the impersonal. For instance:

> Religion, as we have said, in seeking salvation, seeks some form of communication with the master of life. That is, it seeks to come into touch with a power, a principle, or a mind, or a heart, that, on the one hand, possesses, or, with approval, surveys or controls the real nature of things, and that, on the other hand, welcomes us in our conflicts with evil, supports our efforts, and secures our success.[56]

Nonetheless, in his earlier *Philosophy of Loyalty* Royce had supplied definitions of religion, both "in any form" and "in its highest form," which are instructive. Summing up his search for constancies in religious experience, Royce stated, "Religion, in any form, has always been an effort to interpret and make use of some superhuman world."[57]

This 1908 description of "religion in any form" specified two ways in which people express such efforts: they interpret some superhuman world and they make use of it. This delicate balance expressed Royce's absolute pragmatism. As he saw it, religion called a person throughout life to purify his interpretation of the superhuman. This call was as absolute as religion's living bond of the human self to the superhuman world.

On the other hand, Royce's phrase, to "make use of" a superhuman world, might misleadingly evoke ideas of magic or superstitions. His meaning, however, became clear when he later singled out man's concern to be saved[58] or "to win the true goal of life" as the essential feature of religion (1:117). Since the most useful thing a person can win is salvation, he should "make use of" the superhuman world. How? Precisely by allowing it to provide him with his life's true ultimate goal and the way to that goal.[59]

So, by balancing self-interest and objective truth, Royce led his audience through the merely pragmatic to a deeper and more intimate universe where loyal selves encounter "the superhuman, the city out of sight, the union with all life,—the essentially eternal."[60] He had already pointed up the nexus between this "essentially eternal" and the religion of loyalty when he "defined loyalty as the will to manifest the eternal in and through the deeds of individual selves."[61]

Raising his sights from religion "in any form" to religion "in its highest historical forms," Royce defined the latter as *"the interpretation both of the eternal and of the spirit of loyalty through emotion, and through a fitting activity of the imagination."*[62] How did this definition diverge from the former one, yet parallel it?

Differences arise through his substitution here of "the eternal" and "the spirit of loyalty" for his earlier "superhuman world." Moreover, unlike religion in any form, religion in its highest forms requires emotion and fitting imagination. As to parallels, in both definitions the act of interpretation is central. Moreover, the interpersonal union experienced between the superhuman spirit of loyalty and loyal selves in religious community recalls Royce's emphasis on that vital practical bond with the superhuman world which is found in any form of religion.[63]

A few years later Royce showed an even more experiential and operational meaning of religion. In his 1912 *Sources* he was searching for a signpost to guide his investigation into "the ways in which religious truths can become accessible to men." Pragmatically he selected as "the essential feature of religion," "this *interest in the salvation of man.*"[64] A year later in the *Problem* he acknowledged modestly that his work made but a small contribution to a consensus on the meaning of religion. Only the diversified endeavors of many researchers could generate the kind of meaning which would evoke unity (1:6). Yet he offered his mature interpretation of the nature of religion. From history he showed that religion is "a product of certain human needs" and survives only if it meets those needs (1:385). Moreover, he witnessed to the fact that if religion is not communal, it cannot be religion (1:xvi). Since the duty of religion is "to aim towards the creation on earth of the Beloved Community," religion's future task is to invent and apply the arts that will win people over to unity (2: 430). In the *Problem,* then, genuine religion must be rooted in human needs and interests, marked by the character of community, destined to transform humankind from its alienations, and energized to develop the arts of cooperation. Such was the mature Royce's deeply appreciative grasp of religion.

In summary of the way the meaning of religion developed in the mature Royce's thought, we saw that he avoided superficial perceptions of religious experience. In all four stages of developing religious consciousness, he identified finite selves' interpretation and use of an abiding and saving superhuman presence as the living heart of religion. Royce was unwilling to over-specify the living mystery of religion through conceptual overload lest he impoverish his interpretive "close personal touch" with its reality. So he increasingly eschewed a comprehensive definition of religion. Instead, his two 1908 working definitions of religion—in any form and in its highest forms—reveal Royce's intent to wed the absolute and pragmatic factors in these meanings of religion. They also emphasize that interpretation is the activity which effects the essential interaction of religion, forming the living union in which finite selves both appeal to the presence of something superhuman and respond to it. Because this process of communication mediates some teaching or training, the final term to surface for clarification is "revelation."

Revelation

"Whatever intercourse there may be between the divine and the human" is what revelation means, taken in a general sense.[65] Royce was not disturbed when some people simply claimed that they had experienced, in ways as common as the influence of air and sunshine, the ordinary initiatives of the divine reality manifesting itself to them. He acknowledged his own "profound respect for the mystical element in religion" (1:399). Yet the claims of many mystics to an *im*mediate touch with the divine made him uneasy and their frequent lack of loyalty to the whole human community made him regard such mysticism as "the essentially immature aspect of the deeper religious life" (2:401).

However he became quite concerned when others made the additional claim that, through tradition, they had received a special revelation from a divine Revealer who intended to form a chosen people. In his personal reply to this latter group, who often preened themselves on not being like the rest of men, Royce admittedly used measured terms. As he saw it, their claim obliged them to witness to their special revelation with an extra measure of enlightened service to all people.[66] Still, as a philosopher of religion, he recognized that, if he wanted profitable dialogue with people claiming a special revelation, he would have to highlight both the *kind of intent* required of any special revelation and the *presupposition* overlooked by these claimants.

The Jewish and Christian people claim to be chosen by a special revelation. In Royce's view, any group making such a claim is inescapably related to the whole human brotherhood "as part to whole" or "as an organ of the invisible church."[67] Therefore, for a special revelation to become even a coherently conceivable possibility, the benefit of the whole human community would have to be its underlying intent. Hence, any special revelation made to a "chosen people" has to transform this group into a living communal instrument that is inescapably intended to benefit all humankind by becoming a sign communicating this revelation to everyone.

Moreover, each member of such a chosen people would have to recognize and live out a new special responsibility: to serve "man the community" and all human selves through communicating in this special way. They might not see immediately how heavy a burden this is. As Royce put it, the historical fate of religions is determined by both the changing and the constant needs that all humankind has as one community of worshippers. Yet he felt it was equally true that all

> worshippers actually need an everlasting gospel; and that if such a gospel were to be revealed to man, it would not only satisfy human needs, but also contain absolute religious truth. (1:386–387)[68]

Royce believed he had identified just "such a gospel" (unending good news) in his "Christian doctrine of life." He foresaw this doctrine as alone able to show eternal constancy amid the accelerating cultural changes in our world (1:395–397). Therefore, any people chosen to communicate a special gospel bear the responsibility of spiritual life-or-death towards all others.

Royce's second ground of concern was that *presupposition* such claimants usually overlook, which he named "the religious paradox."[69] Knowing that the religious attitude itself involved "an opening toward the divine and some manifestation of the divine presence in human experience,"[70] he did not deny that ordinary or special revelation could or did occur. Yet revelation presupposes that its human recipients already know human nature and destiny. For only thus can they both distinguish the incoming divine communication from the human reality already present and also judge whether this new presence fittingly fulfills human nature and promotes its true destiny. Only thus can they distinguish between the authentically divine and the merely human or even demonic. Royce described what this "paradox of revelation" presupposes as follows:

> Unless there is something in our individual experience which at least begins to bring us into a genuine touch, both with the fact that we need salvation and with the marks whereby we may recognize the way of salvation, and the essentially divine process, if such there be, which alone can save—unless, I say, there is within each of us something of this interior light by which saving divine truth is to be discerned, religious insight is impossible, and then no merely external revelation can help us.[71]

In brief, only a human person who is a qualified interpreter can wisely welcome an external revelation. Royce's emphasis here on the *sine qua non* in each potential recipient of revelation is in no way to be equated with a subjectivistic doctrine of "mere inner light" or of theological immanentism. Rather, he stressed the need to insure the free humane quality of one's religious acceptance of revelation.[72]

When clarifying his notion of revelation in this essay, Royce hinted that the human person is not left alone when interiorly discerning an external revelation. He asserted that "without the witness of the spirit in the heart, no external revelation could enlighten those who are in darkness."[73] Even when treating of the individual human self as the primary, if always inadequate, source of religious insight, Royce pointed to a Community of Interpretation within the individual.[74] It follows, then, that his experiential basis for exploring religion is essentially social and open to the divine. This suggests something of the mystery Royce encountered in the human person and in religion.

The Problem of Christianity clearly develops from the problems, attitudes, and doctrine Royce manifested in his earlier *Loyalty, Essays,* and *Sources.* Of course, he chose different emphases in the *Problem* and omitted much of his previous work. This continuity is particularly evident in Royce's steady efforts to clarify religious consciousness, to employ his methodological positivism in his researches, and to present the human person as bi-leveled. He also built up his own rich meanings for such terms as the human person, religion, and revelation and regarded human experience—at least in the *Problem*—as a process that interprets Signs. The rich results of his researches into religious experience lead one to wonder about the logic guiding the inquiries of his mature philosophy of religion.

3. Creating a Pure Logic and Methodology

After perusing Royce's *The World and the Individual* and after kindly acknowledging the gift copies, Charles Sanders Peirce entreated Royce, "when I read you, I do wish that you would study logic. You need it so much."[1] Royce responded by dedicating himself to more and more logical study.[2] A dozen years later, in the *Problem,* Royce called public attention to this 1901 Peircean correction of himself (2:117). Evidently, Peirce's strong words had been for Royce not only memorable but "epoch-marking." In 1913 Royce could look back at the twelve intervening years of his studies into the foundations and systems of pure logic and feel confident that these logical investigations had borne fruit. He knew that from 1901 to 1912 his progressively deeper and broader logical researches — studies that had been minute, penetrating, and adventurous — had profoundly affected his orientation to the *Problem.* The spirit and findings of those researches provided him with the general direction needed to locate his "problem," to select a fitting overall method, to further revise his plans for the *Problem,* and to make, during its drafting, the series of choices then needed for executing his final plan.

Yet in the text of the *Problem* Royce was thunderously silent about his own technical logic and about its influence in shaping the *Problem.* Although he acknowledged repeatedly the role of Peirce's logic in this work, he never hinted to his audience that just two years earlier he himself had created "The Principles of Logic." Yet C. D. Broad applauded Royce's 1910 survey and synthesis of logic as undoubtedly "the best contribution" to *Logik,* the collection of essays by six outstanding logicians which Arnold Ruge had edited.[3] In his own copy of the 1912 *Logik,* Royce had noted that the issues he discussed in his "Principles of Logic" were more important than the length of this "brief" logical article of sixty-nine pages suggested — and for two reasons. In the "Principles" he had outlined more fully than in any of his previous logical essays just what logic consists in when it is viewed as "a Theory of Order." Even more significantly, as his note continued, in these "Principles" he had discerned "a programme of a future possible Logic; and, *as* a programme [it] has a place in a fairly extensive plan."[4] After the publication of the *Problem,* Royce informed Professor Warner Fite that the Oxford audience's lack of the needed training in technical logic had kept him from sharing with them the logical technicalities of his basic relationship of "membership," called the *epsilon* relation (= ε).[5] Royce had preferred to be tactful. Yet when one considers how much interest, effort, and research Royce had invested in logical studies from 1901 to 1912 and how he had already achieved an important synthesis in his "Principles," his reticence in the *Problem* to acknowledge how his own pure logic determined that work seems significant.

Sensitive to this hidden influence, Bruce Kuklick has directed attention to the fact that the theses of Royce's "Principles of Logic" are connected with those of the *Problem.*[6] Yet Kuklick also states that the exact nature of this connection remains unclear.[7] In the present section, then, we will clarify this relationship as much as we can. In general, we will ask: Which kind of pure logic did Royce choose as a guide when in 1912 he reformulated his plans for investigating "the problem of Christianity"? What kind of influence did his pure logic have upon his general philosophy of religion (his *Sources*) and then upon his philosophy of the Christian religion (his *Problem*)? In particular, we will ask: (1) During the dozen years following his publications of *The World and the Individual* (1901), what were the high points of Royce's growth in the discipline of logic? (2) Did the *Problem* express that highest Methodology which he had described in his "Principles"? (He distinguished this Methodology or Applied Logic both from philosophical method and from the Pure Logic which his General Theory of Order exemplified.) (3) About the time of his publication of the *Problem,* what did Royce's lived experience of "thinking logically" consist in?

Royce's growth in logical prowess from 1901 to 1912 was stimulated both by many logicians, such as C. S. Peirce, A. B. Kempe, and Bertrand Russell,[8] as well as by such Christian mysteries as the Trinity and the Incarnation. Royce's repeated references to his 1905 "Memoir" to the American Mathematical Society indicate his appraisal of it as his then most significant contribution to logic.[9] He entitled it, "The Relation of the Principles of Logic to the Foundations of Geometry."[10] In this Memoir Royce called attention to the largely neglected views of the English logician A. B. Kempe. Perhaps Royce noticed how deeply Peirce had been influenced by Kempe. In any case, Royce *revised* Kempe's principles by adding "a further principle regarding the existence of certain logical entities"—the actuality of any logician's inescapable "modes of action."[11] The result was that Royce found himself "forced to conceive the existence of a system called . . . System Σ [= Sigma], . . . an extremely general order-system."[12]

Beyond the connection of logic to geometry, indicated by the title of his Memoir, Royce was especially interested in the bearing of pure logic on all the sciences. Thus in 1908, when he discovered Peirce's "thoughts about the nature and conditions of the inductive sciences" tucked within a brief passage of the latter's "A Neglected Argument for the Reality of God," Royce became "extremely interested."[13] Two years later, when drafting his "Principles of Logic," he judged that in this essay he had worked out better his intent to promote the sciences than ever before. He here defined a "general theory of order" applicable to "all the order-systems upon which, at least at present, the theoretical natural sciences depend for the success of their deductions."[14]

In approximately the fall of 1911, however, Royce experienced tension mounting between his epistemology and his habitual way of formulating the insight fundamental to his intellectual career, the insight expressed in his 1883 argument from the "possibility of error."[15] He discovered that insofar as his idealism relied on an epistemology of mere percepts, concepts, and their combinations, he could no longer adequately solve the problem of the possibility of error, that problem which had germinated his philosophy. Gropingly, he concluded his 1911 "Error and Truth" article by identifying seven conditions needed for any satisfactory solution of this problem. He emphasized the need for a "revision of Hegel's dialectical method, a synthesis of this method with the empirical tendencies of recent Pragmatism, [and] a combination of both with the methods of Modern Logic."[16] Already in his 1910 "Principles of Logic" he had proposed his preferred approach to "the methods of modern Logic" and had recommended as its highest Methodology an "Organized Combination of Theory and Experience." During the following year, Royce detected that, unlike Hegel who left many matters "profoundly problematic," Charles Peirce, the "father of Pragmatism," cast new light on them by requiring a "very exact logical working out of concepts" (2:184–186; 116). This careful elaboration led Royce step by step to recognize how sharply Peirce's empiricism, originality, and generality contrasted with Hegel's dialectical method. As a result Royce discovered that if Hegel's dialectical method were transformed according to Peirce's ideas and approach to logic, it would satisfy the first part of that crucial "Requirement #7" with which Royce gropingly had concluded his "Error and Truth" article.[17] Furthermore, he could satisfy Requirement #7 completely if he combined his Peircean "revision of Hegel's dialectical method" both with recent Pragmatism's tendencies to take into account how an agent's "modes of action" affect experience and with the "methods of modern logic." Both of these were unknown to Hegel.

This creative combination transformed Royce's mature mode of thinking. It enabled him to become the kind of interpreter who can fittingly apply pure logic to the deductions of the theoretical natural sciences. Royce's choice empowered him to discern and describe that "spirit which is as rare as it is requisite in a man who is to prove a thoroughly good methodologist."[18] Such an interpreter would possess "a certain judicial temper, a breadth of view, a fondness for synthesis, an exactness of intellectual training, [and] a love of the comparative study of his topic." These would be marks chiefly distinguishing him from most "pragmatists, positivists, [and] relativists."[19] Peirce had led Royce to realize that human knowing is, in its deepest life, an interpretive process (2:110). With this help Royce's pure logic of Σ had developed its new and distinctive methodology.

Besides the suggestions of pure logicians, the leading ideas of Christianity's central mysteries influenced the mature Royce's growth in logic. He claimed exclusive responsibility for asserting that the traditional doctrine of Christ's "two natures" was related to his own thesis about the "two levels" of "man the individual" and "man the community."[20] The idea of the Trinity also operated in the genesis of Royce's late logic.[21] He was intrigued by the structure of these two ideas and by their way of developing through psychological necessity into the two traditional basic Christian dogmas.[22] To him the idea of Christ's "two natures" suggested the *Problem*'s fundamental doctrine of "two levels." To him the idea of the Trinity suggested his initial triad of selves sharing life, logic, and loyalty in fecund community. As "leading ideas," these two doctrines confirmed Royce's creation of System Σ.

He had begun Σ by assuming self-identical elements and operations and by co-requiring relations and sets. For Royce, logic's most fundamental relation arises through an element's "belonging" or "not belonging" to a set; that is, being or not being in *epsilon* relation to it: (= ε or $\bar{\varepsilon}$). This relation controls all the element's other relations and, in turn, *epsilon*'s asymmetry both determines all the relations of the set towards this element and qualifies all the other relations of elements and sets in System Σ.[23] Upon these relational bases, Royce worked out his "general theory of order" and then applied it to the logics of geometry and of pure natural science. In this procedure the Trinitarian idea already showed its presence. Its guidance became more clear when Royce's Will to Interpret, in parallel with the Spirit "between" the Father and Word, actualized that triadic relation according to which an interpretive process develops the universe historically.

Moreover, since Christ's human individuality is in ε-relation to the divine Community, the idea of the "two *levels*" of individuals and of community is introduced.[24] Thus, the hint Royce derived from the traditional idea of Christ's "two natures"—one making him a human individual, the other identifying him with a divine community—shows itself no less operative, even if less conspicuous, than the Trinitarian idea in the *Problem*.

In brief, Royce's unique and climactic development in logic from 1901 to 1912 was seeded by his original insights for creating System Σ, by his genius at synthesis, by Trinitarian and christological ideas, and by the ideas of Peirce and other logicians.

As a logician well developed by 1912, the mature Royce probably employed his "Principles of Logic" in some way when creating the *Problem*. Our second question, then, begins to investigate this likely relationship. In the opening section of "Principles," which deals with the application of pure logic to scientific disciplines, Royce sketched the various levels of methodology. He identified the topmost of these as "the organized combination of theory and experience." Was such a combination carried out in the *Problem?*

Royce began his "Principles" by noting that logic is associated popularly with sound methodic thinking. This time-honored discipline of "general or formal logic" no longer stood at the center of logic because a much deeper and broader descriptive discipline, "Logic as the Science of Order," had been discovered, which simply enfolded within itself the traditional logic as a small normative domain.

However, Methodology, that other discipline of traditional logic, seemed to Royce so critically needed in his day that he assigned most of section one of his "Principles" to it. He described Methodology as "a study of the norms and methods of thought used in the various arts and sciences."[25] If the inquiries of the experientially based sciences are to achieve the combinations and comparisons they need for progress, then, to be correct, each of their organically integrated methods, even with its own distinctive diversity, must have in common with the logics of other experiential sciences the four following levels of method. That is, specifically, the overall method in a particular empirical discipline must control and unite serially the three correct subordinate methods whereby this discipline can, first, classify its material; second, discover constancies in those materials once a statistical basis has been gained; and third, form generalizations. Only as supported by these subordinate methods, thought Royce, could an experiential science develop correctly to that fourth level: "the organized combination of theory and experience" which is the "paramount method" of the four levels of Methodology.[26] This was the way Royce sketched Methodology as "Applied Logic" in 1910. Methodology *mediated* between "Pure Logic" (taken as the General Science of Order, such as his System Σ), and the distinctive method suited for a specific discipline like chemistry or philosophy of religion.

The intriguing question thus arises: What happened in Royce's thinking when that interest in religious problems, which had first driven him to philosophy forty years earlier, now after his completion of the "Principles of Logic," impelled him still further into an investigation of religion in general and of Christianity in particular?[27]

Royce's inductive work on religion in some of his *Essays* (1911), and especially in his *Sources* (1912), had actually prepared his materials in much the way these three specific methods do. When he came to create the *Problem*, then, did he concern himself principally with the highest level of methodology described in his "Principles"? I think so.

Generally, in his introduction to the *Problem*, Royce described its Part One as "discussing religious experience" and its Part Two as "dealing with its metaphysical foundations" (1:xxxv). When drawing this work to its conclusion, Royce answered our question more clearly. There he explicitly intended to use comparison to mediate between religious experience and metaphysical theory (2:279–280), and he organized this combination by putting to work his adaptation of Peirce's overall method of interpretive musement.

More specifically, in Part One, using Christianity's central ideas and people's basic ethico-religious needs as his empirical materials, Royce classified the "most essential" ideas. Then in Christian and non-Christian communities he discovered a certain structure of "membership in the Kingdom," which he generalized into the "Christian doctrine of life." To reach this climatic insight of Part One, Royce used interpretation as the living logic that compares and organizes theory with experience. In this way, he consistently combined the communal religious experience of all religions of loyalty (especially that found in genuine Christian communities) with his theory of "the modern mind" (2:6).

In Part Two, Royce only hinted at the methods of classifying and hunting for statistically revealed constant structures.[28] His emphasis fell rather on generalizing the ideas of community and of interpretation, enlarging them into a metaphysical theory fit for the life and process of the whole world viewed as guided by the Universal Community of Interpretation and its Spirit. Then, in his final three lectures, in order to develop a criterion that would test whether the universe is indeed the expression of the Universal Community and of its Spirit, Royce organized the combination of religious experiences of genuine community with his "generalized theory of an ideal society" (2:281). In these ways, then, the highest methodology of System Σ directed his synthetic movement in the *Problem*.

Our final inquiry in this introduction to the late logic of Royce asks what was his living experience of "thinking logically" near the time of his publishing the *Problem* (1913). In dealing with Royce, the mature logician, the challenge is to keep balancing his concrete art of logic as lived with his pure theory of Order, his System Σ. To this end we will observe what

Pure Logic and Methodology   49

"thinking logically" meant to him during his 1913-1914 seminar and how he revised his plans for the *Problem.*

By this time, Royce knew that logic was more than simply an abstract system of ordered ideas. For him, logic was also life as interpretive, life as far more intimately directive of psychic methods and choices than is any objective system of order, even if the latter is an indispensable conceptual guide. The way Royce artfully "rode" leading ideas and inferences during his 1913-1914 Seminar in Comparative Methodology showed how familiar he had become with this living logic. Here he explicitly pointed out that: "Logic stands for becoming conscious of the procedure and not of premises."[29] Seated with colleagues and students around his seminar table, Royce alertly recognized how his and their thought-responses were creating a series of yeas and nays to certain relations, sets, classes, levels, leading ideas, and transformative procedures that entered into the seminar's process. Within this series of both positive and negative modes of assertive action, an absolute pragmatism embodied itself. As a pragmatist, Royce placed primacy on agency, as did James and Dewey; yet as an absolute pragmatist, Royce identified an absolute character in every deed, unlike James and Dewey. For example, these yes-or-no assertions expressed choices which were either right or wrong and which, once made, became irrevocably so. By using dialogic inquiry to co-create consciousness of communal life in this seminar, Royce became directly "conscious of the procedure and not of the premises." These sessions of his seminar in methodology so stimulated intellectual life that he later regarded them as his preeminent experience of community.[30]

By interacting with natural scientists in his seminar, Royce discovered the paradoxical pattern of a process of generalization that leads to greater concreteness. He found this pattern in the living logic of scientists and of "philosophers by interpretation." To bring his specialized learning to maturity, the scientist goes through certain levels of increasing abstraction which prepare his mind for a breakthrough into a new hypothesis. So, too, the logician who becomes sensitive to the various levels of logic advances through certain grades of generalization which prepare his mind for a synoptic insight into what is logically more concrete and vital. Comparing the procedures of a zoologist and those of a logician may clarify this pattern.

The zoologist first has to enter into the process of classifying his specimens. Then he has to gather statistics to discover the frequency of a certain shape, behavior, or development. Relying on rates of greater frequency, he next attempts certain generalizations. Yet all this labor remains sterile unless the zoologist proceeds to assemble and interpret these many classifications, rates of frequency, and general laws. Only by bringing these earlier stages into a unified view does he prepare his mind to suspect and then to discover a *new hypothesis* for zoology. Only through this last step, through a process Peirce called "retroduction," does the zoologist finally reach his maximally significant function. The growth of any natural science depends most of all upon the living logic guiding these retroductive breakthroughs into new hypotheses.

The logician experiences similar stages. His first need is to gain categories. These he achieves by objectifying and classifying the elements in his thought. Then, if he transforms these categories into premises, he can detect certain types of necessary consequence. By simplifying these, he reaches the most general laws of logic. Yet all this remains sterile unless through a synthesis of all these stages he finally breaks through to the life and source of these, his concrete assertions as right or wrong. Then he becomes conscious of how he himself is now giving (or not-giving) himself to attend-or-not, to inquire-or-not, to affirm-or-not. In accord with his adopted fundamental attitude towards life and the universe, and in accord with the consequent exigencies of the living logic he has thus chosen, the thinker will assert certain modes of action. He will allow (or not-allow) a certain leading idea to exert its guidance. He will notice (or not-notice) how his yes-or-no choices are determining his procedure. In all these decisions, by the way the interpreter actively participates (or not) in these choices, he concretely constructs or injures both his future self and his communities.

Did a living logic, similar to that employed in his 1913–1914 Seminar, control Royce's creation of the plans for the *Problem* and of the text itself? In the *Problem* he did not explicitly articulate the *technical* logical methodology whereby he chose the aims and procedures of this work, yet he spoke of "the general plan of our whole inquiry," "glimpses of the course of the inquiry," an overall plan, and a close connection of the two parts (1:xxxv–xxxvi, xl; 2:370). Such remarks suggest that Royce had indeed "become conscious of the procedure" controlling his inquiry. If all of Royce's clues are assembled, one can grasp how intent he was to provide his reader, according to the latter's degree of logical training, with fitting guidance into the logic underlying the *Problem*.[31] Yet these many published pointers seem few indeed when contrasted with the frequent hints about his living logic that emerge from his many *un*published plans and musings preparatory to the *Problem*.[32] For instance, in his first extant plans for the *Problem* he highlighted Bergson and James. Although these drafts referred to logic frequently and explicitly, Charles Peirce received only one mention. The later drafts of his plan, however, reveal how a half-year of intervening musement had shifted Royce's main attention from Bergson and James onto Peirce's ideas, which eventually dominated the published text of Part Two of the *Problem*.

Having experienced how his deliberate choice of certain modes of action ignited an intuitional light for guiding his next step logically, Royce became more precisely interested in this pathfinder kind of "logic of the will." In an early draft of his plan he wrote, "The field of logic is the field of deed."[33] Recognizing the role that even logical motives exert on the will in the choice of its logical "modes of action," he wrote, "A superhuman intuition [is] demanded as the fulfillment of the logical motives [within these deeds]," and again, "Logic thus leads to [an] ideal of intuition; intuition logically leads to an ideal of logical articulation." With their allusions to the role of will, both these excerpts from his early plans for the *Problem* suggest the direction of Royce's late revision of his idealism towards emphasizing the centrality of the will's "modes of action."

To the fifth draft of his early plan, Royce appended a "Note." In it he illustrated how the seriation from logic through intuition to articulation works itself out. In this note he focused on the second and third of his leading "Christian ideas," man's sinful state and atonement. Here, by dialectically purifying the idea of sin's punishment from its accidental accretions, Royce eventually won insight into "the *essential* penalty of sin." Then, to articulate this—or to express it distinctly—he wrote that sin's essential punishment lies simply in placing a disloyal act irrevocably within the entire fabric of one's life, like an irremovable stain.

Royce provided another instance of this seriation when he reviewed his fifth draft. He intuited something he called "Essence of the Previous Plan." His articulation of it followed immediately:

> Essence of the Previous Plan: Defence of a rationalized form of the Atonement Doctrine as the true interpretation of the permanent office of religion in human life.[34]

Here interpreter Royce won "close personal touch" with the "essence" of the plan: to make a rational philosophical defense of religion's mission in people's lives, that is, of involving them in an atonement process.

Radiating through this plan was Royce's familiar dialectical process of clarification. A dozen years earlier, in his *The World and the Individual,* he had serially purified his interpretations beyond the Realistic, the Mystical, and the Critically Rational Conceptions of Being until he reached his fourth and final Individual Conception of Being. Similarly, in this fifth draft of his 1912 plan, Royce listed the Liberal, Mystical, and Traditional Forms of Christianity. This draft shows how he had pushed beyond these inadequate views of Christianity by using his process of insisting serially on further interpretations. When liberalism interpreted Christianity as a merely ethical solution to the problem of character, it showed itself patently inadequate. When mysticism interpreted the heart of Christianity as a "mystical transformation of personality," it clearly omitted Christianity's social dimension. Likewise, when traditional Christianity merely accepted doctrinal paradoxes from the past, it revealed it had not yet reached the reality of the Atoning Spirit who enlivens the Christian Community. In this serial way, then, Royce's living logic led him eventually to *intuit* interpretively that most fundamental transaction within genuine religion: the suffering servant's atoning deed which elevates the morally detached individual to the superhuman life of the divinely loyal community. In accord with his rule ("Logic thus leads to [an] ideal of intuition; intuition logically leads to an ideal of logical articulation"), Royce, after having intuited this basic ideal of atonement, proceeded to articulate it into the brief "rationalized form of the Atonement Doctrine" preserved through his appended note. To himself he commented that it could be "very concretely worked out" in his lectures.[35]

The full text of this "Essence" exhibits the logical ingredients operative in the mature Royce's thought. Two of its elements are related to a "second level": one positively by the ε-relation, the other by its obverse. An assertive mode of action, based on a norm, initiates a function that engages these elements, relations, and levels in one dynamic system.

If these logical terms are transposed into ethico-religious language, the results are as follows. The elements become individuals. The relations become those of loyalty and disloyalty. The levels become that of the morally detached individual and that of the community. The function embracing all these realities is the atonement process. This process is initiated by the Spirit of the Beloved Community whose synoptic and salvific will serves as the norm of this world's process in its every moment of actual change.

In brief, Royce's way of "thinking logically" guided his revision of plans for the *Problem* and culminated in his "Note" on the essence of his fifth plan. His way seems to have been a clear foreshadowing of that living logic we found Royce participating in as he sat at the table of his 1913–1914 Seminar in Comparative Methodology.

To sum up, the present chapter introduced us to the pure logic and methodology of Royce in 1910–1913. It sketched how from 1901 to 1912 he grew toward this logic. It indicated how the methodology from his "Principles" found expression in the *Problem*. Lastly, it showed how his logic of interpretation worked practically when he revised his plans in 1912 for that masterwork and when he took part in his methodology seminar shortly thereafter. These dozen years had made Royce an increasingly adroit rational interpreter. By 1912 he was far more sensitive to the logical claims at work within both his thought-materials and his modes of action in dealing with them than he had been when Peirce corrected him in 1901.

Just as Royce's first section of the "Principles" suggested the approach adopted in the present chapter, so his second and third sections suggest

PURE LOGIC AND METHODOLOGY   53

the main lines of investigation in the following two chapters. If the evidence from our investigation converges to bring to a new level of clarity how Σ influenced the *Problem*'s hidden logical foundations, then the relationship between the "Principles" and the *Problem* will become not only confirmed but also freed from a deductionist interpretation and set within the musement context of mutual illumination of Signs. Later on, in part three, we will turn to a detailed study of the methods Royce devised and employed to create his mature philosophy of the Christian religion—that is, both his subordinate methods and his overall general method. Before that, however, we need to become familiar with his pure logic, which is more fundamental than either his methods or the applied logic of his "Normative doctrine" of Methodology. For when Royce synthesized theory and experience in the *Problem,* System Σ seems indeed to have been that preferred "pathfinder logic" with its ultimate conceptual scheme which was to guide him. To this "Logic as the General Science of Order" we now turn.

4. A General Science of Order, System Σ

The previous chapter reported Royce's identification of "highest methodology" with an organized combination of theory and experience. Now the question arises: Which purely logical theory did he use to organize the combination he intended in the *Problem?* More specifically, after he chose to pioneer a logical path different from that cut by Russell and Whitehead, did he then employ his distinctive System Sigma (= Σ) to organize the *Problem's* combination of theory and experience?

A leading American logician, C. I. Lewis, thought it significant that Royce departed radically from Russell and Whitehead in starting pure logic.[1] Lewis called for more investigation of Royce's theory of a "general science of order," his System Σ, because he believed that the method of Russell and Whitehead had in 1916 already "received a disproportionate share of attention."[2] Royce diverged from the authors of *Principia Mathematica* in three ways. First, he parted from them on the question of how to move from the minimal order of a logical set to some specific type of order, for example, that used in geometry or in arithmetic. Russell had viewed geometric 'points' and arithmetic 'numbers' as conceptual complexes having a definite internal structure, but Royce viewed them as simple and indifferent terms.

Second, Royce chose a different starting point, the concept of any hypothetical self-reflective rational agent. This concept had to embrace all modes of action possible for any rational agent, finite or infinite, and hence had to include the concept of a dense series. Thus, Royce began his most general science of order by simply postulating an infinitely polyadic, symmetrical nexus, his O-relation. He intended it to undergird the traditional principles of pure logic. From the O-relation he could both generate Kempe's 'between' principle with its dense series and also derive an asymmetrical relation from a symmetrical one, through a negative operation.[3]

Last, for Royce the modes of action of any rational agent(s) had to be related to will. By contrast, Russell required a purely objective set of "logical constants" in his *Principles of Mathematics* and regarded any relation to will or agency as "factitious and irrelevant" (*RLE,* 371; #23).⁴ Russell's supposition was that, at least in pure logic, a kind of knowing was possible without its being an *action.* As a pragmatist, Royce countered by proposing a logic in which choices are central because "possible modes of action" and even the traditional elements of pure logic are inconceivable except as related to the will of a rational agent (*RLE,* 338; #16).

Royce regarded Russell's new "logic of relations" as relatively superficial in comparison to his own starting point in any hypothetical rational agent. He thought it arbitrary to exclude relations to will from pure logic since the world of logic needed them at least as much as it needed sets of relations and propositions. Finally, Royce wanted his starting postulate (his O-relation) to show precise analogy with that "earliest exact relation defined by the human mind"; namely, with the ordinary thinker's 'yes-no' relationship (*RLE,* 386). For Russell, such precise analogy and continuity with primitive human thinking seemed insignificant in pure logic. By 1910 Royce already was moving to transform conceptual analysis into interpretational analysis and the latter had to find and/or create an analogy in order to complete its mediation of two contrasting ideas. The foregoing, then, shows wherein and why Royce's System Σ was a *unique* theory of order.

Published in 1905 and summarily outlined in Royce's 1910 "Principles of Logic," System Σ controlled how he translated into the *Problem* Peirce's logic of interpretation and of signs. Although the limits of the present section prevent the kind of scrutiny that Royce's System Σ calls for,⁵ we can so highlight the links between Σ and the *Problem* that the reader will recognize that he cannot reach a "fair understanding" of the *Problem* without an initial grasp of Royce's pure logic. We first focus on the objective order in Σ, taken as a field or class of entities, which Royce defined by postulate to be *as general and inclusive as possible.* Moreover, since a subjective order is also required within any agent's will if he is to be rational, we will focus, secondly, on any rational agent's will to interpret. This two-sided approach to Σ is a device of the present author, using hints from Royce. One result of our two-step inquiry into the pure logic undergirding the *Problem* will be to clarify how Royce's method differs from Russell's. Unlike Russell's method of analysis in symbolic logic, Royce proposes the "method of the pathfinder."⁶ Forging into an infinite field of possible modes of action, the pathfinder gradually determines the actual path of his exploration only through a series of choices, by his successive choices of steps. Royce's break with Russell on this point should caution those biased into thinking that pure logic has to be *only* an abstract objective system or else not exist.

THE OBJECTIVE ORDER IN ROYCE'S O-RELATION AND IN HIS SYSTEM Σ

For A. B. Kempe, whom Royce thought "unduly neglected," any set consists of elements.[7] Certain of these elements are exactly like each other in all their relations, and certain others are not. Throughout the whole set, these like and unlike elements are distributed in a definite way. For his fundamental set, or "base system," Kempe expressed the elemental properties (of likeness, unlikeness, order, etc.) in terms of the triad a c • b, which may be read, "b is 'between' a and c." This was Kempe's powerful F-relation. It can represent the most fundamental relations both in logic and in all types of systematic thinking where serial relations are found. Royce stated:

> Wherever a linear series is in question, wherever an origin of coordinates is employed, wherever 'cause and effect,' 'ground and consequence,' orientation in space or direction of tendency in time are in question, the diadic asymmetrical relations involved are essentially the same as the relation here symbolized by $p \prec_y q$ [= Kempe's F-relation].[8]

Kempe's F-relation is the central logical structure in "certain of our best established practical instincts and . . . some of our best fixed intellectual habits."[9] For this is the relation that our mind grasps or our deeds follow when we become aware of, or carry out, "b is 'between' a and c," or "a precedes c," or "b is the origin of a and c," or "b is the resultant of a and c," or "b is the mediator of a and c," or "a is contained in c," or, in pure logic, "b is the null class," or, in terms of propositions, "a implies c."[10]

Nevertheless, Royce also found that Kempe's F-relation limited a thinker. It required a person to survey nothing but dyadic or triadic relations and to adopt "an arbitrary choice of origin."[11] Royce preferred to overcome both these limitations by defining his basic O-relation "purely by postulate" as a "*sym*metrical" and "essentially *poly*adic" relation that "applies at once to any number of terms greater than one" (*RLE*, 385). This pure postulate created a relation more general and inclusive than Kempe's F-relation. As C. I. Lewis saw it, since Royce's O-relation "expresses simultaneously a whole set of equivalent F-relations," his starting point was deeper and more fecund than Kempe's.[12] Yet Kempe's triadic asymmetrical F-relation "follows directly" from Royce's new starting basis which includes infinite kinds of relations (*RLE*, 408).

As an illustration, suppose that an agent has to decide a course of action. The relation of the possible choices open to him exhibits the O-relation. For, as Royce put it, "the relation in which . . . any set of *exhaustive but, in their entirety, inconsistent choices* would stand to one another" is the O-relation.[13] Since this is the mutual relationship of all possible courses of action that, as wholes, are inconsistent, he transcended an arbitrary choice of origin by including all possible choices in his starting postulate. Thus, by starting from a rational agent with all possible modes of action, Royce found no need as yet to discuss zero collections (or null classes) (*RLE,* 389), since no element can exist without its obverse; for example, no possible course of action can exist without its negation. The O-relation obtains, then, either between an element and its obverse, or between one repeatedly recurring element, or between two, three, or any finite or infinite number of elements, recurrent or not (*RLE,* 385, 388–389).

To identify more clearly the objective order in Royce's O-relation and in Σ, we need to examine the internally experienced analogue of this pure logical relation, study the four ingredients required for this type of order (in the O-relation and in Σ), then inspect in more detail the constituents Royce found in any set, and conclude by examining how this type of logical order organizes the objective structure governing Royce's overall method of interpretation as found in the *Problem.*

To introduce readers to Σ, Royce thought it important to emphasize that the relational properties of his starting O-relation are identical with the properties found in the first exact relation defined by the human mind, the 'yes-no' relation (*RLE,* 386). In all its judgments of true or not-true and in all its choices of good or not-good, the human self moves successively from possible modes of action to an actual series of decisions, each centered on the 'yes-no' relation and each capable of being viewed in self-reflection, social bearing, memory, hope, etc. Which capability will be actualized out of this infinite set of infinite sets of cans, coulds, and woulds depends on the decisions that "select" some possibilities while "excluding" others. These decisions are radically pragmatic 'yes-or-no' choices, the fonts of creativity and surprise in our lives. In Σ, their analogues (namely, all possible modes of action) must include opportunities for free initiative and the arbitrary, for ingenuity and the novel. For as only generally ordered, this System is as yet "wholly indifferent" to further specifications (*RLE,* 390). System Σ thus becomes completely other than a "block universe."

As an example, take Royce's *Problem* in which he "applied" his logic to the philosophy of the Christian religion. He started from "a perfectly human antithesis," the conjugate pair of terms and of ideas: individual and community.[14] Then, tutored by the universal Interpreter,[15] he refused to be confined within this dyadic relation and said 'no' to the adequacy of this pair. In this way he opened up its terms and ideas to that "More" indicated by religious symbolism. He could then speak of "the *sacred pair,*" which he set in upper case as "the Individual *and* the Community."[16] The emphasized term *"and"* expressed the *epsilon* relation (membership in a universal divine community, symbolized by ε). Contrariwise, his negation of such membership seeded the idea of the lost state of the natural individual. By negating this second idea, his transformative restoration of membership led to the idea of the divine plan of redemptive atonement. Thus, by following the guidance of an experienced 'yes-no' relationship, Royce was led to identify his "three Christian ideas." Furthermore, by then negating the adequacy of this "sacred triad," he brought into view the still more general idea of "grace" and formed a "sacred tetrad," his "Christian doctrine of life" (1:343-349; 2:111-113).

In brief, some glimpse of Royce's method of interpretive musement, as employed in the *Problem,* already becomes possible. He experienced these "Christian" ideas (individual, community, alienation, unitive atonement, and grace) as most vital. He united these elements of appreciative interest with his most general yet rigorous theory of the order of pairs, triads, tetrads, etc. For he found these logical forms operating within what he would technically call a "Community of Interpretation" which formed his "ground plan of the World of Interpretation" (2:280). As found in minded beings, the life process of such a "Community of Interpretation" is an interaction occurring between Individual, Community, and Spirit of the Community. The history of this life process is determined by the 'yes-or-no' decisions of the participants.

Psychically, rather than physically, any rational agent experiences at an early age the exact opposition of the 'yes-no' relation. This confrontation parallels that of any logician wanting to think in an orderly way. The logician discerns that the "forms" (or types of order) which he creates freely, yet not capriciously, turn out to be absolute norms for rational thinking. As Royce put it:

> In his study of the Science of Order, the logician *experiences the fact that these forms are present in his logical world, and constitute it, just because they are, in fact, the forms of all rational activity.* (RLE, 338; #16)[17]

To be rational, we have to think, choose, relate, and behave in an *orderly* way. But, asks the logician, "What makes order order?" If he can identify and characterize the "logical entities" without which order is impossible, he can answer this question. Scrutinizing order in his own thinking helps. He finds that four of the ingredients of order are: (a) relation, (b) class, (c) series, and (d) operation. To study these four ingredients is to become familiar with the minimum conditions both for any kind of order and for Royce's System Σ.[18] When his interpretive musement in the *Problem* proceeds according to these four ingredients, they usually function both individually and conjointly as Peircean "Signs" which express minded beings and which call for unending reinterpretations.[19]

"Relation," a term of fundamental significance in philosophy, cannot be defined formally without using presuppositions. Instead, Royce proposed an informal working definition:

> In brief, *a relation is a character that an object possesses as a member of a collection* (a pair, a triad, an n-ad, a club, a family, a nation, etc.), and which (as one may conceive), would *not* belong to that object, were it not such a member. (*RLE,* 339; #17)[20]

Though often dyadic, this "belongingness" frequently is polyadic (e.g., with 3, 8, or infinite terms). In a general science of order, relations are important mainly because in certain cases they "are subject to exact laws which permit a wide range of deductive inference" (*RLE,* 340; #18). These laws enable us to classify relations according to their logical *properties*. "Upon such properties of relations all deductive science depends. . . . and thus Logic as the 'Normative Science' of deductive inference is merely an incidental part of the Theory of Order" (*RLE,* 340; #18).[21]

Thereupon, Royce examined the properties of dyadic relations as symmetrical or asymmetrical, as transitive or non-transitive, as of the one-one or one-many type. Turning next to polyadic relations and making suitable modifications, Royce classified them and showed how transitivity, whether in dyads or by pairs, makes it possible to eliminate intermediaries (*RLE,* 346–347; #18). When relations are related, operations are seeded, such as generalization and variation. Upon a triadic relation, for example, one bases the operations of logical addition and multiplication. These operations lead to deductive inferences "whose range of application is inexhaustible." Royce here opened up only a few doorways into the proliferating paths of valid inference within Σ, paths which his interpretations in the *Problem* could soon follow.

Royce's construction of the *Problem* by uniting the ε-relation of Individual to Community and its obverse relation of Community to Individual to form his basic "sacred pair" (1:343–344) showed how his musement is guided by pairs, then by triads, and then by tetrads. Next, pairs of conjugate relations, chains, resultants, and conjugate pairs of resultants will enter as guides—all to enrich and widen the synoptic vision. Accordingly, the reader of the *Problem* will expect Royce to play with pairs when contrasting manuscript and mirror-script, to fault Spinoza for trying to know reality through only one concept without using a contrasting pair, and to compare and contrast Jesus' doctrine of love with the brethren's communal social experience of loyalty (2:171–173, 275, 359–360). Interpretation starts from comparison-contrast which is based on a pair relation, but it is not completed unless a triadic relation mediates, so that interpretation can be brought to term. The entry of the triadic relation brings consciousness to a new growth (1:130, 243–244).

To treat of relations is inevitably to presuppose a class (or set), Royce's second "logical entity" ingredient in order. The concept of a set has that apparent simplicity, yet actual complexity which marks any elementary "concept." Logically, the "concept" of a set is itself dependent on the four ingredients of individual, membership, assertion, and norm, which we will examine later. Royce's logic of classes reveals his voluntarism:

> Apart from some classifying will, our world contains no classes. Yet without classifications we can carry on no process of rational activity, can define no orderly realm whatever, real or ideal. (*RLE,* 351; #19)

When this classifying will operates, it must employ a norm of classification. Thus it inevitably defines a *pair* of classes: the class and its contradictory (symbolized by Royce as x and x̄). Classifying these sets according to absence or presence of members produces, respectively, the "empty" or null class and the "full" class or "Universe of Discourse" (symbolized by Royce as 0 and 1). Any two classes (x and y) may be so combined that their "logical product" conforms at once to the norms of both x and y, *or* so combined that their "logical sum" conforms either to the norm of x or to the norm of y.

Royce recognized that the relation Peano called *epsilon* (= ε) whereby an individual "belongs to" or "is member of" a set is fundamental to the concept of class. This relation had to be distinguished from the subsumption relation on which the syllogism is built. The paradox of "free interpretability" enters here. In logic, a class itself can be freely interpreted *as* an individual and in this way be viewed as a member of (in ε-relation to) a set of classes. Because of free interpretability, then, if "i ε x" and "x ε y," it is not generally valid to infer "i ε y," just as, when moving to the order of truth-claims, it is not generally true to assert "i ε y." For instance, although California is an individual member-state of the United States and the United States is an individual member of the United Nations, it neither follows that California is a member of the United Nations nor is it true to assert that it is. In this way Royce showed that the most fundamental ε-relation is non-transitive, *un*like the derivative relation of subsumption which is transitive (*RLE,* 351; #17).[22]

Series is the third "logical entity" ingredient in order. Wherever order is found, wherever any activity is rational, there series is necessarily present (*RLE,* 354; #20). The work of Peirce, Dedekind, Cantor, and Russell had provided a common logical definition of series. Within the unity of this definition an infinite variety of serial types were definable. A series can return or not return on itself, and thus be "closed" or "open," respectively. A series is "well-ordered" if it has a first member and a next successor element. For example, a cyclic series is not well-ordered since it lacks a first member. A series is "dense" if it lacks a next successor element.

Since a dense series exhibits infinite divisibility, the concept of "logical continuity" arises and serves as a base for "arithmetical continuity." When Royce studied the logical continuity found in the series formed by relations of subsumption, he saw its parallels both with the series of points that form a dense series and with the continuity of a linear series (*RLE,* 356; #20).

When series are put in correlation, various kinds of "correspondences" become possible, such as the "one-one," "one-many," and "many-many" correspondences. Some instances may clarify this. Since the logical relations within propositions (such as contradiction, implication, etc.) correspond to the logical relations within classes (such as negation, subsumption, etc.), a "calculus of classes" becomes possible. It is analogous both to the "calculus of propositions" and to the "calculus of modes of action" in Royce's System Σ (*RLE,* 353-354; #20). Again, a "one-one" correspondence links the subsumption relation in logic with the "between" relation of geometry (*RLE,* 380). This founds a basis for strict analogy. Finally, if the series of ordinal numbers (1st, 2nd, 3rd, etc.) is set in one-one correspondence with the series of the powers of two (2^1, 2^2, 2^3, etc.), the concept of *levels* arises and even of *series of levels.* This in turn leads to the concepts of *Norms* and *Laws.*

Royce employed the concepts of series, continuity, correspondence, and levels in the *Problem.* He wrote of "series of communities," of his basic doctrine of the "two levels," and of the principle or "norm" employed by the Interpreter-Judge of the Universe.[23] Royce's logical use of *analogy*—both strict and loose—in the *Problem* rested on his logical correspondences.[24] Some examples may clarify this. Utilizing the relation of "believer and object believed" as his basic pair, Royce employed "pairs of pairs" to argue (by strict analogy based on correspondences) first from Professor Minot's belief in the reality of a scientific community, through the two boatmen's belief in the reality of their shared vessel and lake, to our own belief in the reality of a universal community (2:225-249). Again, in Royce's view there is a strict "parallelism between the relational characters of the time-process and those of the process of interpretation" (2:152). Similarly, throughout the *Problem,* his process of generalization rests on relationships of strict correspondence. Finally, he expected that Christianity must increasingly insist upon the fact of analogy between its traditional formulas and the genuine core of its practical faith, between its symbols and its reality, if Christianity, caught in a universe of relentlessly accelerating change, is to keep approaching a true*r* interpretation of its "doctrine of life" (2:426-429).

Besides relations, classes, and series, the logician needs *operations* (or functions) to create and develop his order, his "forms of all rational activity." In pure logic, "operations" are simply "the relating of relations," not psychological movements or deeds. Thus, if sets are correlated, a basis is established for logical transformations and eliminations. If series are correlated, a basis is supplied for mathematical operations (*RLE,* 359–361; #20).

Correspondences exist between these logical operations and Royce's metaphysical modes of voluntary action. In the *Problem* these modes generate and internally govern its central interpretive process. Royce there describes this musement as endlessly fecund of itself (2:160). Thus it helps one to understand the *Problem* if one recalls that whatever mode of spiritual action Royce employs in his musement — whether he compares or contrasts, affirms or negates, adds or eliminates, combines or divides, calculates or generalizes — each mode is supported logically by correlations of objective relations, sets, and series. In brief, all these modes of voluntary action rest logically upon functions that he sketched in his "Principles of Logic."

Thus far we have surveyed the four "logical entities or constants" which Royce judged indispensable for any type of order and, so, for his order-system Σ. C. I. Lewis reported Royce's facetious comparison of Σ to a junk heap or a New England attic which contains almost everything but poses the question of how to get these things out.[25] Regretting no more accurate term, Lewis spoke of Royce's method of "selection." Turning now to the detailed ingredients that Royce found in any class or set, we may find "normed assertion" an alternate term for the rationally voluntary "selection" by which he "got things out" of his New England attic.

Knowing that both his own distinctive Σ and its embodiment in a genuine idea of Community depended on the "concept" of *class* (or collection), Royce wrote trenchantly in his "Principles":

The concept of a Class, in a logical sense, depends

(1) Upon the concept of an *Object,* or *Element* or *Individual,* which *does or does not belong to a given class;*
(2) Upon the concept of the *relation* of *belonging to,* i.e., *being a member of* a class, or of *not so belonging;*
(3) Upon the concept of *assertions,* true or false, which *declare that* an object is or is not a *member of* a given class;
(4) Upon the concept of a Principle, Norm, or Universal which enables us to decide which of these assertions are true and which are false. (*RLE,* 349; #19)[26]

Earlier, Royce had stressed the importance of the felt relation in our primitive 'yes-no' assertions as the psychological analogue of his fundamental O-relation in logic. Here, by such phrases as *"does or does not be-*

long," he inseparably linked the O-relation and its negative E-relation to all four of the ingredients—(1) to (4) above—upon which the concept of a class depends. By this move he tied these ingredients of the concepts of a class and the other three major constituents of "Order" to rational will as elective. Thus he needed a calculus of elective rational will's "possible modes of action," a calculus at least as basic as the calculi of classes and of propositions (*RLE,* 373–376; #24). His four pairs of O and E relations can be variously combined and seriated so his possible modes of rational 'yes-or-no' action generate a pluriform set of systems, each of which contains both well-ordered and dense series in finite and infinite number. Thus, the objective order in Σ provides a parallel in pure logic which can guide into congruency that "infinitely complex Sign," the fruit of Royce's interpretive musement in the *Problem* (2:285–286; 1:204–205; 2:198).

Concerning item (1) above, Royce soon provided his logical definition of an "Individual Object," which deserves notice:

> For logical purposes, an Individual Object is one that we propose to regard at once as recognizable or identifiable throughout some process of investigation, and as unique within the range of that investigation, so that no other instance of any mere kind of object suggested by experience, can take the precise place of any one individual, when we view ourselves as having found any individual object. (*RLE,* 350; #19)[27]

In logic, once we view ourselves as having found an individual object, our *"attitude of will"* enters whereby we propose to treat "an Object, or Element or Individual" as unique, as not exactly replaceable, and as always recognizable within limits. This pragmatic postulate supersedes sense percepts or conceptual constants concerning the individual. In logic, then, Royce's individual (or object or element) functions according to our will to interpret each as *either* a unit *or* a class. Roycean individuals are, as Kuklick says, "not uninterpreted variables, 'simple and homogeneous,' but unit sets."[28]

Concerning (2), we earlier described Royce's relationship to "belonging to" a class as the basic link in his logic. Applied to communities in the *Problem,* Royce viewed it as "a necessary basis and presupposition of all our deeper social relations."[29]

Concerning items (3) and (4), Royce binds his logical universe to a rational agent in many ways. Assertions of membership require an asserting mind and generate logical triads. As declarative, these assertions (or denials) initiate sign-sending communication. "A Principle, Norm or Universal which enables us to decide" between true and false assertions generates logical tetrads, introduces values and disvalues, and establishes a realm governing assertive minds. Moreover, by making the concept of any class—

and thus of itself—depend also upon items (3) and (4), Royce put into his "New England attic" not only true and false assertions that function as declarative signs, but also a Norm that enables us to distinguish between them and provides us with an objective ground for value judgments. Such endowments, however, suggest that Royce's so-called "concepts" are also functioning as signs in an interpretive process. He has already practically transformed his purely conceptual system into a communal process of interpretation, for assertions and signs of assertions require a communitarian process between assertive minds rather than a mere array of concepts. In brief, founded on its initial O-relation, Σ has become a dynamic and unusually inclusive collection.

So far we have surveyed the objective order in Σ according to its four ingredients (relation, class, series, and function) and then looked more in detail at Royce's concept of class with its four sub-ingredients. Before turning to the subjective order in the will to interpret, it is fitting to ask how Σ's objective order embodies itself in the discernible structure of the *Problem*'s overall method of interpretation. Since the interpretive process is: (a) *seriated* in our experience and (b) *related* to essentially spiritual objects, (c) operates according to normative *guides,* and (d) *results* in a fuller assembly or community, Σ's features of seriality, relationship, principled operations, and consequences already come to light. Yet a closer study of these four in succession seems called for.

In the *Problem* Royce asserted, "We live, as selves, by interpreting the events and the meaning of our experience," and "Our experience, as it comes to us, is a realm of signs" (2:284, 289). Royce found that the interpretive process originates in our experience, in its events and meaning. Our experience certainly has its percepts and concepts, but more than this, it has its events and meaningful signs. Since percepts and concepts cannot exhaust the vital richness of this experienced "realm of signs," some nonabstract, intimate, "mind-to-mind" kind of knowing is needed. This third, distinct and irreducible, fundamental kind of knowing is the interpretive process (2:281-286; 152-153). Thus the vital matrix nurturing interpretation is our experience of a "realm of signs." In response to these, our possible modes of voluntary action are to create or not create signs, to attend or not attend, to understand or not understand.[30] Inevitably, then, we generate a series of deep choices that is structured by the O-relation and its negative, the E-relation.

Royce taught, "Interpretation seeks an object which is essentially spiritual," a mind or sign of mind (2:152). The scope of interpretation embraces a wide range of objects. If classified, the *more specified objects of interpretation* would form a list something like the following:

1. *Life,* life's *higher levels* (as being more valuable), *life as social,* and especially, *"life in the unity of the Spirit"* (2:161, 193);
2. Vital human *needs* (2:109);
3. One's own *self,* neighbors' selves, and minded beings (2:127, 137, 160);
4. *"Signs"* through which selves express themselves (2:148, 152);
5. *Ideal values, meaning,* and the *significance of temporal experience* (2:155–156, 160, 217);
6. *Implication* of premises (2:197–199);
7. *Synoptic vision* of two opposed "ideas" grasped together in a completed comparison (2:178);
8. The kind of *truth proper to interpretations,* in contrast with those kinds of truth found in perceptual or conceptual knowings (2: 202–203);
9. *Genuine Reality,* since by interpretation we discern both Being and the value of Being and eventually the Breath (Spirit) of the Universe (2:11, 163, 190, 221).[31]

Interpretation grasps values and disvalues. By interpretation, rather than by perception and conception, one discerns between the real and apparent, the true and erroneous, the beautiful and ugly, the genuinely loyal and traitorous, and, in general, between good and evil. Since our experience is a "realm of signs" in which the above-mentioned "essentially spiritual" objects interact, human minds and their signs live within a communication process that is objectively infinite. In this process, two hidden "guides" exercise their powerful presence in the *Problem.*

Interpretation is guided by a "leading idea" if the latter is understood in Peirce's rather than in James's sense (2:180–182).[32] Such leading ideas are too general and *in*determinate to work as hypotheses from which verificatory tests can be deductively inferred. So nebulous as to seem useless, Peirce's kind of leading idea paradoxically predominates in influence. As Royce realized in the *Problem,* ideas of this kind "determine the whole course of our inquiry" and thus reveal themselves as normative guides (1:3).

For example, in Part One, his three "most essential Christian ideas" and the more general idea of "grace" function as such leading ideas. Again, in Part Two of the *Problem* the three central ideas of "Time, Interpretation, and the Community" along with their more encompassing idea, "The world as a Community" serve as this kind of leading idea (2:422). These eight ideas function, first, as unique ingredient forms for the process of interpretation; then, as pairs, as triads, as tetrads; and finally and most synthetically, as a conjugate pair of tetrads. Especially in this last conjunction, they gave Royce his "synoptic vision" of Christianity within a world coming to birth. They enabled him to create his "organized Combination of Theory and Experience."[33]

A more profound normative guide to the interpretation process is the Spirit of the Universal Community. The Spirit carries out this guidance far more skillfully than the most talented orchestra director gathers his musicians' diverse efforts into a harmonious whole. Even more subtly and masterfully than Royce's favorite composer Beethoven blended sounds, themes, and movements to create his Fifth Symphony does this Spirit of the Universal Community initiate, counterpose, and unite the minds and signs of minds in the process of the Universal Community. As the "Will to Interpret," this Spirit communicates both the "Doctrine of Signs" and the "Christian Doctrine of Life" to all minded beings of all ages, in ways diversified by the recipients' dispositions. By initiating these two sets of signs to all generations in the temporal process, the Spirit-Interpreter, in the strength of its all-encompassing vision, patiently yet powerfully draws all conflicting selves and warring communities towards the unity of the Universal Community.

What *results* from having the interpretation process rooted in experience, related to essentially spiritual objects, and guided in the two ways just mentioned? Along with an ever-present freedom for flexibility in minded beings' diverse communication processes, an absolute self-reinstating constancy reveals itself. To a greater or lesser extent, each interpretation participates in the underlying guidance exercised by the Interpreter-Spirit and the pair of tetradic Doctrines. More specifically, the creative initiative at the center of each Roycean interpreter[34] diversifies infinitely the possible modes of successive action by these finite selves. Meanwhile, under the Spirit's guidance, the ideas of Individual and Community provide a dynamic constancy in the interpretive process and an absolutely irreversible bearing in the message flashed through both of his tetradic "Doctrines." Inside this overall setting of a free flexibility within a fundamental constancy, several negative and positive results can be specified.

Negatively, by adopting his two general "Doctrines" with their Signs (logically, a conjugate pair of tetrads) Royce had to oppose Bergson, James, and Schopenhauer insofar as they accepted particular percepts, "*mere* particulars," as their starting points (2:282, 304–309). Royce's general Signs also made him oppose Spinoza and Russell insofar as these two thought philosophy consisted basically in drawing consequences from abstract concepts, "*mere* deductions" (2:261–262).[35] Since Spinoza and Russell treated their starting "concepts" as if detached from any "will to interpret," he found these thinkers inadequate on this point. Royce's commitment to genuine loyalty made him believe that at the heart of each interpretive deed there *should* be found *that kind* of "will to interpret" which promotes the Universal Community, appreciates fuller life more highly, and dedicates itself to increase the presence of genuine loyalty (2:309–313).

Positively, the very generality of Σ supplied him with the infinite range that his method of *generalization* required in the *Problem*. Already in 1905, he thought Kempe's basic triadic F-relation was too constrictive and chose his polyadic O-relation to provide "the power to survey at a glance relations of more than a dyadic or triadic character."[36] The O-relation, as refined by his "Principles of Logic," enabled him in the *Problem* to *liberate* ideas that were encountered first in some particular historico-cultural setting or that were encrusted with a centuries-long overlay of culture, history, metaphysics, and religious dogma. For instance, in the end, he so interpreted the three so-called "Christian ideas" (originally encountered in Jesus' teaching about the Kingdom of Heaven and in Paul's early Christian communities) that these now-generalized ideas mediated between all minded beings within the universal process of history.[37]

In brief, System Σ, based on the O-relation, exerted its guiding presence upon the interpretive processes that created the *Problem*. As a result, Royce's overall method of interpretation is marked by great simplicity joined with a pathfinder's openness to new ways and procedures. C. I. Lewis wrote, "Involved as the structure of the System Σ may seem, it is, by comparison [with the *Principia Mathematica* of Russell and Whitehead], a marvel of simplicity and compact neatness."[38] Royce took the objective order from his "Principles" as the basis for his "doctrine of the World" in the *Problem*. Yet he there also expressed a "doctrine of life" (2:309, 279). We need, then, to inquire also into his logical basis for the latter.

THE SUBJECTIVE ORDER IN THE WILL TO INTERPRET

We turn from Σ's objective order to examine each self's genuine will to interpret. What conditions and concrete logical order must any genuine, self-reflective, rational agent follow? We first survey Royce's three presuppositions for a genuine will to interpret.

Psychologically, certain human interests must be integrated if the subject's will to interpret is to be genuinely ordered. These are his motives to become self-possessed, to engage in a process that is essentially social, and to introduce unity into life by mediating between conflicting ideas, minds, and purposes (2:193, 159, 286).

Procedurally, Royce's genuine will to interpret presupposes pragmatism's priority of action over theory. From Papini, William James had borrowed the model of "a corridor in a hotel" through which one first must pass. For James, qualified thinkers must both own and pass through this corridor "if they want a practicable way of getting into or out of their respective rooms," that is, their substantive philosophical or anti-philosophical positions.[39] In his own distinctive version of this corridor, Royce required genuine interpreters to make their will-acts as "committed lovers of the whole universe," rather than proceeding in an exclusively self-assertive or self-denying way, without concern for other selves and the Other (2:309).

Temporally, several moments must precede genuine interpretation to forestall misinterpretation. First, percepts and concepts must arise and combine as usual. Next, inquiries into these experienced contents require efforts to compare and contrast them. Only if these conscious moments have preceded can one insightfully grasp the needed mediating idea. The latter makes the explicit comparison genuine by bringing to valid completion at least one stage in the interpretive process (2:148-150, 158-163, 182-184). Similarly, for interpretations at higher levels, a temporally seriated cumulus of dispositive insights are needed. Royce illustrated the latter requirement in his lecture "The Will to Interpret." The ethical and religious interpretations of its final section presuppose the logically ordered accumulation of percepts, concepts, their syntheses, and the series of pre-moral interpretations which he had gradually built up in his preceding eleven sections.[40]

These three conditions (psychological, procedural, and temporal) established the terrain Royce presupposed when he set out as a pathfinder to indicate some of "the principles of this art [of interpretation]" (2:163). With him we ask whether any "artist" at interpretation exhibits a certain logical structure in his will to interpret. More specifically, we ask whether Royce's structure combines imagined ideals with the principles of Σ in much the way that Peirce skillfully combined his empirical aids (symbols and diagrams) with that very exact logic he "worked out."[41]

Royce was convinced that if he successfully defined the ideal of the truth-loving interpreter, then "the innermost aim of the Will to Interpret" would come to light (2:184). Accordingly, we seek the kind of "structure of spirit" which is produced when finite interpreters cooperate with this Will to Interpret. For instance, take the case of a reflective agent who has to decide on one among all the possible courses of action open to him. If this reflective agent were moved by the genuine Will to Interpret, what structure would order his finite will?

When a finite self succeeds in fully comparing two contrasting ideas, he experiences a completed interpretation. His luminous intuition also makes him rationally self-possessed. This successful interpretation lets him find out more clearly what he really means and what he is (2:187). Beyond a finite self, however, one can hypothesize, as in Σ, an *in*finite rational agent whose vision encompasses *all* possible modes of action.[42] What *would* *be* this ideal observer's synoptic vision of his own modes of action and of those in the infinitely numerous finite minds related to him? His selected and asserted mode of acting would constitute the Norm which determines the truth or error of their assertions, just as the primitive O-relation sets a norm for all the constituents of Σ. Objectively, Royce's minimum model of three minded individuals would be linked by the essentially triadic form characteristic of any Community of Interpretation (2:213).

Yet something more is needed in the subjectivity of the individual finite interpreter. First, to engage as a living member in such a community, he must intend to "cross boundaries"; he must search for deep*er* insight into the more vital (2:137-139, 162-163). The Will to Interpret at work in him must send him beyond the boundaries of his worlds of perception and conception into the unique world of interpretation where he can touch the heart of reality; life itself, minds, and value (2:163).

Secondly, this intent to cross boundaries carries with it the desire to create a living union of the participant minds and their ideas. For life ideally consists in the spiritual unity of many minds and their ideas. This desire, in turn, fuels the interpreter's distinctive striving for yet more truth and yet more clarification. The life and unifying bond of a community of minded beings is their interpretational truth. Hence, the intent of the "artist" at interpretation seeks to touch life and life's spontaneous variation and play. Yet, because the interpreter is himself wider than any of his single ideas and because he can thus attain a vision that will look down upon the inner warfare of his ideas, he can also reach interpretational truth *if* he brings his comparisons to genuine Peircean completion (2:203, 181-184). As a strenuous interpreter, he comes to know truths of both the contingent and absolute types. Within his living reasoning he finds absolute truth in the logical nexus ("if P, *then* Q"). Within his living conscience he finds absolute truth in the counsel for a determinate act, a counsel that is irrevocably true or false (2:201-202).

However, when this self-reflective process reveals what one is and what one means, the interpreter also finds himself operating in a community that reflects on what it, as a community, is and means, for interpretation is unavoidably social (2:155, 160). It always addresses itself to a possible interpreter and, in turn, demands to be interpreted. If the sign-sender, the sign-receiver, and the sign-interpreter take part in the Will to Interpret, this common will of theirs unifies these three selves into a community (2:208). Besides the intent of these selves to cross boundaries, their shared intents to become united insert a similar structure in their subjectivities as finite agents.

Being finite, however, these three selves cannot reach that same kind of luminous intuition about the ideas and meaning of the other two members as each can about his own. To reach the truth proper to interpretation at work in their triad, these three selves must at least share in some other intents. They need to become open to the hypothesis of an "ideal observer" and to be opened by it. If they strive to conform more closely to the vision of this hypothetical ideal observer, they will achieve a consciousness in some way near*er* his, in clarity or content or level of knowing (2:215).

We find the objective order of Σ (with its relations, sets, levels through series and operations, like the assertion of norms) present in our triad of interpreting selves as they imagine their ideal observer. Their own way of hypothesizing him creates the primitive ε-relation of themselves to a community. As thus made members, they can share conscious life and truth communally because the ideal observer functions as the norm of their community through his own supposed choice of asserted norm.

However, beyond these rational agents' intents to cross borders and to create union, still more ordering is needed in their subjectivities. More importantly, any agent who is an individual (and therefore incomplete) must be transformed from non-membership into that radically different life of knowing and choosing proper to a genuine member. According to Royce, each of these selves must be transmuted into the kind of agent who personally: a) *grasps* the ideal of interpretation (as hypothesized in the ideal Interpreter and his ideal Community of Interpretation); b) *conceives* this Community of Interpretation both as *inclusive* of *all* individual minded beings and as *unified* by its members' *common hope* of an eventual complete mutual understanding; and c) *lives* by an *awakened love* for this Universal Community (2:220–221). By hypothesizing the ideal observer, by extending acceptance to all without arbitrary exclusion, and by being awakened to loving loyalty of service towards the Universal Community, these finite rational agents are transformed into genuine members of the Universal Community of Interpretation. In brief, their *grasp* of the ideal, their *conception* of catholicity and hope, and their *enlivening loyalty* constitute the remainder of that concrete order needed in the subject's will to interpret. Furthermore, by grasping, in ideal, the meaning of the Universal Community, these transformed finite selves are now effectively oriented towards those realities which religious phraseology designates as Church, Communion of Saints, and God as Interpreter of all minded beings (2:220–221).

Any limited rational agent, however, experiences the sharp difference between merely defining a hypothetical ideal to be sought by a hypothetical truth-loving interpreter and actually grasping and loving a real Community of Interpretation. Since a human self experiences his inadequacy both to gain this love and loyalty and to keep affirming it, and since he feels his need for the saving gift of Loyalty coming from "something more"

General Science of Order 71

than a hypothetical Interpreter, he finds his heartfelt awareness of this difference leads him to "pray that he may interpret" (2:221). This "cry out of the depths" and his expectant openness relate him in a life-giving dependence towards the saving influence of both the Universal Community and its Spirit (1:xvi). He undergoes this ongoing saving influence because of the atoning deeds of some genuinely loyal human self and his community.[43] Only as transformed through atonement can human selves live in community according to that more vital logic which leads them to be playfully alive yet striving to find and communicate more truth, to be such humble atoners in the community that they are leading mediators in it. To be such, the logical structure of their genuine wills to interpret life and the world may not be primarily self-assertive or self-negating but must be a constantly faithful yea-saying to all reality, the fruit of a loyal love of the Universal Community inclusive of all its members and of their own selves (2:309–313). Thus they find authentic ethical and religious life only by living in ε-relation to the Unity of the Spirit of the Universal Community.

5. Genesis of Σ and Its Application

Acquainted in general with System Sigma, we are led to inquire how this system originated and how Royce employed it in the *Problem.* In the present chapter, then, we will first investigate this genesis and look for a reflection of it in the *Problem,* then advance an hypothesis about Royce's way of applying Σ to the *Problem,* and conclude by testing the hypothesis, while inviting others to do the same. Our method for the first step will be to compare two sources. Royce treated the genesis of Σ in the third and final section of his "Principles," entitled "The Logical Genesis of the Types of Order" (*RLE,* 363–378; ##21–24). In it he was so succinct as to be enigmatic.[1] A possibly parallel genesis appears in the *Problem,* in Lecture 14, "The Doctrine of Signs," where Royce finally unveiled the source of his genuine "will to interpret" (2:279–325). By comparing the final section of his "Principles" with this lecture, we may detect how Royce initiated the creation of his "pathfinder logic."

A distinctive feature of the "Principles" was its starting point in any hypothetical rational agent. To be rational, any agent must be able to both act *and* reflect on his possible modes of action. It follows that any hypothetical, rational, self-possessed agent's *capacity to affirm or deny that he intends to do thus and so* is the distinctive genesis of the O-relation and therefore of the entire System Σ. This was the Type of Order Royce selected.

Other Types of Order had arisen from different starting points. In his survey of the history of logic, Royce found three previously proposed starting points (*RLE,* 368–372; #23). Each of them seemed inadequate to him. First, traditional logicians had initiated a type of logical order by claiming *im*mediate knowledge of certain so-called "self-evident" axioms. Yet careful inquiry into the exact meaning of these axioms revealed the presence of inexact or incorrect meanings. Thus their claim of *im*mediate knowing was invalidated.

For Royce, the second starting point was taken by a wide group of thinkers whom he called "logical empiricists" and among whom he included pragmatists like William James. These "empiricists" taught that logical forms have no more internal absoluteness than do items in our world of physical experience. With this view Royce could not concur because he considered certain meanings to be absolute, while others are simply contingent. For example, a denial must presuppose that an absolute relation of contradiction really exists between denying and affirming. By contrast, to be related to another as to a friend is a real but contingent relation.

The third view, proposed by Bertrand Russell, opposed these "logical empiricists." Holding a realistically conceived world of purely logical entities, Russell built his theory of order from *nothing but* "logical constants." He regarded the will's selection of these "constants" as irrelevant to logic. Hence, according to Royce, Russell left unsolved just which entities, laws, and order-systems are so implied by any rational action that the effort to eliminate them would inevitably imply their reinstatement. Russell *had* to leave undetermined just which objects were necessarily required in any system of order.

Guided by his critique of Russell and alerted by the novel endeavors of Kempe, Royce decided to provide Kempe's system with a new foundation: the principle that the modes of action of any self-reflective rational agent form a series which is precisely analogous to a dense series in geometry. Rather than *proving* that any series of modes of action can be dense, he *discovered* this density in the pivotability of choice open to any self-reflective rational agent.[2] Thus, beneath the laws of propositions and of classes in modern logic, he laid the foundation of such an agent's modes of action in a dense series, without implying that the series of class inclusions is dense. By including possible modes of action, he deepened the realm of Types of Order. For his most general theory of order, then, he defined as indispensable "certain possible modes of action that are open to any rational being who can act at all, and who can also reflect upon his own modes of possible action" (*RLE,* 373–374; #24).

In this way, Royce found that the Algebra of Logic applied not only to the Calculi of Propositions and of Classes, but also to a Calculus of Modes of Action. Thus, between possible actions P and R, there is always another possible mode Q, "*in case* there is some rational being who is capable of performing some one single possible act" (*RLE,* 375; #24). The "in case" proviso expresses the one existential principle Royce added to logic: the hypothesis of a possible rational agent. Starting from a possible rational agent with at least one mode of action (*and* the other modes *required* by this one according to the fundamental, symmetrical, and essentially polyadic O-relation), Royce's Calculus of Modes of Action must employ the "dense series" principle with its ever-recurrent "between" to generate a certain, non-totalized set of possible modes of action.[3] For one need not fall into the self-contradictory trap of intending "the totality of all possible modes of action." Instead, with Royce, one can recognize more modestly that it is:

perfectly possible to define a certain set, or "logical universe" of modes of action such that all the members of this set are "possible modes of action," *in case* there is some rational being who is capable of performing some one single possible act, and is also capable of noting, observing, recording, in some determinate way every mode of action of which he is actually capable, and which is a mode of action whose possibility is *required* (that is, is made logically a necessary entity) by the *single* mode of action in terms of which this system of modes of action is defined.[4]

Anyone who holds the concept of rational activity cannot call into question this realm of a rational potential agent's possible modes of action without himself engaging in a *"single* mode of action in terms of which this system of modes of action is defined." Royce's realm provided him with the springboard and ample scope he needed. Any hypothetical rational agent is meaningless without purely logical relations, classes, and modes of action. The modes of action, classes, relations, and co-members which constitute this logically necessary System Σ "exist in sets both finite and infinite in number, and both in 'dense' series, in 'continuous' series, and in fact in all possible serial types" (*RLE*, 377; #24).

Having used this distinctive way to generate Σ, Royce paused to sketch some of its results. As a type of order, Σ embraced objects related to series of all types, such as those found in various number systems and continua, as well as to the types of order found in the various kinds of geometry. Royce claimed that System Σ even linked together consistently all those types of order upon which the theoretical natural sciences depend for the success of their deductions.[5]

Does the *Problem*'s fundamental mode of action, portrayed in Lecture 14, "The Doctrine of Signs," embody the mode of action which generated Σ? Logically, Royce's decision to stand in openness towards the whole universe and in loyal commitment to it was the initiating mode of action from which the *Problem* developed as a philosophy of the Christian religion. This committed mode of action underlies his self-reinstating, fundamental, third attitude of will toward the universe: a loving loyalty to all life and to the whole world (2:310–311). In pivotal Lecture 14 of the *Problem*, Royce portrayed two other basic attitudes which a person can adopt. Both are predominantly exclusivistic of some part of the universe: in the first, a person individualistically asserts his own will to live, and in the second, one individualistically denies his own will to live. Examined logically, each of these two attitudes betrays the lack of the ε-relation to the whole of reality. The first is detached from the whole; the second is absorbed by it through the negation of its own unique individuality. Each of these attitudes has a specious short-term rationality but lacks ultimate consistency. Thus, each reveals its eventual self-destructive tendency, because each is a performative contradiction.

"Between" these two exclusivistic extremes, only one choice is discoverable as a basic attitude of will. A person can insist on his individual uniqueness *and* attend primarily to the universal community. Logically, any attempt to eliminate this third fundamental mode of action implies it. For instance, when one asserts, "The right basic attitude towards the world can't be *only* an intelligent loyalty towards the whole world," he asserts implicitly that it is *more* intelligently loyal to the whole universe to adopt a different attitude. To be fully rational, therefore, an agent must be intelligently loyal to the universe because this is the only basic orientation towards mature life and philosophy which is not a performative contradiction, is critically self-reinstating, and is integrally developmental of both self and community.

Royce's rational commitment in the *Problem* to stand in genuine universalistic loyalty towards the world equipped him with an absolute pragmatic norm, the first principle of both his speculative and his practical philosophy (2:312–314). When making his empirico-historical study of humankind's variety of communities in Part One of the *Problem,* Royce would employ this principle to guide, evaluate, and rectify his steps. This same absolute pragmatic norm would equip him in Part Two to test the truth in any individual or community which claims to be genuinely loyal to the Universal Community. Moreover, since Royce found that this third fundamental "attitude of the will is the *only* decisive one in dealing with the interpretation of experience," he also possessed a criterion for his overall method (2:322).[6] This attitude provided him a living test telling him whether his interpretive musement was proceeding genuinely or slipping into a misinterpretation. A striking correspondence exists, then, between the chosen starting points from which Royce generated his "Principles" and his *Problem.*

From a consideration of points of origin, we turn to examine how Royce "applied" System Σ to the *Problem.* If I show that the logical links within Royce's "Principles" and those within his *Sources* and *Problem* persistently reveal the same structural elements, are organized in strictly analogous ways, and are guided by the same leading ideas, then I will have achieved what the present investigation intends. In clarifying this relationship between "Principles," *Sources,* and *Problem,* Royce's distinctive meaning of "application" and his awareness of the differences created by "levels" of thought (in such various disciplines as pure logic, applied logic, metaphysics, philosophy of religion, and philosophy of the Christian religion) make the tracing of an "exact interconnection" less than a realistic expectation. It seems overambitious to attempt a strict deduction from Σ to the *Problem.* Rather, in the comparison-constrast proper to interpretive musement, the following investigation searches for strict analogies, startling parallels, and yet more fitting embodiments of logical forms as it proceeds from Σ's most abstract to the *Problem*'s most concrete level. Royce's own scattered references to these relationships are terse and cryptic, yet assembling them for study may create light enough to grasp the kind of operations he intended by his key phrases, "apply the principles" and "embody the results."

In the *Sources,* Royce wrote, "I propose at some future time . . . to attempt an application of some of the principles that underlie the present lectures to the special problems which Christianity offers to the student of religion" (*SRI,* 9–10).[7] A year later, after indicating that he had long reconsidered the ancient and modern problems of the philosophy of religion, he foretold that his lectures in the *Problem* would "embody the results of a few of these efforts towards reconsideration" (1:6). In his preface to the *Problem,* written about six months later, when referring to his recent promise in the *Sources* that he would "attempt to 'apply the principles' there laid down to the special case of Christianity," (1:viii) he enclosed "apply the principles" in quotation marks this time, as if alerting his reader to a special sense for that phrase.

To clarify what Royce meant in these three quotations by the phrases "apply the principles" and "embody the results" is to ready oneself to see how he viewed the interrelationships between his *Problem* and his logic (pure and applied). Since the Royce of 1910–1913 was especially interested in logic, one rightly expects that the principles of his distinctive pathfinder kind of pure logic—his System Σ—will provide the basic, even if hidden, leading ideas from logic for the *Problem.* The detailed correspondences that later come to light will support this expectation.

In the *Sources,* when Royce speaks of "applying" a principle or a doctrine, his aim and context show that he means neither a deductive working-out of consequences from pure logic nor an evaluation of a case according to a norm.[8] By "applying," the mature Royce means such a *re*consideration of Peircean "Signs" operating on various levels of greater or less concretion that they mutually illumine each other. Through this mutual illumination of multilevelled Signs, Royce's "application of principles" constituted in one sense an analogue of the "harmonic construction" he sought.[9] This Peirce-inspired interpretive musement was Royce's distinctive procedure and method for effecting that "Organized Combination of Theory and Experience" which was his highest form of methodology in the "Principles" (*RLE,* 321; #8).

Our exegesis of the phrase "apply the principles" is confirmed by a text from the *Problem.* Describing a climactic instance of "mutual illumination," the text by its phrase "nowhere more pronounced" suggests that there are many other less pronounced instances of such illumination. In the setting of the following excerpt, Royce portrays how our major psychic components interact when we, through much pondering and decisiveness, actually adopt and persistently maintain our fundamental orientation towards life and the world. In this process of determining one's fundamental orientation, Royce recognized that

> the intimate relations between theory and life are nowhere more pronounced than in this case, where reason and sentiment, action and expression, throw light, each upon the other as is hardly anywhere else the case. (2:310)

Explicitly, Royce focused on the way "reason and sentiment, action and expression," as four multilevelled Signs in an interpretational process, mutually illumine "the intimate relations between theory and life." Implicitly, he supposed that, in this radically important process, four other Signs were also operating with their distinctive initiatives, namely, the human self, its chosen "cause," the Universal Community, and its Spirit.[10]

In the light of the text above and of his usage of interpretive musement as his general method in the *Problem,* we are led to raise a question. When he wrote of "applying the principles" to the particular case of Christianity, did Royce intend a similar integration of mutually illuminating Signs? Was it through a parallel "Organized Combination of Theory and Experience" that System Σ would win its full bearing upon the *Problem?*

Next, if one tries to interpret Royce's other cryptic explanatory phrase, what did he mean when he described the *Problem* as "embodying the results" of his decades-long efforts to reconsider some of the problems of the philosophy of religion? He added that these results had culminated in his *Sources,* particularly in its lecture "The Religion of Loyalty" (1:6, vii–viii).[11]

Royce's meaning of "embodying the results" of the *Sources* becomes clear if we consider *as* an organized body of ideas that distinctive "Christian doctrine of life," which is the center of the *Problem.* This body of doctrine is organized to some extent by certain *more* general ideas, less specific than the distinctively Christian ones. What Royce found distinctive about Christianity's essential creed was its doctrines of Atonement and of that kind of love which the divine Father has for all human individuals — namely, that love which calls them to become co-members in the Kingdom of Heaven (1:xix–xx, 342). The seeds of these two doctrines became explicit only in the final lectures of the *Sources,* yet these "results" presupposed the discoveries of the *Sources*' earlier lectures. Consequently, when Royce foretold that his lectures in the *Problem* would "embody the results of a few of these efforts towards reconsideration" (1:6), he meant both that the "Christian doctrine of life" is compared to an organized body and that those seven universal "sources of religious insight" (which he found available to *every* truth-seeking human self) find a particular enfleshing in the Christian doctrine of life.

In other words, Royce viewed the *Problem* as incarnating the seven "sources of religious insight" which he had just discovered in his empirical investigation of humankind's keep religious needs and interests. Serving as guides in this investigation were his purely logical principles of Σ and the experientially derived (or "mixed") principles of his reconsidered philosophy of religion in general. To have embodied the results of the *Sources* in the *Problem* called Royce also to embody both of these sets of principles which had led to those results.

I suspect, first, that Royce viewed the *Sources* as supplying a twofold mediation between his "Principles of Logic" and his *Problem*. That is, the two levels of lights (or Signs) provided by the *Sources* are Royce's principles of general philosophy of religion and his sevenfold sources of religious experience in general. Second, I suspect that in the *Problem* Royce's insightful combination of theory and experience in the Christian doctrine of life supplied another twofold mediation between his pre-1912 studies of religion and his 1912 investigation of the "religion of loyalty" as paradigmatically found in Christianity's communal religious life. That is, the two levels of lights (or Signs) provided by the Christian doctrine of life in the *Problem* are that doctrine's essential ideas and those "modes of action" which constitute a right response to that doctrine. Through these further mediators, Royce's System Σ achieved most fitting "application" to that shared life of practical faith which he investigated in the *Problem*.

To initiate some testing of this hypothesis of multiple mediating Signs, I go beyond Royce, who did not explicitly identify his "principles laid down in the *Sources*." I venture to nominate seven specific candidates for the position of these principles and to align them in a one-one correspondence with Σ's principles of pure logic. If one views these sets of correlated principles as mutually illuminating Signs and then compares and contrasts them, he can grasp one phase of Royce's "Organized Combination of Theory and Experience." This may bring him in touch with the process and materials Royce employed while creating and executing the *Problem*.

Royce did not identify one by one his "principles laid down in the *Sources*," yet the seven suggestions above seem likely candidates for these experience-based principles. The question next arising is whether "mixed" principles like these were the *only* mediators between Royce's pure logic and the particular materials of the *Problem*. If so, he would not have spoken of "embodying the *results*" of the *Sources* in the *Problem*. Principles are not results. Moreover, if these "mixed" principles were the only mediators, he would have lacked an experiential basis tailored to fit that distinctively Christian "form of social religious experience" (1:xv), which he wanted to investigate in the *Problem*. This would have prevented him from

Principles of Logic	Principles Laid Down in the Sources
1. The *unity* of Σ's four major ingredients: the *individual as related to a set* by a right (or normative) operation	1. *"The paradox of Revelation"* (or "the religious paradox"), consists in the strange *unity of the individual self with the Universal Community*. This unity presupposes the *right operations* (right discernment through right confluence of three processes: the individual's experienced interior light, the witness of the spirit within, and the inwardly working saving grace of the Universal Community); (*SRI*, 19-25).
2. *Epsilon* relation (of belonging) = ε	2. The human self's *interest* in its highest good. This interest is "the beginning of religion" in the self and of its *"belonging"* to the Universal Community.
3. *Obverse* of the epsilon relation (not belonging) = ε̄	3. The human self's natural state of being *"morally detached"* from the Universal Community and *morally impotent* by itself to reach union with this, its highest good.
4. *Relating of relations = operation* (through a triadic function)	4. The *teleologically directed process or operation* whereby the self's interest in its highest good reaches towards ever more reliable sources of religious insight, even to ones authenticated by union with the Universal Community.
5. Operation on a *higher level* (forming a series that transcends the individual element)	5. On the human side, *opening up* to a higher level of life; on the divine side, the *inbreaking of the Deliverer* into the "detached individual" to save him from his impotence by the gift of the Spirit of the Universal Community.
6. *Series of levels* of operations	6. The *mediation* – through the loyal human community (-ies) and their loyal human servant(s) – of this Deliverance by the Spirit of the Universal Community.
7. *Norm* (or principle) in its authenticating operation upon assertions, negations, classes, relations, etc.	7. The Universal Community with its Spirit is the *Supreme Norm* that authenticates the highest three sources of religious insight (universal loyalty, the religious mission of sorrow, and life in the unity of the Spirit), makes these sources necessarily reliable *norms* of genuine ethico-religous life by its unseverable union with them, and through these sources solves the "religious paradox" authentically.

suitably carrying out his own highest normative methodology, "The Organized Combination of Theory and Experience" (*RLE,* 321; #8). Rather, it seems that Royce used the "results" of the *Sources* as additional mediators. His seven "sources of religious insight" more fittingly guided the "application" of his two sets of principles (pure and mixed) into the particular data of the Christian creed. What, then, would another crosslisting reveal if Royce's principles of pure logic were this time compared in a one-one correspondence with these "results" of his *Sources* (*SRI,* ix–xvi)? The following list of conjugate pairs seems significant:

Principles of Logic	Royce's Seven Experiential Sources of Religious Insight, Regarded as Results to be Embodied in the *Problem*
1. Individual	1. Individual religious experience
2. Class	2. Social religious experience
3. Relation	3. Rational religious experience—such thinking as relies on relations of consistency and cogency
4. Operation (as a relating of relations)	4. Volitional religious experience—such as rises from a rational agent's operations of willed decisions
5. Transformative operation, moving through a negation of an ordinary ε-relation into a higher and authenticized ε-relation to a normative set	5. Religious experience of transformation into the life of genuine Loyalty, by the denial of one's morally detached individuality and his elevation into membership in a genuine Community. Loyalty thus becomes the first source authenticated by a union, at least incipiently genuine, with the Universal Community.
6. Dialectical correlation of various series, based on a one-one-one correspondence between members in these series (*RLE,* 359)	6. Vs the "all too human" series of: A1) seeking broader vision, A2) encountering difficulties, and A3) thus inferring that the world's ruling principle is not good, there arise from the same felt evils, B1) religious hints, B2) that certain sufferings are essential to humankind's higher moral life, and B3) that these sorrows are missioning one into the way of salvation. If one idealizes adversities in this latter way, the religious hints grow into a series of insights: C1) that human life is involved in larger spiritual processes, C2) that "stark evils" (now unintelligible to mortals) may yet have their reason, and C3) that the eventual triumph of the good may not be an illusion.
7. Norm, principle, or a universal	7. The supremely normative religious experience is Life in the Unity of the Spirit and the Invisible Church.

When placed in the context of the first set of conjugate pairs, this second set with its similar one-one correspondences reveals too much sustained order to be a merely chance correlation. Our hypothesis develops into the position that Royce's seven "sources of religious insight" functioned as another set of mediators (along with the "principles laid down in the *Sources*") between Σ and the Christian religion.

However, the most particular matrix to which Royce applied Σ's light in the *Problem* is that "doctrine of life" common to the Christian people amid all their variety of life-styles, traditions, and formulas. Accordingly, to carry the present hypothesis to its fullest extent, I inquire whether Royce applied Σ to the problem of the Christian reality by combining the *Sources*' results with the experientially rooted "Christian doctrine of life." To test this third and final stage of my hypothesis, I examine whether each of Royce's seven sources of religious insight allowed something of Σ to be embodies *more* readily into that Christian experience and metaphysics which he treated in the *Problem*. Presupposing from the foregoing paired lists some familiarity with Royce's pure and applied *principles* (those of his "Principles of Logic" and of his *Sources,* respectively), a third list suggests how Σ was most concretely mediated by certain Ideas and Modes of Action into Royce's interpretation of the Christian religion. Differentiated by its three-membered one-one-one correspondences, this list compares Royce's "Results" from the *Sources* with both the essential Ideas of the "Christian Doctrine of Life" and those Modes of Action needed for responding *rightly* to the "Christian doctrine of life." Royce held that the "most significant choice for the modern man, in dealing with Christianity, lies between accepting and rejecting the Christian doctrine of life" (1:404). (By this doctrine's essential Ideas he synthesized Part One of the *Problem,* and through these Modes of Action he indicated the practical thrust of Part Two of the *Problem.*) By comparing and contrasting these essential Ideas and religious Modes of Action he carried out his projected "Organized Combination of [metaphysical] Theory and [religious] Experience" by means of his general method of interpretive musement.[12]

In brief, then, my hypothesis is that, through his method of interpretive musement, Royce "applied" his System Σ to the *Problem*. In order to carry out his interpretive musement, he employed mediating Signs to illuminate each other mutually and that distinctively Christian "form of social religious experience," which he had chosen to investigate (1:xv). In this musement, he selected and organized the combination of the following Signs: the purely formal starting points of his "Principles of Logic" (1910), the materially mixed principles of his general philosophy of religion (1911), the experientially discovered "results" or "founts of religious insight" (1911), and then, most particularly, the Ideas and Modes of Action ingredient in a right practical response to the Christian doctrine of life (1912). These dovetailing Signs reveal detailed correspondences which heighten the probable accuracy of the hypothesis, which Roycean scholars are invited to confirm or disconfirm.

The *"Results"* or Sources of Cumulative Religious Experience	Essential *Ideas* in the *Problem's* "Christian Doctrine of Life" – Signs Royce uses for his "Organized Combination of Theory and Experience"	The *Problem's* "Modes of Action," suited for a fitting response to the "Christian Doctrine of Life" – Pragmatic Signs in Royce's Process of Interpretation
1. Individual Life	*Individual Self* with its unique priority as counterbalancing the Idea of Community in Temporal Process	*Self-initiative*, expressed by extensions, postulates, and identifications which, as right, move toward community (2:40, 60–61)
2. Communal Life	*Community*, an idea recurring as a series of Signs extending from Self as community to the Universal Beloved Community itself	*Communal Strivings*, creative and promotive of community-consciousness, through genuine communication and effective co-operation (2:67, 82–83)
3. Rational Life	*Relation of Membership in a community* or lack thereof is the basis for either loyalty to a higher level of existence or one's "lost state," respectively	*"Christian" Discernment* – that distinct kind of progressively rational yet eventually insightful interpretation which life in a genuine community needs – can and does detect the presence of the Spirit of the Universal Beloved Community (2:220–221, 361)
4. Voluntaristic Life	*Temporal Process of Will* responding to duty in the hopefilled "endlessly constructive love of all mankind" (1:330, 345)	*Decision for an active attitude of resolute will* that creates values for an actual meaningful life, a will that expresses itself in a distinct mode of appreciating both itself and its realm of actual or of possible deeds, which cannot lack universal meaning (2:291–297)
5. Higher Life transformed by Loyalty	*Loyalty* as the *transformative process* that radically alters the "morally detached self" into union with a genuine community and its Spirit in "genuine freedom" (1:345, 363)	*Radical Attitudinal Choice to stand in genuine Universal Loyalty towards the whole world* – an attitude that makes one imagine and practically acknowledge as real a universal and divine community (2:293, 311)
6. Life in the Religious Mission of Sorrow	*Atonement* as the climactic expression of the creative will that the Spirit shall triumph (1:xx, 378)	*Atoning Deeds* by the genuine community and its heroic atoners – deeds that heal the traitorous violations of the "Christian" community (2:376–377)
7. Life in the Unity of the Spirit and the Invisible Church	That unique *Unity of the Beloved Community* whose diverse unique members share in a pluralism of one Life and one Spirit. Teleologically identified with this unity, "the ideal Christian community is to be the community of all mankind" (1:346)	Such wholehearted *Belief in this Unity of the Spirit that members "symbolize and realize the presence of the Spirit in the Community"* (2:428). This practical acknowledgment of the Spirit of the Universal Beloved Community consists in a devotedly loyal and critically discerning service of a genuine community (2:425–427)

To engage in at least one test, beyond the columnar lists of correspondences above, we will examine more closely whether and how each of Royce's seven "sources of religious insight" allowed something of Σ to be embodied more readily in the Christian experience and metaphysics treated in the *Problem*.

The *individual* is an irreplaceable element for Royce's pure logic. In the *Sources*, his "religious paradox" enshrines the individual's unique role in religious experience because individual subjectivity enjoys primacy in discerning whether a revelation is genuine. Not surprisingly, then, in the *Problem* Royce attributes a similar priority to the individual human self. It is the primary analogue both for other subjects of the ε-relation and for our genuine understanding of communities of memory and of hope (2:60–64). Similarly, in the *Problem,* the moral development into freedom by the human self consists in an individual rational agent choosing and committing himself to an intended life-plan and then serially embodying it. This selected internal meaning of the individual self generates an infinite sub-set within system Σ.[13]

Royce's second source of religious insight is *social* religious experience. The creedal form of such experience is the main topic for investigation in the *Problem* (1:xv). As social, religious experience reflects the mature Royce's use of logical pairs in Σ. Initial instances of these pairs are ε and its obverse ε̄, O and E, F and F̄, while the system is developed through transition by pairs and by pairs of conjugate resultants. In his living logic of the *Problem* Royce's usual more fundamental procedure is to compare and contrast a pair of contrary ideas to gain guidance through the mutual enlightenment which these ideas generate. Similarly, if the religious experience of two or more distinct human selves becomes *shared,* its quality can be, and often is, enhanced. So, too, even the shared experience found in that merely exclusivistic (or "natural") loyalty which often marks a family or a nation surpasses the quality of experience had by atomized individuals. Even the clouded religious experiences found in such natural groupings at least illumine members about, and purify them from, many of the extravagant fancies and untrustworthy insights which the simply solitary self is prone to accept (1:66–74).

Royce's third source of religious insight, *"the concrete use of reason,"* closely approximates his process of interpretation in the *Problem* (*SRI,* xi).[14] Conceiving human experience as an integral meaningful whole, reason searches for insight into it and finds *something* no human individual as such personally experiences or confirms, the living unity of two or more minded beings sharing in that meaningful whole. In its concrete use, then, reason recognizes that, *if* our notions of truth and error are to hold, this something must be actually experienced and verified. Unless the whole real world of human experience is an object of some all-knowing grasp of facts as they are, our opinions cannot even have the privilege of being false. Our concepts of truth and error depend upon the concept of an appeal to a superhuman insight had by divine wisdom. Thus Σ's hypothetical infinite, all-seeing, rational agent becomes the foundation (reiterated in the *rational* religious insight of the *Sources*) for Royce's metaphysical claim in the *Problem:*

> It belongs to the nature of things to involve an interpretation of its own contrasts, and a mediation of its own antitheses. To the world, then, belongs an Interpreter of its own life (2:276).[15]

Fourth, the *free choices of a will that seeks fuller truth* are guided by, yet go beyond, rational direction. A choice becomes free for Royce insofar as it expresses one's unique individuality (*SRI,* 160). When making his exploration into Σ, the pathfinder freely chooses his steps into a subset of it by his series of choices whose factual connection lies beyond any inferable deductions. Counsels of abstract reason stay sterile unless authentic will-acts translate them into truth-guided deeds. In this way they further constitute the consciousness of one's genuine self. System Σ emphasized the rational agent's assertions and other chosen modes of action. The *Sources* emphasized the endless striving of such an agent's will to adjust to a "higher reasonableness" (*SRI,* 149). Similarly, the *Problem* emphasizes a rational agent's deeds that build genuine community.

In brief, Roycean pragmatism depends upon a world of wills made up of rationally directed counsels and of the decisive deeds which embody such counsels. In Royce, concrete reason and willing so combine a "wide outlook" and a "well-knit plan of action" with a serious and strenuous commitment to realize the plan that from this synthesis "freedom of spirit" arises (2:5–6). This triadic combination does not remove, yet profits by, the paradox that one's freedom can become genuine only by committing oneself to serve the universal community in some way.

Genuine loyalty is Royce's fifth source of religious insight. Royce acknowledged that the ε-relation really is the "*most* elementary logical problem involved in my theory of 'community'."[16] Unless the human person's thinking is directed by the ε-relation towards the idea of belonging to a community, he can neither recognize his own moral impotence as a "detached individual" nor acknowledge the Universal Community's saving influence towards himself. Yet he needs to do both if his life is to be fundamentally meaningful (or, in religious terms, if he is "to be saved"). Furthermore, only by acts wholeheartedly in accord with the ε-relation can there arise a shared life of communication and cooperation that promotes unity with other loyal members of one's community and service towards all those not yet enlivened by genuine loyalty.[17]

Loyalty also brings the O-relation and the concepts of class and levels into the *Problem*. Royce's logic is based on the O-relation and its obverse. Similarly, in the *Problem*, the human will's yes-or-no modes of action towards genuine community are the most fundamental choices modern man can make towards Christianity. Such choices accept or reject the Christian doctrine of life and its supporting metaphysical doctrine of the two levels (1:404, 409–410). Similarly, the *Problem*'s leading ideas of Community, Grace, Process, Time, and Interpretation have a *communal* dynamism which mediates reconciliation and union to otherwise opposed minds and signs of mind.[18]

The *Sources' religious mission of sorrow* is the sixth result Royce embodied into the *Problem*. His logical system can develop only if negation pairs up with every positive ingredient. So, too, in the *Problem*, one cannot be genuinely loyal unless the possibility of treason is real and unless risk, adversity, and tragedy put one's loyalty to a series of tests for its greater growth. The human self cannot have freedom for choosing rightly unless it also can misuse its freedom. If we abolished every possibility of misusing our choices, we would also remove the "conditions which are logically necessary to the very highest good that we know" (*SRI*, 251). However, our very misdeeds can be transformed by astute interpretation into springboards for creating still higher good. Thus the logical triad from positive through negative to a higher level of the positive was the pattern Royce followed in the *Problem* to reach "the most vital of all Christian teachings," the climactic idea of Atonement.[19]

The *Sources*' seventh and culminating result is *Life in the Unity of the Spirit and the Invisible Church*. This result mediates the fullness of Royce's logic to the *Problem*'s highest level of reality. If System Σ is infinitely rich and fertile, so, too, is the *Problem*'s Realm of Grace with its Interpreter-Spirit of the Universal Community. Just as Σ is "one conscious spiritual whole of life" as infinite Sign of minded being, so the *Problem* points to a far more vital and actual "conscious spiritual Whole of Life," the Universal Community with its Spirit.

Within Royce's overall method of interpretive musement, the seven results of the *Sources* functioned as third-level Signs illuminating Christianity's social form of religious experience. Meanwhile, he drew his most specific, fourth-and-fifth-level, illuminative Signs from Christianity's distinctive doctrine of life and from the distinctive modes of action forming a fitting response to that doctrine. (See accompanying chart of Royce's series of Levels and of Signs.) From the concrescent mutual illumination created by these Signs, he experienced that novel, radical way of knowing which is genuine interpretation. It actually resembled that illumination which he had found when "reason and sentiment, action and expression, throw light, each upon the other" in the radically human process of de-

Royce's Series of Mutually Illuminating Signs

1. → SYSTEM Σ,
   SIGNS from Pure Logic.

2. → MIXED PRINCIPLES OF THE PHILOSOPHY OF RELIGION IN GENERAL,
   SIGNS in "human nature" underlying Royce's 1911 study, *SRI*.

3. → SEVEN EMPIRICAL SOURCES OF RELIGIOUS INSIGHT, the "results" of his 1911 study,
   SIGNS that Royce intended to embody in his 1912 study of a particular religion, *PC*.

4. → IDEAS ESSENTIAL FOR HIS "CHRISTIAN DOCTRINE OF LIFE" in *The Problem of Christianity*,
   SIGNS that are the doctrinal form of the social religious experience found in genuine Loyalty.

5. MODES OF ACTION REQUISITE FOR RIGHTLY RESPONDING TO THE "CHRISTIAN DOCTRINE OF LIFE," modes which are
   SIGNS OF PRAXIS that concretely organize the life of genuine Loyalty within the Beloved Community.

Levels

ciding what shall be one's fundamental orientation towards life and the world (2:310).

By applying to the *Problem* those seven principles of his mature philosophy of religion and the seven resultant "insight[s] into the need and into the way of salvation," Royce was allowing Σ to function as the hidden guide of his philosophical investigation of the Christian religion (*SRI,* 17). C. E. Lewis' prediction that "system Σ may — probably does — contain new continents of order whose existence we do not even suspect" looks increasingly accurate.[20] By realizing this, a reader will grasp what a dangerous understatement it is to describe Royce's style of thought and expression in the *Problem* as "deceptively simple."[21] If one carefully studies the "Principles" and then, after probing the *Sources,* searches through clues like "pair," "level," and "one-one correspondence" for the logic underlying the *Problem,* one will come to recognize that this work is an intricate and fertile masterpiece in logic and that, from a logical point of view, it is one of the most succinct and profound works in American philosophy. In the *Problem* a vitally tense logic directs everything and discerningly selects the thought-structures, procedures, kinds of questions, leading ideas, and even the type of phraseology. Pragmatically, all this logic of Royce the interpreter conspired towards a "fairer understanding" of the philosophy of the Christian religion.

We have seen how Royce was prepared for his prophetic interpretation of problematic Christianity. His life schooled him in Christian community and philosophy, in suffering and prayer. His forty years of studying the philosophy of religion fashioned him into a competent interpreter. Undergirding and guiding this competency were his dozen years of intense logical studies which discovered and followed a path different from that of Russell and Whitehead and which became crystallized in his 1910 "Principles of Logic" with its pragmatically based System Σ. Overall, then, Royce was being formed and forming himself into a seer who could interpret Christianity from a secular viewpoint, that is, "from the human side, only."

PART TWO

*Royce Explores the
Human Interests That Produce
Religious Experiences*

6. The Seven Sources of Elementary Religious Experience

We have next to discover how Royce's problem of Christianity arises out of elementary and complex religious experiences. It is one thing to propose a problem attractively; it is quite another feat to establish experientially and historically the actual sources and branchings of this problem. This and the next chapter will detail Royce's two-year investigations of elementary religious experience which culminated in his Bross Lectures of 1911,[1] published as *The Sources of Religious Insight*.

A person can disregard *Sources* on the plea that they are too popular and simple and then rush into the *Problem* claiming that Royce's late masterpiece deserves all his time and energy. Such a tactic is questionable. Part one has already raised justified suspicions about Royce's "deceptively simple" style. His presentation in the *Sources* hides profound insights, and the current widespread neglect of this work inclines a reader to slide over Royce's own caution that in the *Problem* the principles to be applied had already been laid down in his Bross Lectures.[2] Soon after completing the *Sources,* Royce wrote that this work "contains the whole sense of me in a brief compass" even if it is "one of the easiest of my books to read."[3] Lacking time to develop any comprehensive philosophy of religion, he had concentrated his inquiry on elementary religious experience and thus won both depth and clarity.

We can forestall possible misunderstandings if we try to distill this "whole sense of Royce" into still briefer compass. In the present chapter, then, we will clarify Royce's basic terms and aims in the *Sources* and rapidly survey the work as a whole. Doing so will let us grasp how from his seven sources of religious insight he synthesizes one, fully complete, elementary religious experience. Our main endeavor, however, occurs in the next chapter where we accompany Royce as he, like a skilled boat-captain taking soundings to explore an unknown river, investigates the two most elementary of these seven sources of religious insight. Our exploration of elementary religious experience will then enable us in chapter 8 to enter deeply into Royce's central topic in the *Problem,* complex religious experience.

Royce's distinction between the "elementary" and "complex" kinds of religious experience depends, respectively, on the absence or presence of a communally held doctrinal "form of social religious experience" (1:xv). Much of the labor of the *Problem* is needed to identify accurately just what this "form" is which makes religious experience "complex." Basically, the difference consists in whether or not a particular religious experience is marked by a communally conscious sharing in a single religious doctrine of life. If so, it is "complex"; if not, it is "elementary."

For example, in a nationally televised Memorial Day ceremony, many adult Americans find some kind of religious experience during the moment of silence honoring their country's deceased servicemen. But not all who experience the moment share the widely held doctrinal faith that somehow these dead live on, because among the participants are some skeptics and disbelievers. These latter participants may have some kind of religious experience by becoming aware of their life-ideal as endangered and by receiving a saving light. Their spirits may be uplifted by an emotional and even complicated experience. Yet because of the lack of a consciously communal doctrinal faith Royce would regard their experience as elementary.

In contrast, a handful of early Christians sharing a liturgy with the apostle Paul knew they participated with each other in one doctrine of life, in one eucharistic faith. Their religious experience was "complex" because of the doctrinal faith that each knew was communally shared and held by all. If they occasionally manifested their "one conscious spiritual whole of life" by jointly professing one identical creedal formula, then what made their experience "complex" was their conscious sharing of one doctrinal faith, rather than their joint profession and formula—however much the latter two raised their awareness of sharing one doctrine of life.

One would misread Royce, then, if he interpreted this Roycean distinction between elementary and complex religious experience to run in strict parallel with other, more familiar distinctions. It is not the distinction between simple and complicated religious experience, nor between individual and social, primitive and developed, or even pre-loyal and loyal. The bases and intents of all these distinctions are different. As Royce's investigation of religious experience develops in this and the following chapters, his distinctive sense of elementary and complex religious experience will become clear.

Religious consciousness is, of course, far more than the essential structure of insightful knowing that Royce discovered in the *Sources*. To be wholesome, religious experience also has to embrace human feelings and tendencies. He had reflected for decades on the ways ordinary people try to balance the ingredients needed for living their religion—whether they viewed it as a life-stream composed of knowings, feelings, and tendings or as a skillful blending of sensitivity, docility, and initiative. By the time of writing the *Sources,* Royce had finally succeeded in weaving the many colorful threads of religious feelings, tendings, and knowings into one rich, intricately balanced tapestry vibrant with life.

BASIC TERMS IN THE *SOURCES*

Seven basic notions and terms directed Royce's exploration of materials in the *Sources:* religious experience, religion, salvation, interest in salvation, religious insight, religious paradox, and source. What did he mean by these ideas and how did he use these terms when he delivered his Bross Lectures?

In a *religious experience* one's psyche moves from less to more light about overall issues. Since religious experiences are "common to a very large portion of mankind" (*SRI,* 37), they are in no way confined to religious geniuses such as those William James selected for his cases in the *Varieties*. Religious experiences, which are forestalled by a merely routinish or shallow life-style, occur in the daily lives of serious-minded people in both their difficult and pleasant circumstances (*SRI,* 40).

Moreover, as Royce said, "they are great and, in certain respects at least, simple experiences" (*SRI,* 37). They are great on several counts. A person's paramount need operates in them. In them one meets one's salvation (or "Deliverer," if taken both religiously and personally). And one gains insight into the *way* of salvation. This requires that in these experiences one also learn the way of salvation for all one's brethren because all men and women are members one of another (*SRI,* 34). At the same time there is something simple in these experiences. They have one fundamental motive (interest in salvation) and a regular triad of objects (ideal, need, and Deliverer). Accordingly, Royce could postpone "complex" religious experience for study in the *Problem* and concentrate on elementary religious experience in the *Sources.*

Religion underlies the latter part of the title *The Sources of Religious Insight.* For Royce, the eternal refers ultimately to the divine will as it constantly intends the total plan of life and achieves this in and through the flow of finite experiences. For instance, in 1908 he detected that ordinarily one who undergoes a deep religious experience gains through his interpretation a union with the divine intent and with the spirit of loyalty. He defined religion in its highest forms, then, as "the interpretation both of the eternal and of the spirit of loyalty through emotion, and through a fitting activity of the imagination."[4] Humanistically, he supported religion's interpretive union through a nourishing context of fitting affections, symbols, and commitments. Philosophically, he generalized the higher religion of Christianity into his "religion of loyalty." As a salvific process of interpretation, this latter grows by alternating between a sacred pair of ideas and by winning increasingly vital contact with both: the idea of the Individual at one level of uniqueness and the idea of the Beloved Community at another. The Logos-Spirit of the Community guides these processes of alternation and increasing contact even while it instructs through this sacred pair of ideas. During Royce's final years, this pair increasingly characterized his references to his "religion of loyalty."[5]

When one searches to adjust himself to the supreme will, he seeks *salvation* (*SRI,* 159). But he can do this only if transformed into a community that is itself transformed by genuine loyalty. Contrary to the popular sense of something won by the individual, salvation meant for Royce a process promoted by a genuine community in its union with its highest goal. Only derivatively did the term "salvation" apply to one who *as member* participated in the saving community's process of receiving from its Interpreter the needed union with its highest goal. This idea of the "salvation of a community through a universally significant human transformation, without which no salvation of an individual man would be possible . . . became the most essential and characteristic idea of the Christian church."[6]

The human self's *interest in salvation* is the taproot of religion in both its primitive and its higher forms. This interest signals that the transformation towards genuine loyalty has at least started. Royce described this interest as a person's peculiar and overriding need to be freed from some universal burden and from the danger of missing his highest good (*SRI,* 8-12). Factual support for this description arose from surveys of religious experience carried out by himself, his audience, and William James (*SRI,* 11-17, 27-28). Royce's own survey ranged from elemental experience that lacks a communal form of belief to the kind found in such higher religions as Buddhism and Christianity. Since he found this interest in salvation experientially verifiable, primordial, and ubiquitous, he reached his research decision: "Now, for my present purposes, this *interest in the salvation of man* shall be made, in these lectures, the essential feature of religion is so far as religion shall here be dealt with" (*SRI,* 8).[7] Then to insure that his research kept in vital touch with this interest, he clarified his remaining terms (such as "religious insight" and "religious paradox") by making them depend tightly upon man's concern for salvation.

As a special kind of interpretation, *religious insight* called for technical precision of language in the *Sources.* Here Royce used "insight" without qualification to point to a third kind of knowledge, fundamentally distinct from perception and conception. Insight is primarily a "knowledge that makes us aware of the unity of many facts in one whole, and that at the same time brings us into intimate personal contact with these facts and with the whole wherein they are united" (*SRI,* 5-6). For him insight has three marks: "breadth of range, coherence and unity of view, and closeness of personal touch" (*SRI,* 6). This third mark suggests that insightful knowing requires firsthand experience. It also implies that the object known by insight is personal and not abstract; that is, it is a minded being or sign of some self. Hence, neither mere percepts nor mere concepts nor second-hand learning (whether by rote or by hearsay) suffice to produce insight.

The interpretive grasp of insight becomes specifically religious when it is "insight into the way of salvation and into those objects whereof the knowledge conduces to salvation" (*SRI,* 9). The species of religious insight examined in the first two chapters of the *Sources* is that occurring in an individual who is as yet not transformed by genuine loyalty. He is viewed first by himself and later in relation to others. At this level of the most elementary sources, religious insights can be at the same time both intimate, fundamental, and indispensable but also crude, capricious, and fallible. At the intermediate level of development, religious insights accrue from synthetic reasoning and decisive choice. Contrasting with these religious insights of lower quality are those mediated by Royce's three highest sources: loyalty, religious sorrow, and felt unity in the spirit of community. The higher level insights can develop only out of the indispensable lower insights. Yet as the serial insights correctively supplement each other, the natural motives of religion gather strength. With decreasing caprice and illusion the mysterious objects of religion appear: the ideal-goal, the need of salvation, and, especially, the union with one's Deliverer. Developmental wholeness and authenticity culminate when the highest sources bring an individual's religious experience to its rich fullness.

The *religious paradox,* or paradox of revelation, is the central problem Royce investigated in the *Sources* (*SRI,* 20-26).[8] This paradox lies in the deep puzzlement about just which conditions in the finite self allow it to assert validly that it hears the divine voice certainly or recognizes unmistakably the divine autograph upon some supposedly religious experience or even upon a special revelation (*SRI,* 22). Without some principle of discernment intrinsic to the human self, religious experience and revelation cannot be authenticated and therefore lie prey to illusion. What then, if any, is this principle of discernment? If people come equipped with this spiritual radar set rightly attuned to the Spirit, can they know certainly that what they meet in religious experience is, at least sometimes, truly "the Master of Life" and not an illusion (*SRI,* 32)?[9]

Coming to his final notion of a *source,* Royce knew he was dealing with a primitive insight of common sense. So, abandoning his way of explicitly clarifying basic terms, he simply let his audience infer what he meant by "sources" from several clues in his opening remarks. For instance, he spoke of "ways in which religious truths can become accessible to men" (*SRI*, 4) and of his intent to stress "those perennial sources from which human insight has flowed and for ages in the future will continue to flow" (*SRI*, 18).[10] Excluding special revelations and focusing instead on insights that are religious, he concentrated on certain founts within natural religious experience. To the persons having such experiences, these originals emit religious light which illuminates the motives and objects within people's religious awareness. From the start Royce made it clear that these sources function only within an ongoing communication between the human and superhuman (*SRI*, 19). At the close he made this explicit when speaking of the invisible church — "The sources of insight are themselves the working of its spirit in our spirits" (*SRI*, 297). In sum, by the term "sources" he both pointed to the natural fountainheads of religious experience and postulated a triadic sign-sending process occurring between human selves, the universal community, and its Spirit.

ROYCE'S AIM IN THE *SOURCES*

Deliberately moving from an inital indeterminacy to more determinate goal-setting, Royce stated his aim in the *Sources* as generally to "make some comments upon the ways in which religious truths can become accessible to men" (*SRI*, 4). To identify these ways or sources he first had "to understand the great common features and origins of the religious consciousness" (*SRI*, 18). This meant penetrating to "the origin of that deeper sense of need [of salvation], which is indeed the beginning of religion, . . . [to] the basis of the religious interest" (*SRI*, 48).

To get in touch with this origin, he concentrated chiefly upon the mature form of religion found in the higher religions rather than upon the embryonic form of religion exhibited by the primitive religions. Royce recognized that differences in people's cultures, temperaments, experiences, and basic attitudes necessitate the "many various and apparently conflicting forms" of religion and "the apparent chaos of religious experience" (*SRI*, 41). Believing that "the underlying motives of the higher religions are, after all, much more in agreement than the diversities . . . would lead us to imagine," he wanted to sift through the latter in order to lay bare "this deeper unity of the higher religious life of mankind" (*SRI*, 41). His faith in this deeper unity was of a piece with his radical trust in the basic soundness of modern man, a trust he described as a fundamental religious act.[11] His hope was that if he identified the interior light of religious discernment in every human self he would lay bare this deeper unity. In doing so, he would provide a basis for revelation and promote ecumenical understanding and cooperation so that people of differing religious traditions could live in unity of spirit by sharing this common interior light.

To verify this deeper unity, he investigated "those perennial sources from which human [religious] insight has flowed and for ages in the future will continue to flow" (*SRI,* 18). These sources would direct him towards the human self's inner power of distinguishing between authentic religious experiences and illusory ones. This power of discernment was what unified "the ways in which religious truths can become accessible to men" (*SRI,* 4). In brief, Royce's intent was to investigate people's preadapted sense for sifting between a genuine and a non-genuine divine communication. His seven perennial sources served as a series of accumulated clues that cast increasing light on the higher religions' deeper unity. That unity lies in each human self's power of religious discernment which has its own motives and objects (*SRI,* 41-42).

Whatever naturally moves a person in any way towards salvation is a *motive* of higher religious life. These natural motives include the spiritual needs, ideals, and interests common to every human self, his orderly and disorderly tendencies, habits and associations, along with the basic desires, fears, hopes, and joys common to mankind insofar as these are concerned with salvation. If Royce could show that these motives were indeed natural, he would make evident "the unity of the religious concerns of mankind" and also solve the religious paradox. Moreover, if, through his methodic self-limitation only to what is experientially describable, he could show that people's "principal religious motives are indeed perfectly natural and human motives," then he would have explained their presence adequately and rendered superfluous James' explanatory hypotheses about "mysterious movings from another world" (*SRI,* 41-42).

When these natural motives move our consciousness, they put us into the path of salvation (*SRI,* 26); they thrust us towards religious *objects*. The motives "force us to seek for relief from spiritual sources," to enter the definably superhuman. As part of the higher religious life which is dialogical, these mediating objects are threefold: the religious ideal, the need for salvation (in each self and in the whole of humankind), and also that saving "something" or Deliverer (*SRI,* 29, 41-42).

Being naturally ignorant and fallible, we fail "to conceive readily and to grasp adequately the religious objects." To us they have to appear mysterious, supernatural, and naturally baffling (*SRI,* 42). Perceived through differently acculturated mindsets, these baffling objects produce a vast variety of religious experiences and people's still vaster variety of interpretations of them. Natural religious consciousness is charged, then, with mystery because the ideal, the need, and the saving process we know are all superhuman. Accordingly, Royce's aim was to so employ both the natural religious motives and these mysterious religious objects as signs pointing to "the deeper unity that underlies all our nobler religious needs" (*SRI*, 42).

Carrying the hope of this aim into the public forum of his Bross Lectures, Royce investigated seven different "sources" or "elements"[12] which produce religious experience by serially developing the inner light. He began his psychic sounding by scrutinizing the factors in religious experience which come from a human self when viewed (1) as uniquely individual and (2) as social. These two sources are the *most elementary*. Later he studied the other five ways of coming to salvific insight. Though dependent on the two most elementary ones, these five complementary ingredients develop, strengthen, correct, and transform the original pair of sources. Religious experience cannot become fully integrated without these remaining five sources; namely, those elements making one's experience (3) synthetically rational, (4) volitional, (5) loyal, (6) redeemingly patient, and (7) communally shared in the unity of the spirit. He claimed no completeness to this list of seven sources. In fact, when speaking privately and less formally, he added two other sources of religious insight: man's response to beauty and his natural cult of the dead.[13] In all of his seven publicly investigated sources he was searching for authentically divine sources which the self's principle of discernment would recognize by an unseverable bond with "the Unity of the Spirit and the Invisible Church." That is, by trying to deny the authenticity of each of his seven sources, he used his interpretive logic to discover whether the attempted denial itself implicitly testified to the unseverable bond with the universal community. His research revealed that the final three sources reinstated themselves as authentically divine by being unseverably bonded to the unity of the Spirit.

When peering into human religious experience, then, Royce centered his attention on its natural motives and its seemingly mysterious objects. This pair of signs point revealingly to that deeper mediator, the inner light of discernment within each person yet common to all. By distinguishing between authentic and inauthentic divine communications, this discerning light or natural interpreter does two things. As an embodiment of a uniquely teleologized form of the ε-relation, it brings each human self "into touch with a Power or a Spirit that is in some true sense not-Ourselves" (*SRI*, 32). As a common identical gift at work in all people, it also unites the entire human community into a genuine second-level reality, into "one conscious spiritual whole of life" (1:406).

By selecting the two most elementary sources for scrutiny in the next chapter, we risk obscuring the overall continuity which Royce portrayed in the *Sources*. Roycean elementary religious experience requires for its fullness the synthesis of all seven sources of religious insight. This full experience has only its beginnings in the two "most elementary sources" (the individual and social fount of this illumination process) (*SRI*, 18) because a natural concrescence tends to develop all seven sources into an integral yet elementary religious experience. To avoid a misemphasis, then, we need to get the feel of the rich texture of elementary religious experience in the fullness of its seven sources. Like Royce, we begin with the most elementary, even if most capricious, ingredients and then move towards a cumulative synthesis of the other five sources of religious experience.

SEVEN FOUNTS OF AN INDIVIDUAL'S RELIGIOUS EXPERIENCE

A strange rhythm marks the way consciousness ebbs and flows in the unique individuality of each finite itself. Routinely, a person daily attends to definite tasks and social amenities, generally unaware of any overall meaning to her life amid the stream of ordinary events. Yet occasionally, perhaps when struck by the unexpected or when isolated from others, a broad and deep vision momentarily looms up in her consciousness to give meaning, purpose, and wholeness to her life. She then sees in contrast with this broad but passing vision that her usual experience of life is fragmented and disorderly. The contrast alerts her to her daily captivity and leads her to "cry out of the depths." This is the individual source of most elementary religious experience.

Correlative to this is the social source which enlightens a person when he discovers that by himself alone he cannot get meaning, purpose, and wholeness into his life. To be saved from his usual fragmented life, he must have sisters and brothers helping him towards a unity of life and he must accept their help when they support, guide, and correct him with human affection. His experience is no longer that of relating to a mere collectivity or bare social pressure. Instead, companionship and love have transformed his previous loneliness and loveless social world. They have revealed to him, through the loving face, smile, or gesture of a friend or of one in need, a hint of a mystical vision of something superhuman, of a divine process (*SRI*, 74). Social religious experience has dawned but, as mediated through our literal social relations, is never enough to satisfy the religious need of people.

Upon this twofold, most elementary basis, Royce moved straightway to probe the ultimate meaning within any opinion, doubt, error, or true judgment. Within reason as synthetic he rediscovered his thirty-year-old religious insight into the reality of the all-knowing Other so that the opinion be validated in this Other's wider experience as either true or false.[14] As Royce put it, "if we err, we simply come short of the insight to which we are aiming to conform, and in the light of which our ideas get absolutely all of their meaning" (*SRI,* 115). No merely possible Seer, but only an actual all-seeing Reason could adequately account for any actual error of a human self. The finite rational self can neither grasp intellectual meaning nor grow to fuller truth without the responding normative knowing of an actual all-seeing Insight.[15] Even "in every error, . . . we are still in touch with the eternal insight. We are always seeking to know even as we are known" (*SRI,* 115). Whenever the human self, then, creates the rational synthesis of adopting an opinion as its own, there is an implicit religious awareness of the Knower of the universe (*SRI,* 113-114).

Knowing that many in his audience would regard synthetic reason as a source "too contemplative to meet vital religious needs," Royce turned to the volitional side of human consciousness (*SRI,* 116). What people want is to get in touch with reality as a whole. They want to escape meaninglessness, to avoid pseudo-values, and to make decisions in line with the way the world is moving. By willing in these ways they reveal their implicit intent to adjust themselves to the supreme will that is running the world (*SRI,* 159). This means, more specifically, that the finite will, in setting its values, establishing its rule of life, and estimating the relevance of its purposes, is actually, even if unconsciously, striving to act in ways that fit into the basic processes of the whole universe and its overall direction.

Light comes from a contrasting example. Ask a person to try thinking seriously that he can undo a past deed. If he so tries, he finds himself foolishly trying to reverse, even destroy, the time process of the universe, a process in which his own series of choices is inescapably embedded. So, the human will cannot realistically avoid this much minimal conformity to the temporal universe's bearing into the future and its unchangeability of the past. These irreversible features of our universe are expressions of the will of the all-Knower.

However, beyond this minimal conformity, the meaning of the universe can be interpreted differently and each minded self must adopt a preferred basic interpretation of it — for example, as "just for me" or "ultimately a deceit" or "for all of us called to a loving loyalty towards the whole universe."[16] Without this free basic interpretation, the human self could not make any ultimate sense either of itself or of its decisions. But in all its other choices, the finite will can successfully score a hit and avoid a miss only if its fundamental interpretation of the world is basically correct.

Suppose a self has adopted the correct fundamental interpretation of the world. How does it, in its ordinary nonbasic choices score hits and avoid misses? One's ordinary choices arise either from the self's uniqueness or more superficially from mere habit or disordered impulse or just group thinking. If the choices arise from the self's uniqueness, they become genuinely free since by this route they conform to (or hit) the will of the divine all-Knower (SRI, 160). He wills to evoke finite selves to fuller genuine freedom by their making decisions that arise from individual uniqueness and are guided also by the true basic interpretation of the universe.

What, then, has Royce's investigation of will discovered? He had probed his previous insight of synthetic reason until it also revealed that since the self's fundamental interpretation of the universe is valuational; it cannot lack an action-guiding character. Consequently, he realized that the Seer also had to be the supreme appreciating Self in the community of all finite minded selves. By examining this Self's universal appreciative intent in the time process, Royce discerned how highly he values and loves these unique finite selves and calls them to more freedom through choices rising out of their uniqueness. Because of his complete insight into his own intent for the world, this universal Appreciator sets values, establishes the fitting rule of life for human selves, and estimates their purposes (*SRI,* 159). When the will and conduct of the finite self coincide with this intent of the Supreme Will, the finite self can experience an enlightening touch (or volitional religious experience) arising from contact with the "Great Companion" (*SRI,* 135). In these nonbasic choices, even if the finite self's intent misses the divine intent, the finite self still maintains a continuing, though attenuated, touch with the divine will (thanks to the radical non-free conformity of finite will with the "Will that wills the universe," described above) (*SRI,* 115, 159). This distinctive fourth source of religious insight, then, issues from the human will when by its choices it meets the divine will as lovingly appreciative of all minded selves and as deserving reverent response.

So far Royce has shown four sources of religious insight. The first lies within the felt contrast between an individual's narrow and broad ranges of consciousness while the second impinges through the loving presence of human others. Then the implication of an all-Knower is revealed through synthetic reason, and the requirements of the superhuman Appreciator and caring Lover of all are touched by a finite will when the intents of its choices reveal a similarly evaluative response. Impelled by these two conjugate pairs of sources, Royce next rose to a completely higher level that combined them all. For he now showed how a fifth source, the transforming experience of genuine loyalty, organically assembles his first four sources into a living synthesis of religious interests (*SRI,* 166, 206).

But the urgent question arises: What makes Roycean loyalty so different that it can claim to be the *genuine* or true loyalty? Its distinctive point is the will to love and to serve the universal community *as* community. This loyalty leads to the universal community of all minded selves and thus to the felt presence of the divine (*SRI*, 206–210). It may not exclude any self insofar as that self is or can become universally loyal. Ordinarily, through what are often called one's "loyalties to other persons," one desires to love and serve other individual members of his community. Valuable and indispensable as these desires are, they are inadequate for genuine community life because their object is the human individual *as* individual, rather than the proper object of Roycean Loyalty: the universal community *as* community. By the insight of genuine loyalty one recognizes a morally sound human community as "one conscious spiritual whole of life."[17] Loyalty becomes genuine, then, only if it is that unique love which relates a morally transformed person to the second level of man's spiritual existence, the level of man the community.

Converting a genuine loyalty and growing in it require of the human self a peculiar blending of activity and passivity (*SRI*, 181), and of fidelity to both his own individual uniqueness and his multileveled responsibilities to others (*SRI*, 198). Sensitive to self and others, docile to the Spirit's voice and movement, the loyal self also initiates wholehearted deeds of community service. Paradoxically, these deeds allow him to find his true self and promote its development (*SRI*, 198, 209). In a thoroughgoing and practical way he devotes himself, no longer with merely natural loyalty to a naturally exclusive community (like a tribe or nation), but by genuine loyalty to the interest of the universal community.

The causes of genuine loyalty fit both the finite and infinite dimensions of the human self. One needs a special personal cause, for example, his beloved, or his home, or his life-calling, and he also needs his true cause, namely, "the spiritual unity of all the world of reasonable beings" (*SRI*, 205). When he makes both levels of causes his own, he does more than expand his consciousness, find his true self, and promote its growth. From the superhuman unity of life thus contacted, he receives a fuller light, undergoes the transformation of his moral self-identity, and enjoys life-giving union with a genuine community. In other words, by dedicating himself to that conscious whole of life shared without exclusion by those he serves, he is implicitly and unavoidably intending his ultimate true cause (*SRI*, 205). In this way Roycean loyalty becomes a human self's concretely experienced source of morality and religion (*SRI*, 206).[18]

But to find your true cause, "you must find it in human shape. And you must love it before you can choose its service" (*SRI*, 206). Psychologically, the only way a self can discover the true cause it needs for genuine loyalty is through another person, already genuinely loyal, who exemplifies loyal deeds. Through that human face, the self learns how to love a human community, not as a mere collection of other human individuals, but as "a life of many brethren in unity" (*SRI,* 201). Being touched by another person's embodied service of a community, the self can experience the interest of its "true cause" even within its special personal cause and yet transcending it. Through this genuinely loyal human mediator, the true cause of the universal community appears as a religious object that both saves one from one's own "lost state" and calls to that kind of dedication which a genuinely religious object deserves (*SRI,* 206).

From genuine loyalty, as the fifth source of religious insight, flow many benefits. Viewing it as a moral principle, one can derive from it the whole of a moral code (*SRI,* 203-204). It requires one always to promote authentic loyalty in all others, howsoever different, and to avoid anything leading one to exclude, disdain, manipulate, or prey upon them. The orientation inserted within a self by one's dedication to the interest of the universal community is unique because it is more than a steadfast direction in the face of movements as yet not transformed; it is even self-reinstating in the face of attempted denials.

Religiously, in this dedication of the loyal self a beneficial commerce is found. The universal community searches out the lost individual, calls him, and bestows upon him this free gift of true loyalty as "from above." In Royce's words, "This free gift first compels your love. Then you freely give yourself in return" (*SRI,* 206). Roycean loyalty, then, contains its own unique interior light from the divine side. This lived union with the universal community, however incipient, contains its own authentication and thus first solves the religious paradox. For in such dedication the loyal self who

> addresses his word, not to a human individual, but as unto the master of life, and then, sincerely and persistently and lovingly lives that word out in his life, has solved the religious paradox. (*SRI,* 209-210)

Despite all his limitations, such a person successfully "has heard the voice of the Spirit. He has heard, and—however unlearned—he has understood" (*SRI,* 210). In such an insight, he knows his Deliverer, just as he is known. "Crying out from the depths" and carrying out his dedication, the loyal self has become *opened* in his very existence to hear the only Self-authenticating Spirit and to value its contribution to ethico-religious life as lying beyond anything provided by the four previous sources. Having reached the living source of morality and religion, Royce employed the energies of his two final sources (assimilated sorrow and felt unity) to add strength to his loyalty-solution of the religious paradox.

The problem of evil assaults human selves whether loyal or not. In the *Sources* Royce limited himself to the general philosophy of religion and so refrained from using the Christian idea of atonement, even in his pre-1912 grasp of it, to peer into the problem of evil. Instead, by focusing on the religious mission of sorrow, he addressed the tribulations which flesh is heir to and which seem to hinder religious insight.[19] To humans the manifold presence of evil seems either to doom religion to failure or to identify it with the moral struggle. For evils apparently show that the world's ruling principle is not good (and thus religion cannot but fail) or all evils are to be wiped out (and then religion's aim becomes that of morality).

Although many evils are so narrowing (because of tragic fortune or irrational chance) that they cannot at the time be assimilated, there are higher tribulations inextricably woven into the life of genuine loyalty. Loyal selves are prone to the abortive misunderstandings and to the thwarting loves with which finite, inconstant, ignorant, and often passion-led other selves burden the loyal self. Such ills need not be totally destroyed but can become part of a

> constructive process, which involves growth rather than destruction — a passage to a new life rather than a casting wholly out of life. Such ills we remove only in so far as we assimilate them, idealise them, take them up into the plan of our lives, give them meaning, set them in their place in the whole. (*SRI*, 235)

Royce calls these evils we can assimilate "sorrows." These are "not only clouding but revealing" because they "show you the way into the spiritual realm and the nature of this realm" (*SRI*, 240). Loyalty and adversity are inseparable companions since one could not become spiritually effective "without assuming the risk involved in taking personal responsibility for some aspects of the lives of our fellows" (*SRI*, 251). Through sorrows we can grasp how deeply significant are our social relations and win "those goods which can only be won through such sorrow" (*SRI*, 252). In this way we experience a religiously insightful union with God by desiring "to be one with God through bearing and overcoming the sorrows of a world" (*SRI*, 254).

The religious mission of sorrow brings us near, but not quite up to, the fullness of Royce's elementary religious experience. Fullness is achieved only when human selves, having mutually dedicated themselves to a common human cause beyond particularism, rejoice in their communion of love whose life-blood is fitting communication and cooperation. Such selves experience the felt presence of a unity of spirit which is interpretively known to be co-present in all the members of such a community. Here is the

Elementary Religious Experience 105

"highest sort of religious insight" (*SRI,* 7–8), the kind that synthesizes all the foregoing six sources.

When this life in the unity of the spirit is contrasted with a bare social union or mere institutionalized uniformity, one finds a display of differing special loyalties evoking and supporting each other. Some members of this genuine community are committed to special personal causes which are not shared by other members who promote still other special causes. Capitalizing on this rich diversity, and not captivated by it, the loyal self dedicates itself, because of the felt unity of the Spirit in the universal community, to promote yet more intensely the loyalty of these members by respecting their differences from himself. Each is illuminated by this communion of the invisible church which bestows its crowning insight on full elementary religious experience.

To solve the religious paradox in the *Sources,* Royce made elementary religious experience his sole concern. In its fullness he found seven interconnected founts or sources which together constituted a felt union with the eternal through loyalty. The relation of this felt union to the objective creedal form structuring communal religious experience was to be investigated only later in the *Problem.* Because the richness of this elementary religious experience in seven sources could lead us beyond our goal of preparing to read the *Problem* intelligently, we limit ourselves in the next chapter to the two most elementary of Royce's seven sources.

7. The Most Basic Structure of Elementary Religious Experience

Since pertinent terms have been clarified and the *Sources* surveyed, we can now do a slow-motion study of the way Royce explored the two most basic sources of elementary religious experience, its individual and social aspects. To accompany Royce on this exploration, the reader does well to tailor his or her expectations to fit the mature Royce's view of the triadic human self and of inductive method in the *Sources*.

Even when Royce temporarily disregarded the human social relationships unavoidably present and operative in the human self, he still viewed this artificially isolated individual as a "Community of Interpretation" — and that in two senses.[1] The human self is a triadic process which constitutes itself by creatively interpreting both its past remembered self and its hoped-for future self to its present self. Second, as Royce asserted, "Without the witness of the spirit in the heart, no external revelation could enlighten those who are in darkness" (*SRI,* 24). Here he indicated within the individual self a second triad of "minded beings" (or Signs) taking part in a communication process: a spirit who witnesses some message, a self who receives that witness, and a religious object symbolized in the message. Thus when Royce starts peering into the religious experience of an individual, viewed at first "in isolation," he focuses on a historically processing self, a "dynamo of ideas," with its own creative initiative, discerning light and relation to its Deliverer. This Roycean self is far more than either a mere aggregate of consciousness reacting to external stimuli or some monad sealed off from the social communications that will constitute his second source.

Concerning his inductive method, several facts invite the reader to expect Royce to use it less deftly in the *Sources* than in the *Problem*. As yet he had not undergone his "Peircean insight" of 1912 which rendered his interpretive method explicit. Limited in the *Sources* to only seven lectures (not to sixteen as in the *Problem*), he could only indicate most generally the seven founts and not expose the doctrinal content they conveyed (*SRI,* 3). Then, too, since the *Sources* was Royce's first strictly empirical investigation in the philosophy of religion, he provided his audience with fewer and less explicit signals of his methodic choices than he did in the *Problem*. Finally, in the *Sources* he chose to present two explorations of religious experience as had by the individual (*SRI,* 26-34, 44-54). Apparently the intricate intimacy of this first source called for a plurality of approaches and for a variety of methods, at least of exposition.

In the opening pair of the Bross Lectures Royce first pondered the meaning of an individual's religious consciousness when he is alone with the divine and later explored ordinary social experience as a fount of yet richer religious insight. His order sets the two major considerations of the present chapter.

EXPLORING FOR THE ESSENTIAL STRUCTURE OF INDIVIDUAL RELIGIOUS EXPERIENCE

Concerning religious experience as had by an individual, Royce identified his target: "I shall discuss the sense in which the individual experience of any of us is a source of insight into the need and the way of salvation" (*SRI,* 18). Implicit in the setting of this aim were three distinctive methodic choices. He would understand salvation as the human person's union with his supreme good, imperiled as that union presently is. Rather abruptly but with practical usefulness, he would confine the term "religion" to center upon the human self's interest in salvation, understood in a sense generalized beyond the specific meaning of salvation in Christianity (*SRI,* 8-9). He would focus the insight within religious experience upon both the need of salvation and the way to it.

To reach his goal, Royce first gave a thorough description of individual religious experience. Then, searching like Husserl for its essential structure, he came upon its "great common features and origins" (*SRI,* 18).[2] Only thereafter did he raise the critical question of whether such experience could be known to be genuine. In this way he came full circle to the central problem of the *Sources,* the religious paradox. His order of procedure directs the following three sections.

Careful Description

After his introduction, Royce's first methodic move was to describe ordinary individual religious experience in careful detail. To let such experience signal the meaning both of the religious ideal and of the correlatively felt need for salvation, he employed two approaches: the first, clarificative; the second, interpretive (*SRI,* 26, 44).

In the first approach, he started with an ordinary flow of human experience that rhythmically manifests not only wanderings and rich variety but also a contrasting "insight, as intimate as it is fragmentary, into one absolutely valuable ideal" (*SRI,* 30).[3] To provide instances of such ordinary human experiences, Royce combed life and literature for people of strikingly different affective stances towards the world; the cynic and the lover, the rebellious and the placid, the dissolute and the seeker of further wisdom (*SRI,* 13-17, 31). In his experience each person exhibited a similar pattern. The usual flow of partially clear experiences is interrupted by a clear*er* awareness of his life ideal. This latter stands in corrective contrast to his customary ways. Momentarily confronted by his life ideal, a person becomes sharply aware how tragically disharmonious is his ordinary life and how much he needs liberation from his naturally chaotic and divided self. He recognizes that such a transformation to the fuller integrity he desires could occur only if he gains effective "touch with a Power or a Spirit that is in some true sense not-Ourselves" (*SRI,* 32). If such a direct mystical touch occurs, the healing dawn of revelation would have "precisely its most intimate significance, as an appeal of the divine spirit directly to the interior light" (*SRI,* 33). To win and to increase this kind of enlightened union, and thus to be saved from a murky, fragmented, and meaningless life, becomes for the individual self a supreme life-goal clamoring to be made real through its future choices. Thus, by employing in his first approach the images of groping for an effective touch and of moving from partial darkness to true light,[4] Royce clarified how the religious interest arises in the presence of the three religious objects: one's life-ideal, his need for liberation, and his union with the Deliverer (*SRI,* 28-29).

In his second approach (*SRI,* 44-54) he tried to show more fully how our awareness of our highest good and of our need of salvation arise *naturally* in our "unaided private experience" (*SRI,* 41, 44). However varied be the forms in which the life-ideal and need are interpreted, Royce believed his generalized formula of our highest good underlay all the higher religions (*SRI,* 45). He recognized that his way of defining the religious paradox "depends upon the fact that the principal religious motives are indeed perfectly natural" and "need no mysterious movings from another world" (*SRI,* 41-42). Once conscious, however, these motives cannot be satisfied by any natural good but only by a truly supernatural source. How then could Royce clearly distinguish between the conscious natural origin of the religious interest and its fitting satisfaction?

He discerned between various explanations of the rise of people's longing for salvation. One traditional view held that a mysterious revelation from without first teaches the isolated self that it is out of harmony with God's will. From this recognition arises in the self a religious interest whose ideal is to conform oneself to the divine will. Secondly, William

James explained the rise of the religious interest through the effect of superhuman beings upon our subliminal selves (*SRI,* 47). By contrast, Royce found both explanations excessively mysterious. By simply grasping a would-be and the suggestion it carries, we can far more naturally become conscious of our life-ideal and need for salvation.

To explain more naturally how these two objects originate in our awareness, he began from the same contrast-effect between our usual narrowness of view and our rarer moments of broader visions (*SRI,* 48–49). These latter moments of insight reveal, sometimes with painful contrast, our need for integrity of spirit both in vision and in action. He acknowledged that the satisfaction of this better vision could come about only if we got in touch with an order of spiritual existence lying far beyond our naturally isolated selves. Nevertheless, each individual's own better grasp of the meaning of his or her life is enough to explain the interior origin of this broader vision. Our interest in religion grows out of our personal vision of what a harmonious life that triumphs over our chaotic natural life *would be* like (*SRI,* 52). The suggestion thus grasped in our clear moment leads us to strive to win in reality the integrity we know in ideal (*SRI,* 53).

In this sense, then, "religion is, indeed, our own affair" (*SRI,* 52) since for it we need neither the opportunity to come under the influence of some arbitrary external revelation nor some capricious upsurging from the subconscious. All we need is simply to glimpse the meaning of spiritual harmony and power, to grasp the meaning of genuine freedom and peace as the truest reading of our own lives when contrasted with our usual, hopelessly remote fulfillment of this ideal in our natural lives. Such a contrast makes it clear that if we are actually to approach the fulfillment of this ideal, we must come into close personal touch with "a real life infinitely richer than our own," with something genuinely supernatural (*SRI,* 53).

As Royce said, these moments of broader vision "come to us sometimes when our friends die, and when memory reminds us of our neglected debts of love or of gratitude to them" (*SRI,* 50). Through these stretches of rhythmic experience we are taught the difference between two kinds of needs. In contrast to our needs for particular objects (food, power, sleep, pleasure, and so on), there comes to consciousness in these glimpses that other "peculiarly paramount" need of attaining something "more important than all other aims," of not missing the greatest good man can attain (*SRI,* 12). No matter where one is situated in history and civilization, in psychic normalcy, organized religion, literacy, and politico-economic status, *if* he becomes aware of this overriding concern, he feels the need of salvation; that is, he begins to have a religious interest.

In sum, then, the need for being saved emerges into conscious awareness when a human self feels two facts simultaneously: (1) he cannot escape from his usual insensitivity to his occasionally glimpsed supreme goal, and (2) even given sensitivity to it, he cannot translate this ideal into a reality without continuous aid from beyond himself, from something genuinely supernatural. Although both the ideal and the need of salvation arise naturally from within the self's interior, this union with the saving Other enters religious consciousness from beyond the human self. This third factor is felt to arise only when "we come into genuine intercourse with a spiritual realm that is above man" (*SRI,* 42). Religious insight into a saving union with this superhuman Other is marked by "closeness of personal touch" (*SRI,* 6, 32) within, yet beyond, the individual. Religious intercourse of this kind is felt either within one's longing for one's Deliverer when felt as absent or within one's enjoyment of the Deliverer's approach or presence or communion (*SRI,* 28-29). Royce leaves the Deliverer to be interpreted personally as Spirit or impersonally as a divine power or principle (*SRI,* 220-221).

Search for the Essential Structure

On the basis of his repeated description of private religious experience, how did Royce come "to understand the great common features and origins of the religious consciousness" when viewed in its individual aspect (*SRI,* 18)? Although recognizing the actual inseparability of his method and content, we will attend first to his choices of methodically searching for these "great common features and origins" and later to the essential structure he thus uncovered.

Methodic Choices

Royce set forth his prerequisite orientation, his philosophical intent to clarify common sense, and his commitment to avoid unneeded hypotheses. Attention to these three choices sufficiently manifests his method in the first two lectures of the *Sources.*

He began by consulting experience and invited his audience to consult theirs (*SRI,* 17). The more varied his and their experiential base became, the less likely it was that some non-essential meaning and structure would distract them and the more likely it became that they, as humans together, would "catch a glimpse of this universal form of the need for salvation" (*SRI,* 16) and "get insight into the true nature of this need and into the way toward the needed salvation" (*SRI,* 17). Whether rebellious or reverent, cynical or scientific, sentimental or traditional, their experiences would reveal one common thread, one supreme goal underlying all, because all were human, "all members one of another" (*SRI,* 34).

Was any special faith, any supernatural creed, or at least the hope of finding out some way of salvation a prerequisite in addition to one's experience? No. Anyone joining Royce on his investigation needed no extra equipment (*SRI,* 37–38). A fellow researcher only needed himself and his experienced contrast-effect between his usual narrowness of view and his occasional broader vision.

Yet this contrast-effect, as interpreted, would seed insights into the way as well as into the need of salvation. While on its objective side the contrast-effect would reveal a threefold object, on the side of the subject it would evoke a transformation essential to religious consciousness.[5] The new intentionality in this transformation would orient the now religiously interested inquirer not only towards his overall ideal and need but also towards his Deliverer. Explicit reflection on this orientation would make the inquirer aware that the *direction* within this distinctive process of insightful religious knowing bears him towards his Deliverer with a sense of urgency and of self-betterment. By becoming aware of this direction, he would win "insight into the *way* of salvation" (*SRI,* 17). Through this awareness of a direction that is overall more healthy, one can detect Royce's strategic method in so defining "religious insight" that it must be double-barreled. He stipulated that "religious insight" must include insights into both the need *and* the way of salvation. Thus, while differentiating these two ingredient lights, he made one's recognition of the way as important as one's recognition of the need of salvation.

For Royce, "insight into the *way* of salvation" seems to have meant an insight that causes a shift in the self's basic orientation or attitude. Certainly he was not talking about glimpsing some specific means to salvation; for example, insight into this or that virtue or church or career or deed as "the way." Instead, he was concerned with that moment when it first dawns on a person that he can be saved. The sunlight of this new idea turns and opens the person towards thinking about a "higher, helpful Something." By this primal shift of perspective, the person sees the real likelihood of a higher than human Helper. By thus gaining what William James identified as "a new dimension" in one's life (*SRI,* 27), a person undergoes a radical change of attitude whereby he feels the warmth of a hope beyond the helps and hindrances of limited human beings.

Beyond choosing experience with its conscious contrast-effect, Royce also chose to interpret the task of the philosopher to be that of trying to clarify the deep meanings of common sense. Ordinary people surmise that all their clamorous needs, ambiguous turnings, and conflicting feelings possess some sort of unity. However, they usually cannot formulate accurately the underlying meaning that unites all their psychic experiences. Royce regarded philosophy (and thus his own endeavor in the *Sources*) as concerned "with what common sense means but does not express in clearly conscious terms" (*SRI,* 46). As a philosopher, he intended to identify this underlying meaning of common sense and to articulate it with technical precision.[6]

Finally, Royce's method in the *Sources* was marked by his own kind of naturalism and positivism, one that shunned unnecessary hypothetical entities. He adhered positivistically to the naturally experienced needs and interests of ordinary consciousness. This meant choosing *not* to follow William James' lead of postulating subliminal passageways through which dynamic higher powers effected conscious changes. This meant avoiding transempirical explanations such as willed leaps to faith, touches of grace, activities of the Holy Spirit, or other non-natural, non-ordinary factors. Royce wanted to stay closer to the experienced facts than James had done in the latter's famous chapter that concluded his *Varieties of Religious Experience.* He would *not* imitate James in creatively *thinking up* hypotheses to explain our experienced "sense that there is *something wrong with us as we naturally stand.*"[7] Rather, he would stand in the flow of natural experience and *let its facts dictate* a fitting explanation.

Essential Structure

Attending to the two poles of individual religious experience, Royce directed his analysis subjectively, to show the "unity and naturalness of the religious motives" and objectively, to "emphasize the mysterious seeming of the religious objects" (*SRI,* 44). At this point his analysis began putting him in touch with the essential structure he sought: the triad of temporally processing self with its subjective consciousness and its objective consciousness. Its subjective consciousness exhibits rhythmic variations of vision and a longing for salvation and insight. Its objective consciousness exhibits its life-ideal, need of salvation, and its Deliverer. Presupposing Royce's view of the individual human self, we follow his investigation of its subjective and objective consciousness.

Viewing the human self as subject, Royce found him "an infinitely needy animal" (*SRI,* 11) and "naturally a creature of wavering and conflicting motives, passions, desires" (*SRI,* 44). Each human self experiences a constant longing to be freed from this chaos, to arrive at a coherent unity that makes life meaningful. Within this universally experienced cry of humankind, which arises in varied voices, Royce detected a single meaning. Radical in each human self is its need for some supreme good which is currently endangered. Failure to attain this highest good makes the whole of any human life "a senseless failure" (*SRI,* 12). Here, in this need for salvation as motivating a human subject, Royce discovered a great and universal origin of religious consciousness (*SRI,* 18).

The subject's concern for salvation drew Royce to investigate the psychological first dawning of religious interest. He asked how a person undergoes the change from being consciously a-religious to religious. How does a person who for many years has been uninterested in religion gradually find the problem of religion starting to become consciously real for him? In detail, how does this burgeoning of religious interest occur in him (*SRI,* 38)?

In response, Royce found such a person must experience two facts before a religious interest can start to dawn: first, that human life has some highest end; and second, that "man, as he naturally is, is in great danger of failing to attain this supreme goal" (*SRI,* 38). From the united experience of these two facts, a person's interest in his own salvation arises naturally. (Implicit in this interest is an interest in the salvation of all other people.) This conscious emergence transforms a person into a fundamentally genuine religious inquirer, even though calls to many a future moral conversion lie ahead. As hidden, this transformation lacks the trappings of any extraordinary conversion in revival tent or in ecstatic rapture. Rather, the intimate thrust of religious life has emerged out of the inmost dynamism of the self through the light, warmth, and working of rational common sense. On the basis of this individual source of religious insight all the remaining sources can accrue and develop naturally.

A contemporary reader may boggle at Royce's bold claim that the two causes of basic religious interest are experienced facts: "I personally hold them to be facts whose reality you can experience" (*SRI,* 38). Royce assumed that his audience would recognize in the context of the Bross Lectures that he referred to what we may call "facts of real meaning" and not simply to "facts of real events." For him, "facts" are data permeated by true interpretation—a position hardly consonant with an empiricist's theory of allegedly "bare facts." Given the assumption, then, that human experience is permeated by interpretation, the mature Royce's claim becomes quite clear. These two "facts" (of man's supreme goal and of its possible loss) can be experienced by ordinary persons. So, Royce's factual claim and tenets lose their seeming brusqueness and emerge quite naturally as valid readings of our ordinary experience.

Royce went on to demonstrate more fully this natural emergence of the religious interest. He examined what the usual result is when a contrast-effect impinges on the human self's inner light, on its power of religious discernment. To support his claim that any adult human self naturally experiences man's supreme goal and its possible loss, he had to clarify how these two religious facts or objects arise from a self's basic needs, interests, awarenesses, ignorances, and affects. If consciousness of these two united facts arose regularly and unavoidably, he would have found one simple and universal form, or essential structure, of religious consciousness (*SRI*, 54). Not only could he find no human consciousness that lacked the key contrast-effect between narrower and broader range of vision, but the very attempt to deny the nexus between one's conscious life-ideal and his basic need for integrity involved a performative contradiction that reinstated the nexus. The two facts were regular and unavoidable. Thus when the human self's inner light of discernment reads this contrast between the self's narrower and broader visions, the interpreted contrast itself becomes the natural root of religion, the "basis of the religious interest" (*SRI*, 47).

Correlative to the subject's interest in salvation is its objective pole with its derivative triad of the three fundamental religious objects. All the basic meaningfulness and value of the life of a human self depends on its grasping its personal life-ideal (*SRI*, 28). This grasp of its highest good, its goal in life, is its first religious object. Along with its ideal, the individual human self also experiences the gap between this ideal and the life it actually lives. Whether its felt inability to close this gap comes from ill fortune or lack of decisiveness or moral baseness or from all these and more, the individual feels that by himself he can never attain his ideal. Furthermore, he witnesses this "tragedy of natural human failure" not only in himself but also in the people he meets (*SRI*, 40). Only too clearly and tragically do such experiences dramatize to him, and to all, each human self's need to be saved. This need of salvation is his second religious object.

In addition to these two objects, each human self can become aware of a third and most mysterious object: a felt *union* with a "saving Something," whether the union is felt through the absence or presence of this Something. Different human individuals, or the same individual at different times, interpret this "saving Something" diversely, perhaps as a Power saving her or as a Light dispelling her darkness or as a reliable Truth showing her the way out or as the great Companion or, to adopt a most general and yet a one-sided formula, as her Deliverer (*SRI*, 29). When most accurately identified, however, this third object is the human self's experienced *union with* a saving Something.

In sum, then, a threefold object—ideal, need, and union with a Deliverer—structure the essence of individual religious consciousness on its objective side. What warranty did Royce produce to support this universal statement? He appealed to the personal experiences of his audience, to the witness of world literature, and especially to William James' rich collection of cases in the *Varieties* (*SRI*, 29)

But the self knows these three objects differently than it knows its own interest in salvation. It knows the latter factually, without mystery, just as clearly as the non-mysterious fact of its own ignorance (*SRI,* 42). But the three objects it partially knows even while finding them partially far beyond its knowing. They go beyond its grasp and appear as in part mysterious. Why, then, do these objects emerge into human consciousness with this "mysterious seeming" (*SRI,* 44)? Clearly, these objects transcend our limited powers of comprehension, but do so in different ways.

Royce noticed that the first two objects (ideal and need) appear in consciousness with a more natural ordinary presence and with far less mystery than James had portrayed them to have (*SRI,* 48). Meanwhile, the third object (one's union with the saving Something) appears most mysterious and is most diversely interpreted. For each person interprets these objects, particularly the superhuman third object, out of his own unique self and out of a diverse mental set which a different culture, tradition, and education have produced. Hence, although human selves are united as subjects by their common concern for salvation, they are objectively diversified by their different interpretations of these naturally baffling objects, especially of the genuinely superhuman one (*SRI,* 43). This explains people's differences in faith.

Royce was called to scrutinize more profoundly people's claims of knowing that third object—their especially mysterious union with a superhuman power or spirit. How *could* individuals know their Deliverer with certainty? Here Royce was confronted by the religious paradox. He accepted as factual the description that in religious experience a natural revelation is mediated through one's concern for salvation and that this concern expresses itself in a consciousness of the three objects. Yet how can even natural religious revelation occur unless some prior process of recognition is at work within one's interest in salvation? That is, some inborn discerning light and prior assurance must be required to enable one to judge the genuineness of his individual religious experience. The problem is that such so-called individual experience cannot be *merely* individual but "must become some sort of intercourse with Another. . . . [which] must be in some sense the Master of Life" (*SRI,* 32). Mystics of all ages claim that this experienced union is possible for human selves and has happened in their own case. Without denying the mystics' claim, Royce stressed that for a direct touch with the "saving Something" to be possible, it had to be distinctly recognizable. Otherwise, a natural revelation's most intimate significance would be lost; namely, the divine spirit's direct appeal to the interior light of the individual "alone with the divine" (*SRI,* 33). Even if such individual religious experience were a factual and genuine occurrence, the individual human self would only know *that* he or she was so touched and *not how* it had happened. The inference Royce drew from all these experiences, claims, and critical appraisals was the balanced judgment that the human self's "individual experience remains a source of religious insight *as* indispensable and *as* fundamental *as* it is, by itself, inadequate and in need of supplement" (*SRI,* 33).[8]

In review, individual religious consciousness is that series of acts in which the self interprets its flow of experiences according to its interior light for discerning between genuine and non-genuine divine communications. This light guided Royce's phenomenological search for the essential structure of religious consciousness. He found the "great common ... origins" of that consciousness to lie in the rhythmic variation of narrower and broader visions; second, in the contrast-sparked interest in, and longing for, salvation which is the beginning of religion (*SRI,* 46); and third, in certain insights both into one's need for salvation and into that hope-filled shift in perspective towards a superhuman Helper—a recognized shift that is insight into the *way* of salvation. Then, on the objective side, he found the "great common features" of religious consciousness consist in an ever-present triad of objects: one's ideal, need of salvation, and union with one's Deliverer. Both subjective and objective poles presuppose the paradoxical individual human self in intimate religious intercourse with superhuman Deliverance, in some form. In brief, then, the goal Royce sought, the essential structure of individual religious consciousness, displayed a triadic form in general: the self, its motive, and object.

During his inquiry into the essential structure of individual religious consciousness, Royce sometimes asked about its openness to other than individual influences and sources. Such queries drew him on to explore the ascending series of the six remaining sources which build upon and enhance this most fundamental experience of the individual's religious intercourse with the divine. Before doing so, however, he had to test his findings. Did this essential structure put the individual self in genuine touch with reality? Was it true?

Raising the Critical Question

Royce acknowledged that religious experience when had by an isolated individual alone with the divine is the crudest, most fallible, and most illusory source of religious insight (*SRI,* 27). But concerning the first two religious objects (the ideal and the need), such experience can produce genuine insight. This occurs when one truly knows through his own intense intimate personal life that his ideal is an ideal and that he is too frail to attain it. He finds his ideal and need coming into consciousness together in an insight marked by breadth of range, coherence and unity of view, and closeness of personal touch (*SRI,* 6, 31). As certain of them as of his own ignorance, he knows the relations of these two objects to each other and to himself.

MOST BASIC STRUCTURE   117

However, beyond an individual's true insightful knowledge, his private feelings, changing trends in life-style, and varied perceptions produce in him favorite opinions and one-sided approximations. If the ocean of his fluxing human feelings were the only source of these over-beliefs, they would be about as valuable as sea foam (*SRI,* 30). For although intense and intimate personal feeling is indispensable for grasping the valuable truths about life, nevertheless, *something more* than feeling is also needed. But bare knowledge of this ideal and need is also unsatisfying since such knowledge neither "transcends the boundaries of any merely individual experience" nor lets him "find the presence that can give this unity and self-possession to the soul" (*SRI,* 32). This brought Royce to test one's felt union with the Deliverer.

Is individual experience adequate for such felt union? Is it also critical enough to distinguish genuine communions with this Other from illusions of such communions? More exigent on this point, Royce held that *only* by transcending the boundaries of any merely individual experience can there occur "some sort of intercourse with Another," who is actually no other than the "Master of Life . . . the revealer of final truth" (*SRI,* 32).

In his fuller reply, Royce acknowledged that some people perhaps have direct mystical experiences and recognize them as such, but this helps only the mystics, not the vast majority of people. Moreover, not even the mystics can remain content with their experiences alone with the divine. Insofar as any mystic remains a humanly isolated individual in these experiences, he has not yet won the whole of any genuinely true insight. A true insight would teach him three things: that we are all members one of another; that no one can have a genuine insight into the way of salvation for himself *unless* in it he also learns the way of his brethren's salvation; and that there is no unity of spirit *unless* everyone is privileged to enter it once they recognize and appreciate this unity (*SRI,* 34).[9] Hence, individual religious experience calls for corroboration at least through ordinary social religious experience. In fact, it is only through such social experience that one first begins to see the meaning of the religious experience one had as an isolated individual (*SRI,* 34). In this way, then, Royce began to expand his natural foundation for religious insight.

In synthesis, an individual finds some union with his Deliverer through the rhythmic contrast of his narrower and broader views. But this union, insofar as it is had by an isolated individual, is inadequate and needs to be supplemented by social experience. These two sources of religious insight are, in turn, further strengthened if the socially related individual becomes rational and then willfully commits himself to genuine values. Even then, these four sources need to be synthesized into a practical life of loyalty before one knows one's Deliverer as one is known.

Is there any sense, then, in saying that individual religious experience gives true insight? According to Royce, the union with a saving Other attained by individual religious experiences may be valid. If valid, these mysterious unions are weakly authenticated by solely individual experience and are hardly adequate to dispel any illusion present. Hence, if one is to solve the religious paradox and exhibit religious experience as genuine, he needs to integrate other sources into this indispensable base. Of these sources, the social is the next and most fundamental.

SIFTING FOR AN AUTHENTIC SOCIAL APPROACH TO ELEMENTARY RELIGIOUS EXPERIENCE

By our ordinary social experience Royce meant our usual relationships with other individual human selves. Through them we meet a greater social self that both teaches and disciplines us since in these relations we find companionship and conflict, bickering and support. This experience also includes our natural non-universalistic loyalties to family, clan, and nation but does not include that rare dedication of genuine loyalty to the universal community—a topic Royce reserved for his fifth source of religious insight.

This second source brought him to the borders of the unending squabble between individualists and collectivists (*SRI,* 60–61). It also called him to tell his audience that William James, despite his pluralistic universe, had rigidly excluded ordinary social experience from his *Varieties* (*SRI,* 62). James and Royce both recognized how ambiguous ordinary social experience is for religious insight. But whereas James read this ambiguity as always inserting conventionality into group meetings (e.g., in common prayers or in church services) and thus precluding the genuinely religious experience, Royce recognized that ordinary social experience can go either way. It can channel or obstruct authentic communion with the saving Something.

He also noticed that as he began his scrutiny of ordinary social experience he was approaching some contemporary fads among certain Christian preachers. They felt that "It is love that saves" or that Christianity had to be taught as "a religion of social consciousness" (*SRI,* 56). He knew personally both those advocating such versions of Christianity and their opponents. Would his examination of natural social experience contribute to the school of "salvation only through love" or to the cause of Christianity's "social engineers"? Royce had his reservations.

After surveying the pros and cons of a purely social theory of our awareness of religious objects and values, he began analyzing this second most elementary source of religious experience much as he had done the first. Just as he had previously insisted that the isolated individual must discover two meaningful facts within his experience, so he now pointed out two considerations prerequisite to a balanced interpretation of social consciousness as a source of religious insight (*SRI,* 65). On examination, both considerations seem to form another pair of ideas for comparison-contrast much as the two meaningful facts functioned as a pair required for genuine individual religious experience. Although both considerations are familiar, they are "easily misinterpreted" (*SRI,* 65). All agree "no salvation without love" but many confuse a love of mere individuals with a love that contains a superhuman dimension.

Royce's first prerequisite consideration is that even though solitude may occasion some insight, a person cannot be saved alone, since he is "bound to his brethren by spiritual links that cannot be broken" (*SRI,* 65). For a genuine religious experience that saves, therefore, love of other individual human selves is always required, yet never enough by itself.

Royce's second prerequisite consideration revealed this inadequacy:

> So long as man views his fellow-man *merely* as fellow-man, he only complicates his problem, for both he and his fellow equally need salvation. Their plight is common; their very need of salvation chains them together in the prison of human sorrow. (*SRI,* 65)

Here Royce highlighted the need for "the more than *merely* human" in our ordinary social experiences if they are to be religious without illusion. This "more" is the superhuman dimension, a mystical element within human love that makes it genuinely liberating, that brings down some angel from above to loosen the chains of any pair of merely human lovers, who are mutually powerless to fulfill the other's need for salvation (*SRI,* 65).[10]

Thus, as a religious guide, our social experience can be weak or strong, can have a pathetic limitation or irresistible authority (*SRI,* 66). To support this pair of complementary considerations, Royce thought it best to use three types of cases illustrated by various instances drawn mainly from literature. His examples exhibited a sense of guilt that grew into a feeling of overwhelming loneliness, a sense of companionship born of friendship-love, and a patriotic spirit of devotion to country (*SRI,* 66–73). In all these cases, only if something beyond mere commonplace social relations, only if something apparently mystical and superhuman was also operating therein, did these social relationships function as religiously saving experiences (*SRI,* 74).

If human beings are ever to enter into salvific relations, a new kind of love must enter which will sufficiently reveal a superhuman process at work in at least one of the lovers. Such love must lead one individual to view his human other as somehow more than merely human. Furthermore, his human other must actually function as the sign of a superhuman process of salvation. Otherwise, no saving divine Other will be met (*SRI,* 74–75). In other words, unless one's friend or beloved has been transformed through grace-mediating love and also has been recognized as so transformed, no genuine religious insight will take place in this social experience (*SRI,* 71, 74–75).[11]

To further clarify his second prerequisite consideration, Royce turned to human affectivity. When a genuine friendship functions naturally as a religious motive, it reveals a mysterious religious object, a saving path to the divine. In social experience transformed by love, a new kind of affective knowledge is mediated and a new strength communicated. One discovers the "miracle that the nearest movings of affection are also a revelation of the highest powers of the spiritual world" (*SRI,* 73). Clearly, one needs to test which highest powers are at work in these affective changes or, as Royce put it, one must "try [or test] the spirits that pretend or appear to be religious" (*SRI,* 286).

If one's social experience is to become a source of religious insight, he must correctly interpret the pair of considerations. Since many types of ordinary social experience lack genuine love, Royce disqualified them as irrelevant for religious insight. However, he also insisted that if an ordinary smile or friendly gesture is animated by genuine love and is read as a revelation of a divine process, then such ordinary social experiences function as authentic sources of religious insight (*SRI,* 74–75).

Despite its limitations, then, our usual social life contains a unique revelatory power. Affects have the natural capacity to signal divine purposes. On the other hand, Royce gave warning to those preaching a mere social gospel as the essence of Christianity:

> the religion of love is no religion at all, unless it conceives its human object not only as this creature, or as this collection of needy men and women, but as a hint, or revelation, or incarnation of a divine process. (*SRI,* 74)

He went on to caution that the only persons who can read such a hint are either the mystics or those "rationally enlightened enough to know that human life is indeed a revelation of something that is also superhuman" (*SRI,* 74–75). This inserted certain qualifications and discipline within Royce's religion of love. It also drove him to search within rational enlightenment for a third source of religious insight. We would, however, go beyond our stated aim if we accompanied him farther as he proceeded to analyze and synthesize the remaining five sources of religious insight.

In the present chapter, then, we have peered into elementary religious experience. With Royce, we found its individual essential structure, its natural origin, and its necessarily social dimension. Thus prepared, we can enter his study of complex religious experience as analyzed in the *Problem*. Elementary religious experience is the basis for complex religious experience. In turn, complex religious experience is the secondary foundation upon which Royce built his mature philosophy of the Christian religion in the *Problem*.

8. The Social Form of Complex Religious Experience

Royce, the son of a California 49'er, was an intellectual prospector digging for the ore needed for his anticipated philosophy of the Christian religion. In the *Sources* he had mined elementary religious experience. He had fairly exhausted its dimensions that link subject to subject and self to community. He viewed such experience as still "elementary," even though all seven sources enriched it and the communal unity of the Spirit enlivened it. In addition, Royce recognized that sometimes a group of people also share an awareness of this Spirit's presence and action in their community *as a community,* rather than as in individuals simply. They sense that their community itself is the "Beloved" both of the Spirit and of themselves in a unanimity of genuine loyalty. Then their religious experience is of a different kind than that which they have simply as individual members who are not yet bound together either by the Spirit's doctrine or life or by their mutually making it their own personal belief. When such doctrine and gift of the Spirit raise religious experience to this new level, Royce calls it "complex." Then the members have a religious awareness, not only as individual minded beings, but also as participants in the minded being and doctrine of their community and its Spirit.

Penetrating still deeper, Royce detected that the mother lode of this complex religious experience lies in the set of beliefs which these members share. Accordingly, as a mental prospector, he staked off this communal sharing in one doctrine of life, called it "more complex religious experience," and shifted his methodic tools to bore into it. From such experience he aimed to bring to light a nugget of great worth: the "object form of community," that is, "this social form of experience . . . upon which loyalty depends" (1:xv). This aim led Royce into those varieties of religious experience which William James had carefully avoided (1:xv–xvi). Unlike James, however, Royce was equipped with powerful logical tools (his concepts of ε relation, set or class, series, operation, and conjugate pair like "Individual *and* Community") to aid his digging into communal religious experiences.[1]

What were the ingredients distinctive of this more complex religious experience? To identify these, Royce chose to examine the shared religious experiences actually found in three groups of people: 1) today's Christians caught in challenging changes; 2) early Christians of the Pauline communities struggling to live their faith; 3) all universally loyal persons who live in a genuine community of interpretation (2:335-336). Royce believed there was one meaning central to the communal religious experience of these three groups. Clearly to identify this meaning was the aim of his refined interpretation of it in *The Problem of Christianity.*

THE MORE COMPLEX RELIGIOUS EXPERIENCE OF TODAY'S CHRISTIANS

In Royce's view, Christianity, like all other religions, is inescapably human. Christianity survives and grows only insofar as it keeps in touch with people's ever changing needs and their constantly emerging hopes. To stay alive, then, Christianity must attract people's interest and keep winning their support. For any religious community this is a law of life. Royce pointed out that an archaeological team can verify this law quite vividly, simply by scanning the forgotten temples of a past civilization. Each abandoned shrine suggests a twofold message. As a temple, it reveals how a particular tribe once placed vibrant confidence in a divine source and pledge. Abandoned, it tells how confidence withered because, custombound, the insensitive religion failed to adapt to the tribe's changed needs when other interests began to lure those tribesmen away. Christianity must meet this same challenge or die (1:385-390).[2]

Royce further pointed out that existing religions must adapt not merely to the changing expressions of man's basic psychological needs and interests but also to his basic ethico-religious needs and their consequent values. In Royce's judgment, anyone "can experience . . . that human life has some highest end; and that man, as he naturally is, is in great danger of failing to attain this supreme goal."[3] However, he can attain this goal only if he loyally serves a genuine community. Yet such service is blocked by his natural self-preference which cannot be overcome unless his two deep ethico-religious needs are brought to his full attention, accepted by him, and then lived out. It follows that he must encounter an ever-constant good news (1:396) and, guided by its truth, must undergo a radical transformation of his way of life from that of one individualistically preferring himself to that of one loyally serving a genuine community. Only by going through this transformative process can he grasp the ultimate significance of his life. To grasp this, however, is to be set upon the way of salvation. Taken cumulatively, then, everyone's inescapable, basic, ethico-religious need is to enter into that new level of human conscious life which is called higher loyalty.

Like all human beings, today's Christians live amid a variety of communities (family, neighborhood, nation, humankind) and can experience any of these as representative of that Beloved Community which can save them. If Christianity fails to arouse and effectively to fulfill this basic ethico-religious need, its members must walk away and search elsewhere for the good news and the transformation which alone can make their lives meaningful.

To meet these psychological and ethico-religious demands and thus to stay alive and grow, Christianity must today do at least two things. First, it must make fresh contact with each person's basic need to be saved and unremittingly cultivate this need. To do so, Christianity must recognize in this need the human taproot that is indispensable for its own life and renewal. However, within contemporary culture Christians can reach this recognition *only if they so radically adjust their ways of perceiving and valuing the present world and humankind's situation in it* that they actually succeed in adapting to the changed and changing mentality of contemporary society.

Second, because the interests of twentieth-century people are strongly engaged in finding effective ways to liberate and develop all persons, the loyalty at work within Christianity must be embodied in deeds that free and promote the whole human race. Christianity will either pour its energies of loyalty into structuring a more human society or else be abandoned.

Yet in 1913 Royce asked himself: Was Christianity actually growing more and more anemic? It seemed to move languidly amid an ever more de-Christianized culture. Its efforts to heal the alienations and disloyalties causing society's lesions were feeble. No wonder modern man questioned whether Christianity was any longer alive. Or, if he granted that it somehow was still alive, he asked himself just where he might most accurately locate that life. This puzzlement deepened when modern man found Christians fighting among themselves about their mission and practical needs or quarreling over different ways of formulating Christ's message. Thus, Royce was impelled to study more closely how practical and theoretical rifts caused these doubts and hesitancies in contemporary Christians.

In his estimate, the experience of modern man ordinarily has at best a muted religious tone to it. The crescendo of technological, scientific, economic, cultural, and sociological changes that are transforming people's ways of experiencing, valuing, and acting almost totally preoccupies and dominates the consciousness of modern man. Although he knows that the actual vitality of Christian religious institutions is not to be underestimated, modern man also knows that the life-centers of today are science and business, education, government, and communications. Indeed, these life-centers occupy the attention and receive the support which people once invested in religion. Consequently, as Royce wrote:

> In the modern world, religion no longer has the effective institutional support of the whole collective social will, but lives more apart from the other great social interests, and dwells more in a realm where internal faith rather than publicly administered law determines the range of its control. (1:391-392)

Hence, "the process of estrangement between the Church and modern life is constantly accelerated" (1:395).[4]

Under these influences, modern man comes to experience Christianity as a puzzling problem, rather than as an embattled faith to be defended. Or he may view it as a cultural relic to be treated with studied indifference, if not to be discarded from civilization (1:7-9). His experience swings back and forth between the positive and negative contributions of Christianity. This generates in him those questions, doubts, and philosophical issues which already have marked the history of Christianity with tragic divisions and sinful conflicts. Indeed, modern man's numerous superficial formulations of the problem of Christianity further confuse the situation. Moreover, when modern man faces this problem under the pressures of his deepest psychological, ethical, and religious needs, his anxious quandary deepens because then, for the first time, he encounters "the religious problem of the future" (1:393). Will the hearts of coming generations, formed in the swirl of ever accelerating change and "stirred by countless new cares and hopes" turn for life to Christianity? Or will they regard it as another dead fossil of the past?

When modern man shifts his puzzled gaze from the external structures of Christianity to his own personal interior life, two new questions loom up: Does Christianity meet people's deep interest in being saved? Does Christianity offer that kind of union with the divine which today's humanistic life-style requires? Royce's modern man is convinced that Christianity is as good as dead if in practice it emphasizes "the Kingdom of God within" so exclusively that it identifies itself almost entirely with individualistic mysticism (1:402). Man's social nature requires that the basic meaning (the saving) of his life come in and through a community. So, if Christianity becomes a religion of mere interiority, it will neglect the many ills racking society. If Christianity fails to promote a more humane way of life through social reform and enhanced institutions, then it divorces itself from the present needs of people and cannot in this way adjust to their new cares and hopes. Little wonder, then, if people lose interest in such a Christianity and gradually stop supporting it.

Royce pictured modern man not only as torn by these practical tensions but also as caught in the crossfire between divergent theoretical interpretations of the Christian religion. Among its warring sects and denominations, modern man finds opinion divided over the central meaning of Christianity itself and over the most basic intent of its founder. The Liberals say that it is enough simply to imitate the founder morally. The Orthodox say that one must also accept certain dogmas (1:xxiv–xxvi).

While the mind of modern man is torn on the dilemma of whether Christianity is solely "the Kingdom of God within" or is also a commitment to restructure the social order, both Liberals and Orthodox try to heal this rupture by appealing to their own view of the founder. But if such people formulate the problem in terms of Christianity's individual human founder, then, in Royce's judgment, they miss the point at issue. He held that the basic issue was *whether or not reality has two levels of minded beings:* individuals and communities. The source of the solution lies, he felt, not at the individual level where the founder is as human, but at the second and deeper level of Christian community (1:xxi, 30, 33).

As Royce saw it, all these practical and theoretical conflicts were putting his Christian contemporaries through a stiff test of their religion. They were confronted by the following questions which called for affirmative answers if modern Christians were to remain consistent. Could today's Christian, then, still discern the living center of his faith beneath the thick shell of Christianity's many obsolescent traditions and creedal formulas? Could he even penetrate to the perduring human need for salvation? Could today's Christian, in an era of ever accelerating change, discern precisely those ideas that are most vital to his faith? Royce felt that most Christians could not answer each of these questions with the "Yes" needed for consistent living.

Responding to this problem of Christianity, Royce alerted his audience that his approach was "from the side, not of metaphysics and of traditional dogmas, but of religious life and of human experience" (2:5). Fresh from his research in the *Sources,* he certainly responded in his present investigation to the feelings, sentiments, and intuitions which all people experience in their religious lives. But while acknowledging and welcoming the influence of such affective reactions, Royce paid special attention to the role played during such experiences by the set of beliefs which people hold in common. He found that generally, in the midst of a communal religious experience, people make implicit judgments about its worth.

For them, it is of high value that these religious experiences are *had in a group,* develop unity among the participants, cohere with previous experiences, and point to future ones. Furthermore, these participants treasure the truth of their shared basic beliefs for only their truth, *as* held in common, allows such distinctive unity to develop. Contrary to William

James's working hypothesis in his *Varieties,* they prefer these communal qualities to that uniqueness in religious experiences which solitary individuals can enjoy. Instead, they respond to the commonly held, vital values of their communal religious experience with a calm, far-seeing judgment of conscience—something Royce treasured highly (2:3-4). Next they stretch their judgments of conscience to the ultimate horizon to discern whether these personally shared values further realize the universal community. Royce treasured this even more because such interpretations unite them to their ultimate goal—union with the Spirit-Interpreter—as well as to each other.

From this general philosophy of religion, Royce turned to its department of Christianity and specifically to the life-giving role played by the Christian creed. He recognized that, *as shared,* the basic beliefs of Christians held the key to the social structure of their communal religious experience. Hence, anyone who searched through these shared beliefs for their inmost meanings could discover Christianity's "leading and essential ideas" (1:xxxv).[5] And these ideas would account—at least from the human side— for the perennial life in the Christian religion.

This heuristic reasoning led Royce to search for criteria whereby he could identify the live and leading "ideas" of the Christian creed. After carefully discerning things of the spirit, he eventually judged that such living ideas would have to: (1) develop a further and richer interpretation of the master's teaching about the Kingdom of God, (2) unify people in the Spirit, and (3) satisfy the human need for salvation (1:36-39). Within his aim of investigating "the social form of [religious] experience," Royce's discovery of these criteria served to direct his entire development of the *Problem.* These standards enabled him to identify the three "Christian ideas"—Community, Lost State of the Individual, and Atonement, "together with the somewhat more general Idea of 'Saving Grace'" (1:xxxvi) —that as a collected whole form the Christian doctrine of life. In this way these criteria guided his exploration of *how* the Christian doctrine of life was related to the real world—the profound problem he had selected for research in 1912.

THE MORE COMPLEX RELIGIOUS EXPERIENCE OF EARLY PAULINE COMMUNITIES

Royce knew that the idea of a universal community had been at work in the world long before Christianity began. Philosophically, the Stoics had fashioned the abstract rational concept of all humankind as in ideal a single community (1:74, 99). Militarily, various tribesmen had often committed themselves to loyalty to their own group, occasionally to strangers, and more rarely even to such foes as proved themselves heroically loyal. Religiously, the tribes of Israel, led by Deborah and other prophets, had been gathered into a unified people whose divine mission was to announce to all nations the message of a saving God.

According to Royce, however, only in the Christian communities of the apostolic age[6] did the idea of a universal community first become highly developed, definitely concrete, and effectively practical (1:36-40, 99-104). These Christians believed and felt that the Spirit was daily working in their midst, uniting them into one body, rendering Christ present to their assemblies, and guiding them in their loving deeds of cooperation (1:104-105). By their experiences, works, and deepening reflections, these communities were further interpreting their master's teaching about the Kingdom of God. By fulfilling the above-mentioned criteria, particularly the first one, these communities directed Royce's attention to the essential ideas of the Christian creed.

But *how* the Christian community or Church originated was a topic on which Royce offered no opinion, except one concerning an evident psycho-social prerequisite. The extant historical evidences were, in his judgment, simply too meager to form any grounded interpretation (1:xxvii). Clearly, the human motives which led the earliest Christians to unite in communities had to be social, as well as individual, motives. And regarding these communities *as* communities, he emphasized that the "psychology of the origins of Christian experience is thus social, and is not an individual psychology" (1:419).[7] These origins had to involve a real, even if dim, consciousness of the second level of reality, that of "man the community." Yet neither historical materials nor social psychology allowed anyone to fathom precisely just which psycho-social motives had led the earliest Christians to constitute themselves as a community (1:419). Accordingly, Royce abstained from asking just how the Church originated and instead inquired into its doctrine of life.

Should he turn his investigation to late first-century Christian communities and their documents—for instance, to the Johannine Community and its Fourth Gospel? Royce knew that this Gospel had been "nearest to the heart of the Christian world during many centuries," despite its relatively late origin and its being least literally historical about Jesus' earthly words and deeds (1:206). Impressive because of its wholeness, the Fourth Gospel "faces the central practical problem of Christianity—the problem of grace, the transformation of the very essence of the individual man" (1:207). Christian tradition interpreted this latest of the four gospels as having uniquely won through to a close personal touch with the living center of Christianity. It had, in Royce's words, "perfectly united . . . the Pauline conception of the Church as the body of Christ, and of Christ as the spirit of the Church . . . with the idea of the divine Word made flesh" (1:206).

Nevertheless, even with due recognition of the Fourth Gospel and occasional use of it, Royce preferred to base his investigation upon the earliest extant signs of Christianity. This meant usually employing only the letters of the apostle Paul. Royce judged that "we possess, in the Pauline epistles, information which is priceless, which reveals to us the religion of loyalty in its classic and universal form" (1:xxix). Even among the Pauline epistles, however, he preferred to restrict himself almost entirely to the proto-Pauline letters (those to the Thessalonians, Corinthians, and Romans).[8] This subgroup of documents, written approximately between 52 and 57 A.D., is the earliest extant set of signs emitted from Christian communities. Through these privileged signs, then, Royce chose to focus on the earliest Pauline churches in their day-to-day communal life in search of the "actual life" and "essence" of Christianity (1:xxix).

Accordingly, Royce preferred generally *not* to rely on signs originating from communities of late second- or third-generation Christians (for example, from the deutero-Pauline letters or the synoptic gospels). And with the exception of the Fourth Gospel, he would rely even less on the Christian Scriptures of the late first century—such as the Apocalypse, the Acts of the Apostles, and the pastoral letters.

Employing rather the "priceless information" from the early Paul, Royce aimed "simply to expound the essence of the Christian doctrine of life, and the relation of the Christian ideas to the real world" (1:xxix). He believed that if his "simple considerations" were sufficiently recognized, then ethical, religious, and christological ideas would be transformed.

Perhaps it suffices here simply to summarize Royce's interpretation of the Pauline communities' more complex and problematic religious experience.[9] He found that the earliest records revealed the deepest experiences of Paul's first Christians. Without ever physically seeing or hearing their master, they relied upon reports of his parables, deeds, and mission. Responding in loving gratitude to him, they committed themselves to become his followers. But they felt that their new way of life needed a basic thrust which was steady and shared. Since such a thrust would be lacking unless they made sense of their master's person and mission in general, they experienced the need to form a communal interpretation of him that was fitting and coherent. Furthermore, they believed that, as they discussed their master's meaning for themselves, his Spirit was the Interpreter who was revealing new things to them and guiding them in due time into all truth (1:34–35).[10] Within their Christian life together these Pauline communities had early experienced an unavoidable contrast between the master's person, deeds, and mission on the one hand, and, on the other, the interpretations which Christian communities had from the start formed about his person, work, and mission (1:22-26). So, because the master's deeds and teachings about the Kingdom of heaven had not fully revealed his whole view of life and salvation, these Christians gradually discovered and developed their own interpretations.

While musing over Paul's letters,[11] Royce found that the early Christians had rhythmically undergone a cycle of experiences during the several decades following their master's death. When Pauline Christians assembled, they sometimes experienced the Lord's Spirit perceptibly. More often they experienced how wayward, contentious, and unloving they themselves were. Periodically they felt the need to be reconverted and reconciled. As they encountered other Christians who served the community generously, who forgave and healed the self-centered members, they found themselves restored to friendship with their brethren and God. In experiencing the newly deepened unity of their shared life, they recognized that this Christian community and its Spirit were continually converting them. As morally weak members of the Church, they felt themselves lifted from their previously frayed, self-centered, and miserable existence into a genuine life healed by the founder's Spirit and centered now upon Him.[12] He called and empowered them not only to gracious sentiments toward individual members but also to orderly discipline in upbuilding the divine community (1:101).

Feeling this sharp contrast between their past and present lives — a contrast that each of their conversions again and again brought to light — they eventually recognized that they were being directed along a pathway toward the divine, that they were "being taught by the Lord." In this way, the members of the Pauline churches found that they actually lived as members of one real body. They now shared in the social life of a whole which had its own life distinct from that of any mere individual (1:102). Their Christian love had a specifically new object, the sacred community (*koinonia*).

Paul referred to the mystery of this corporate unity in the body of his letters, but in his conclusions he took care to treat its individual members with warm and tender concern. For example, his church at Rome was indeed "the body of Christ," a corporate unity with its super-individual life, needs, and mission, yet it was also Phoebe, Prisca, Aquila, Rufus, Mary, Nereus, and dear Persis.[13] Such was Paul's two-leveled experience of mystery in everyday life. In Paul's portrait of this life, each member's tender love for every individual brother and sister had to be united with his distinct disciplined love for the whole community. Both loves had to be integrated in each member's daily life in his Christian community. Only if these two kinds of practical love worked together, could the two levels of reality in the Christian community—its individuals and its distinctive super-individual communal life—actually interpret and enhance each other (1:101).

In sum, then, Paul's early Christians had communal religious experience that was both complex and problematic. It was complex because their shared belief oriented them to certain experience through which they perceived the factual presence of the master's Spirit. For they felt Him working powerfully among themselves, guiding them interiorly to deeds of loving loyalty toward God, neighbors, and their community. It was *more* complex because, by thus living as "the body of the Lord," they gained a sense of living mysteriously in "the divine unity of its spirit in all the diversity of its members and of their powers" (1:101). For they all shared in the belief that the master's Spirit was operatively present and guiding them through the doctrine of life he communicated to them.

Nevertheless, their experience was also problematic since their shared life also made them aware how religiously wayward and capricious they themselves were. Unhealed of individualistic tendencies, they showed self-preference, inconstancy of will, and resistance towards doing what was needed to maintain and increase their community's shared life and mission. And their experience became *more* problematic because, unlike their situation prior to becoming Christians, they could now become even traitors against this new realm of grace by yielding fully to their individualistic tendencies. This was the problematic and complex way in which Paul's early Christians experienced their own problem of Christianity.

As a philosopher of religion, Royce scrutinized the communal experience of these Pauline Christians. He sought to identify not only the shared interpretations that they made of their master's person and mission but also the human motives, ideals, and efforts that led them into this shared life. These items constituted what he called the "human side" of religion—the side which he would next try to verify in any universally loyal self who took part in any true community of interpretation. In this way Royce gained "close personal touch" with the deepest and widest principles of ecumenism.

THE MORE COMPLEX RELIGIOUS EXPERIENCE OF ANY UNIVERSALLY LOYAL SELF IN ANY COMMUNITY OF INTERPRETATION

For his third sample of more complex religious experience, Royce looked beyond Christian communities, whether contemporary or pristine. Wherever he found genuine community, he explored its members' shared life and consciousness of unity (1:61–74). He did *not* find such life and consciousness in merely natural communities whose loyalties were restricted simply to family or race or nation. Rather, he found genuine community life arising only when members, who had previously been alienated or at least limited in their scope, were transformed deeply enough to somehow take conscious part in the life of the whole human community and to let universal loyalty direct their moral choices.

Elsewhere I have suggested how Royce described the conditions and levels which mark the development of the consciousness of genuine communities.[14] It suffices here to highlight the religious dimension in that evolution. For this I draw upon Royce's careful delineation of that process, as found chiefly in Lecture 10 of the *Problem*, entitled "The Body and the Members" (2:57–105).

In Lecture 9 Royce had left behind the rubberband senses of the term "community." His usage would not stretch to embrace herds or flocks nor even include human groups as simply living in the same location under the same government. He added, moreover, "Not every social group which behaves so that, to an observer, it seems to be a single unit, meets all the conditions of our definition" (2:57). Rather, by building shared conscious references into his more precise and stipulated sense of "community," Royce required that each of the distinct members of the group consciously identify himself with the same definite past or future event or deed. This specially restricted sense of "community" had a definite objective structure along with great intersubjective significance (2:50).

What kind of religious experience, then, can members of a "community of memory and/or of hope," reasonably expect to find? Such members undergo a profound change when they are moved and move themselves from being only naturally loyal or even radically alienated to being authentically ethical and religious through their dedication to universal loyalty. To enjoy the authentically ethical and religious life of a genuinely loyal community, people must fulfill three conditions *and* also rise from a first to a third level in their consciousness of community (2:60–69, 79, 83–105). The doctrine of levels in his System Σ was expressing itself in yet another way in his philosophy of religion.

Royce's *first* condition addresses the problem of how to transform a present momentary self into one worthy to become a member of a significant community. If viewed as merely the flicker of the present moment, a human self so lacks history and hope that it is generally meaningless. As such, it cannot participate in the time process required for a deed-doing community. In Royce's sense, a community both lives as a conscious temporal process and intends to achieve practical deeds in time through its members (2:64). Hence, if such communal actions are to occur, each potential member must extend the consciousness of his life—yes, to the real past and future events of his own life as a unique individual—but especially, to those events and actions, persons and objects which generally lie beyond his individual life. He does this by identifying those items as "part of my own ideally extended life." For example, a person consciously creates his self-identification as an American by taking in, *as* part of his ideal self, the past events of the Declaration of Independence and of Gettysburg as well as the future days when all citizens will have unimpeded access to equal opportunity and when big money will not skew due process. If a person somehow identifies his or her ideal self with the whole universe, as mystics and stoics do, then a religious tone is already resonating in his or her consciousness (2:62–63).

For Royce, a genuine community is not primarily an object of contemplation but essentially a doer of deeds, a seeker and achiever of ends. So he added a formal restriction to further clarify his meaning of community: the only way the idealized events and objects of an individual self can belong to a community is if they are "bound up with the deeds of the community" (2:65). Each time-bound human self, then, ideally conceives his or her extended personality as in symbiotic union with a deed-doing community and thus as winning richer meaning through the story of its idealized communal past, present, and future. By making one's own these idealized events and objects that are inseparable from a temporally processing pragmatic community, each member discovers the way to secure his or her own identity as a meaningful self. The destiny of such an ideally extended self may indeed be worthy of the interest of beings lying beyond the level of human individuals (2:67). By their ideal extensions, then, human selves "form a community . . . in so far as these personalities possess a life that is for each of them his own, while it is in some of its events, common to them all" (2:65).

This consciously possessed life is both individual and communal in another way, as specified by Royce's *second* condition: a number of *distinct selves* can and usually do engage in social *communication.* The community's life consists in this exchange of signs by its irreducibly distinct members. Each member is so individually unique that no passing emotion or felt mystical union can constitute the unity of the community. Its unique members cannot be absorbed into some undifferentiated super-self. Instead of allowing oneself to melt mindlessly into a fused feeling of oneness, each member serves the common life *better* if he intelligently contributes (or communicates) to that life his own constructive gift in its uniqueness (2:68).

Meanwhile, other potential members are also making their own ideal extensions and consciously appropriating some of the *same* idealized past and future events, actions, persons, and objects. They, too, identify these same items as "part of their ideally extended lives." So Royce concluded, "The *third* of the conditions for the existence of the community . . . consists in the fact that the ideally extended past and future selves of the members include at least some events which are, for all these selves, identical" (2:68). That all these members' past and future ideal extensions coincide in some *same* past and future items creates the basis for these selves' sharing in at least almost the same interpretation of these items with each other. For example, each of the Pauline Christians extended his consciousness back to their master's dying and rising as part of his own life and then stretched it forward to his own future bodily resurrection in the Lord. Since all these Christians included at least these two events in their ideal extensions, they could, according to the earlier second condition, communicate their nearly identical interpretations of them to one another. As a result, Pauline Christians enjoyed the sense of sharing life together. Each member possessed the same idea or doctrine; each read its practical interpretation in the same way; and each member mutually recognized that the other members were making the same kind of ideal extensions to the same events and interpreting them similarly, thus forming one body of many members (2:69).

For Royce, a community is at least as much a person on the second level of reality and of consciousness as an individual human self is a person on the first level.[15] A human community has its own mind, will, and historico-cultural products. All these arise from its common life which in turn arises from the spirit in that community (2:35, 49-50). Accordingly, like the types of consciousness that can arise from the living central identity of an individual human self, so, too, the consciousness that arises from the life of a community can develop properly or be arrested or even become perverted.

In its proper growth, the community's own consciousness of itself develops fittingly into its ethical and religious stages (2:79). Its first stage or degree is reached when a "community of memory and/or hope" is created. When this is enriched by shared understanding, identification, and mutual acceptance, it has evolved to its second degree. A transformation into the climactic third degree occurs when genuine loyalty animates this consciousness of community. Such a peak is as precious as it is difficult to achieve (2:100). Interpreted in secular terms, this highest stage of the community's consciousness of itself enables each of its members to love the universal community as a community, in addition to loving all minded beings in it. Interpreted in Christian terms, this stage is marked by that divinely graced *caritas* which is wholeheartedly practical in serving all the Church's actual and potential members. A prerequisite for this *caritas* or genuine Loyalty is to have fallen in love with the universe (2:102).

Once having taken part in this highest degree of community consciousness, the genuinely loyal member deeply appreciates this supreme shared life as his "Beloved Community"—that is, as the one he selects and adopts as his own. He recognizes that this community and its Spirit have first loved and rescued him as their "beloved." However, his consciousness of community can be arrested even before it evolves to Royce's first degree. Selves organized for a joint task can settle superficially into a shared awareness of cooperating in a merely mechanical way. Workers on an assembly line often produce items this way. So, too, do people who are aware of cooperating to the extent of simply queuing up for a bus or ticket. Their social consciousness has not yet reached a "community of memory and/or of hope."

Ironically, however, a band of robbers often achieves this first degree of consciousness of community. They share memories of various "jobs" they performed together and hopes of others to come. They often develop a disciplined *esprit de corps*. Yet a "community of hate," as Royce calls it, marks their type of community consciousness. It is inauthentic and perverted because it is parasitical. The self-identity of a robber as a member of his band requires the mutual acceptance of his own and his fellows' intents to pillage the very people who want to obey the law of the land and thus promote the common good of all.

The crude illustration of the consciousness of a robber band can serve as a rough indicator of those far more sophisticated forms of arrested or perverted communal consciousness which can occur on any of Royce's three degrees. For example, if one engages in either the Communist Party or a capitalist "free enterprise" corporation that lacks effective concern for the integral development of all its workers (especially those in the Third World), his starting point is not fairness but self-preference. He starts from that aggressive will-to-live the natural life and to win in its great game which is the first of two willful attitudes that destroy genuine community (2:298–300). The opposite attitude that seeds an arrested or even perverted consciousness of community is the will-to-withdraw from life. Fed by such negative moods as pessimism, discontent, escapism, and misguided sympathy with the escapists, this second destructive attitude lacks a courageously loyal embrace of the universe as it is (2:101, 305–308). The only attitude, or "spirit," that leads truly to the authentic development of consciousness of genuine community is the wholehearted loving loyalty of a community which is ethically structured and religiously oriented.

This open-ended non-exclusive loyalty eventually grows to embrace the whole community of humankind. The catalyst that propels the leap to this third stage of genuine communal consciousness originates in a mysterious gifting "from above," from the antecedently loving universal community and its Spirit. Only this third degree of consciousness is fully religious and genuinely salvific. Yet the first and second degrees, when taken as simply less mature forms rather than as arrested or perverted ones, foreshadow true religion in their inner desires for overall meaning and for release from moral bondage.

At all three degrees of consciousness of community, the members' monotonous toil, divergent interests, conflicts, failures, and frictions becloud their conscious sharing of common memories and hopes. This threatens the maintenance of the sense of community needed to preserve that degree. Moreover, the will of an individual or of a group that prefers itself can breed cooperation only by stifling interest in any true community. To grasp *why* this opposition exists between the true development of community consciousness and its arrested or perverted forms — between the "spirit of the genuine community" and the "natural social order" that is arrested or deviant — Royce says one must "sound to the depths the original sin of man the social animal, and of the natural social order which he creates" (2:85). If one makes such soundings, he will appreciate the sinful dynamisms and the strength of certain institutions that make people and groups prefer themselves and treat other individuals and communities as "mere things."

Hence, to counteract the downdrag which human limitations, monotony, and original sin exert on the consciousness of a community, its members need periodically to celebrate their common memories and hopes and to renew their commitment to engage practically in cooperative deeds. Within the cooperative processes formative of community life, deeds done together and communication about them are what create genuine common life in a community (2:83). Let us grant this need for a rhythm of communication that becomes both more articulate at celebrations and yet more vital in people's ordinary deeds of conscious cooperation. Still, *just how* does conscious cooperation arise within the awareness shared by the members of a *genuine* community?

This question calls for a more detailed examination of how consciousness of community, having reached the first degree, gradually mounts to the second and then can be lifted to the third degree. We start, then, presupposing the existence of that first degree of communal consciousness found in any "community of memory or of hope." Regarding each of the two higher degrees, we will first indicate its required ingredients and then add some needed qualifications. The overall pattern which Royce seems to reveal through his sketch of the evolving degrees of community consciousness is that its ethical and religious aspects are foreshadowed increasingly in the first and second degrees but reach their authentic form only in the third.

If consciousness of community is to develop from its first to its second degree, each member must "interpret his own individual self in terms of the *largest* ideal extension of that self *in time* which his *reasonable* will can acknowledge *as worthy of the aims* of his life" (2:105).[16] Royce taught that the life-aims of each human self cannot realistically exclude the longed-for eventual harmony of all wills since just that is the necessary ideal of every human self.[17] Consequently, *as reasonable,* each human self needs to open up and stay open to that whole human community which embraces the human selves of all times and places—the one which Royce designated technically as the "great community"[18]—so that the life and efforts of each human self may fit in with this community's overall meaning. Without this "largest ideal extension" to all human selves the second degree of communal consciousness cannot be attained. Negatively, this means that when reaching its second degree, communal consciousness excludes no human self arbitrarily. Positively, it means that communal consciousness must be enlivened by an appreciative interpersonal understanding and be structured by a mutual commitment to interdependent living.

Suppose, then, that many uniquely distinct members with their various talents actually fulfill the above requirements. Their communal life will then become a conscious moral art of so cooperating to defend and promote the basic values of the entire human community that no one is arbitrarily neglected or excluded. To illustrate this, Royce drew a parallel from the world of aesthetics. When members of an orchestra cooperate, their harmonious playing creates an experience of musical beauty for all actual and even potential listeners. They are *so* ordered in their cooperative deeds, *so* disciplined in following directions and in timing themselves, and *so* sensitive to everyone—both in the orchestra as it produces its creative venture, and in the entire audience. The kind of consciousness which these artists of musical collaboration achieve is an instance of that rich complexus of communal consciousness which Royce meant by his "second degree," including its relation to all humankind.

Can greater clarity be brought to this "appreciative interpersonal understanding" which marks the second degree? For it Royce taught that community members must have *enough understanding:*

> to be able, first to direct their own deeds of cooperation; secondly, to observe the deeds of their individual fellow workers; and thirdly, to know that, without just this combination, this order, this interaction of the coworking selves, just this deed could not be accomplished by the community. (2:88)

These three kinds of understanding presuppose more than the shared ideal extensions of the first degree. Each member must now consciously adopt the life of his community *as a communal* life; that is, each member's understanding must be enriched by a twofold appreciation. He must "view these present cooperative deeds as linked to the community's historical life and hopes" and he must identify his own life with the on-going common life of the community.[19] The required understanding, then, is not merely conceptual and rational, but also appreciative. That is, it gets in touch with and treasures values rather than mere concepts and implications. This understanding is also interpersonal in both of Royce's senses of unions lived — between individual persons on reality's first level and between a community and its members on personhood's second level. Exemplifying the first union are two selves who mutually recognize their identical interpretation of some ideal past event. Exemplifying the second union are those cooperating members who concur in saying of their community's cooperative life-process, "That cooperation, in which many distinct individuals take part, and in which I also take part, is, or was, or will be, an event in my life" (2:83). As a final ingredient in this appreciative understanding, each member needs to identify his own life with the common life of the community. This he does by viewing himself as a part of the concrete and treasured life of the community *and* by wanting to *be* directed by its values, future goals, and cooperative process.

Besides this richly socialized and value-laden understanding, Royce requires for the second degree an ingredient from the *wills* of members: *their mutual commitment to live interdependently.* This mutual commitment arises when each person who offers himself to the community is *genuinely accepted* by all his fellow members. They genuinely accept him when they personally and cooperatively consent to his offer of seeking his self-identification through the union of his life with that of the community. This mutual commitment, however, can be thwarted in many ways: they may reject him; their acceptance of him may be only superficial and functional, not personal; or, if they accept him as a person, they may so restrict the ideal extension of their lives that the worth and influence of certain persons is excluded from their "own self writ large" (2:85–86). Rather, to keep the acceptance genuine, they must somehow acknowledge all human selves and avoid any arbitrary exclusion of any of them.

In other words, the community both is, and knows that it is, "a community conscious of its own life" on the second degree when that life is enriched with the following ingredients. All the members share this threefold understanding. Sensing the community's time-flow and its deed-doing thrust, they identify their lives with its life and in turn agree in accepting others' identifications with the community's life. Since no arbitrary exclusion is allowed and sinced an openness to all human selves is required, ethical universality is found inseparably involved in this second degree of communal consciousness. Thus the idea of the "great community" and a disciplinary usage of the idea of a "morally detached individual" have already articulated themselves into the "social form of experience" examined in the second degree of communal consciousness.

Not just any consciousness of cooperation suffices for the second degree of communal consciousness. Each member needs to make the community's life part of his own life and in turn identify himself with it. This he does only if he equivalently says, "This activity which we perform together, this work of ours, its past, its future, its sequence, its order, its sense, — all these *enter into my life, and are the life of my own self writ large*" (2:86).[20]

But these mutual identifications presuppose that the members are in touch with their ideal selves and are, in the deepest sense, "*artists* of cooperation." Each member becomes such an artist when he is genuinely in touch with his ideal self within and finds that what actually gives practical expression to his life as ideally extended are the cooperative deeds done with and through the community (2:90). In brief, the members who create Royce's second degree of communal consciousness are artists in genuine ethical life. They have personally appropriated their inner ideals. They want to express these in cooperative deeds coordinated with others. For this they value and respect all human selves and exclude none as such. Thus their ethical universalism, rising from the shared idea of universal community, already contains at this second stage of communal consciousness a religious seed for the next stage.

But most people find it difficult to achieve this second degree of communal consciousness. Its requirements of an appreciative interpersonal understanding and of a mutual commitment to interdependent living are too exacting — especially for people in our highly complex contemporary life. In business and politics, for example, world-wide movements and organizational structures, along with the complex procedures they require, often reduce intelligently wrought cooperation to mere mechanical performance. To counteract these depersonalizing forces effectively, some new energy must enter the consciousness of community so that it can make a quantum leap to a new level beyond these obstacles. The very special kind of love which Royce called "loyalty" is the needed transforming energizer, the new tie-in with the transcendent Spirit. Certain individuals, responding to their experience of some genuine community's prior love of themselves and thus oriented towards membership, are further moved to dedicate themselves in love and service to this community as to a second-level reality itself, as well as to its individual members. This kind of self-gifting orients them towards openness to the universal community of all minded beings and this openness generates a unique consciousness that makes theirs a morally genuine loyalty.

Partaking in this third degree of community consciousness, each of these members recognizes that the highest fulfillment of his ideal self lies precisely in some perfectly cooperative deed of this community. Hence, each genuine member eagerly loves the successful cooperation of all its members even more than his own initiatives. To be genuine, loyalty needs its base in the human affectivity and the sensitivity for others that it fosters even as it must be open to mystical touches. It also needs true interpretations and a resolute fidelity to maintain and promote the community's life (2:98). But also indispensable, if loyalty is to be genuine, is a cogent and critical shared intelligence to form clear plans that direct the cooperative deeds.

This insightful, rational, and appreciative love for the community as such constitutes the third and highest degree of consciousness of community. Perhaps Royce's own words that balance the unique vocations of individual members with their hoped-for communal deed which fulfills each self, deserve attentive study:

> If a social order, however complex it may be, actually wins and keeps the love of its members, . . . then indeed love furnishes the basis for the consciousness of the community which intelligence, without love, in a highly complex social realm, can no longer furnish. Such love—such loyalty—depends not upon losing sight of the variety of the callings of individuals, but upon seeing in the successful cooperation of all the members precisely that event which the individual member most eagerly loves as his own fulfillment. (2:91-92)

When this highest stage of consciousness permeates the members of a community, they begin experiencing the religion of loyalty. Through the interactive processes at work in this genuine community, the participants encounter authentically loyal deeds and words that function as religious signs promoting religious insight. Experiencing the true loyalty of other members and a "love of the ideal community of all mankind," they find themselves empowered "from above" with the gift of a similar love and are thus rendered sensitive to the presence and influence of the Spirit-Interpreter of the Universal Community (2:102-105).[21]

How, then, does genuine loyalty's total gift of oneself to the community and to its members through cooperative deeds affect the consciousness of community at this highest stage? Since this consciousness is sown by *caritas*-loyalty, the community's awareness of the *present* is moulded in a distinct way (2:95). In his distinctive loyal "love of a community, the individual obtains, for his ideally extended self, precisely the unity, the wealth, and the harmony of plan which his sundered natural existence never supplies" (2:99-100). Thus this third degree of consciousness of community rings with a religious tone because in it the voice of the Deliverer-

Spirit is heard. Royce clearly saw how our natural alienation makes us impotent to love the genuinely saving community which is so radically linked to the basic religious needs of each individual. Near the close of his investigative lecture, "The Body and the Members," he synopsized: "The problem of love is human. The solution of the problem, if it comes at all, will be, in its meaning, superhuman, and divine, if there be anything divine" (2:102).

CONCLUSION

Three kinds of complex religious experience, then, provided the data for Royce's late philosophy of the Christian religion. These were the experiences had (1) by modern man confronted with a problematic Christianity, (2) by Paul's early Christian communities as they interpreted the Christian mission, and (3) by any universally loyal self in his multidimensional total experience of forming a genuine community. Complementing these rich experiential sources was, of course, Royce's late theory that the real world is a directed process of serial interpretation (2:264, 373–374). The overall situation within which he sought to do his mature philosophy of religion was the perennial decision-making dialogue going on between the peoples of the world, cosmic events, and history. He said that his method in *The Problem of Christianity* consisted in uniting philosophical reflection with a history that showed the world advancing along definite lines (1:45). His methodic use of the "social form" induced from his analysis of three more complex religious experiences produced important results in the overall method and content of Royce's late philosophy of religion.

Thanks to his new transformed method of philosophizing by interpretive musement (that is, by reflective interpretation based on experience, history, and his new metaphysics of interpretation), Royce had finally succeeded in integrating human affections into his philosophic enterprise. He recognized how a person's emotions and impulses were integral factors in any "fair understanding" of the whole of human living. Yet he maintained his insistence on the overall importance of logically consistent ideas, of practical dedication, and of a genuine community led by the Spirit of interpretation. Enriched now by affectivity, his method of interpretive musement was found eminently suited to the Christian reality. If this reality called him to reconsider ethics and metaphysics, far more did it call him to search and to evaluate the complex religious experience of Christians for its new and distinctive features. Royce's interpretive musement suited him well for a study both of man as a finite individual self and of "man as a community of grace."

Moreover, because his late philosophic method included an overall search for a communal goal, it had the intrinsic tendency to develop an eschatology and a constructive ecclesiology centered on the ideal of a hoped-for Community.[22] Royce's method also promoted a fuller realization of the Beloved Community by fostering freedom among selves, by directing the communication processes within communities, and by attracting community members to a fitting sending of signs. For the life of the community depended on such communication by words and especially by deeds.

On the other hand, the content of Royce's late philosophy of religion rested upon the acknowledgment of "two levels of human existence": man as individual and man as community. This philosophy gave structure to itself by defining how man's highest good was a transformation of his individual nature through loving union with an essentially higher grade of being, namely, the spiritual community (1:405). These "two levels" served as the bases for the mystery of the genuine community (or, in Christian terms, of "the Kingdom of heaven"). Out of this mystery arose the "three ideas" which constitute the "Christian doctrine of life." This doctrine, in turn, accorded with that continually emergent doctrine on community which the education of the human race down through the ages is bringing to fuller and fuller consciousness in people.

At the same time, the mature Royce had discovered a most sensitive and highly accurate line of interpretation for "finding the nature of God." He resonated to a fundamental hint within the Christian creed's distinctive article about the Holy Spirit: the "divine Interpreter." Human selves can experience the contrast between the Beloved Community of this interpreting Spirit and "man as a community of hate." This experience can awaken them to various fundamentally different life-orientations and especially to the one which leads to the divine. Finally, as Professor Collins observed, since "Christian religious experience is social in its sources and in its intended goals," and since the church is a distinctive type of socially organized religious experience, Royce did not "regard the church as a perverting or an artificial form imposed from the outside upon private religious life."[23]

In sum, Royce's study of religious experiences—both elementary (chapters 6 and 7) and complex (chapter 8)—exhibited his full experiential resources. The present chapter has highlighted the various ways in which he studied "the social form of [religious] experience." To be rooted in these experiential bases is essential for a philosopher of religion; yet such empiric evidence remains inadequate unless, with a definite mastery, one responds to these materials and works them into a creative synthesis. Royce's mastery came from his philosophical method. But before examining the fundamental choices and bold initiatives by which he created his mature method, we need to enter into Royce's chosen approach for investigating his problem of Christianity and scan his mature masterpiece as a whole.

9. Orientation to *The Problem of Christianity*

By 1912 Royce considered himself competent to investigate the problem of Christianity. His recent decade of logical studies had equipped him with an order-system to guide his appraisal of the "social form" underlying the creed of that particular religion. His experiences of life and his forty years of inquiry into the philosophy of religion, which he intensified from 1907 to 1912, had made him familiar with this field. He now recognized that he had a "distinctively new interpretation of the 'Problem of Christianity'" (1:xii). Yet he also saw that most of his audience were not professionally trained either in pure logic or in the philosophy of religion. He decided, then, to devote his entire first lecture to orient them effectively towards understanding his problem, aim, and method.

By clarifying Royce's compact first lecture, "The Problem and the Method" (1:3-45), we map out the immediate approach to his problem as designed by Royce the interpreter. To become at home with Royce's distinctive approach we need: to adjust our minds in three ways to his unique approach; to take into account his own three kinds of orientation; to examine how his distinctive terms function in his serial formulations of the problem; to understand why he emphasized the second of Christianity's two indispensable foci; and to grasp how and why he selected the three ideas "most essential" for his "Christian doctrine of life." By taking these five needed steps, we can become readied for "a fair comprehension of the problem of Christianity" (1:34).

WE ADJUST OURSELVES TO THE APPROACH OF AN INTERPRETER

A Bias for Only the Definite?

When Royce is deliberately vague and general at the start of the *Problem*, the contemporary reader may tend to accuse him of slack thought. Such a judgment would overlook the mature Royce's discipleship under America's "Exact Logician," Charles S. Peirce, who argued that we must

ORIENTATION TO THE *Problem* 145

cultivate vagueness and generality to achieve the indeterminateness our minds also need.[1] If a person confuses being clear with being determinate, he insulates himself from Peirce's insight that our minds have a rhythmic need to be both determinate *and* indeterminate.

The rich indeterminacy of Σ awaits the pathfinding logician's choices of postulates to create determinate order systems. When devising the *Problem,* Royce saw that, within its rigorous logical movement, vague and general ideas and terms do have important roles to play. For instance, general ideas let a thinker be adequate to the fully complex nature of a problem without prematurely foreclosing the issue and without falsely simplifying the living mystery of reality. If at first ideas are kept general, they forestall a precipitous exactness that would cramp the mind's "free play" among paradoxical and mysterious realities. Again, felt vagueness not only helps lure the mind to quest for the accurate determination it needs but also gives it room to roam in its opposite quest for generalization.

Presupposing creative thought's initial need to be indeterminate, Royce used his skills to wrestle with the mind's contrary tendencies to grow both in generality and in determinacy. While serially formulating his problem of Christianity in increasingly general ways, he also sought ways to sharpen his focus on its central factors and to make them specifically more determinate. Even in his opening chapter where he progressively generalized his problem, he already sought to hint at it as a sign of the whole universe — a sign to be clearly revealed only in his final chapters. Accordingly, his first chapter shows how deliberately he chose vague and inadequate expressions for his initial formulations of the problem (1:14, 19, 21). Even in his early use of terms like "church" and "Christian," he wanted some indeterminancy to be felt. Knowing his intellectual passion to become more determinate and exact, he judged he could give rein to that passion in later chapters. On the other hand, although his starting context was the determinate situation of twentieth-century Christianity, he knew that in the end he would have to generalize about the whole universe and any self in it, whether either of these were viewed as an individual or as a community.

In short, we can confuse clarity and definiteness. We can also start with expectations proper to linguistic analysis. To impose either mentality upon Royce's different mode of philosophizing in 1912 would be needlessly to impede one's understanding of him. Another hindrance would arise if one failed to take into account the exact stage of thought Royce had reached when creating his work.

Just What Was Royce Asking about Christianity in 1912?

In late 1912, Royce's growing insights into Peirce were transforming his intellectual development. Only then had he reached the precise stage of consciousness that permitted him to create "a distinctively new interpretation" of problematic Christianity (1:xii).[2] The kinds of questions he asked about it in 1912 show a significant change from the kinds of questions he asked of it in 1909.

In his 1909 address, "What is Vital in Christianity?" Royce used his "individual approach,"[3] but, by 1912, he had made the significant shift into his "social approach" to Christianity. These two approaches provided different portraits of an individual's relation to God. In 1909 Royce based this relationship on the distinctive Christian doctrine that God is a loving Father of each human person because of his appreciation of each one's infinite worth.[4] Although Royce continued to regard the individual's relation to God as vital to Christianity, by 1912 his social approach stressed membership in the universal community as indispensable to the individual's now triadic relationship to God. The new form of his question was: In human nature what is the *communal* basis which Christianity must presuppose when formulating a creed for its community?

Royce had just finished exploring how human feelings, attitudes, and reason make religion vital and social.[5] Presupposing these findings about religion, he could in 1912 concentrate solely on *ideas* drawn from experience, viewed not merely as abstractions but also as practical interpretations at work in the world. Drawing these ideas from people's great common religious interests, needs, and ideals, he would discover the essential creed that gave Christianity its fundamental social structure. Taken together, these essential ideas formed a determinate and well-adapted plan of Christian living, "the Christian doctrine of life."[6] This doctrine was constituted by the following three fundamental ideas: a spiritual community exists; separated from it, a mere individual cannot unburden himself of his self-ruinous aloneness, hostility, and sinfulness; and he can be rescued (or saved) only through the atoning deeds of the loyal servant community. The community's atoning influence can transform the lost self or traitor into a loyal member of humankind who in his new life loves the community, himself, and all others through genuine deeds of service.

Why did Royce in 1912 stress *ideas* and their union in a long-range doctrine? Contemporary happenings on the American Christian scene made him uneasy. Largely stimulated by William James and Henri Bergson who were emphasizing religious feelings and intuitions, people were then becoming both enthusiastic and yet confused about religious life. Recognizing the need for a strong counterbalance, Royce decided to take a position different from James's (2:3).

Just as Royce required philosophy to arise not from any temperament but from one's "essential temperament," so he required religion to arise not out of unrefined human experience but from something more than uninterpreted spontaneities. Refusing to identify religion with experience, he required critical discernment and practical dedication in it, too. For genuine religion, a person had to slough off the inauthentic urges and insights he experienced and integrate his genuine impulses and intuitions into a commitment to a long-range plan of action. To adopt Royce's metaphor, were these spontaneous processes to pass uncriticized, they would disturb our compass and get us lost in a "wilderness of caprices" rather than guide us to a home of wisdom (2:4). His problem, then, was to discover an *un*disturbable religious compass by which *all* people could test whether their inner and outer religious impulses and intuitions were heading towards authentic loyalty. He found such a compass in his Christian doctrine of life. Even non-transformed hearts could at least recognize that its presence had salvific meaning for them (*SRI,* 21-24).

Which Experience of Christianity Is Needed to Formulate Its Problem?

Royce's many ways of formulating the problem of Christianity (1:14, 19, 21) arose from his different ways of meeting that problem. His ways of artfully advancing to more and more determinate formulations can so preoccupy the reader that he misses the obvious point of Royce's personal and dialectical experience of paradoxical Christianity. Royce appreciated its many positive contributions to humankind; he factually faced its failures, divisions, and problems (1:9-13). For him, to experience Christianity meant seeing, smelling, and tasting its "good *and* bad fish."[7] This held true whether one's net brought up Christianity's traditional doctrines or its organizational structures or its Western cultural attachments or, more painfully, its members. In each and every such experience one met "the problem of good *and* evil" in an intensely gripping way. Royce's deep and many-sided experience of Christianity thus empowered him to reformulate its problem in many ways and to regard that problem as pregnant with a metaphysical generalization.

He sketched his experience of this dialectic of good and evil near the start of the *Problem* when he described the two main crosscurrents that generate the problem of Christianity. Positively, Christianity's spirit has called for sympathetic interpretation all through its ages. "The fact that the Christian religion is, thus far at least, man's most impressive vision of salvation, and his principal glimpse of the homeland of the spirit" calls for fair appraisal (1:11). Negatively, however, Christianity occasions questions, doubts, and even tragic divisions not only in history, theology, and philosophy, but also and especially between persons and between their groups. These unresolved difficulties afflict Christianity's very life and plague those who expect healing from it rather than wounds. They find that, although Christianity enlightens our troubled world, it "has thus far brought, not peace, but a sword" (1:12).

TOWARDS THIS PROBLEM ROYCE TAILORS A SUITABLE ORIENTATION BY CAREFULLY FITTING TOGETHER HIS SELECTION OF NEEDED ATTITUDE, STYLE, AND ASSUMPTION.

Which Attitude towards Christianity Is Most Suited?

According to Royce, "The man who considers the interests of religion may choose any one of three attitudes towards Christianity" (1:6). Each of these arises out of a basically different, freely adopted orientation towards the Christian reality. Sensitive to most persons' mixture of motives, Royce avoided presenting these attitudes as pure extremes. He spoke of each grouping as composed of persons "predominantly apologetic" or of those "in the main hostile" or of those principally problematic (1:9, 12). He also described these three groups in a deliberately general way so that each psychic stance might include as many variations as possible.

Those who have the predominantly apologetic attitude choose to live within Christianity as its special advocates. Such apologetes take Christianity to be so true, important, and necessary for people that they feel they must defend it and must make it effective for all people, inside and outside Christendom. Convinced of the truth and gifts which it possesses in itself and for them, they do not experience any pressing need to acknowledge its shortcomings or their own imperfections. They are less than eager to point out the Spirit's saving influence in other great world religions or to labor for the ever-needed deeper healing and renewal of themselves and Christianity. These promoters of the faith are perhaps too securely rooted in the deposit handed down and, therefore, too rarely ready to be trimmed clean to increase their yield.[8] Before Bultmann, Royce diagnosed that the weakness of traditional apologists arises "because they misread the symbols which tradition has so richly furnished" (2:390). Therefore, they generally fail to express *in an authentic and balanced way* Christianity's *basic* doctrine of life; namely, the fundamental doctrine of the universal saving community.

Those who have an attitude in the main hostile choose to take a position outside of and aloof from Christianity (1:7-9). Of these, some are positively hostile to Christianity because it opposes what they call genuine religion or human progress. Others feel sure that Christianity falls beneath their high standards or are coolly indifferent to it since to them it seems a clinging but withering vestige of a barely surviving form of religion. These critics find nothing vitally good in Christianity. According to Royce's diagnosis, persons adopting this second attitude are generally either "ignorant of the meaning of the ideal of the universal and beloved community" or "unaware of what salvation through loyalty signifies" (2:390).

Those who have the principally problematic attitude prefer to be sympathetically sensitive to the human and divine elements in Christianity's history, actuality, and hopes and who wish to relate fairly and adequately to it as a whole. Choosers of this third attitude regard Christianity as basically a mystery, as a beautiful but murky blend of good and evil. Whether as members or non-members, they desire to keep on experiencing it as paradoxical. They regard it as both suffering and yet victorious, as wounded yet healing, as transient yet eternal. By always dealing with Christianity as mysteriously problematic, this group succeeds in maintaining balance.

These three attitudes towards Christianity are so basic and mutually exclusive that whenever a person freely adopts his orientation to Christianity, he enters into one of these ways. Fundamentally, he judges Christianity as true and good or as erroneous and bad or, by postponing judgment, insists on a more basic antecedent interpretation of it as problematic, and thus as calling for a more adequate understanding.

Freely and explicitly Royce chose this third psychic stance towards Christianity (1:13; 2:383-386). He recognized that this careful choice controlled his method of philosophizing about the Christian religion (1:3, 13). It also controlled his selection of a *title* for his 1913 opus. To it he assigned neither the title of "The *Truth* of Christianity," nor its "*Power*," nor its "*Triumph*"—titles echoing the first attitude. Nor on the other hand did he call it "The *Anti-Humanism* of Christianity," nor its "*Philistinism*," nor its "*Vestigial Nature*"—titles echoing the second attitude. By contrast, Royce quite deliberately selected as his title, "The *Problem* of Christianity" (1:3, 12; 1:384). This choice bespoke his commitment to keep experiencing Christianity in its wholeness as a mysteriously problematic reality.

Is the Herald's Style What Best Fits a Philosophy of the Christian Religion?

Royce further recognized that, by adopting the predominantly problematic attitude towards Christianity, his style of philosophizing had to steer between the isolating monologic way of a Pilate and the conflictive dialogic mode of those who get mired in traditional controversies. He could not be like Pilate who had merely uttered a question and then by withdrawal prevented discussion.[9] Pilate's style violated both the trust essential for cooperatively investigating a question and the loyalty befitting genuine persons in community (2:383-384, 388). Royce's rejection of this monologue manner spoke volumes about his belief that only the endeavors of a genuine community could seek and win philosophical truth.

Entering public philosophical dialogue, Royce also knew he had to avoid that wrangling which for nearly twenty centuries had stretched discussions about Christianity to the breaking point and beyond. He detected that the basic attitudes of the apologete, the assailant, and the studiously indifferent critic of Christianity invariably evoked the traditional stalemated controversies and provoked unfruitful methods of philosophy.

Hints of a fitting path arose from his recent reading of Peirce and his childhood memories. Peirce's doctrine of icons, as a type of signs, suggested the need of a model for the problematic attitude Royce preferred towards Christianity. Royce's memories of Bible reading in his Grass Valley home and often thereafter brought to mind John the Baptizer's response to Jesus.[10] With the puzzling cry, "Behold the lamb of God!"[11] the Baptizer had identified and witnessed to that problematic stranger from Nazareth — partly known and partly unknown. Hence, by adopting John the Baptizer as a model both for himself and for the Church which interprets Jesus, Royce revealed that one of his main interpretations of himself and of the Church was that of *herald*.[12] Part of Royce's critically selected strategy, then, consisted in identifying with a herald's orientation (2:388). The choice seeded his unique method of generating a philosophy of the Christian religion.[13]

He, too, would be a *prophet* for Christianity, a *voice* crying in the wilderness. He would often voice the theme "that a religion, long needed, is yet to come" (2:386). He would announce his interpretation of the essential message of this religion. To those with ears to hear, he would communicate the word of wisdom — specifically, that each temporal deed and happening is both fact and sign in its own unique way. As he eventually made clear, the message within each event and within each choice is both a prophecy that the Spirit will triumph and a revelation that its near and ever faithful insight interprets and victoriously overcomes the dialectical tensions of our lives and of the world (2:386).

This mention of intrinsic prophecy may hint at something more in Royce's method and doctrine of 1913 but at least his choice of the Baptist's orientation towards Christianity clearly determined his mature method of philosophizing. It became a search for the insight of a prophet and for the wisdom of a witness who respects the dignity of his audience even as he proclaims his message. Underlying this choice, too, is a traditional yet startling assumption.

Does the Christian Creed Imply an On-going Universal Pedagogy?

From the start Royce frankly admitted that for his investigation he was employing a working assumption. It was indeed a traditional postulate but one as yet untested by his inquiry.[14] Postponing the completion of the test to his conclusion, he assumed

> that the human race has been subject to some genuine process of education, that the ages have taught man some more or less connected lesson, and that the modern man can read this lesson. (1:20)

Here Royce employed "process of education" and "teaching" to refer to any communication of ideas occurring serially between any minded beings who function within a community of genuine dialogue, "a Community of Interpretation" in his technical phrase (2:109–163).[15] In this more general sense, teaching takes place not only between people on a one-to-one or a one-to-many basis but whenever an interpretation is successfully communicated. Instances arise whenever an individual or a group effectively appropriates a message, whether it be through mass media, group influence, civilization, language, religion, culture, or nature. Whenever ongoing genuine education occurs, a community arises because minded beings are being united in life by the message communicated.

The assumption that world history implies a universal teaching process functions as a central nerve in Royce's philosophy of history and in his metaphysics (2:38). Only gradually does he identify the "more or less connected lesson" of this process as the "doctrine of signs" to all selves and as the "Christian doctrine of life" to all finite minded beings (1:374–380; 2:324, 422), and only at the close of his work does he suggest clues corraborating the truth of this assumption. He started from Christianity's ongoing teaching, as found between its master's Spirit, his disciples, and those receiving their word. Then he extended it through all loyal communities wherever a similar call has arisen or arises for a more loyal commitment to a still more comprehensive truth. Finally, he reached the broadest and deepest scope of this pedagogy when viewing the time-process of universal evolution as mediating the sending of signs to *all* selves.[16]

At this fullest extent of evolution's educative process, Royce was also assuming that the developing universe, although a pluralism of different selves (2:52) and of tendencies that from many aspects are fragmented and chaotic, is yet fundamentally a unified cosmos having its own self-identity. For this fullest extent of evolution, he had strategically preferred *not* to assume that his three "Signs" (the Christian doctrine of life, the best of modern civilization, and the entire processing universe) *could* be radically out of harmony with each other. If he, like James, had reversed the assumption, his investigation would have had a vastly different orientation. Royce assumed that these three Signs *could* be consistent, as his initial formulation of the problem of Christianity had suggested (1:14). From this formulation he successively extended the scope of his assumption until it reached to ultimate convergibility of the meanings within any loyal human community and the whole of evolution.

Underlying all this is Royce's ultimate idealistic supposition of a radical unity of meaning and of truth. With emphasis, he wrote, "Our fundamental postulate is: *The world is the interpretation of the problems which it presents*" (2:323). Here Royce's triad of metaphysical ideas ("Time, Interpretation, and Community," as unified by the more general idea of "The World as a Community") intercommunicate to form Royce's fundamental postulate, his "doctrine of signs" (2:324, 422). Significantly, this postulate and the *kind* of "will to believe" which it expresses is absent from William James' philosophy. For James, pluralism is so radical that meaning and truth *can* be non-convergent, can be basically inconsistent, can diverge into an ultimately absurd pluriverse. This diversity in the fundamental philosophical faiths from which James and Royce generated their different "wisdoms" locates a fundamental choice in philosophy.

USING DISTINCTIVE TERMS, ROYCE FORMULATES THE PROBLEM SERIALLY

Royce recognized that "a fair comprehension of the problem of Christianity" required great care (1:34; 44–45). He was acutely aware of the imbalances operating in others' earlier formulations of the problem. Painstakingly he moved towards a first statement of it, knowing that the whole course of his work would be largely set by even a quite general statement (1:14). He could have approached the problem of Christianity through religious feelings, moral codes, or cultic practices. He chose instead to focus upon the set of religious beliefs that a Christian community accepts and the problems this creed occasions for them (1:15). He aimed to explore "the reasonable consistency of certain possible religious opinions" (1:14).

He was also sensitive to the gap that people felt between religion and science. So, he chose this point of concern as the nest in which he would situate his first formulation of the problem. It would let him combine his own philosophical quest for consistency among certain religious opinions with his audience's sense that the modern mind had turned scientific and areligious. Molding his first formulation of the problem of Christianity in a way that touched his audience, he asked, "*In what sense, if in any, can the modern man consistently be, in creed, a Christian?*"[17] He admitted that this opening question was vague and deliberately inadequate (1:14), and cautioned his audience that its terms, "in creed," "Christian," and "modern man" were as richly complex as was the religious life they mirrored. He immediately proceeded to clarify these specific terms and then to generate new formulations of the problem.

To those in his audience who wanted the opening statement of a problem to be free from frills Royce's qualifier "in creed" seemed a needlessly jarring over-specification. Yet he wanted from the start to lay bare the dynamic center of the Christian life as he saw it and to distinguish it from whatever accrues to this center. His "in creed" began the process that trimmed aside all those "illuminating but capricious" historical accidents in Christianity whether they rise from one's culture, race, or sect or from one's uniquely personal experiences, training, and opinions (1:38; 2:428). Eventually it became clear that by inserting "in creed," he was actually setting six requirements for the "form of social religious experience" which was his main topic (1:xv). These were: (1) the traditional meanings encased in symbolic creedal terms need to be freed from the limits of their traditional dogmatic categories, that is, generalized, or, as some say today, "demythologized"[18]; (2) common religious experience must be the source and norm of a creed; (3) in this creedal form there must operate an intentionality towards a higher realm of values which are more vital than those people usually seek; (4) an intellectual content greater than that which William James prescribed for his "faith state" is needed for communal religious experience; (5) in the latter experience one's commitment must be expressed in deeds for the common good; and finally, (6) a rational will must organize life in community in such a way that disorderly impulses are recognized and countered.

In the opening formulation, does the term "Christian" function with a distinctiveness equal to that of "in creed"? For Royce, a "Christian" had to be more than an admirer of Jesus' example and of his moral code. He had to be more, too, than one shopping for such of the master's teachings as seemed most suited for himself (1:24). From the start Royce required that a Christian see himself as at least also a *member* of the Christian community (1:25-29, 37-38).[19]

Finally, by "modern man" in his opening phrasing of the problem, Royce created a symbolic construct which indicated both the individual historical result and the significant summary of the religious teaching of the ages. In "modern man" Royce beheld no arbitrary fiction, but actually "the present minister of this treasure of wisdom which the ages have stored and which our progress is still increasing" (1:19).[20] Hence, he freely used the term "modern man" to refer to selves, not only of the present and future, but also of times long past—for instance, to the educated apostle Paul (1:19) and to Royce's Athenian Christian, imaginatively brought back to life and education in the twentieth century (2:370). Since the term functioned as a concrete symbol for the contemporary communal consciousness of all persons entrusted to develop and pass on to future generations the most cherished elements of wisdom, "modern man" could and did refer to certain persons of the past, present, and future. "Modern man" both carries the Christian doctrine which these persons are destined to teach and possesses the modern *mind,* that treasure house of living tradition. Little wonder, then, that Royce felt anyone grasping his sense of "modern man" would get "a bearing on permanent religious concerns" (1:17).

He acknowledged that by using "modern man" in his opening formulation, he was introducing his postulate of universal pedagogy.[21] This assumes three things, as we have seen: (a) that humankind is historically growing in wisdom and religious truth; (b) that this truth teaches us the lesson that humankind's life is as a whole "no mere flow and strife of opinions, but includes a growth in genuine insight" for building a highly significant community; and (c) that persons can read this lesson (1:19, 21). The term "modern man," then, implies both a universal pedagogy and a communal doctrine. Together they should serve as the basic criterion for testing any historically emerging religious creed and, if necessary, for revising it (1:19).

After this clarification of terms Royce moved in his first chapter to further formulations of the problem. Here the scope of his process of generalization began showing itself. Although his opening question at first seemed to ask simply about the consistency of the overall present religious education of a contemporary individual, Royce was actually inquiring about the entire past and future religious education of the whole human race. Only a few pages later, he confessed that the true depth and scope of his problem of Christianity are better revealed in the following more careful reformulation of it:

> When we consider what are the most essential features of Christianity, is the acceptance of a creed that embodies these features consistent with the lessons that, so far as we can yet learn, the growth of human wisdom and the course of the ages have taught man regarding religious truth? (1:21)

ROYCE REQUIRES A GRASP OF BOTH ASPECTS OF CHRISTIANITY, BUT IN LOYALTY EMPHASIZES THE SECOND ASPECT

To experience and formulate the problem of Christianity is not enough. One must also choose which aspect of the problem to emphasize.

Basically, what was at issue was *how* one should describe Christianity. Is it a religion taught by the master? Or is it the doctrine whereby his disciples interpreted the master's life, message, and mission? Or was Christianity somehow both of these aspects?

Convinced of time as an essentially human category, Royce showed that the time-process creates a life-giving tension between the founder's message and evolving Christianity's interpretation of that message. He detected that many Christians, unwilling to accept this tension, are inevitably drawn into oversimplifications of the problem of Christianity. Thus, some regard as *the only* basic question, "What say you of Jesus?" Others insist that *the only* basic question is "What is the Church?" (To answer this question will, they believe, determine the Jesus question.) Yet all such approaches based on one idea only preclude a fair comprehension of the whole problem.

So Royce faced up to *both* of these "principal and contrary characteristics" of Christianity: the master *and* the Christian community's interpretation of him (1:22). For him, Christianity is like an ellipse whose two foci are indispensable and irreducible. Yet some reductionists keep trying to tighten Christianity into becoming a circle that centers on one element, either making this focal point the master with his life, teaching, and spirit or the present Christian community with its doctrinal interpretation of the master, his message, and mission (1:24). Both schools pay the price of drastically reduced truth (1:24–29). By contrast, Royce preferred to hold both sign-sender and sign-receiver in his embrace and to keep meeting the dialectical tension generated by these "two sharply contrasted aspects" of Christianity (1:30).

Nevertheless, one must face the fact that many of the master's ideas about the Kingdom were simply seeds which, however potent, would have remained sterile without the Christian community's interpretive process as guided by the Spirit. So, one has to meet the evaluative question about Christianity's two foci: Which is "the more essential, the more permanently important aspect?" (1:30). Is it the pre-resurrectional Jesus with his teaching *or* the Christian community with its interpretation of Jesus, his teaching, and mission? Royce chose to emphasize the second aspect.

This choice arose from Royce's loyalty to the Christian community and its reality (which included the individual pre-resurrectional Jesus as, in one sense, its founder). The individual mortal Nazarene, his work, message, and whole religion are enriched and deepened by the community's continuously developing interpretation, mediated by tradition (1: 26–27, 31–32). Royce knew that only through the community's interpretation of its master, its members, and itself, could there arise the Christian community's self-identity and its loyal response to its master's presently experienced Spirit. Consistent with this choice, then, certain ways of formulating the problem of Christianity were ruled out (1:409–415).

He shifted from descriptive language ("Christianity has two foci") to evaluative language ("Christianity's second focus is the more essential and more permanently important"). Producing this shift was the powerful attraction of his metaphysical doctrine of the two levels (of man the individual and of man the community). He would later acknowledge explicitly that this doctrine controlled his entire work (1:405; 2:57–58, 99). According to his pure logic, System Σ has the priority of an integrating process over any individual element in it. According to his metaphysics with its view of community as one conscious whole of shared life rather than as a set of societal structures, genuine community has ontological priority over any finite individual. According to his ethics, loyal commitment to the more universal community transfigures the will to live and makes it authentic for the first time. All these lines converge to reveal the attractive power of the *communal level* of reality and of consciousness.

Since his principle of the "two levels" had, in his opening chapters, no more status than that of its author's belief, Royce promptly alerted his audience to its controlling presence (1:33). He insisted on not surrendering either of Christianity's two aspects yet he preferred to stress the temporally developing interpretive actions of the Christian community. Through such an emphasis he tightened Christianity's bond with the rest of the world.[22] He thus put the temporally processing Christian community in a one-one correspondence with the ongoing human community as with another historical process. Then, using this interacting pair as a basis, he would insert it consistently into the expanding conical helix of the total process of world evolution.

ROYCE FINDS AND IDENTIFIES
THREE CENTRAL CHRISTIAN IDEAS

A final major ingredient in his approach to the problem of Christianity was his meeting with, and identification of, its three "leading and essential ideas" (1:xxxv). Royce knew that his selection of these ideas would guide his entire investigation (1:38). Investigating their meaning and truth would be his distinctive contribution to the problem of Christianity (1:44).[23]

The vitality, power, and universality of these "most essential" ideas had more and more won Royce over and convinced him of their supreme value and indispensable role. Along with the influence of the over-arching idea of Grace, the three ideas — Community, Lost State of the detached individual, and Saving Atonement — were the central dynamisms in his rich experience of "the mystery, the elementary human significance, and the beauty of the problem of Christianity" (1:xxxviii, 40). His rich and continuing experience of this "central, . . . intensely interesting, life-problem of humanity" (1:12) revealed itself in his mental procedures adopted in the *Problem*. There one finds the attitudes of attentive receptivity as well as of inquisitive initiative towards these ideas. They support Royce's claim of not inventing these ideas, but encountering them. "They found me. I did not devise them" (2:335). Through his alertly passive investigation of various communities of genuinely loyal people, Royce arrived at the following identification:

> The idea of the spiritual community in union with which man is to win salvation, the idea of the hopeless and guilty burden of the individual when unaided by divine grace, the idea of the atonement, — these are, for our purposes, the three central ideas of Christianity. (1:44)

For an initial clarification of the role played by these ideas in Royce's approach to his problem in 1912, we inquire during the remainder of this section: why he called these worldwide ideas "Christian" which criteria he used to identify them, and how they led him to articulate the "essential parts" of the *Problem*.

Even without Christianity, all the ideas in the so-called "Christian" doctrine of life "would be needed to express the meaning of true loyalty, the saving value of the right relation of any human individual to the community of which he is a member, and the true sense of life" (1:xx). When Royce called these ideas "essential," he meant indispensable for any genuine human religion. But then why did he refer to them as "Christian" if they themselves have nothing distinctively Christian, at least at first glance? Royce explained by way of simple historical designation. These three ideas had first been noticed and formulated together in early Christian communities. Royce called these universally present ideas "Christian" simply for historical reasons, much as we call universally present forces "Newton's laws" for historical reasons.

To identify his three leading and most essential "Christian" ideas Royce employed, as I find, three criteria: a) the concepts the early Christians used to interpret their master's teaching on the Kingdom; b) the inner thrust within the historical development of the Church; and c) the fit between these ideas and humankind's radical religious needs and interests.

Royce recognized that the early Christians believed that their master's spirit was guiding them to interpret the not yet fully clarified doctrine of the Kingdom. Their apostolic and post-apostolic communities gradually came to discern both that a certain real but mysterious, universal, and divine spiritual community was currently operating in their midst, and that without membership in it salvation was impossible (1:39). Somehow they learned a kind of identity between three realities: the Kingdom which the master had proclaimed, this universal spiritual community, and their own local Christian church. But they could not have identified their own Christian community as an expression of the Kingdom without also discovering two other ideas: the morally detached individual's lost state and the ongoing saving atonement. They found the inner connection of these three ideas as well as a need for the idea of gracious initiative "from above."

Next, Royce delved beneath the many historical accidents that mark Christianity's course through the centuries. He asked what was the inmost thrust and meaning within the Church's development through history (1:38). His research showed him that at the center of Christianity's historical life and doctrine pulsed that vital interpretive process through which principally these three ideas, integrated with grace, had worked themselves out.

Finally, he tested whether "the Christian doctrine of life" actually dovetailed with humankind's deepest religious needs for salvation and for a way to salvation. Here he discovered an amazing fit. Where these ideas operated most clearly was where the noblest forms of loyalty informed and redeemed secular or religious communities. But what determined the degree of loyalty which any community had? *Precisely* the degree to which its members had already "learned to live the life of the universal brotherhood" (2:335-336). Such learning cannot be done without grasping and practicing the Christian doctrine of life for only this doctrine fittingly meets people's needs for redemption by mediating that redemption.

Once identified and selected, each of these leading ideas guided Royce into recognizing an "essential part" of his discussion and clarification in the *Problem*.[24] The ideas also suggested questions that helped him further articulate each part. To clarify the *full* meaning of the master's teaching about the Kingdom, all three ideas, united by the idea of grace, were needed (1:43-44). Yet each idea had its own role to play in the process of interpretive musement Royce intended to carry out.

Thus, by using the idea of Community, he found himself asking questions closely paralleling those which the first Christians had asked when, in this religion's first decades, they tussled with their own problem of Christianity. For instance, when he inquired into the idea of a saving community, he found such questions as the following: Did this idea point to an existing and indispensable means of salvation for each individual? Was it the sole means of accurately translating the master's teaching about the Kingdom? Did it imply that Christian virtues could be effectively practised only in Christian community? Or turning to the present and future, he asked: Today, what is the significance and value of this idea of the saving community? Is this the idea destined to direct the course of the future?

Royce followed the lead of the second essential idea, namely, that of the individual's inescapable moral burden and lost state. So he inquired, as had the early Christians: Have natural inheritance and personal sin entrapped each individual in a spiritual death? By himself alone, is the individual truly powerless to escape this state of a lost soul? Is the only way out of "hopeless guilt" some divine intervention that works "a raising from the dead"? Recognizing the increasing aversion generally felt towards this second idea, Royce added significantly: "Can the modern man make anything of such an idea [of the individual's lost state]?" (1:43).[25]

By using the third idea of atonement, linked with grace, Royce probed a third essential part of the problem. Is the basic security of the human individual found *only* in a divine plan for redeeming mankind? If so, is the plan such that without atonement no one can be saved? Is the achievement of the atoning deed the only way in which the spiritual community can unite to itself a lost individual and thus save him? Does a person fully grasp the master's essential meaning of the Kingdom of heaven *only* when he first divines what atonement means? (1:43-44). By raising questions like these, Royce rendered more determinate his inquiry into the several "essential parts" of his problem of Christianity.

In review of the present chapter, some specific factors fashioned the immediate orientation of Royce's mind for its investigation in the *Problem*. He insisted on holding in vital tension both aspects of Christianity (the religion of the master and his disciples' interpretation of him and his message), even while stressing the latter's greater importance because of its rising from the second and deeper level of reality. Royce had his characteristic ways of serially formulating the problem and of using terms with distinctive meanings. Towards Christianity, he preferred the problematic (rather than the apologetic or hostile) attitude and selected the style of a pointing herald in order to philosophize about it. He acknowledged his radical assumption that an ongoing universal pedagogy was uniting all minded beings into a dynamically growing universe of Signs. He was met by, identified, and selected the three central ideas of Christianity while they, in turn, completed the orientation of his mind and set for it the major tasks of interpretation to be worked out during the remaining fifteen lectures of the *Problem*. So equipped, Royce was ready for his investigation. Before accompanying him, we may be helped by a rapid survey of the whole course of the *Problem*.

10. Overview of *The Problem of Christianity*

After his first and wholly orientational lecture, Royce investigated in his next dozen lectures the *meaning* of his Christian ideas in their historical, psychological, ethical, religious, and metaphysical dimensions. Thereafter, in his three concluding lectures, he completed testing the *truth* of his underlying assumption that the world is a universe of interpretation. His question then became: Was the great Interpreter of the universe using the "doctrine of signs" and the "Christian doctrine of life" to persuade all finite minds towards wholehearted promotion of the coming of the Beloved Community?

Royce chose "temporal process" as the medium suited for getting in proper touch with these Christian ideas. By "temporal process" he meant mainly the interpretive process of interacting minds insofar as they engage serially in successive communications. The physical process of natural and cosmic evolution was only a secondary and derivative meaning of the term. Still less central and more derivative was the popularly imagined sense of time. Our mutual acceptance of some standard (for instance, the motion of the earth relative to our sun or the number of years since some event significant to a human community) presupposed more fundamental processes at the levels of physical nature and of minded beings. In this present chapter, then, we will survey the whole course of the *Problem* by studying how his twofold quest for meaning and truth had "time" as its nutrient matrix—understanding time in Royce's principal sense of the temporal process of successively communicating minded beings.

Three years after writing the *Problem,* Royce acknowledged how important this process was for his mature thought. He wrote of that

> process which has been going on, in human thought, ever since Heraclitus remarked that the Logos is fluent, and ever since Israel began to idealize the life of a little hill town in Judea.
>
> I stand for the importance of this process, which has led Christianity to regard a community, not merely as an aggregate but as a person, and at the same time, to enrich its ideal memory of a person, until he became transformed into a Community.

The process in question, is not merely theological, and is not merely mystical, still less merely mythical. Nor is it a process invented merely by abstract metaphysicians. It is the process which . . . [is found in any genuinely loyal, community-rooted individual] whose life has its unity in its restless quest for death on behalf of the great good cause — its ever living Logos in its fluent quest for the goal.[1]

This process, although requiring myth and metaphysics, theology and mysticism, is far more intimate, vital, and communal. As the source of these four needed modes of expression, Roycean process is a concrete questing to overcome alienating disloyalties and to further the cause of unity by using the series of one's dyings in atoning ways that mediate entry into a life of yet higher and richer community.

Participating in this process, Royce devised his overall method for the *Problem*. In general he described it as a "union of an effort to read the lesson of history with an effort to estimate, upon a reasonable basis, the philosophy of the Christian religion" (1:45). Just as in his 1910 "Principles" he had said that the highest methodology consists in an "organized combination," so here he points to a "union." When he here identifies one member of that union as his "effort to read the lesson of history," he is referring to this search for the meaning of the Christian ideas as they work themselves out in world history. When he here identifies the union's other member as his "effort to estimate, upon a reasonable basis, the philosophy of the Christian religion," he is looking ahead to his concluding quest for the ultimate truth of the Christian ideas. Hence, before surveying in this chapter the highways of these two major quests (or "efforts") in the *Problem,* we need to focus briefly upon that dynamic which produces their "union," the process of interpretation which "organizes their combination" and characterizes Royce's mature mode of thought.

For him, truth lies in the eternal conspectus of the All-knowing Self. Each finite minded being is led towards fuller truth by influences inescapably social. This free growth towards more truth is generated by a type of interpretation, in which the object interpreted also functions as a sign calling for further interpretation. Meanwhile, at a more interior level of this process, each participant's mind likewise functions as something to be interpreted, that is, as a sign calling for further interpretation (2:160, 270). However simple this interpretive process, it must circle between interpreted object and an interpreting mind. Yet, as part of the process, each of these must function as both thing and sign. Hence, an endlessly broader spiral of interpretation is initiated. Accordingly, one should expect a Roycean object of interpretation to lead ever onward to wider ranges of objects and to more comprehensive communities of knowers.

For example, we saw that the term "modern man" in his opening question refers directly to a present-day educated person. Then, giving his audience clear signals about expanding its scope, Royce uses this term as a sign to point to the entire human race, first as currently existing, then as having existed through all past generations, next as about to exist in future generations, and finally, as including the fullest ambit of all humankind (1:15–18). At a more interior level, the audience's very response to Royce's interpretation of modern man is itself a distinct act of interpretation which itself is to be taken as a sign calling for further interpretation. Clearly, for Royce, the evolving temporal process of minded beings' serial interpretations is necessarily a dimension of the reality known.

Many of Royce's key terms, then, refer to realities as both things and signs and elicit audience participation in the interpretation process. In this way the terms themselves and the responding audience propel the serial process of interpretation. Since both the thing interpreted and the act of interpretation lie within the intentionality of the interpretive process, they endlessly call for further interpretation. This is unlike the seemingly arbitrary nexus between one perception and another, between one conception and another (2:160). Expectably, then, Royce's opening formulations of the problem of Christianity will not only enjoy their direct face-value sense but also point (by the power of Σ's expanding logic) to some broader and deeper interpretations within the temporal process.

From the start of his first major effort, Royce assumed that the basic creed of the contemporary Christian *could* be consistent with the highest wisdom of contemporary thought. Yet, when he expanded his perspective, could the basic creed of the nineteen-hundred-year-old, ongoing Christian community be consistent with the highest wisdom in the entire human community of all times and cultures? This question led him to try to identify one doctrine of wisdom common to all genuinely loyal men and women. He thought that he could identify it authentically if he detected a unique set of beliefs which brought into consistency and basic human accord three kinds of communities: those of Paul's Christians, of today's Christians, and of all people who promote the advent of the Beloved Community. This led him into a close study of how evolving temporal process affects both Christian communities, the whole human community, and the universal community of all minded beings. Concurrent with his study of evolving temporal process, he produced a series of further generalizations of the problem of Christianity and further revealed his own method stage by stage.

This series of reconsiderations forms the body of the *Problem,* Lectures 2 to 14. Here it suffices to mention that in Lectures 2 to 8 Royce successively investigates complex religious experience as it occurs in a variety of communities (whether composed of Christians, or of loyal non-

Christians, or of all the genuinely loyal). In this first major part of the *Problem*, then, evolving temporal process is just as much the matrix of his thought as it is in that work's latter major part. So, although both parts are integral to his "effort to read the lesson of history," we now turn to the *Problem's* latter major part—that is, to Lectures 9 to 14—in order to notice more closely there the role of evolving temporal process.

READING THE LESSON OF HISTORY

In his efforts to generalize the problem of Christianity, Royce situated the Christian phenomenon within the broader compass of human evolution. During previous decades he had critically explored human evolution in its various forms: biological, anthropological, psychological, psychosocial, and such cultural forms as the ethico-religious. As a result, he persisted in his estimate, that, although in all its forms human evolution was chancy, it showed in its general direction a constancy and an overall "total meaning" (2:422). As he pondered the whole of human development, he detected that human consciousness first underwent a major transformation at the start of the Christian era, noticeably in the Pauline churches (1:xviii). He also recognized that the subsequent centuries of Christianity could have been genuinely Christian only if they retained the vital core of this new consciousness.

Naturally, however, Christians are bonded to all the human race. So Royce turned to consider how that far lengthier and broader process, the evolution of the entire human race, had affected Christian life and consciousness in its nineteen hundred years of development. He observed that the rate of ever-greater change marking human evolution enters inescapably into Christianity and that the Christian community of the future may realistically expect ever greater and ever accelerating changes in culture and institutions. Humankind, and Christianity within it, is being transformed by multileveled temporal process.

Yet, by taking this transformative and purifying process into account, Royce rendered more difficult his own search for that "one doctrine of life" which he postulated as the constant source of Christianity's self-identity.[2] By the permeating presence of evolution, that living nerve of doctrine would have both to resound in the wisdom of all humankind and to perdure throughout all these ever more profound and increasingly more rapid changes. For instance, today's educated person envisages the universe in a way radically transformed from that of a Pauline Christian. So, too, in 4000 A.D., the world view of an educated person will be strikingly different from that of today's Christian. Under these conditions, could

Royce discover any experience that would be identifiably the same in the religious life of Christians in the years 50, 1913, and 4000 A.D.? And, supposing this identifiably constant experience to be discovered, could he further detect within it one basic doctrine of life which would account for this constancy amid religious experiences that are in other ways so strikingly different? If so, would Royce then have identified the creed that has always been and always will be "Christian"?

Referring to any loyal person, whether consciously related to Christianity or not, Royce had proclaimed in his introduction:

> whoever has learned what it is to "do the will" of the loyal spirit has a right to endeavor to "know the doctrine" which shall teach whether, and in what sense, the Spirit, the Community, and the process of salvation are genuine realities, transcending any of their human embodiments. (1:xxxix)

Royce looked into all ages to examine the experiences of any person doing the will of the loyal spirit. In this way, he tried to find one identical doctrine which would continuously guide all such experiences and make them meaningful in any age. His search became more difficult when the historical divisions in culture, education, and religion heightened the already vast differences of diverse time-worlds. For example, the historically divided Christian churches had introduced varying traditions, dogmas, laws, and rites which had further differentiated the religious experiences of Christians.[3]

As Royce searched amid the many past, present, and foreseeable "historical" embodiments of evolving Christianity in order to find its enduring self-identifying core, he referred to his problem as that of "the historical and the essential" (2:329-379). Christianity's ongoing journey through time presented a rich panorama for his scanning: the life of the early Pauline communities; later developments in code, creed, and cult; and those subsequent dogma-formulations, divisions, and decisions which were often motivated more by church politics than by mission to the world. By contrast with the ages of faith, twentieth-century people had major needs and interests that no longer centered on religious institutions and dogmas. Projecting this trend, Royce looked ahead to a probably de-Christianized future. In it he expected that most of the so-called Christian structures of his day would be discarded. This estimate of the future led him to develop his basic question as follows.

Suppose that the future civilization prides itself much less on "being Christian" and much more on meeting humankind's deep needs for worldwide justice and peace and thus on unifying the entire human community. Suppose, too, that the civilization of the future largely succeeds in this mission while our present civilization, still partly church-related, has largely failed to so unify humankind. Then the question arises: "Where is the spirit of early Christianity present more genuinely?" Is it in today's denominations which claim to possess the "fullness" of the Christian life even while their hardening divisions prevent them from communicating that justice and peace which would unify the human race? Or is this spirit present more genuinely in tomorrow's more secularized, less churchy civilization which succeeds more effectively in unifying the human community through its worldwide structures for justice and peace? Putting the question that way made the shoe fit more tightly (2:369–373). From a foreseeable path of human development he had reformulated the problem of Christianity in a telling and poignant way.

Through time's educative process, Royce's personal interpretation of the relation between religion and science underwent development. Back in 1875, as we saw, he became acutely aware of the conflict between his preacher's version of Christianity and his teacher's science of evolution. Later, he discovered a deep harmony between science and religion.[4] Still later, he came in his final years to the more profound discovery that science serves as a positive instructor which disciplines ethico-religious persons to a still more authentically religious response. So instead of launching the *Problem* from a supposed opposition between religion and science or even from the premise of their consistent co-existence, by 1912 he had discerned that the natural sciences were in their deepest dynamism "one of the principal organs of religion" (2:431).[5] In his opinion, the natural sciences more successfully evoked human needs and interests and more effectively schooled people to build the human community than did the visible institutions of religion.

Similarly, through the evolution of culture, Royce found that the "social arts" functioned as another "organ of religion." Through their intrinsic freedom and inventiveness, the social arts discovered ways to render dialogue humane and to insist on civility in rational discourse between persons of vastly different viewpoints. It is significant that Royce, with the aid of some suggestions from Peirce, fashioned this interpretation of the sciences and the social arts well in advance of the generally similar view of a later Teilhard de Chardin.[6] The expanding outreach of interpretation, however, did not allow Royce's mind to rest with the evolution of humankind or of its sciences and arts. As a philosopher, he had to investigate the entire process of evolution to detect whether its fundamental plan of action resembled that of Christianity's essential creed.

So Royce eventually broadened the scope of his interpretive pondering to embrace the entire universe of all finite evolving "selves" in community, whether these selves were atomic, organic, simply conscious, or minded.[7] He pondered how so many diverse selves were developing in such widely ranging kinds of communities. In this way he approached all the distinctively mental processes occurring in the entire evolving spatio-temporal universe. By such gradation in tracing likenesses and unlikenesses, he broke through to the climactic stage of his comparisons.

No longer did he inquire about a one-dimensional fit between the evolution of humankind and that of the universe. Looking above, below, and beyond human beings, he inquired whether a multidimensional fit were likely among all the evolving communities of non-human beings (whether minded or not) and the evolving cosmos. From this latter perspective he further asked whether one basic plan of action united and gave direction to all the world's processes. He asked this even while facing up to all the changing events, pluralisms, and chance diversities at work both within physical evolution and, especially, within the evolution of all communities of minded beings (actual and possible, human and non-human). He particularly inquired whether any plan governing actual human communities also governed the possible communities of extraterrestrial minded beings.

TESTING THE TRUTH OF THE PHILOSOPHY OF THE CHRISTIAN RELIGION

Having embraced the entire evolving universe of mind and matter, Royce next faced the critical question of testing the truth of his interpretation. This led him into the second and concluding effort in his clarification of the problem of Christianity.[8] Earlier he had promised that eventually he would test the truth of his two working assumptions: that a cosmic educational process underlies world history and that this schooling of the universal community is guided by a great interpreter.[9] Now was the time to put these assumptions to the full test. When focused more sharply, his hypotheses stated that the ethico-religious education of all finite minded beings (human and non-human) was gradually leading them to a clearer consciousness of the three, most fundamental, saving ideas (the trio of "Christian" ideas) and thus to a fuller participation in the Beloved Community (the Kingdom of God, in Christian terms). By his redeeming presence, the great Interpreter of the universe (the Spirit of Jesus, in Christian terms) was artfully guiding all this schooling through highly diversified means. The question then arose whether evidence was on hand to confirm such hypotheses. Were the evolving communities of finite selves handing on one doctrine of wisdom which was consistent with the evolution of life and of human mind in the universe? Such was the meaning of Royce's problem of Christianity when transposed into its final formulation.

Being a mature philosopher by late 1912, however, he no longer sought, in his dealing with this problem, *the kind of* demonstrative proofs or "solutions" which he had employed in his youth and middle age. Without providing a "solution" to the problem of Christianity, he would clarify it (1:xxiii). And to those problematic issues endemic to Christianity—its Christologies, dogma in general, and the relations between the true interests of religion and philosophy—he would bring a great simplification. Hence, he would not attempt to coerce his audience's minds by syllogistically arranged demonstrations. Rather, he would invite them to ponder the assembly of evidences, clues, and signs that he presented to them. To the new kind of main interpretive evidence offered in his lecture "The World of Interpretation" these added signs would not "prove" but simply *illuminate* his hypothesis (2:393).

Royce first applied his concluding truth-test to the one principle that undergirds his whole philosophy (2:313). Lecture 14, "The Doctrine of Signs," is the *Problem's* most important chapter from the criteriological viewpoint. In it Royce described three basic attitudes of the human will towards the universe—the will to live, denial of the will to live, and the will to stand in loving loyalty to the entire universe. Of these three fundamental attitudes of will, which is right and true? He brought to light the ultimately self-destructive character of the first two attitudes. This let him show that only the third attitude of will—that absolute voluntarism of universal loyalty—can be correct and true. Any theory of practice lacking this attitude has to be tainted. "Unless this principle [of the converted will's loyal commitment to the universal community] itself holds true, there is no real life or real world in which we can find success" (2:314).

Building upon this third attitude of will, Royce saw his next task to be the verification of his overall hypothesis: that the world is a Community of Interpretation to which we should be loyally dedicated. Set in close paraphrase, his truth-seeking question first asked theoretically: Is it true that the real world is a universal community of interpretation and that it is guided by a great interpreter who knows the goal of the universe and who schools all finite selves towards fuller unity in community? The Athenian Christian of Royce's fiction (2:344-369)—that symbol of the contemporary educated person—was called upon to identify the most essential faith of his religious life. Using interpretive comparisons and contrasts of his former and present existences to sift the historical accretions away from Christianity's essential core, the imagined Athenian finally professes his basic creed this way: "the divine redeeming spirit that saves man dwells in the Church" (2:363). In like manner, the temporal process, that is taking place throughout the entire developing universe, calls forth a similar kind of faith from minded beings everywhere—namely, that a divine Spirit of interpretation is present in the universe, guiding its processes, saving alienated selves by purifying minds, and leading all towards a more genuine community.

What evidences pointed to the *truth* of this universal faith? Principally, Royce pointed out the *strict analogy* between the unavoidable postulate that the mind of one's neighbor is real and the belief that the world is a real Community of Interpretation which alone gives ultimate meaning to one's life (2:314–315, 322–325). Furthermore, Royce pointed to that highly persuasive *fittingness of the signs* offered by the natural world, by the human mind, and by the logic of science—a fittingness C. S. Peirce had highlighted in his impressive article "A Neglected Argument for the Reality of God" (2:395).[10]

Calling his audience to ponder the clues, Royce sketched Peirce's argument more fully (2:406–418) than does the following précis. In the history of science, especially since Galileo, the rate at which scientific geniuses have invented their seemingly unlikely, yet highly successful hypotheses about nature is too close-packed, connected, and orderly to be brought about by *mere* chance. Such successful serial discovery of fruitful scientific hypotheses, at a rate beyond mathematical probability, suggests that human minds have been "attuned to nature." This further suggests some attuner of human minds. In addition to the mechanisms of natural selection employed for biological survival, this nonbiological attuning and its attuner are required to make sense of the world's evolution.

Thereupon, Royce further confirmed this evidence by pointing to the work of his colleague, L. J. Henderson (2:420, n. 1). For according to Henderson's *The Fitness of the Environment,* biological evidence strongly points to the thesis that non-organic elements and structures throughout physical nature reveal traits that are *more,* rather than less, *suited* to become an environment for living organisms. This kind of preadaptation shows a "biocentricity" which, as Royce put it, "illustrates the teleology of a spiritual process" (2:420). Something deeper than biology, deeper, too, than mere vitalism shines forth from this evidence. Operatively embodied in this biocentricity is an appreciation for life itself and for the ordering of materials towards the betterment of life.[11] Such valuation and intention manifest the goal-seeking that is distinctive of a minded (or spiritual) being.

The evidences from Peirce and Henderson made it clear that both the natural world and mental life possess inbuilt dynamisms that give signs of preferring life (rather than non-life) and that seek values (rather than operate only by chance). But these significant dynamisms are so arranged that from them minded beings will form the interpretation that the world is developing according to a coherent universal plan and is thus manifesting an immanent total meaning. For if minds are not attuned to make this interpretation, why can they interpret all reality *only* in a valuational and goal-seeking way? (Even in apparent denials of this, in the explicit claims that reality is valueless or absurd, the actual denial seeks value and a goal, thus reinstating this interpretation.) Hence, these preadapted structures in minds and in infra-organic matter are signs that something in the universe has spiritual knowledge of its overall direction and is effectively drawing all finite selves in that direction.

The late Royce here displayed much more realism of a moderate kind than is usually associated with a self-professed idealist. He was not attempting to reassemble those crude eighteenth-century teleologies which crumpled under Kant's critique and under Darwin's mechanisms for natural selection. Instead, as the locus of his own refined kind of teleology, Royce focused on the inner ordination of human minds towards real signs to be known in nature.[12] He then interpreted this ordination within human minds as itself the distinctive sign of an orderer or of an immanent divine guide. This great interpreter directs all mental and physical processes in the universe somewhat as a conductor directs his full orchestra. However, rather than employing some previous composer's fully prearranged score with all its details pre-fixed in advance, this unique director is also composing and evoking the ever new melody being presently created by his orchestral community. In their conjoint creation of this melody, both director and his players are opening paths and pilgrimaging into an open future. Guiding them are the basic themes created by this composer-director while the variation of these themes arises from his evocation and his member's spontaneity and freedom.

If Royce's theoretical "doctrine of the universe" thus tests out true, how does one practically live truly in accord with this doctrine? We can summarize Royce's practical recommendations in response to the generalization of his theory of interpretation into his "doctrine of Signs" if we imagine him giving to the genuinely loyal the following directives concerning our visible, but now jurisdictionally divided, Christian institutions (2: 421-432). First, situate these institutional structures and forms within the many millennia of physical and mental evolution. Next, recognize factually that ever more accelerating rates of change are permeating our whole evolving universe. Then, within such a setting, focus on some individual whose main hope is that one, certain, visible form of the Christian Church will triumph. Lastly, let his hope occasion a critical question in yourself: "Is this individual out of harmony with the central hope of the world's entire process, the coming of the Great Community of all human beings of good will?" Royce's answer would be a strong "yes.".

Becoming more critically practical for his largely Christian audience, Royce brought his lecture series at Oxford to a close by shifting from the question just mentioned to a series of four imperatives (2:428-431). First,

"Simplify your Christology!" (For historically, you have sown divisions in the Church by extending your Christology beyond the Pauline faith-based perception of Christ as the divine redeeming Spirit in the community.) Second, "Give up your unrefined hopes for the human and visible triumph of your particular form of the Christian church!" (Instead, prefer to emphasize the hope and practical promotion of the coming of the Great Community.) Third, "Hold fast to the Pauline faith!" (The redeeming Spirit is in your midst unifying.) Fourth, "As your criterion for every decision, use the query: Does this help towards the coming of the universal community?"

Clearly, he proposed these as four rules of thumb. He knew the careful nuancing each of them requires when one encounters deep-rooted evils and backward communities. Yet these personal directives form his constructive practical response to the problem of Christianity. His philosophy of the Christian religion pivoted upon that conjugate pair of the "Christian doctrine of life" and his "doctrine of the universe." Thus its pragmatic truth-test lies in a loyalty genuine enough to fulfill the four imperatives and in this way to contribute to the further realization of the Beloved Community.

The present chapter has offered a brief preview of Royce's main movements in the *Problem*. Having adopted a Peirce-like pondering as his own method, Royce united his "effort to read the lesson of history with an effort to estimate, upon a reasonable basis, the philosophy of the Christian religion" (1:45). He tried to decipher the meaning of temporal process in the evolution not only of Christian and non-Christian communities of the loyal but also of all humankind, of the sciences and social arts, and even of the entire cosmos of nature and of all minded beings. Upon this reasonable basis of reality considered as a process of sign-sending, sign-interpreting, and sign-receiving, he constructed an estimate of the truth of his philosophy of the Christian religion. For this he devised an elaborate truth-test which he brought to completion only in his three final lectures. He there assembled the negative argument of a performative contradiction with several clues to support his basic metaphysical thesis that the universe is a community of interpretation with its own interpreter. This thesis formed his theoretical response to the problem of Christianity. Yet since a bearing on right action is needed to complete the truth-test of his pragmatism, he issued four directives to serve together in daily life as practical guides for determining (through the consistency of one's own modes of action) which kind of estimate Royce's philosophy of the Christian religion deserves.

PART THREE

Royce Develops His Mature Method

11. Introduction to Royce's Method

A careful reader of the mature Royce is impressed by the emphases he placed on the formal consistency of ideas and on true doctrine. Nevertheless, Royce set even higher store on a thinker's winning reflective awareness both of the values he had selected or relinquished and on the ongoing steps he was taking to realize his chosen purposes. To the members of his 1913–1914 Seminar on "Various Types of Scientific Method" he witnessed this mature setting of priorities, "Logic stands for becoming conscious of the procedure and not of premises."[1] The mature Royce put top priority on reflectively controlled procedure. During 1912, through a radical shift in his method of philosophizing, he offered rich gifts to philosophers. For these reasons, I consider a careful examination of his mature method the most important part of the present work.

Part three focuses directly on the overall and subordinate methods which Royce devised and employed when he explored his problem of Christianity and clarified its doctrine of life. This focus is on *how* Royce formulated his problem of Christianity and especially on *how* he investigated it. Part three, then, is not concerned either with his Methodology (his applied logic of 1910) or with his methods of exposition and rhetoric.[2] Nor is it concerned, except incidentally, with his usage of a fascinating array of philosophical techniques.[3] Rather, we will focus positively on his unique *way* in 1912. He had his way of selecting the "social form of [religious] experience" (1:xv) as his main topic then. He had his way of discovering that this social form of religious experience was structured and integrated by certain "leading and essential ideas" that were unified under "the somewhat more general idea of 'Saving Grace'" (1:xxxvi). He had his way of attending so simply to the historical processes within human communal religious experience that he could avoid theology and dogma and postpone metaphysics. In this way he found the basic psychological motives in people's deep need for ultimate sense (or salvation).

After the present introductory chapter, chapters 12 and 13 will examine how he used his three "leading and essential ideas" to so illuminate people's basic psychological motives that he could estimate the value of the ethical and religious motives that arise from these basic ones. Then chapter 14 will explore how he came to view Reality as the universal Community of Interpretation and how he employed the resultant transformed metaphysics as his theoretical and practical truth-test of the Christian doctrine of life. These three chapters will show that Royce had to develop two specialized and widely different methods: his empirico-historical and his metaphysical methods (1:45). The problem then becomes how did Peirce's example and suggestions provide Royce with a path to unify these two specialized methods. Finally, in chapter 15, we will observe how Royce broke through to one underlying general method of interpretive musement which provided a pervasive unity of method to his entire endeavor in the *Problem*. From this list of chapter topics, then, the reader can detect the series of goals that guided Royce through his two main endeavors in the *Problem*.

Before launching into his empirico-historical method, however, and in order to prepare the way for a just estimate of Royce's contribution to philosophical method, we need a context and perspective. The present chapter, therefore has as its purposes: to view his philosophical method as a process of self-limitation (according to "negativity in operation"); to highlight Royce's fundamental decision, critical for his mature method, to start his philosophy of religion by standing in loyal love of the universe; and to compare and contrast this method with those of his contemporaries, William James and John Dewey.

ROYCE'S METHOD: A SERIES OF SELF LIMITATIONS

One of Royce's favorite sayings was "In limitation alone can mastery be displayed" (*RLE,* 201).[4] Without ceasing to emphasize the positive, he saw the indispensable role which negation and exclusion play in life and in valuation since "all the preciousness of life depends upon it [limitation]" (*RLE,* 199). How, then, did the power of negativity—of self-limitation and restraint—affect Royce's mature person, his interpretive musement generally, and its zeroing in on the *Problem*'s precise target?

Few philosophers of religion have striven as much as Royce to become explicitly aware of how one's previous basic choices limit his approach to philosophy and of how further self-limitation plays a subsequent role within that philosophy (1:15). Few, too, have surpassed the mature Royce in recognizing how the successive adoption of limits required him to become more reserved, tentative, and dependent on the community's validation. He acknowledged that his own philosophical habits, metaphysical interests, and chosen idealistic viewpoint inevitably limited him from making that kind of contribution to the philosophy of religion which other types of philosophers or thinkers might make (1:4). As a result he considered his *Problem* to be one small contribution to merely one department within the philosophy of religion; and he saw his work on Christianity as calling for completion, correction, and confirmation by professional theologians, church historians, and specialists in comparative religion (1:5-6).

In general, *negativität* permeates interpretive musement. In late 1915 Royce tried to identify the main drive behind his working out of his mature doctrine of life, truth, and reality. He described this drive as "a fondness for defining, for articulating, and for expounding the perfectly real, concrete, and literal life of what we idealists call the 'spirit'."[5] In that season, however, he had just drafted or was still drafting his "Monotheism" article.[6] In it he stressed the Oriental apophatic (reticent) tradition as a counterbalance to the West's kataphatic (assertive) traditions about God— who is essential Form for the Greeks and ethical Will for the Hebrews. The apophatic tradition emphasizes the needed presence of an awareness of what can*not* be said, defined, or otherwise articulated in our knowledge of God. Divine life and even human life are realities too rich for logic to grasp fully. To reach such realities we need both logic and spirit, even though neither logic nor spirit can express life fully. This is why both the speakable and unspeakable awarenesses (the kataphatic and the apophatic) complement each other in Royce's interpretive musement.

As examples: discernment happens; someone detects the Deliverer; someone experiences with a fright or a thrill the difference between life without a genuine community or within one. Knowing these realities with "close personal touch," Royce stood as a witness, pointing to them; but he would not and could not define the unspeakable aspect of these presences. In his interpretive musement, he was conscious of operating in a community of *finite* knowers. This meant he had a fringe awareness of *not*-knowing the way the all-knowing Community knows. Negativity at work in interpretive musement requires an interpreter to regard his achieved interpretation as *not* the final answer and spurs him forward to seek a still richer and more comprehensive interpretation. Negativity imposes self-limitation on the human knower, keeps him from claiming to have *the* answer (even when it is confirmed by the community and its spirit). It requires him to confess his dependence on these if he is to be rescued from his next error. Because interpretive musement has the community as its matrix, it negates any centering on oneself as more important than the community. Hence, too, negativity leads to the climactic act of atonement in which the suffering servant limits his life and its possibilities so that the straying of disloyal agents may be countered effectively and both straying and loyal selves be raised to a yet higher life. These are a few ways, then, in which truth and the freedom which truth generates are achievable only through negation.

Specifically, how did the negativity of self-limitation function in identifying Royce's precise target for the *Problem?* Since his high school days he had studied philosophy of religion. In his final decade he passed by philosophies of other particular religions to focus upon Christianity. On this topic he explicitly spoke of his enterprise's "chosen limitation; not undertaking to contribute directly to religion itself but only to an understanding of some of the problems which religious creeds suggest" (1:15). Passing by the problems of Christianity's code and cult, he focused on its creed. Within the creed, he passed by its fullness of "overbeliefs" in order to focus on its most essential ideas. Within these essential ideas of the creed, he restricted himself to their "human side"—that is, to the universal human needs and interests which give rise to these ideas, to the ideal values following from these ideas, and to the human destiny intended by them. In this way he chose not to attend to the "divine side"—that is, to a study of how God may be revealing himself (and thus engendering and increasing either Christian or some other Faith that responds to divine initiatives towards the human family), of how Faith-filled theology researches these initiatives, and of how it generates various systematizations of Christian or other revealed Faiths.

Viewing Christianity's most essential creedal ideas from the human side, Royce further narrowed his research by limiting himself precisely to studying these ideas' consistency with each other, with human nature, with civilization, and with destiny. Since for four years he had used his "individual approach" to study Christianity,[7] in 1912 he further restricted his study by taking only a "social approach" to the Christian reality. Just one aspect of Christianity, then, became his carefully delimited target: namely, the consistent community of fundamental ideas insofar as these unite finite selves into a living whole of life and call these selves to promote the coming of the Great Community. Thus his precise concern was a community of ideas that intended a community of persons.

In brief, Royce chose a social and teleological approach to the most vital Christian ideas. He felt that such a method of exclusion, such a negation of possible courses of action, was the only pathway to a responsible freedom when investigating further into the philosophy of the Christian religion. Yet, as we saw, the precision and narrowness of this chosen topic made him invite the complementary contributions which other philosophers and scholars could make to the study of the Christian religion, "man's most impressive vision of salvation, and his principal glimpse of the homeland of the spirit" (1:5-6, 11).

THE BASIC CHOICE THAT DETERMINED ROYCE'S METHOD

We saw that in pure logic Royce's choice of the O-relation determined the remainder of his System Σ. In philosophy of religion, Royce's choice to stand in radical love and loyalty towards the universe determined every subsequent step in his method as genuine or not, as basically right or not.

For Royce the most radical practical question was: Which fundamental orientation should one take towards the universe? He identified three irreducible attitudes of will towards the world: simply assert oneself, simply deny oneself, or so gift oneself in loyal love of a genuine community that one develops both the universe and oneself (2:293–295, 309–310). He justified his choice of the third attitude by advancing negative reasons and positive experience.

If one chooses to desire and assert oneself above all, he expresses "the natural solipsism of the individual will" (2:301). However, when this self-asserter encounters an assembly of similar self-asserters, his resentment and hostility towards his fellows and their society must grow (2:302). The primarily self-assertive attitude, then, counters each human person's irrepressible interest in the ultimate harmony of selves. But this interest unavoidably reinstates itself whenever anyone tries sincerely to prefer the ultimate disharmony of selves, as Royce's "moral insight" of 1885 had shown. Thus, if one follows out one's bare vital impulse of self-assertion, eventually one will come to the painful recognition that such a life inescapably vexes oneself and is vain.

Reacting out of fear of such a life, one can choose the opposite extreme: to withdraw from the world as a chaotic struggle of wills and by denying any desire, to seek resignation. This second basic attitude of will, which Royce found exemplified in early Southern Buddhists (2:306), also follows mere vital impulse, this time redirected by reaction. It, too, is self-defeating since it finds no goodness in desire or in the will to live or in creativity. If consistent, it would negate even the desire to withdraw. This attitude certainly frustrates the irrepressible interest in an ultimate harmony of selves. How, then, can this deadlock of merely individualistic impulse be broken?

The human self needs the transforming gift of a loving loyalty which redirects the will to dedicate itself to the service of a genuine community and thus to the universal community. As a third irreducible attitude of will, this genuine loyalty supposes that one believes he is involved in a world of interpretation, and that between himself and it a mutually beneficial life-process goes on which develops the community and himself, at least ethically. If one tries to deny that such loyalty is the only viable radical orientation towards the universe, he performatively asserts that his denial is a more loyal way of developing the world and himself. Therefore, Royce held this third attitude to be the only right one towards the world. Hence, it is the only basic attitude that can generate a philosophy that is genuine and true (2:293; 102–103).

Only with this fundamental choice to stand in loyal love of all reality (i.e., the universal community) can interpretive musement take place in any valid way. Interpretations arising from a self-asserter or a self-denier will be misinterpretations. The direction, power, and spirit of Royce's third basic attitude of will determines whatever philosophy of religion is done in the *Problem* and whether each intent and procedure in the *Problem* is genuine or not (2:293-294). For example, this attitude of genuine loyalty exposes the "closed" minds in both the apologist defender and the hostile impugner of Christianity. It also casts its philosophical vote for the researcher who is open to Christianity's problematic nature and who, like a witness, points to its undeniable and significant presence (1:6-13).

COMPARISON AND CONTRAST OF THE METHODS OF ROYCE, JAMES, AND DEWEY

The mature Royce's experience, background, and skills for a philosophical investigation of the Christian religion were far above the ordinary — even superior, as I see it, to the same three factors that James and Dewey brought to their philosophies of religion. Royce's forty-year "apprenticeship" in philosophy of religion served him well. His decade-long experience in logical research and in chairing his seminar in scientific methods had honed him to discern mastery when method was fittingly in control. Then, too, for his study of the Christian religion he had an uncommonly broad acquaintance with the writings of Ritschl, Loisy, Renan, Strauss, Feuerbach, and Sabatier, along with those of Kant, Hegel, Schopenhauer, and Nietzsche. To prepare for the *Problem,* he had done, as he acknowledged, "much reading of literature,"[8] which included the writings of Weinel, Troeltsch, Matthew Arnold, Master Eckhart, Percy Gardner, and Harnack. His preparatory readings also included the works of such contemporary dogmatic theologians as held that Jesus is God; namely, R. H. MacIntosh, R. C. Moberly, and William Sanday. Most of Royce's philosophical colleagues would not consort for ideas with writers in these latter two groups. Yet knowing his was a new research topic, Royce wanted to reach for greater breadth and depth. So he listened carefully and critically to these theological scholars in his desire to help build bridges between various disciplines. All these experiences trained him to recognize sound disciplined thought on religion and on the Christian reality when he met it.

In this context, then, we can begin a comparison-contrast of Royce's method in the *Problem* with the methods of some of his contemporaries. William James' *Varieties of Religious Experience* preceded the *Problem* by a decade and had at first inspired Royce (1:xiv) while John Dewey's *A*

Common Faith followed the *Problem* by about two decades, without explicitly attending to it.

One recalls that in the *Varieties,* after supplying case histories for most of his first nineteen lectures, James had, in his final twentieth lecture, summed up all the preceding empirical data and supplied a source of deep insights that is still not exhausted. Regarding his method, however, we may attend to a trio of James' moves: how he described his method and practiced it, how his method of "summing up" proceeded, and how he determined his topic.

When examining James' method in the *Varieties,* one might say fairly that, like Marcel's, it consisted in having no reflectively held method except that of simply expressing the insights found through being rigorously in touch with one's deepest feelings. Accurate enough. But such keen intouchness with one's feelings still leaves unfaced the critical question: How to discern whether a certain religious affect is genuine or illusory? James took up neither the "religious paradox" Royce found so fundamental nor any set of tests needed to certify the operation of one's "inner light."

James described his own as a "purely empirical method of demonstration."[9] His case studies are clearly empirical but I find neither pure empiricism nor demonstration. Can a method be purely empirical? Other non-empirical elements are the subconscious self to which James recurs as a psychological fact rather than as a postulate, his hypothesis about "a MORE" to which one's "higher part is conterminous and continuous," and this "MORE" itself with its "farther" as well as its "hither" sides. Perhaps Royce's uneasiness about James' subterranean passages and subliminal forces has some merit (*SRI,* 47–48). Concerning James' "demonstration," he shows (or "demonstrates") that his examples generally seem to converge in support of his formulation of the essence of religious experience — an "essence" Royce in turn builds upon (*SRI,* 12, 27–28, 46–47). But James offers no methodic demonstration if, by that, one refers to an argument by deduction or by performative contradiction or by an extension of criteria to religious experiences that are more than individual and personal because they are also social or playful or quietly peaceful or institutionally organized. It seems, then, that only in a non-ordinary and quite narrow sense may one accept James' description of his "purely empirical method of demonstration."

As mentioned, James' method of "final summing up" sparkles with insights. In Lecture 20 his time-pressed mind breaks through to intuitions and flashes forth his insights in a display as fascinating as a sparkler on the Fourth of July and with a minimum of presentational order. But his "summing up" comes across simply as a shift from a long look at trees to a brief look at the forest. One feels no full fruition of a process of serial criticism and planned coherent expansion and practical concretion, such as marks the close of the *Problem*. James's method in Lecture 20, then, being simple generalization in fidelity to feeling, eschews long-range planning, careful organization, and executive integration.

James acknowledged seeming "so bent on rehabilitating the element of feeling in religion and subordinating its intellectual part."[10] Yet despite this anti-intellectualism, he wanted his philosophy of religion to be reasonable.

This tension in his method arose from his view of intellection, which he thought could know only generalities—those merely pale reflections of life as experienced. Here was that traditional view of knowing, confined to percept and concept, a view that imprisoned James in its tight dyadic framework of just subject and object. Had Peirce's view of triadic intellectual knowing broken in on him, James could have held a close personal intellectual touch with concrete human selves.

In his search into religion, James intentionally stressed feelings. This precluded his raising the question whether some set of creedal ideas might be indispensable for authentic religious experience. It also led him to focus so narrowly on "rapturous" religious experiences that, at the very least, he downplayed the reception of ideas and responsible decisions in religion. For step by step he sharpened his focus on religious experience to include only the "personal religion" of *"individual men in their solitude,"* whose experience is not only "solemn, serious, and tender" but is had "in its acutest possible form" of "rapturousness" or "the enthusiastic temper of espousal."[11]

This publicly untested method of stipulative selection of his target forced James to examine only "those violenter examples" of more bizarre religious experiences. Granted, he personally found religion in church groups conventional, bland, and boring. But from this to universalize the uncriticized assumption that all social religious experience had to lack depth and sincerity was tragic (1:xv–xvi). James was faithful to the spontaneity of his feelings but it led him to tolerate without test a truncated specimen of religious experience. Understandably, then, Royce appraised James's disregard of communal religious experience as "a profound and a momentous error in the whole religious philosophy of our greatest American master in the study of the psychology of religious experience" (1:xvi).

Turning from the *Varieties* to the *Problem,* one learns by contrast that Royce used method purposefully and reflectively from start to finish. Sensitively he adjusted in interpretive musement to different materials and contexts, by devising subordinate methods, by ordering tasks, by nuancing procedures step by step, and by raising all these moves to the light so that public criticism might be solicited. In sum, Royce lived out and expressed his "deliberate plan of the whole book" of which the result had to be that some portions became "technically metaphysical" while others became empirical or ethical or directly practical as called for (1:xiv).

John Dewey's *A Common Faith,* his only published work in the philosophy of religion, is more reflective and organized than is that of James in the *Varieties,* but it pales when compared to that of Dewey's own *Logic.*[12] There Dewey's keen fidelity to the unique quality of an experience and his living rigor in analyzing the way logical forms emerge from within a problem-solving experience are breathtaking and life-giving.

In *A Common Faith* Dewey shows that he has not been working the pertinent materials for forty years. He often relies on the empirical work of others, such as James. He quickly assumes general directions either without referring to the bases which might warrant his assertions or without inviting the responsible dissent of others. For instance, so much does Dewey emphasize the differences between the religions of the human race that he persuades the unwary to believe that "any common element that can be extracted" from these religions must be factually meaningless.[13] Neither in *A Common Faith* nor elsewhere, to my knowledge, did Dewey bother to test whether or not the common elements which Royce extracted—those ideas of community, moral burden, and gracious atonement—were factually meaningless.

The method Dewey evidenced in the assertive dogmatism of *A Common Faith* shows far less control and mastery than Dewey displayed so outstandingly in his carefully disciplined handling of empirical materials in his *Logic.* Dewey did not publicly examine reports of experiential encounters with a Holy Other. Yet these reports were backed up by such contemporary scholars as Rudolph Otto, by the classic mystics, and by the present and past leaders of various communities of faith through their centuries-long concurrence of judgment on this point—through the *"consensus fratrum et patrum,"* as Royce put it. Dewey's method in *A Common Faith,* then, is far less articulately grasped and clearly communicated to his audience, far less tentative, heuristic, and humble than is Royce's method in the *Problem.*

Our comparison-contrast of Royce's method with that of Dewey and James in the philosophy of religion has, therefore, let us see the significance of Royce's mature method. In 1912 he was on the cutting edge in the discovery of a new method. He was not yet caught, as some contemporary methodologists seem to be, in long habits of adopting the "right" approaches. The contributions within Royce's method that make it worth examining include his interpretive pondering (as a third irreducible kind of knowing), his situating loyalty at the heart of his method and establishing loyalty to a genuine community as his norm for sound interpretation — something many individualistically minded thinkers omit — and his emphasis both on teleology and on a perspective that is ever greater and broader as requisites for wisdom.

12. Empirico-Historical Method: First Stage

How did Royce come to select his three fundamental Christian ideas?[1] Assuming his choice was rational and responsible, I infer that he made it: 1) from a particular frame of mind; 2) on the basis of values found within the ideas he chose; and 3) with a foresight of the connections and consequences of his choice as a test of its reasonableness. These three dimensions of his choice outline our way of responding to the main question.

ROYCE'S PARTICULAR FRAME OF MIND FOR MEETING AND SELECTING THE THREE CHRISTIAN IDEAS

Royce knew that he could not succeed in winning a *fitting* grasp of problematic Christianity unless he selected its most central ideas *methodically* (1:34). He also realized that this selection would determine and guide his whole study (1:38; 2:335). Nevertheless, he balanced his statements about "selecting" these ideas with an equal insistence on "receiving" them (1:36; 2:334-336). Encountered in experiences of genuine loyalty, these ideas were neither abstractions nor inventions. As Royce put it:

> Such Christian ideas as I have tried to interpret, I certainly did not invent. They found me. I did not devise them. . . . They come to us from human life, from the life both of the Christian Church itself, and of those communities, secular or religious, which the noblest forms of loyalty have informed, and have redeemed, precisely insofar as men have yet learned to live the life of the universal brotherhood. For us the metaphysical meaning of these ideas has occupied, in our discussion, the second place. (2:335-336)

One's frame of mind is heavily influenced by one's consistent set of goals and the example of outstanding persons. Three goals and three personal examples gave an orientation to Royce's mind for meeting and selecting his most essential ideas.

His Series of Three Integrated Goals

In the *Problem* three interrelated goals became explicit guides of his work. One overall goal was "to help others to share in the gifts of the spirit" or "for the strengthening of hearts" (1:5, xiv). These formulas crystallized his life's aim of promoting the Great Community by developing "himself and his brethren" integrally. Two obstacles blocked his path to this goal. Both the apologists and the critics of Christianity "almost wholly misunderstood" its central ideas, despite their familiarity with them (1:44–45).[2] They neither discerned things of the spirit nor grasped the doctrine of the "two levels" (of the individual and of the community). Hence they missed genuine insight into these ideas.

As Royce saw it, they viewed intersubjective knowing simply in a subject-object way, which omitted the community's influence upon such knowing (1:xxix). They needed to reflect adequately on the three fundamental ideas central to *any* genuine community—the ideas of the saving community, of the lost state of the individual, and of the process of atonement through grace (1:xxxvi). For this reflection, they needed to become aware that they were actually using a triadic pattern in their intersubjective knowing rather than a simple subject-object pattern. Prior to this, however, they needed to recognize that both reality and consciousness have two levels—individual and community. This recognition, if personalized, would transform their basic perspective on life. Royce was inviting them to this transformation. His first goal of mutually sharing the gifts of the spirit, then, involved no small challenge.

Royce's second goal was to sift Christianity's most vital and most essential ideas from its less essential and historically contingent ideas (1:20–21). Carrying out this discernment challenged Royce. His 1912 apoplexy limited him physically yet his groundbreaking readings of theologians and philosophers of religion excited him to engage them on their basic philosophical options. Meanwhile, his daily deepening insight into Peirce's thought and method both made his mind more free and resilient even while it summoned him to so adapt Peirce's triads to these new materials that a quantum-leap in interpreting the Christian reality might be created (1:xxix). This challenging intellectual adventure excited a "trembling hope" for great results (1:5–6).

Royce's third significant goal in the *Problem* was to search for the social form of the creedal ideas most essential for communal religious consciousness (1:xv). If he succeeded in finding this treasure, he would have discovered Christianity's most essential idea—his second goal. And by such a fitting application of the principles of his philosophy of religion, he certainly would have engaged in a mutual sharing of the gifts of the spirit and thus strengthened hearts—his first and overall goal.

When Royce researched the individual form of Christian consciousness in 1909,[3] his "individual approach" had uncovered three natural factors vital to Christianity: the divine Father-child relation, the sense of each person's infinite dignity based on God's creative love for each, and the individual Christian's personal commitment to the Lord and his message.[4] Although the Christian life essentially requires of each Christian some acceptance of traditional teaching and some kind of mystical response to God, Royce soon found that both of these descriptions failed to convey *adequately* the mysterious life of an entire belief-practicing Christian community. By 1912, then, he had shifted his interest to the master's teachings about the Kingdom and had adopted as his precise goal that inmost structure of the shared experience which the Christian people have as a community of practical faith.[5]

Shared religious experience, however, can grow stale and fail to save as the history of religions showed in its display case of once-flourishing, now defunct, religions (1:385-394). For example, the shared religious life of the Greeks, Aztecs, or Incas had somehow lost contact with their devotees' ineradicable religious needs and interests. These casualties confronted Royce with two research tasks: to identify humankind's most basic taproot of religion (underneath any religious movements or fads), and to probe whether only one human resource effectively and unceasingly satisfies this taproot—and if so, to identify this resource. Conscious of the ever accelerating pace of change permeating the human race, Royce felt the urgency of this double task of identification.

Royce investigated his precise target: people's fundamental ethico-religious needs which express themselves in the three central ideas of Christianity. He discovered that in their social form these ideas were just as irremovable from human nature as were each person's basic ethico-religious needs (1:397). In his words:

> Whatever creed or institution or practice may lose its hold on the modern mind, the Christian doctrine of life is the expression of universal human needs. . . . No progress . . . can remove from the human mind and the human heart these needs, and the ideas that alone can satisfy them. (1:396-397)

These basic religious needs and the Christian ideas were bonded to each other and irremovable. Yet Royce saw more here, as his "alone" shows. He discovered that since the human self's basic need of salvation expresses itself in the idea of "saving grace" *and* that idea's three necessarily implied ideas, no other idea which excluded the Christian doctrine of life could satisfy the human need of salvation. Hence, *only* this set of ideas could meet the requirements of humankind's basic ethico-religious needs. So, in his experience of the fact and necessity found in this pair-relation between these needs and the Christian ideas, Royce discovered the empirical and logical taproot for Part One of the *Problem.*

Thereupon, Royce made explicit the politico-social and theological corollaries of his momentous assertion. He added that "the very life of every social order depends for its worth and for its survival" upon the satisfaction of these universal human needs (1:396-397). Unless these needs are continuously satisfied by the ideas which comprise the Christian doctrine of life, people will lack an enduring basis for progress in industrial arts, for responsible economic and demographic growth, for building communities and maintaining civilization, and, in brief, for supporting the entire forward-and-upward direction of the human evolutionary process.

Further still, unless God fittingly relates to these irremovable needs and ideas, he cannot effectively communicate with human beings.[6] Indeed, when focusing on "the human side" of this communication process, if human nature lacked its inborn sensitivity for the divine message, God could not insure that a faithful tradition would keep mediating to successive generations any communication through which he might choose to teach and guide the evolving human race (1:26-27).

In sum, the social form of religious consciousness which Royce sought could lie only in the set of most essential religious ideas. He would select only that set of ideas which expressed people's most basic religious needs insofar as these latter functioned through human nature's radical need and inborn sensitivity for the divine message. Only such a unity of ideas could be enduringly reliable. Certainly, all creedal formulas, all systems of philosophy of religion, of metaphysics, and of theology, and all human institutions had to be consistent with, and be judged by, this set of ideas. Furthermore, whatever is essentially made up of matter, energy, and time had to be shot through with the flux of change. Hence, from the human side, what would be *most* vital in Christianity would be its most essential ideas. Only in the doctrine of Christianity's most essential ideas could Royce find that inmost unchangeable meaning of genuine community, of "life in the unity of the spirit." Only in this message would he find that meaning which keeps reinstating its true absolute direction into humankind's future evolution—so chance-ridden and tragic yet resilient and hope-filled (1:xix).

Royce's frame of mind for selecting his central ideas was fashioned by more than his series of goals and his focus on the pair-relation between people's basic religious needs and ideas. He also set up *criteria* to test whether a particular idea or set of ideas was most vital and essential when viewed from the "social approach" to Christianity that he was making in the *Problem*. The two criteria already mentioned may well deserve closer attention. They are the questions whether certain proposed ideas: a) *promote a "fair comprehension"* of Christianity viewed as problematical, and b) are *inseparable from humankind's universal religious needs*.

Royce recognized that every single great idea and most sets of leading ideas provide inadequate bearings upon what is most vital in Christianity (2:275). As inaccurate meanings, they would ultimately mislead his inquiry for they would tend to reductionism or individualism or mere mysticism. Or they would put excessive emphasis on the master or church or humankind or time or eternity. Or they would imply experiential bases or epistemologies or syntheses that were insufficient.

Royce's criterion of "comprehending Christianity fairly" let him see the inadequacy of many candidate ideas. For instance, beyond the unbalancing ideas of egoism or altruism, or of command or counsel lay that more comprehensive idea of community life. Beyond the ideas of human worth (conceived as belonging to a detached individual as such) and of human depravity (conceived as capturing an unhealable and despairing atomic individual) lay the idea of grace (or superhuman powers) saving the detached individual from his moral burden. Beyond the ideas of aggressive free enterprise (based ultimately on an individual's self-interest-and-reliance) and of resigned endurance of aggravated injustices (based on an ultimate absurdity of the universe) lay the idea of loyalty that achieves its supreme act by engaging in a hope-filled saving process of atonement (1:xx).

Second, Royce tested whether that set of ideas which did lead to a fair comprehension of problematic Christianity—namely, his three "Christian" ideas—showed *inseparability* from humankind's ineradicable religious needs. He found that any attempt to deny such a bond only reasserted the vital nexus of idea with need. For instance, people's common desire for an ultimate harmony of selves is irrepressible.[7] But this desire expresses itself irrepressibly in the idea and ideal of an ultimate spiritual community which saves people's lives from being isolated and meaningless. Again, the frequent and inevitable failures of a finite individual or community make inescapable the idea of a person's lost state. One cannot long avoid recognizing that as a self, either isolated or in a merely natural community, one is again and again impotent to know, love, and faithfully serve others the way one should if one is to promote the spiritual community of humankind. Finally, when a person is transformed into a loyal servant of a genuine community, that individual cannot help but see that always to enhance community life means to sacrifice unilateral self-preference. In other words, the loyal servant of the community must undergo suffering which, if entered redemptively, cannot but become life-giving. Here Royce touched a central insight of Christianity's founder, "but if the grain of wheat die, it brings forth much life."[8] In planning the *Problem,* Royce had become clear that such suffering servants counteract the infectious alienating forces within community and build its health through atoning deeds.

In sum, then, he found that these three ideas not only led to a fair comprehension of problematic Christianity but that attempted denials of them only reinstated their inseparable bonds with basic human ethico-religious needs. In this way he demonstrated that these ideas and their unity were essential to the communal religious life of the human race. This set of ideas, then, secured for him that living contact with the essential form of social religious experience which was his precise target in the *Problem.* Having this target, along with his previously mentioned general and specific goals, he took on a specific mindset. This was reinforced by three powerful models.

The Attractive Models of Peirce, Paul, and the Spirit-Interpreter

In 1912, Royce first realized definitively how "our American logician" Charles Sanders Peirce had chosen to concentrate upon "a few fairly simple and obvious ideas," had devoted all his energies to inspecting ever more minutely his original trio of categorical ideas, and had allowed them, amid musement, to "work themselves out" with very exact logic (2:186).[9] At long last Royce realized that all of Peirce's fertile insights and illuminating essays had sprung *from this way* of "pondering" (2:395). With this friend serving as a model, Royce hoped by similar pondering to achieve similar results in his philosophy of the Christian religion. Royce's pathfinding in Peirce's essays had uncovered the latter's basic logical categories of "first," "second," and "third" and his epistemological correlatives in the universal, the individual, and the sign, respectively (2:282-284). Royce generally followed suit by selecting universal community, individual self, and Spirit-Interpreter as his basic metaphysical categories.[10]

Yet, if Royce depended on Peirce (1:xi), he would also be independent (2:282). He would not exactly parallel Peirce's method and three categories. If Peirce worked primarily in logic and theory of knowledge, Royce would pioneer with these ideas in philosophy of religion, using historical interpretation and metaphysics as supports. Royce would transform his triad of ideas into a logical tetrad by admitting "grace" as a most general "leading" idea that was linked with, yet lay beyond his three basic Christian ideas. Still more originally, at the center of his overall strategy, Royce would place the life of loyalty and of spiritual discernment.

If Peirce's musement attracted Royce, the apostle Paul's sensitivity to the Spirit attracted him even more powerfully (1:xv-xxix, 78-98). In

Paul's descriptions of how the early Christian communities were formed, Royce encountered their belief that the Spirit of Christ guided their process of interpreting his message. To keep surviving, then, the Christian community had continuously to pass on from generation to generation a basically coherent account of the founder's doctrine of the Kingdom. Which seminal ideas had the Spirit-Interpreter first developed in the minds of the early Christians (including Paul) for achieving this faithful tradition (1:26–31)? Did not Paul's writings testify that in their interpretation of the Kingdom these early Christians had first been led to an awareness of a saving Community (or Church), a lost state of one detached from such a Community, and a planned process of restoration and elevation? Furthermore, later on, whenever the Christian message had restored life to faltering humankind, had not the vitalizing strength come through these three ideas (1:35)? These ideas were the ones most needed to be faithful to the founder's teaching on the Kingdom and to transmit that message faithfully. Would Royce be wise, then, if he built independently of this original interpretation of Paul and the early Christians?

However, this Spirit-Interpreter himself was the most powerful model attracting the mature Royce.[11] Here we concentrate only on Royce's images and ideas of this Spirit and on the bearing they gave his mind.[12] Royce believed that Paul had identified the risen glorified Lord with the guiding Spirit, or Interpreter, of the Christian community (1:158, 212, 354).

Around 1912, then, what were Royce's dominant images of Christ? Tentative research indicates that, although the mature Royce intermittently relied upon other Scriptural images (such as Vine, Seeker of the Father's Will, and so forth), his leading images of Christ were Interpreter-Spirit who gives life (mediator), master (teacher), and suffering servant (redeeming atoner). Shimmering with its wealth of connotations, this trio of principal images strongly influenced Royce's interpretive musement and played a central role during his selection of the three leading Christian ideas.

In turn, these ideas affected Royce's late interpretations of Christ as the Spirit of the community of the loyal, the Deliverer of lost individuals, and the chief Atoner for disloyal members of his body. Royce's continued reading of the Christian Scriptures also nourished these ideas of Christ, which led him to the themes that "all people are being taught by God" and that "the *Logos* is enlightening every person coming into this world."[13] But, as Royce realized, the *Logos*-Spirit cannot be teaching without communicating certain basic ideas to all finite minds. Royce's quandary was: Which ideas? To him, ideas like canonical Scripture, jurisdiction (including magisterium), and concupiscence seemed tinted with Western culture (2:362–369). Rather, he had to seek transcultural ideas as the basic signs being sent by the Spirit-Interpreter of all human selves however diverse their culture, race, and religion. Royce's sensitivity to the Spirit that works in and beyond Christianity helped guide his selection of the three fundamental ideas.

In summary, the attractive examples of this Spirit-Interpreter, of Paul, and of Peirce dovetailed with Royce's general, specific, and precise goals in the *Problem*. Because of these six influences, his frame of mind in 1912 favored his selection of a particular trio of ideas as most essential to the life of genuine loyalty that undergirds the "Christian" creed. But besides extrinsic factors leading to a sound choice, Royce had solid intrinsic reasons for selecting his three Christian ideas. To these reasons we turn, asking first what the mature Royce meant by an "idea"; then, how he saw the role of ideas in morality and religion; and finally, which reasons led him to select just the three ideas he chose.

ROYCE'S INTRINSIC REASONS FOR SELECTING HIS THREE IDEAS

His Mature Meaning of "Idea"

Throughout his career, Royce made "ideas" the center of his idealistic philosophy. An idea for him was clearly neither a simple universal concept, nor a mere content of consciousness, nor a detached Platonic form. His middle period understanding of ideas had been transmuted by being grafted on his Peircean insight of 1912[14] for by then ideas had become the living centers of minds and of mental signs. They were "wills to interpret" (2:184) or intents to bring unity among other members of a community — whether a community of minds, of ideas, of systems of nature, or of the sciences. An idea "is a conspectus . . . a realm of conscious unity which constitutes the very essence of the life of reason" (2:188).

In his exposition of William James's and Charles Peirce's different meanings of "idea," Royce revealed how sensitive he was to various other usages of this term in contrast to his own distinctive usage (2:180–188).[15] His mature usage is far closer to Peirce's complex meaning of idea than it is to James's usages.[16] Yet into his own usage of "idea," Royce usually inserts both a human ethical heart and a divine Presence. That is, the self thinking the idea must sincerely seek truth and the community's good *and* the idea must mediate the presence of the Interpreter-Spirit, operating as the universal community's Will to Interpret.

When Royce focused on fundamental Christian ideas, he thought of very powerful dynamisms which were alive, essential, and leading (1:xxxvi).

One can approach some grasp of the life, non-deviant aim, and potent influence of such a "leading idea" if one considers the role played by the idea of "man" in other traditions. What would biblical tradition be if man were not "a living image of God"? Or what would Thomistic philosophy be if man were not "a rational animal that is free and social"? The biblical and Thomistic ideas of man are so alive, essential, and leading that a fairly comprehensive view of the Bible and Thomism can be gained simply by trying to convey their ideas of man in as full and integral a way as possible. Similarly, for Royce, "Man is an animal that interprets; and therefore man lives in communities, and depends upon them for insight and for salvation" (2:168). Here he is speaking of an idea that no philosophy or creedal formula can grasp adequately and that no institution can embody fully (1:396). For philosophy, with its necessarily abstract statements, can offer only a *sketch* of an idea, and institutions, given human limits and frailty, have to be partial and defective embodiments of their governing ideas.

It may help clarity to suggest how alive and complex is one leading idea of Royce — that of the Church — by developing his simile that an idea is like a multi-membered personal organism (1:54).[17] The universal aim of an idea is like a person's head, its varying expressions like his face, its precious longings like his heart. Its living memories of the past are a kind of backbone, and its hope of promoting the universal community a kind of outstretching of welcoming arms. Since the idea lives to express itself, it solicits interpretation, like an organism demanding the interaction of breathing. Morally, the idea steadily supports and comforts the faithful subject who adopts it as his own. Yet the idea also calls strongly and sternly to duty, setting up an ideal that challenges one and commands efforts to meet the ideal. The idea's inmost core is the resolute will to serve creatively all minded beings and their community — much like the deepest desire of a person's heart. All these meanings — tendential, affective, cognitive; social, moral, pragmatic — belong to Royce's idea of Church as well as to his other leading ideas.

Hence, because it is so wealthy in meanings, tendencies, and processes, a leading idea first looms up mysteriously, and then, because of the conflicts of its interpreters, it baffles many. Yet the truth of such an idea lies in its inmost bearing through which it is related to all other such ideas and selves. For, as mentioned, each Roycean self and minded being arises from an idea as from its living center. Hence, when Royce volunteered to investigate Christianity's "leading and essential" ideas (1:xxxvi), he became a pilgrim interpreter searching for insight from the redeeming Spirit of the Great Community (2:168).

Ideas, the Enduring and Potent Sources of Morality and Religion

If one examines Christianity "from its human side," what is *most* essential in it? In the *Problem* Royce answered by preferring certain central ideas over leaders and heroes, over social institutions, and over the inner life of prayer. He knew that leaders, social organization, inner habits, and prayer are as essential to group religious life as food is to human bodily life yet he also detected that the accelerating rate of change made these things vulnerable. Royce's preference for ideas as *most* essential meant that for him there was a significant difference between the essential and the most essential. His preference, then, did not stem mainly from his bias as an idealist (1:4) nor from his career as a university professor. Rather, this preference arose principally from his radical appreciation that certain "leading ideas," viewed precisely as human, are the most enduring and potent sources of morality and religion. His selected ideas, designated "Christian" simply by historical origin in communal consciousness, but eternally sown in the Universal Community by its Interpreter *Logos*-Spirit, stand in the truth and are true, whatever changes come.[18] For without the truth, spirit, and life which these ideas give, morality and religion are moribund. *Guidance by truth,* that quality-factor most critically needed, is at the heart of each person's ethico-religious decisions insofar as these are supported by a genuine community. What Royce found, then, was that *only* his so-called "Christian" ideas supplied this most essential factor without fail.

In the past, group ethico-religious life was supported by a conservative cast of mind, by externally impressive symbols and rituals, and especially by the political, economic, and educational institutions that were generally cooperative. But ever more rapid changes in technology, science, and secularization have transformed not only these formerly supportive cultural factors, but also the evolving conscious tendencies that newly express people's underlying, irremovable, religious need. Ethico-religious life, now finding its past worldly weapons ambiguous and unreliable, must depend simply on the "sword of the Spirit" (1:392), on precisely that unity of the three basic Christian ideas. As humankind's most essential medium of truth, that set of ideas empowers people to discern the misleading "angels of light" from the Holy Spirit's "kindly light" which shows them, not the distant scene, but just the "step" they now most need to see "amid the encircling gloom" (2:388).[19]

This relation of the leading ideas to the Spirit suggests how crucial are people's responses to the Spirit.[20] In differing ways each human self suffers from the moral burden, that inner-dividedness of a self-assertive will which both complies with, yet resists society's demands. The genuinely loyal servant of the community suffers through residual habits of crafty social training and the potential for treason (1:148-155, 252-253, 278-279). So, while the quality and strength of one's alienating forces differ, each self has a radical tendency to avoid the needed "openness to the Spirit." Sensitive to this on-going peril in everyone,[21] Royce underscored each individual's two-sided need. Through these basic bonds, then, Royce showed how intricately interwoven are the three Christian ideas with his other doctrines of the two levels, of the need for human transformation, and of the Spirit's guidance within the whole communal salvation process (1:404-405).

The Three Most Enduring and Potent Ideas

When confronted with Christianity's broad spectrum of competing basic ideas, why did Royce select specifically the ideas of community, moral burden, and atonement as "the most vital Christian ideas" (1:52)? One may feel the thrust and relevance of this question so keenly as to overlook its misleading assumption and omission. It assumes Royce's selection was like that of some shopper who has three separate items to buy. It omits any reference to Royce's deepest conviction that the most vital message of Christianity, like that of Jesus, is the good news that the Kingdom of heaven is at hand with its Spirit's "saving grace" available to everyone, who are all destined and called to this Kingdom. Or, to transpose such Faith-talk into its "human side" proper to a philosophy of religion, the initial question omits any mention of the synthesizing and regulatory ideas of the Universal Community, its Interpreter, and Loyalty. But these "somewhat more general" ideas form that integral whole of Royce's "doctrine of signs" within which *alone* functions his "Christian doctrine of life," provided that its trio of most essential Christian ideas are synthesized by that "somewhat more general idea of 'Saving Grace'" (1:329).

Instead of viewing the three ideas individualistically, as happened in the opening question, one can view them as inseparably interacting members of a "community of ideas" which, as a regulative connected whole, guides all temporal process towards the universal community (1:331; 2:387). Thus one can initiate a new inquiry which is led by two main questions: Why did Royce select loyalty, and not love, as Christianity's central idea? Why did he select precisely the ideas of community, moral burden, and atonement rather than some other trio of Christian ideas which seems to be at least as vital, or even more so, for Christianity? These questions can be treated in order.

First, instead of the traditional idea of "love" which is widely regarded as Christianity's most life-giving notion, Royce inserted the transformed idea of that special kind of love, called "Loyalty" (1:xviii). He saw the need to negotiate about this "top-quality" kind of love. This kind had to go beyond three lower kinds of love found in human selves: animal affection, the mutual self-gifting by individuals uncommitted to a genuine community, and the sympathetic sentiment for the whole human community viewed simply in itself. Royce sensed that the term "love" usually means the affective self-gift of one morally detached individual to another similarly detached individual. Not yet morally joined to a saving community, these individuals cannot through their loves offset the alienating forces at work in each of them. If two finite sinful individuals love each other without also dedicating themselves wholeheartedly to a genuine community, they receive no healing influences from the saving community and so cannot mutually help each other grow. Hence Royce's insistence on the need of that top-quality love which is the undeserved gift of being enabled to make a total and practical dedication of oneself to a genuine community—that is, to that kind of community which is open to the universal community and promotes its coming. Such Loyalty loves all individuals—others and oneself; all members, whether actual or potential—but it also and essentially requires a love for a genuine community as a saving community. This means that kind of love which eventually takes part in the community's saving and atoning activities. This was Royce's "reconsideration" of Pauline *caritas*. He came to it by reinterpreting the meaning of Christianity's central prayer, "Thy Kingdom come!" as follows:

> The central doctrine of the Master was: "So act that the Kingdom of Heaven may come." This means: So act as to help, however you can, and whenever you can, towards making mankind one loving brotherhood, whose love is not a mere affection for morally detached individuals, but a love of the unity of its own life upon its own divine level, and a love of individuals in so far as they can be raised to communion with this spiritual community itself. (1:357)

Hence, before asking about a set of three general Christian ideas, it is wise to notice the overall regulative function of Royce's Christian doctrine of life as a whole. It is connected by the Christian idea of *caritas* which "from above" appears as "saving Grace" and "from below" appears as "Loyalty." Such was Royce's reinterpretation of Paul's transformation of Jesus' doctrine of love.[22]

Second, why did Royce prefer to regard the ideas of community, moral burden, and atonement as "the most vital Christian ideas" within Christianity's doctrine of *caritas* (1:52)? The ideas of love, mission, and service of humankind are essential and vital Christian ideas. So, too, are the Christian ideas of Trinity, church, and baptism. In Christian moral life, the ideas of divine imperative, sin, and Christ-like decisions are indispensable. What claims, then, could Royce advance that, for his approach in the *Problem,* the ideas of community, moral burden, and atonement were "*the* essential ideas of Christianity" (1:45, 106)? To understand his answer, a contrast with the Royce of four years earlier may help.

Already in 1909, Royce was using his "individual approach" to find what was vital in Christianity, examining it first in its purely primitive form and then in its mature form structured by its most central doctrines.[23] In primitive Christianity he found three ideas were "vital and essential": Christ, the Father, and repentance.[24] (Royce interpreted these, respectively, as the teacher of an interpretation of life, the one whose love gives infinite worth to each human individual, and the transformation needed for new life.) Turning to mature Christianity and letting its doctrines of the incarnation and redemption guide his study, Royce found that the Essential Christ is even more vital to Christianity than the Historical Christ.[25] (For Royce, the Historical Christ was the human individual Jesus who lived from Bethlehem to Calvary and who is known mainly through the Synoptic evangelists. By contrast, the Essential Christ is the *Logos* who now works abidingly in each heart, in humankind, and in the entire world, and whom John the evangelist and the apostle Paul mainly portrayed.)[26] Royce preferred to focus on the *Logos* and to regard this Word Anointed as the One who carries out his contemporary atoning mission through his suffering servant role in and through those loyal human hearts who are being developed morally and spiritually because, as his members, they accept suffering with him for others' good.[27]

In sum, four years before writing the *Problem* and without reducing Christianity to the ever-vital ideas of its primitive form, Royce viewed the Essential Christ's contemporary incarnation and redemption as "more vital" to Christianity than the historical Jesus' incarnation and redemption—particularly, if the latter were regarded as merely ancient events. As a result of this second, dogma-guided study of mature Christianity, the Royce of 1909 selected as its *most* vital triad of ideas: incarnation, atonement, and the early Church's right interpretation of its founder.[28]

However, in 1912, when employing his new "social approach" to Christianity in search for its "form of social religious experience" (1:xv), Royce had to select its essential ideas differently. He used historical and metaphysical reasons to identify this new set of ideas. It constituted the fundamental life-giving form of communal religious experience in Christianity.

Historically, the apostle Paul's account showed that the early Christian communities had interpreted the master's message of the Kingdom into a recognition that the saving Kingdom was present in their own community. Upon this shared interpretation depended their group-identification as a Christian Church. Royce inquired which ideas were indispensable for their reaching this interpretation which first constituted them as a group communally aware of its distinctive Christian identity. By his analysis, the early Christians could not have come to this Church-constituting interpretation unless they had used the ideas of community, lost state, and atonement. This trio of ideas, then, seemed most essential and vital to Christianity, when viewed from his social approach of 1912.

Metaphysically, Royce held that "in the whole world, the divine life is expressed in the form of a community" (2:388). But the individual human selves whom this divine life calls to live in this community and to believe in it are limited, ignorant, and self-preferential. Necessarily, then, they will breed alienation between themselves and their institutions. Only a divine plan and process of reconciliation could intrinsically heal these estranged selves into a wholesome and growing community. Hence, if people were to believe that a gracious expression of divine reconciling life was occurring in their midst, they had to be guided into that belief by a pedagogue Spirit who used the ideas of community, lost individual, and atonement—ideas united by the more general idea of saving grace.

Not clarified as much as the other three, the idea of grace points to mysterious origin, operation-salvation, and the Spirit. Viewed superhumanly with Paul, grace is the power that gives to the individual a new life, spiritual gifts, and a bonding to a superhuman community. Viewed humanly with Royce, grace is the *new life of genuine loyalty,* a life of inexplicable origin (1:172-173, 185-187). Viewed superhumanly, the *"realm of grace"* has three requisite elements: a special unity-bond, the Spirit of the community (present both as Jesus the Master and as this community's proper activity), and that mutual love between this Community and its every member which is charity. Viewed humanly, this loyal life employs perfectly human motives and bases, correlative to these three elements (1:192, 209). The idea of grace, referring to humankind's new life in the unity of the spirit, also indicates the gratuity of the saving and reconciling activity of the Spirit of the Community. Being so general as its synonyms "pure favor" and "saving spirit," the idea of grace fittingly unites Royce's three essential and leading ideas. This synthesized set of the three "Christian" ideas, insofar as communicated by the pedagogue Spirit, is what both directs and explains the spiritual evolution of human finite selves and of the entire universe into community (2:387). In sum, the foregoing historical and metaphysical reasons led Royce in 1912 to regard his grace-integrated triad as "for our purposes, the three central ideas of Christianity" (1:44).

Of course, his selection had its implications. For instance, his centering on the individual's relation to a saving community committed him to the basic doctrine of the two levels (in human consciousness and in reality). His idea that the Deliverer-Spirit transforms individual hearts to genuine loyalty required him to regard the doctrine of human moral transformation as fundamental and to value this spiritual process as humankind's way to its highest good (1:405). Again, by his regarding the temporal process whereby human selves make loyal decision as so central, Royce was led to hold that a divine pedagogy is at work schooling loyal human hearts how the Kingdom advances and how hope for further realizing the Kingdom is gradually fulfilled by the "ever-living *Logos* in its fluent quest for the goal."[29]

TESTS FOR THE CONSISTENCY OF THE THREE IDEAS

A third dimension of Royce's method for selecting his fundamental ideas was his way of checking their consistency within his overall system of thought. Before basing all his research in the *Problem* on his selected ideas, he had to know how they reverberated throughout his philosophy.

His introduction of these ideas in the *Problem*'s first lecture revealed their close connections and contrasting differences and thus evidenced the intrinsic consistency of these ideas among themselves (1:36–45). Later he found a similar consistency in any coherent complex religious experience, which could not occur, cumulate, and repeat itself if its constitutive leading ideas were inconsistent (1:61–74, 98–102).

Royce tested the extrinsic consistency of his set of three ideas by turning especially to their ground in logic, as well as to their psychological roots and the implications for epistemology and metaphysics. We already saw how he investigated the psychological roots of these ideas in chapter 7 and in the next chapter we will examine how he explored the empirical bases for his three ideas. We turn, then, to their grounds in logic and later to their implications for epistemology and metaphysics.

The ϵ-Relation Test

Royce was convinced that he could not be understood unless his audience underwent a paradigm shift away from the view that ultimately the only realities are individuals to the view that two levels of reality (the individual and the community) are mutually co-ultimate. This new paradigm had its logical ground in the ϵ-relation. Royce highlighted the mental entrapment of those limited to one-level thinking, when he wrote:

> Now that is in brief why the whole lore of "salvation," "atonement," etc. — in brief the whole lore of community relations, can never be rightly approached by one who simply proceeds as if such problems could be solved by considering "one individual" and "another individual," etc., without ever explicitly facing the ϵ-relation.[30]

The all-pervasive importance of the ε-relation comes to light if we discover how ε works in some practical situations. Royce found it governing the following cases: a) when we direct ourselves to cooperate responsibly according to the orderly processes of communication and service; b) when we prefer to promote the common good rather than to follow our uncoordinated urges and desires; c) when we pay attention to the community's interpreter and his directions rather than let ourselves become absorbed in our own interest as such; d) when we insist on maintaining ourselves more as members than as individualistic agents—for example, by preferring to seek insight communally; and e) when we prefer to love enduringly rather than to opt out of a basically good but frail community representing the Beloved and Redeeming Community. All these sound moral choices are directed by the ε-relation rather than by its obverse, ε̄.

The ε-relation is presupposed then in every volitional process, in every theoretical activity, and in every relationship of an individual member through a system of various communities to a highest community. Of course, the ε-relation sprouts a rich context of other kinds of relations. For instance, an individual member may be related to another member, to a non-member, and to a clique, even while his community may be related to himself, to each other individual member, to non-members, to an inside or outside clique, and to a higher community. All these relations are distinct and derivative from the ε-relation. Unfortunately, according to Royce, theoreticians of community often fail to distinguish these different kinds of relations. "My view is," wrote Royce to Professor Fite, "that the ε-relation is a necessary basis and presupposition of all our deeper social relations." And among those deeper relations he especially included our moral and religious relations.

In itself, the ε-relation is the unique membership relation which an "individual entity" has insofar as it "belongs to" a set, assemblage, or community. The ε-relation requires two characteristics: 1) the *membership* of the individual entity in a non-individual type of reality (i.e., in the different level of reality proper to a set or community); and 2) a *direction toward* this non-individual type of reality. Underscoring how fundamental and unique among all relations is the ε-relation, Royce informed Fite, "If I am a member of a community, *all* my relations to that community depend upon my ε-relation and upon its context."

Hence, the ε-relation can never be identical with any of the following relations: individual to itself, individual to another individual, individual non-member of a set to that set, set to itself, set to individual member, set to individual non-member, set to set (as such), and set (as non-individual)[31] to an assemblage of sets.

Embodied in human living, the ε-relation is the link between the human self's two levels: individual and community. This relation has an asymmetrical (one-way) direction from the member towards the level of community. But unless functioning within the transforming realm of grace, this direction leads to a self-preferential community, a merely natural community. As transformed by grace, however, the ε-relation directs a human self into vital union with "one conscious spiritual whole of life" (1:406) which distinguishes a genuine community. As one-way, this direction inserts teleology and a norm, for the individual human self is called to accept and follow out this direction by his or her wholehearted dedication to a genuine community. And the community's life of loyalty is genuine only insofar as, according to the direction of the graced ε-relation, this life transforms morally separated selves into genuinely loyal ones and develops its loyal members to fuller life. It follows that the loyal love of a member for the genuine community as a community differs greatly from either the loyal love of such a community for its member or the "loyal love" of one member for another human individual-member of the same community. For Royce had logically established the distinctiveness of the first kind of loyal love through the distinctiveness and priority of the ε-relation and its transformability within a realm of grace. Having found the ε-relation so characterized, he then employed its asymmetrical bearing to direct individual members through their particular genuine communities to the divine.[32] (What does not follow, however, is that, on its side, the Community's love for, and loyal care of, any individual member is unimportant and hardly worth mentioning in our day.)

Equipped with some understanding of the ε-relation, we can inquire how Royce tested his three selected ideas by the ε-relation. That is, did his trio of ideas presuppose and fit in with the ε-relation? Since a member's relation to the community is the ε-relation, the idea of the saving Community cannot be thought or embodied without accepting this relationship and its transformation by grace. In its turn, the idea of the moral burden of the detached individual (the lost state) represents the practical attempt to deny the control and direction of the ε-relation as graced. Finally, the idea of atonement expresses how the graced ε-relation is restored by the suffering community's loyalty to the isolated individual and to the coming Universal Community. Clearly, then, each of the three essential ideas (community, moral burden, and atonement) presupposes and points to its distinctive logical foundation in the ε-relation. Besides consistency in logic, however, there is consistency in truth and reality. Looking at the lived relations between subject and object in a community context, Royce asked whether his set of three ideas consistently led to true knowing and opened one to take part more fully in the interactive reality of Universal Community.

The Epistemological Test

A perduring theme in Royce's writings is that the deepest intentionality of the human self is its radical hunger to be lifted out of one's narrow-mindedness, mere self-assertiveness, lovelessness, and social conflicts into a completely higher mode of life. Suppose, however, that the will of a knowing subject has not yet undergone this saving liberation, this transfiguration into genuine loyalty. Such a knower may win glittering insights and generate spectacular theories. Nonetheless, he is starting from a radical alienation that biases all his thinking.[33] If his knowing arises from a basically alienated self, it cannot be integrally true for his knowing operations must arise from a subjectivity transformed by a loving loyalty to the universe and to all persons within it.[34] But the set of Royce's three basic ideas consistently point to and promote this saving moral transformation because of the teleology of their leadings.

Again, Royce's three ideas go beyond perceptual and conceptual knowing into interpretive knowing. They lead to an intimate personal "in-touch-ness" with real minds and signs of minds—things which percepts and concepts cannot appreciate. These three ideas generate a conspectus marked by a breadth and coherent unity that is consistent with the whole universe (*SRI,* 6). If a human knower makes these three ideas his own by finding his personal identity through them (2:89, 92, 187), they open up for him a new and deeper level of reality—the communal conscious life of memories, hopes, interests, values, commitments, and actions, *as shared* by human minded beings. Through the "close personal touch" of such knowing, there is introduced into his knowing "that homeland of the human spirit" (1:xviii) as a vision, a hope, and a longed-for ideal, consistent with the knowing of the Spirit Interpreter of the Universe.

The Metaphysical Test

Royce wanted to extend his discussion of Part One of the *Problem* into a "metaphysics of the Christian ideas" (1:xxiii). Could the modern mind consistently accept the position that the Christian doctrine of life had *more* than a human meaning and foundation? Might it also consistently refer to, and be based on, the whole processing world and its God (2:7)?[35]

To test whether his three Christian ideas, united by the idea of Grace, could be expanded consistently into a theory of the universe, Royce strove to provide evidence giving an affirmative answer to a series of three questions: 1) Could these ideas be *generalized consistently* into a metaphysics? 2) If so, could this metaphysical theory be *technically proven* consistent with the unavoidable life of the human mind? 3) Could experiential signs be advanced which *strongly confirmed* this metaphysical theory? His method kept in close touch with his selected set of Christian ideas, since their bearings, interconnections, and truth had to guide the generalizations comprising his metaphysical theory if the latter was to be consistent.

By devising a technical definition (2:50), he moved towards a generalization of his idea of community. This definition, as both precise and generalized, would be the "sign" revealing the whole temporally processing universe as the "Universal Community of Interpretation." (If integrated with the idea of grace, this sign would reveal "The Beloved Community.") He would also generalize the idea of the Lost Individual (of the finite human individual as individual) so that, thanks to the obverse of *epsilon* ($\mathcal{E}$), it would refer to all "*non*-belongings," to all metaphysical evils, such as inadequate knowings, misinterpretations, exclusively self-aggressive, or self-denying wills (2:203, 374–376). Finally, he would generalize "Atonement" into that eventually healing kind of temporal process that supplies reconciliations. In this way the cosmic process would be no mere flow of conflictive and chaotic forces but would include a meaningful spiritual communication through a community-forming "Doctrine of Signs" (1:19; 2:312, 324). Thus a genuine development of the processing Universe would be insured because of the guidance of the Spirit Interpreter of the Universal Community (2:374). The presence of the Spirit would be generalized from the ideas of the atoning Deliverer and of Grace. Royce found these four generalizations making consistent connections and dovetailing into his general metaphysics (2:220–221, 324–325, 422).

This metaphysical theory would pass the test of "technical proof" when it reinstated itself amid a battery of denials attempted in Lectures 13 and 14 (2:276, 323, 392). His fitting illustrations in the closing Lectures 15 and 16 would provide the needed experiential confirmation. Three of these illustrations or clues lay in Royce's fiction of the learned early Christian from Greece who came back to life in the twentieth century, in Royce's use of Peirce's argument that the scientific human mind is attuned to nature, and in Professor Henderson's theory of the evident fitness of the natural environment for originating and developing organic life (2:342–379, 406–420, 420–422, n. 1).

In sum, besides their intrinsic consistency, made evident in his first lecture, Royce's three selected ideas passed the tests of logic, epistemology, and metaphysics and thus revealed their extrinsic consistency with his religious philosophy and whole theory of the universe. So, these basic ideas proved that they could sustain the brunt of the empirico-historical and the metaphysical investigations in the *Problem* as well as of the extreme flexibility required by his general method. Royce knew that his selection of "essential ideas" would guide his entire investigation (1:3, 38). His three convergent goals and his three personal exemplars provided him with good extrinsic reasons for his choice. More importantly, he knew the sound historical and metaphysical reasons intrinsic to his choice (2:334-335).

SOME MAIN ROYCEAN LINES ALREADY EMERGING

FIRST STAGE OF THE EMPIRICO-HISTORICAL METHOD*
(governing Royce's First Lecture:
"The Problem and the Method")

ITS AIM: To encounter experientially, to select carefully, and to test for consistency "some of the leading and essential ideas of Christianity" which will guide our study of the creedal "form of social religious experience . . . upon which loyalty depends" (1:xv, xxxv; 2:11).

FIRST STAGE: From within the experience of Graced Communities, that save or reconcile otherwise Lost Individuals, fittingly to encounter, select, and test leading ideas essential to a religion of loyalty.

First Task: Choose such a set of goals and such a set of exemplary interpreters that Royce's mental set is suited for properly selecting these ideas.

Second Task: Identify the intrinsic reasons for selecting the Ideas of Community, Lost Individual, and Atonement, under "the somewhat more general idea of 'Saving Grace'" (1:xxxvi).

Third Task: Check the consistency of these ideas by tests that are psychological, logical, epistemological, and metaphysical.

*For the outline of Second and Third Stages, see p. 217.

First, even though many world religions employ the same fundamental ideas of community, lost state, salvation, and redemption, Royce wanted his philosophy of the Christian religion to be *distinctively Christian* (1:xii; 2:15-16). He presupposed a transformation by loyalty to a new life on the second level of spiritual existence. Royce discerned this two level doctrine in the distinctively Christian mystery of the Incarnate Word—the human individual Jesus in ε-relation to the divine Community—and then extended this doctrine to the "Spirit of the Beloved Community" who promotes ethico-religious conversions of lost individuals into genuinely loyal members of his body (1:203). Distinctively Christian is this union of conversion (*metanoia*), of belief in the "good news" that the Spirit is salvifically present in the Community and of that kind of practical life in the unity of the Spirit required of a new creature (1:114, 174). Furthermore, Royce suggested that the characteristically Christian symbol of the Holy Spirit provided the best way of interpreting God. Finally, he insisted, "In this [fourth Gospel's] doctrine of the spirit, lies the really central idea of any distinctively Christian metaphysics" (2:16). Implying both unique individuality and triune community, *Logos*-Spirit has distinct Trinitarian connotations (2:219).

Second, Royce expected that the accelerating rate of change in the world would transform our ideas of nature and supernature (1:420). Within human selves, however, he found *an irreversible constant* that could and would survive future shock. Deep changes are to occur in Christian theologies, institutions, practices, and creeds. All people possess a few basic ethico-religious needs in common and only the three essential Christian ideas can satisfy these needs. So, interacting in vital mutuality, these needs and ideas steadily generate for humankind its basic meanings and values (1:420–421).

Third, by overlooking *a basic presupposition,* a reader can easily become irritated by Royce's frequent usage of "right," "true," and "genuine." For example, he never tires of insisting that the human individual should have the right relation to the community, a true loyalty, and a sense of genuine life (1:xx). Royce's method and doctrine presuppose that everyone's spiritual transformation is most fundamental and urgent (1:xx). If the reader has neither noticed this basic presupposition nor personally undergone this transformation into a genuine community (1:xv), Royce's normative assertions will at least seem unclear, and more likely seem gallingly cocksure. But genuinely loyal persons will hear echoing through Royce's frequent usage of normative language his basic claim: so heavy is the detached individual's moral burden that no one can become genuinely honest and an authentically true human being unless he is transformed to genuine loyalty. If one dedicated himself loyally to a genuine community, he has been set on the path of salvation and thus mediately united to the universal Beloved Community. Transformation is fundamental in the mature Royce's ethics and philosophy of religion. Yet most descriptions of Royce's late ethics have failed both by not "defining the highest good of man in terms of a transformation of our individual nature" and by not recognizing that this transformation follows from applying his doctrine of the two levels to ethics (1:405).[36]

Finally, I suspect that Royce created a *radical shift in philosophical method* by both employing interpretive musement and by moving loyalty to the living center of all his mature philosophy. Throughout his life, philosophy somehow remained a search for wisdom. In his earlier periods, this search consisted mainly in his seeking to generate theories. But in his mature period, the indispensable basis of a sound search for wisdom became the spirit-guided life of a genuine community converting selves to loyalty. By subordinating theory to a person's ever-present call to make genuinely loyal choices, the mature Royce relativized the importance of specific metaphysical, theological, and dogmatic theories and systems. Moreover, if consciousness is converted to genuine loyalty, it distinguishes between technical metaphysical theories and those deep metaphysical truths which point through loyalty to a more than human significance. Genuinely loyal consciousness makes such a discernment thanks to the distinctive teleology and wisdom at work within Royce's philosophy of loyalty. That teleology and wisdom are distinctive because they operate within the interpretive Process of the universal community whose central figure is the Spirit-Interpreter.

Hence, the teleological considerations that mark the distinctive philosophical methods of William Ernest Hocking and Alfred North Whitehead derive more from the radically revised absolute pragmatism of the mature Royce than from other pragmatisms. Hocking was Royce's student and later the colleague he most influenced. Subsequently, Hocking's influence on Whitehead showed itself in wooing the latter to Harvard and in the faculty interchanges that followed. All three thinkers presupposed that if one wants to philosophize wisely, one should start from that transformed affectivity of "standing in loyal love of the Universe." Those teleological considerations which dominate Hocking's and Whitehead's distinct philosophical methods seem, then, to derive directly or indirectly from the mature Royce. Similarly derived, at least in part, is Whitehead's shift from a mathematically modeled method of essential form to a teleological method open to such ingredients in process as "subjective aims" and God's "primordial and superject natures."

Because Royce's mature philosophical method has been influential and presupposes a radical shift to an ethico-religious starting point and to a basic procedure, his mature method calls for careful reassessment.

13. Empirico-Historical Method: Second and Third Stages

Royce's mature understanding of the second and third stages of his empirico-historical method arises from his experience-based interpretation of human selves' inescapably communal life. Since various peoples, and humankind in general, search irrepressibly within their deepest communal life for the human *basis, value,* and *truth* of the ideas guiding their conscious cooperation, these three interpretive searches naturally form a series of three procedures within their overall musement.

Within this overall process of shared interpretation, Royce's problem was to find out experientially whether his set of selected Christian ideas would first cast light on these three deepest processes in the communal life of human selves, and then, aided by the idea of graced loyalty (or, in Christian terms, of "Saving Grace"), direct the integration of these processes to form that conscious whole of shared spiritual living which distinguishes a genuine community (1:406). Committed to an empirical and historical starting point, Royce saw his overall task was to identify in the deep communal religious experience of humankind throughout history "the basis in human nature" for the Christian ideas he had selected; that is, their psychological foundation (1:xxxviii, 113). Next, upon this basis he would move to estimate the significance of these ideas for human life — their ethical and religious value — and finally, their truth (1:52).

Foreshadowed here is his general design for the second and third stages of his empirico-historical method — for his entire investigation of communal religious experience in Part One of the *Problem*. Near the start of his third lecture he offered a far fuller description of his intended procedure. This major text clearly provides a key both to his overall method and to the two subordinate methods which his different experiential and metaphysical materials called him to devise (1:xxxv). In this text he began with his design for the empirico-historical method, as operating within his all-pervasive interpretive method. The text so clearly reveals his "deliberate plan of the whole work" (1:xiv) and is referred to so frequently in the following pages that it deserves to be quoted here in its entirety. Contextually, Royce is forestalling an objection: it is premature for him to begin interpreting a second Christian idea when he has as yet not sufficiently interpreted the first idea of Community to really clarify, criticize, and correlate it, as needed. Supporting his advance into a new idea, Royce said:

> I answer that the three Christian ideas which we have chosen for our inquiry are so closely related that each throws light upon the others, and in turn receives light from them. Each of these ideas needs, in some convenient order, to be so stated and so illustrated, and then so made the topic of a thoughtful reflection, that we shall hereby learn: First, about the basis of this idea in human nature; secondly, about its value,—its ethical significance as an interpretation of life; and thirdly, about its truth, and about its relation to the real world. At the close of our survey of the three ideas, we shall bring them together, and thus form some general notion of what is essential to the Christian doctrine of life viewed as a whole. We shall at the same time be able to define the way in which this Christian doctrine of life expresses certain actual needs of men, and undertakes to meet these needs. We shall then have grounds for estimating the ethical and religious values of the connected whole of the doctrines in question.
> There will then remain the hardest part of our task: the study of the relation of these Christian ideas to the real world. So far as we are concerned, this last part of our investigation will involve, in the main, metaphysical problems; and the closing lectures of our course will therefore contain an outline of the metaphysics of Christianity, culminating in a return to the problems of the modern man.
> Such is our task. (1:112–113)[1]

The modest tone of this key text disguises Royce's breathtaking intent and method. To unveil these, the present chapter engages in some textual analysis, pointing out three major movements in the text which will disclose three major movements in Royce's overall strategy, and then concentrating on the first third of the text to bring the major features of his empirico-historical method into sharp relief.

MAJOR MOVEMENTS IN THE TEXT

In the quotation above, Royce presupposes that the three Christian ideas have been selected—the first stage of his empirico-historical method. If we then regard his text in approximate thirds—using "At the close . . ." and "There will then remain . . ." as the places of division—we discover the three different topics proposed by Royce for thoughtful reflection: each Christian idea, then the synthesis of these ideas, and, finally, the relation of these ideas to the whole of reality. Corresponding to these topics are, respectively, the second and third stages of Royce's empirico-historical method and his development of a metaphysics. Since his study of how the Christian ideas relate to all reality requires him to go beyond human nature into metaphysics in order to work out the ultimate meaning of the Christian ideas[2] and to submit them to an elaborate truth-testing, it calls forth his metaphysical method. But before attempting any metaphysical investigation of ultimate questions in Part Two of the *Problem,* Royce wants in Part One to restrict himself simply to human nature. Thus, in Part One, he wishes to be independent of any metaphysics, dogmatic system, or theory of history.

As seen, Royce has already selected his three fundamental Christian ideas and set the limits of his investigation. He did so by the first stage of his empirico-historical method, found in Lecture 1 of the *Problem.* In the second and third stages of this method he intends, through the seven remaining lectures of Part One, to get into ever closer personal touch with the depths of human communal living by means of progressively deeper and more interrelated interpretations of the three ideas. To carry out this intent, he engages in a series of cyclic interpretations, each with three phases. For Royce wants to search successively for the experiential *basis,* then for the *value,* and finally for the *truth* of either a Christian idea or the whole set of these ideas. He unites the cycles by an alternation process that compares and contrasts a single idea's forms, a pair of ideas, or their relation to the more general idea of "saving grace." In sum, by persisting in this three-phased procedure during each of the successive advances of his reflective reconsiderations of the Christian ideas, Royce intends in Part One to learn serially three particulars about each idea and their synthesis: 1) its basis in human nature, 2) its ethical significance as an interpretation of human life, and 3) its worth and coherence with humankind's nature, history, and destiny.

Thus the overall series of interpretations that build Part One resembles a gradually advancing and expanding helix. Within this entire series, each of the three-phased cycles of interpretation has to be fragmentary (1:111, 113). Each has to be dependent—both on the completion of Part One's overall process and on that more elaborate and critical truth-test of Part Two. Royce estimated, however, that when Part One was completed, the coherency form of truth-test, which both recurs as the third phase within each interpretive cycle and also wholly dominates the nature of Part One's concluding stage (Lectures 7 and 8), would already have supplied enough truth for most of the serious purposes of people's lives. Accordingly, Royce could postpone to Part Two his elaborate truth test by metaphysical critique (1:328).

Moving from this overview, we zero in on the first third of our major text: its sketch of the second stage of Royce's empirico-historical method.

In this stage, Royce sets as his first task to take each Christian idea individually and muse upon it carefully. He starts, then, with the Christian idea of Community and begins his three-phased cycle of interpretation. That is, he searches first for the natural origins of the idea of community in humankind's deep communal consciousness, viewed experientially and historically. Then he observes how this idea gives birth to basic ethical and religious values. Finally, he gathers some signs of the truth of this idea by measuring its consistency with the other two ideas and with persons' basic ethico-religious needs. Thereupon, employing the same three-phased cycle of interpretation, Royce intends to advance towards his second, and then towards his third idea.[3]

Turning to the middle third of the text which starts, "At the close of our survey," we find Royce synthesizing the three ideas "through the somewhat more general idea of 'Saving Grace'" (1:xxxvi). This "connected whole" forms the most essential Christian doctrine of life. By shifting from viewing an idea as an individual sign to viewing this "connected whole" as a community of ideas, Royce initiates the third and final stage of his empirico-historical method. Its goal is to discern, through a comparison and contrast of Buddhism and Christianity, what is most essential to Christianity's doctrine of life: graced Loyalty in the Spirit. By searching out the experiential basis, value, and truth of this Christian doctrine of life, Royce again exhibits his three-phased cycle. In this third stage he uses experience and history both to identify the whole of duty essential to Christian life and to slough off its historical accretions. By such discernment he comes in touch with the "sword of the spirit" (1:396) upon which alone depends Christianity's human hope for the future. Finally, he shows the validity of that hope by checking out whether the Christian doctrine of life coheres with the expectable exercise of humankind's basic ethico-religious needs and with human civilization's genuine advances in science and in the social arts.

SIGNALS OF ROYCE'S METHODS IN THIS TEXT

The foregoing selected text has displayed Royce's "deliberate plan of the whole work" (1:xiv) and thus his overall strategy for the *Problem*. In its first lengthy paragraph, this text offers an overview of the three major movements of interpretation in the empirico-historical method which Royce wants to employ in Part One. His other and final paragraph sketches the metaphysical method he will use in Part Two.

We now subject some phrases in the first third of this text to a more detailed exegesis, expecting that Royce's underlying method of interpretive musement will disclose itself. When his interpretive process encounters experiential materials within a temporal process, as described in the first two thirds of the text, interpretation adaptively metamorphoses its life to function according to its subordinate empirico-historical method.

Some Adverbial Signals

In this text Royce first speaks of a "thoughtful reflection" on "the three Christian ideas which . . . are *so closely* related *that* each throws light upon the others, and in turn receives light from them." These phrases refer to Royce's overall method of interpretive musement. He here insists on those aspects which objectively determine this musement. It needs interrelated ideas (signs). It operates because, through progressive interpretation, these ideas illuminate each other. It depends on the degree of closeness of these ideas ("*so* closely related"). As mentioned,[4] the ideas of Royce's pure logic and of his philosophy of religion generate mutually illuminative processes that find or create new ideas called "beyonds" or "thirds" for the further advance of the interpretive process. So here in Royce's philosophy of the Christian religion, a similar processing "community of signs" is found. These Christian ideas are signs that clarify each other and that lure their viewers to see clos*er* interconnections by finding binding "beyonds" or creating mediating "third" ideas. This is the objective side of Royce's overall method of interpretive musement, or, as he here calls it, of his "thoughtful reflection."

By such pondering reconsideration, he can observe humankind's basic spiritual needs expressing themselves in the three ideas and in turn see how these ideas move to satisfy those needs. By making this alternating life-process the object of his continuing musement, during the many phases of his method, Royce can eventually render two truths convincingly clear: first, that amid the world's accelerating changes the only thing that can satisfy humankind's basic ethico-religious needs is the Christian doctrine of life, and, second, that this doctrine furnishes a consistent everlasting basis for integrating a person's life. In fact, if carried out faithfully to the completion of the empirico-historical method, his thoughtful reflection will eventually validate the concluding conviction of Part One: "The most significant choice for the modern man, in dealing with Christianity, lies between accepting or rejecting the Christian doctrine of life" (1:404).

Royce continues by asserting that each of "these ideas needs, in some convenient order" to be dealt with. Behind this modest assertion lies that "deliberate plan of the whole work" (1:xiv) which he had so often redrafted. The phrase, "needs, in some convenient order" reveals his conviction that a clear grasp of method must guide his philosophizing. He knows that the expected fruit of his efforts can come only if they are ordered both by overall direction and discipline as well as by simple naturalness and convenience.

More specifically, "convenient order" hints at the three-phased interpretive cycle whereby Royce guides his serial musing upon the experience and "natural history" which he and others have had of the three Christian ideas. This three-phased cycle of interpretation is characteristic of his empirico-historical method (1:52, 112, 175, 213, 331, 384).

"Convenient order" also signals the step-by-step strategy of purifying an idea. This purifying strategy will enable Royce to slice neatly through the many historically conditioned, non-essential tissues of Christianity to its vital organs of belief. This strategy will so order his thoughtful reflection of each of these Christian ideas (both in itself and in union with the other two) that he can gradually work out the essential meaning of each idea and then generalize it. His order will indeed be "convenient" (or fitting) if he can, while carrying out this purification, also avoid the thickets of historical controversy and of complicated Scriptural exegesis.

Even more centrally, his "convenient order" refers to that series of living syntheses which guide his interpretive musement. They do this by uniting Royce's own subjective intents with objective relational structures. Subjectively, as we saw, interpreter Royce intends a threefold deeper penetration into each of the fundamental Christian ideas. That is, in each idea he looks for the meanings distinctly proper to its experiential source, to its value, and finally, to its truth. Objectively, between people's radical ethico-religious needs and the three Christian ideas, as well as between these ideas themselves, there emerge mutual bonds vital to morality and religion. Consequently, the interpreter's subjective order of questions is attuned to these concretely experienced objective structures. In this way the series of living syntheses is generated. These "thought-marriages" constitute the living forms of "logic as procedure" which guide and propel Royce's musement through the three phases of each cycle in his empirico-historical method, both in its second stage (of clarifying an individual idea) and in its third stage (of clarifying that "connected whole" of these ideas which is the Christian doctrine of life).

Finally, if one goes on to look ahead into the method of Part Two of the *Problem*—a method that is sketched in the final paragraph of the text presently under analysis—one finds that Royce's "convenient order" will in Part Two make him generate a "doctrine of signs" as his metaphysical theory. With it he can then elaborately test the truth of the Christian doctrine of life (2:285). His last task, then, will be to use this metaphysical theory to search out the ultimate bearings of these Christian ideas upon theory and practice for the good of "modern man" (2:312-343).

Within the same second sentence of our central text, Royce tucks the phrase, "*so* stated and *so* illustrated, and then *so* made the topic of a thoughtful reflection, that we shall hereby learn. . . ."[5] These three "so's," while not a bugle call, should alert an attentive reader. Meaning "in just such a way," Royce's "so's" are central to his method of discerning the *right* way (and of avoiding less helpful ways) of stating, illustrating, and turning each of these Christian ideas in a particular phase within a particular stage of the entire process into a sign that is suited for the interpretation then needed. These "so's" are also centrally important for Royce's audience. To wean an audience from their habits of subject-object (dyadic) thinking and to invite and support them in walking along the new paths of interpretational (triadic) thinking requires a *right* procedure — orderly, gradual, and reinforced.

For instance, how does a reader of Royce manage both to shift into interpretive knowing and to adjust expectations and attention to suit Royce's cycle of investigating the meanings first in the experiential base, then in the value, and finally in the truth of each of the Christian ideas? Only by entering Royce's "right methodic way," his path of well-ordered reflective reconsiderations, will a reader gradually learn the three phases characteristic of each cycle in the advancing, expanding helix of Royce's empirico-historical method. Although Royce frequently signals to his reader about this triadic rhythm (through which each idea needs first to be posited as a universal, then experienced in an individual example, and finally transformed into a sign suited for the kind of interpretive process that teaches a learnable doctrine), these signals are usually as jejune as the present "so stated and so illustrated, and then so made." Perhaps only the alert reader, then, easily finds in such a reference to three activities the hint that Royce will move beyond concept and percept to a sign rightly suited for an interpretive process that advances through the alternation of comparison and contrast.

Royce's following clause of intended result, "that we shall hereby learn," taken in conjunction with his triple "so," uncovers his underlying communication process that teaches more by procedure than by content. This combination also suggests the need that "we" have — both philosopher Royce and his audience — to be guided by the inner dynamic of his interpretive process which simultaneously communicates life-giving doctrine and procedure.

Some Substantive Signals

In the first paragraph of our major text, Royce uses the expressions: "the Christian ideas," "the basis of this idea in human nature," and "its ethical significance as an interpretation of life." The ideas of Spirit and of Community so permeate these phrases that the latter can be "fairly understood" only within the context of the overall temporal process that is directed by the universal community and its Spirit towards creating or enhancing genuine community (1:xxxvi).[6] Therefore, so long as these two most dominant ideas lie hidden from notice—perhaps through a failure to shift one's knowing from a dyadic mode into that of loyal interpretive musement—both Royce's language and his method must remain unintelligible.

Since his meaning of "Christian idea" is primarily that of a unity-promoting "will to interpret," an idea is Christian insofar as it tends to unify all humankind. What Royce concentrates upon within each Christian idea are its fully reasonable and universal intents which promote any human self's life in genuine human community. Put negatively, since Royce's meaning of a Christian idea does not function primarily as a classifying concept but as an interpretive process, it does not create a separate enclave, but a reconciling and unifying process. If sometimes he employs the distinctively Christian dress of that meaning, it is simply to focus more clearly upon the transcultural values it carries. For example, in order to focus better on higher human loyalty wherever found, he examines the Charity at work in Pauline communities (2:315).

Consequently, despite Royce's *calling* an idea Christian because historically it first arose to explicit communal consciousness in the early Christian communities (1:xviii, 10–11), what he *means* by "Christian idea" is something more essential. He means that kind of leading idea which, because of its reasonableness and universality, has as its distinctive mission *to promote whatever is more genuinely human.* The norm of what is "more genuinely human" lies in the ε-relation as graced; that is, in the teleology to the universal community as beloved. Since this norm has reached its closest realization in authentic Christian life (1:xviii–xx), an insight into a genuine Christian expression of such a leading idea may more fully disclose the transcultural human values at its heart.

However, just as one cannot grasp what Charity means unless he lives in personal touch with the Christian community and its Spirit, so a philosopher of the Christian religion cannot get insight into the specifically Christian form of an idea unless he gets beyond perceptual and conceptual thinking and enters a life of loyal interpretation wherein he can get in touch with what Royce calls "the spirit of that idea" (1:58). For, if a person "senses" or "feels" the spirit of a Christian idea during his interpretive musing on that idea, he will find the idea revealing itself as profoundly universal and reasonable. Thus, the more thoroughly a person appreciates the spirit of the Christian ideas, the more he sees these ideas as "simply and impressively human" (1:56). In practice, then, Royce equates the spirit of the Christian idea with that intentionality which most fully humanizes a person. Of course, such interpretation requires that one pray earnestly for the ability to discern the things of the spirit. As Royce saw it, this discernment-ability is the indispensable gift without which one cannot responsibly do philosophy and religion (2:221).

"The basis in human nature" is another phrase which can easily be misunderstood when studying Royce's empirico-historical method. His use of "human nature" displays an adroit positivism, at least in his first volume where he severely restricted its usage to the confines of social psychology. In this he paralleled a favorite teacher of his, the German psychologist William Wundt, who used linguistic positivism to deal with the construct "*Volk*" (1:64). Since a people acted as a minded being and produced mental products like a language, culture, and religion beyond the capacity of any individual minded being, a people (or community) can be considered and spoken of *as if* it were a minded being. So at the start "human nature" indicates merely psychological phenomena. Only after he has shown psychologically how the interests of individuals and communities together generate the ideals which produce both values and the ethical life that follows them does he allow "human nature" to function with ethical connotations (1:66). Furthermore, even in his metaphysics of Part Two, the term "human nature" functions only within a metaphysics of signs, without being allowed to carry ontic claims.

For Royce, then, "human nature" indicates a construct from social psychology. In no way does it carry the sense of either an Aristotelian *ousia* ("substance") or a Lockean pincushion. "Human nature" means for Royce the socially formed human consciousness found both in the individual self and in the community. The unavoidable basic structure in such consciousness arises from human selves' continuous making of decisions. Their cooperative deeds are guided by shared memories of common past events, persons, and deeds, and by shared expectations of common future events, persons, and deeds. The basic shared expectations set the direction towards our common human destiny and carry within them a particular sense of risk and hope that alerts humankind's consciousness and spurs its pursuit of this goal. The structure of human nature is a continuous flow of decisive choices, memories, and expectations, unified by one central teleological meaning because, for Royce, human nature is inseparable from the history and destiny of humankind.

Moreover, human nature is a conscious conflict of spirit and letter (1:59). Despite its contrary tendencies to self-centeredness, human nature also contains the persistently arising idea of communal life that keeps inviting human selves to co-create community. The original sin of human nature is a type of alienation, its tendency to separated individualism. This is intensified by personal sin, human selves' acts and consequent habits of unloyal or even disloyal choices. These two kinds of sin cause recurrent tragedies in the human history of the Christian ideals (1:58). And yet, although human nature is naturally wayward on its individual level, it is relatively constant on its community level where the pull of the common good is felt more strongly. As communal, human nature has relatively stable customs, languages, laws, and religions which promote the common good. In brief, relying on his positivistic approach, Royce first viewed human nature in the limited terms of social psychology, then turned to its ethical dimension, and only in his second volume began examining its metaphysical aspects with his non-ontological "doctrine of signs" (2:285).

If a person is insensitive to this serial enrichment of meaning or to the two levels of conscious existence, he or she may be misled by the term "*basis* in human nature." By "basis" Royce means the fundamental needs of the community self and of individual selves. Too often, perhaps, Royce's talk about needs is heard as if these are had only by individual selves. For him, needs also express themselves in communal consciousness where they surface as common interests, motives, and ideals and interact with the individual's interests.[7] The interest of the community is the "cause" by which the community unites many selves into one self by eliciting from various individuals a loyal dedication to the community (1:68). Through this spiritual embrace of "cause" and the dedication of individuals, the community as a super-individual self shares its one communal life to all these loyal individual members.

But this loyal dedication could not arise unless some basic life-giving (or "Christian") idea were generating the awareness of value needed for such dedication. In the major text under examination, Royce had pertinently explained that a Christian idea has "ethical significance as an interpretation of life." He thus pointed to a new kind of meaning—the ethical—and hinted at its indispensable function in developing genuine loyalty. Royce's use of this phrase, then, marks his methodic transition from social psychology (with its natural history of communal and individual consciousness) into an investigation of the rise of normative ideals, whether ethical or esthetic or religious. This phrase also signals his start of the second task within the second stage of his empirico-historical method. In other words, within this second stage, his first task was to survey life as factually human; his second task is to interpret it as appreciatively human.

In this evaluative second task, Royce countered the tendency to view ideals as rising like free balloons. Instead, he turned the wealth of ideals back into human nature, "as an interpretation of human life." In his maturity he was convinced that just as human nature suggests ethical ideals, so in their turn, ethical ideals must reenter the natural history of human society to modify it (1:61).[8]

Moreover, rather than speak of a transition from the level of fact to that of value appreciation, the mature Royce judged it more accurate to talk of a-thing-with-value or of a-being-with-goodness. A person's first judgment of reality is also a value judgment. As Royce taught explicitly in the last lecture of his life,

> The world isn't first given to you as a datum and afterwards estimated in virtue of the fact that you as a being with certain interests, and standing outside of that whole realm of existence, find some things in it good and some things evil. *The very recognition of Being is itself an estimate.*[9]

Which kind of estimate this will be depends upon how one chooses to stand towards the universe. For Royce, the human spirit's basic ethico-religious needs are so inseparably linked to its ideal that there is only one right attitude of will towards the whole universe: genuine loyalty (2:293).

Because Roycean human nature includes not only the history of the human family with its wisest lessons from the past, but also our destiny with its intelligently disciplined hopes for the future, Roycean evaluation feeds upon a doubly rich source. When loyal interpretation touches this rich treasure—namely, the full temporal process of human life in the world—then things unveil themselves as values and ideas reveal themselves as also ideals. So, in this second task of evaluation, when Royce interprets a Christian idea for "its ethical significance as an interpretation of life," the idea is seen *along with its ideals* as an irremovable ingredient of human life.

A Final Signal that Points to the Third Stage of the Empirico-Historical Method

Without subjecting the second and third divisions of our central text to a similar detailed analysis, we conclude our inspection of Royce's design of methods by focusing on his phrase "about the truth" at the close of the first division of the text. This phrase points to the third and final stage of Royce's empirico-historical method. And when viewed with its companion phrase "about its [the Christian idea's] relation to the real world," it also points further still to the entire enterprise of Part Two.

Royce enters into this third stage by transcending his pattern of considering a Christian idea individually and by shifting his topic to interpret "the connected whole to which they [the Christian ideas] belong" (1:331). This shift produces a *holistic* consideration of "the Christian doctrine of life," in which this synthesized whole becomes normative for validating the interconnections of the three ideas themselves "together with the somewhat more general idea of 'Saving Grace'" (1:xxxvi). This whole set of ideas is also normative for the ethico-religious life of modern man, of his destiny, and of the destiny of the entire evolving universe. Royce's aim in this third stage is to bring the essential Christian ideas together as expressing basic human interests, to elaborate the ethico-religious meaning of this synthesis, and to test how it fits both the lessons taught by the history of religions and the scientifically educated modern mind (1:329, 384; 2:6). In this third stage Royce's holistic consideration interprets serially three wholes: the whole of the Christian doctrine of life (as expressing basic ethico-religious needs), then the whole lesson of religious history, and finally, the whole of the modern mind as the unifying interpreter of these two previous wholes or "signs."

In sum, then, in his third and final stage of the empirico-historical method, Royce's first phase is to integrate the three Christian ideas by means of the idea of saving grace as his mediating and synthesizing "sign." Guiding this synthesis is that higher triad of the ideas of any genuine ethico-religious community, of the "life-spirit of Christianity" (1:355), and of saving grace.[10] This higher interpreting triad of ideas is under the overall influence of Royce's highest triad, his most vital and significant ideas: Community, Spirit, and the temporal interpretive process of salvation (1: xxxix).[11] Thereupon, in the second and concluding phase of the third stage, Royce tests the Christian doctrine of life for its coherence with humankind's basic ethico-religious needs and with the lessons of the history of religion as well as with the modern mind.

If one scans the *Problem* in its entirety, then, one can identify three kinds of truth-tests. In the previously examined second stage of the empirico-historical method, Royce closed each cycle of his three-phased interpretive musement by testing whether each particular Christian idea is a "true idea" (1:54, 106). That is, he measured the consistency of each idea with its basis in human nature and with the ethical ideals it generated. Similarly, in our present final stage of the empirico-historical method, Royce closes his methodic investigation in Part One by testing whether the whole set of essential Christian ideas is a true doctrine. His second truth-test measures the consistency of this doctrine with people's deeper life of loyalty and with the lessons they have learned from the history of religions. Functioning within an overall serial process of interpretation, this second truth-test employs only historical human nature as its limited norm. So, for completion it looks forward to a third and final elaborate truth-test (1:328). For this, Royce must construct metaphysically both a different method and a fitting "doctrine of signs." With this paired instrument he can transcend the human limits he has observed in Part One and move to test whether the Christian doctrine of life is consistent with the whole universe and true in it.

We have rapidly sketched the third stage of Royce's empirico-historical method by considering the phrase "about the truth" from his major text

THE EMPIRICO-HISTORICAL METHOD*
(governing Part One of the *Problem,*
"The Christian Doctrine of Life," according to 1:112.)

ITS AIM: To interpret the historical lesson revealed in the communal religious experience of both problematic Christianity and all religions of loyalty. This lesson, with its meaning for the future, is to be read according to the "doctrine of life" in these religions — a doctrine synthesized from their three most vital ideas.

SECOND STAGE: Royce's positivistic search into historical communal religious experiences for the natural and ethical motives of each of the three selected ideas — a search propelled by interpreting these ideas individually at first and later as paired; (see Lectures 2-6).

First Phase: Search for the natural needs and interests which are the motives of these "Christian" ideas.

Second Phase: Search for the ethical values which arise naturally from these natural needs and interests.

Third Phase: Test the coherence of each of these "Christian" ideas, viewed individually, with humankind's natural ethico-religious needs and its contemporary educated mind.

THIRD STAGE: Holistic consideration of "how the modern mind stands related to the human interests which the [whole of the] Christian doctrine of life expresses" (2:6).

First Phase (Lect. 7): To bring together the essential Christian ideas [into a connected whole] and to state, as a result of a synthesis of these ideas, some aspects of the Christian doctrine of life (1:329).

Task One: To so compare and contrast Buddhism and Christianity as to identify the most essential doctrine of Christianity.

Task Two: To propose genuine Christian moral teaching on duty, as an expression of this most essential doctrine.

Task Three: To show how this Christian doctrine of life, as a WHOLE, puts people in touch with humankind's basic ethico-religious needs and interests.

Second Phase (Lect. 8): To summarize some of the lessons which the history of religion seems to have taught humankind and to make a general study of the bearing of these lessons upon our estimate of the present and the future of the Christian religion (1:384).

Task One: To summarize the key lessons of the history of religion in order to define the religious problem of the future.

Task Two: To estimate how these lessons bear upon problematic Christianity in the present.

Task Three: To predict how these lessons bear upon the future of the Christian religion and of all religions of genuine loyalty.

---

*For an outline of First Stage, see p. 202.

on method. After surveying a summary outline of both the second and third stages of his empirico-historical method, we need to watch Royce exemplify this method. To do so, we turn in the next chapter to observe how Royce developed the Christian idea of community during the second stage of empirico-historical method.

14. An Instance of the Second Stage: Royce Muses on the Idea of Community

If a child and a biologist look at a tall green tree, both can see it simply as a pleasant and beautiful whole. But the more sensitive the biologist is, the more puzzled he will become as he recalls all the dynamic exchanges occurring inside and outside the tree—the mystery of its life. The same holds for Royce's empirico-historical method. When we simply experience it during a reading of Part One of the *Problem,* it appears to be a beautiful and simple whole. But if a scholar should subject this method to a slow-motion study, he would probably find himself puzzled. He would wonder: Is Royce musing about the idea of community, or its ideal, or its reality, or all three of these? Is he considering the spirit or the letter, the process or the structure, of community? Is he speaking of community in general or in its specifically Christian form? Is he experiencing, or conceiving, or interpreting the idea of community, or doing all three? At first, questions like these may disconcert an inquirer; yet by articulating them, he can develop a better feel for the mysterious life of interpretation with its many interacting dynamisms, as it wrestles with these empirico-historical materials.

To experience and understand this method, a person needs some special epistemological and ethical equipment: first, a highly alert historical sense, and second, a talent for discerning ideals in their relationships to other ideals, to human destiny, and to practical living (1:59). Moreover, one's interpretive skills should have attained the higher stages of the art of living (1:55). That is, if one is led increasingly by the ethical, aesthetic, and religious ideals of higher civilizations, he will be more interiorly disciplined and sensitive and thus more able to recognize in human nature the sources of the ideas of community and of Church. A poor ethical position can impede this recognition (1:58). For example, if an individual is morally detached from a community, he will often accept a literal formulation of the idea of community rather than struggle to win touch with the spirit of the idea. Yet interpretation becomes possible only if one keeps in touch with this spirit. Hence, disciplined intelligence and ethical loyalty are needed if one intends to enter Royce's empirico-historical method.

Royce applied this method to the idea of community in his second lecture of the *Problem* (1:49-106). Here he reflected on the history of evolving communal consciousness. He searched for the real meaning contained first in the natural basis, and then in the ethical value, of this idea (1:52). Meanwhile, by a series of comparisons and contrasts, he mentally penetrated this idea so concretely that it allowed him to form a more fitting generalization of it—paradoxical as that may seem.

What sparked and directed Royce's ongoing interpretive musement on this idea of community? Much as intriguing pair relations fed his development of System Σ, so a fascinating series of paired signs drew him to further *re*consideration of them. Thus he felt the gaps and links between the idea of community and its ideal, between the spirit and the letter of this idea, between the general form of this idea and its specifically Christian form. The call to identify the source of both likeness and difference in these pairs teased his mind into musement. In addition, he was moving in an overall direction by his choice of goals: first to gain theoretically a connected view of the ideal of the Beloved Community and then practically to contribute to its coming. This disciplined commitment prevented Royce's interpretation from rising into airy abstractions or from spreading out in poisonous dialectics. On the way, during all his provisional cycles of interpretation, he shared life with this idea of community, accepting it as both baffling and yet precious, as both incomplete and yet growing (1:54-55).

To follow Royce in his particular methodic procedures, we invite the reader into the first and second phases of Royce's second stage of the empirico-historical method and to pause with him to note the significant transition he made between them. Then, instead of again sketching the third phase—his initially simplified truth-test—we will close by synthesizing what Royce achieved in finishing these first two phases.

FIRST PHASE: SEARCH FOR THE NATURAL MOTIVES OF THE IDEA AND IDEAL OF COMMUNITY

The main query uniting Royce's first two phases of this second stage is: In human experience, which natural and ethical motives provide rationally significant grounds for the idea and for the ideal of the universal community? To answer this question "in some convenient order," Royce postponed the ethical topic and made his first effort the search for the natural motives in certain natural needs and interests common to all people and to all human communities. For this first phase, he sought three sites to win an adequately diversified sample of communities. The results of his three "digs" into these sites—his three tasks—would form a triad of signs to be compared and contrasted. Connecting these three tasks was his aim to investigate which natural motives had historically led to the development of communal consciousness in the entire Christian community during its nearly two thousand year history, then any human community, and finally, that early Christian community of the apostle Paul.

During its long history, the mind of the Christian community has fed upon the Kingdom-message of the master. This contains both a promise of salvation for the individual and a social meaning (1:49). From the start, this message of the master utilized two natural motives: hope for an ideal future good and present commitment to cooperate practically in embodying the Kingdom. Then, through a series of interpretations formed during its first twenty-five years of life, the early Christian community had come to identify itself both with this Kingdom as beginning on earth and with the master's Church as missioned to all peoples (1:104–105). Only then did the Christian community achieve its first *fully* developed interpretation of the master's Kingdom-message. Then, performing a validation test within himself, Royce found that he, too, could win close personal touch with the spirit of this idea of Church only if his mulling of the idea of Church were accompanied with this idea of "missioned to all." That intimate touch revealed the spirit of this idea of Church to be universal, reasonable, and impressively human (1:55–56).

Next, while surveying how this Christian idea of Church evolved through the centuries, Royce noted its tragedies and encrustations. He attributed these more to growth processes in human nature than to wayward individuals or sects. That is, the unhealthy tensions and tendencies within group consciousness were the chief obstacles to a straightforward development of this dynamic idea of the true Church. As for present responsibilities, people should rediscover this true idea. Even more imperatively, they should bring this idea more into reality by responding loyally to that ideal of the New Jerusalem which has perennially stimulated the Christian community's awareness (1:58).

Royce's first task, then, had unearthed and identified three natural psychological motives for the idea of Church: the *spirit* within this idea, the *dynamism of commitment* to cooperate for the temporal embodiment of the idea (even though wayward tendencies provide obstacles), and the *ideal of being missioned* to all humankind. This third natural motive— the ideal of being missioned—calls Christians to behold the vision of the Church Universal, to long for it in hope, and by deeds to strive for its fuller realization (1:xviii, 58). As a further result, Royce's sketch of the "natural history" of how the Christian community's communal consciousness grew through the centuries offered intimations of the psychological motives needed for the idea of universal community—intimations that later could guide the technical definition of that idea which Royce needed (1:66; 2:49-50).

Consequently, Royce next searched for those spiritual needs and interests exhibited by *all* people and by *all* their communities. He found that the natural history of community consciousness shows the latter creating, maintaining, and developing language, religion, sets of customs, and other communal products which no individual as such can create. These underlying cooperative processes reveal that the community acts as a unity, with a life and a mind of its own. Unless some communal interest were felt, individuals would not unite cooperatively to create, maintain, and develop their language, religion, and sets of customs.

This factual cooperation of the members of a community also reveals how, in each individual participant, there operate a certain need for community and a certain sense of the community's interest. Royce further noticed that individual members not only belong to their community and regard it as a unit with a mind of its own, but also take "active attitudes of love and devotion" towards it. As evidence, he pointed to persons loyally serving their family, their circle of personal friends, their home, their village community, their clan, or their country (1:67). The active attitudes of these loyal people make it clear that they love these very communities as a real but different kind of person from themselves. Moreover, they regard these communities as having a life, power, and worth of a higher and nobler kind than is found in any isolated individual morally detached from community (1:68).

Finally, Royce noticed how loyal members of communities, despite all differences in nationality, race, creed, sex, and age, experience one and the same spirit at work in all loyal people. It was precisely their experience of this spirit that explained why they now prized both themselves and every loyal person, and why they were aware of a different spirit uniting themselves that was found among individualists who had separated themselves from a community. Because of the new spirit, these members experienced, precisely through their differences, that "the loyal are, in ideal, 'essentially kin'" (1:71). In this way each member's basic need for deep human harmony was met as was the community's interest in this harmony. Together, then, all these natural motives satisfied each member's basic need for deeply meaningful human living and the community's own interest in having human selves enabled to live this way.

In sum, then, Royce had uncovered in all community participants certain common natural motives needed for the rise and growth of any community consciousness: 1) cooperative impulses which create communal mental products; 2) requisite beliefs declaring that the community has a life, mind, and interest of its own; 3) loyal dedication to the community given in response to the community's felt interest toward them; and 4) the spirit of loyalty which unifies the members and raises them to a previously non-existent level of loyal life in the unity of the spirit.[1]

As his final task, Royce described the three periods which he found in the early Christian community's development of its doctrine of love. The master had given his message on love to his disciples. Then, after the master's death and reported ascension, the first Christians found that, although the master's doctrine was excellent for their individual inner lives, it occasioned doubts about social implications since it lacked a practical program for social reform. Lastly, Paul came and explicitly taught that the objects of Christian love were not merely God and individual human persons, but also the Christian community itself, the "mystery" (1:76–92).[2] Thus came to light that need and interest whose bearing is upon a community as such, rather than upon other individuals. In this way, Royce showed three things in the Christian doctrine of love: the command to love individuals (God, self, and neighbors) is preserved; another need and interest was harmoniously at work transforming this command into a demand for loyalty toward the Church, the community of the Christian people; and this transformed community also required loyal service to the whole community of humankind as such because the Church is missioned to all people.

Thus, in his first and third tasks, Royce examined how the communal awareness of both the centuries-old Christian community and of the early Christian community fed upon the master's Kingdom-message, then developed the notion of Church, and finally produced the Pauline interpretation of also loving the community itself. These historically developed interpretations were inescapably linked to the idea and ideal of the universal community.

In his second task, Royce sketched the growth of communal consciousness in any human group where loyalty arises. This development again led to the idea and ideal of the universal community. Thereupon, Royce estimated that his bringing together of these Christian and non-Christian ideas of community would be "of the utmost importance for our entire enterprise" (1:60). By comparing and contrasting the two natural histories (of the idea of universal church and of the idea of universal community), Royce found both ideas pointing forward to the *ideal* of the universal community. With its spirit, this ideal would guide the whole Roycean endeavor in the *Problem*.[3]

PAUSE FOR REFLECTION: ROYCE'S SHIFT FROM A NATURAL TO AN ETHICAL SEARCH

Through cooperative group experiences, both individual and community become aware that the idea of community will eventually suggest how universal the scope of this idea is and thus how pregnant it is with ideal values. What this shift from a natural to an ethical search for values fully implies can be brought to light only gradually through a series of reconsiderations, as Royce himself recognized.[4] In general, he started with the natural history of an individual's consciousness and soon compared it with the natural history of a community's consciousness (1:66-70). Both individuals and communities recognize that successes and failures fashion their histories. If they compare and contrast these ups and downs, they will soon be led to evaluation, and eventually to ethical awareness.

Royce, however, wanted to see this emergence of ethical consciousness in greater detail. He began his analysis by inquiring why the conception of community as a real unit can be ethical in its purposes (1:66). Once a person (or one's community) acts on the hypothesis that a community is a living being with a mind of its own, many human motives lead him to interpret the community as precious and noble (1:66); that is, induce this person to create ethical values. To identify these common natural motives, Royce examined two types of experience found in all individuals and groups: (a) the feeling of frustration at the failure of natural self-will and of mere morality to satisfy a person's longing for one's highest good in social relationships; and (b) the startling recognition of how differently one feels the spirit of unity among genuinely loyal persons over against that more commonly found spirit of predominant self-will and mere conformism (i.e., non-loyalty).

Once an individual has experienced these two spirits, he or she senses in the spirit of genuine loyalty how the community's interest exerts a distinctive appeal and how the community's influence supports oneself. He or she also feels oneself responding differently from one's previous way of responding simply to one's own interests or only to those of a few friends. If this once morally detached individual comes, through these contrasts, to experience the meaning of loyalty, then that person will find oneself starting to touch a deeper level of human life. That is, one will enter an intimate experience of life in a Beloved Community. One will understand, in a personally lived way, the saving idea of "man the community" (1:405-407). One may even find oneself lured on to superhuman realms and values (1:408).[5]

By such comparison and contrast, an individual or even a group that was previously separated from genuine community can get in intimate touch with that communal level of human existence and consciousness without which genuine ethical life is impossible (1:69, 408). But such getting-in-touch requires several stages of development. In the natural histories of individual and group minds, Royce noticed that people's natural loyalties are usually limited by an exclusive concern for family or clan or race. From these naturally restricted forms, a lower loyalty needs to develop through stages, such as those of chivalry and true sportsmanship, to a transcendent form, called universal loyalty. Eventually, when the individual adopts unrestricted universal loyalty towards every human self, as his or her conscious ideal, then the person has arrived at the essentially new type of self-consciousness from which genuine ethical life takes its start (1:158). But this breakthrough to such an unrestricted commitment requires that the individual be transformed. The transformation starts when the person receives the gift of that spirit which is essentially the same in all genuinely loyal people however diverse they may otherwise be (1:71). This special gift empowers a person simultaneously to love the community as a person and to prize oneself (1:158).

Royce's shift from the natural to the ethical motives provides a test for his empirico-historical method.[6] Moreover, its import for moral reflection is momentous — namely, the establishment of community as the paramount ethical value. It seems worthwhile, then, to reapproach this shift, even if from a slightly different angle this time.

The individual who lacks moral attachment to any genuine community feels disintegration occurring both in oneself and in one's natural social groups. This heightens one's sense of needing both inner healing and group reconciliation. The idea of community is already radiating with ideal significance. It does so particularly when this individual encounters others whose steadfast deeds express loyal dedication to their community. Then, sensing a distinctive spirit at work in their genuinely loyal community, one feels and appreciates the attraction of the deeper level of human living found in such a community. In this kind of appreciative experiences one "tastes" both the loyal spirit itself and one's newly rich life of membership.

When the individual makes the value and ideal of genuine community one's own, it transforms one's life. First one recognizes one's former state as lost; then one discovers the logic in the value of genuine community as it attracts one to the ideal of universal community now seen as absolutely loveable in itself (1:71–72). As Royce put it, "To act as if one were a member of such a community is to win in the highest measure the goal of individual life" (1:73). But this presupposes that one is logically universalizing the ideal of community and at the same time making the promotion of the universal community one's supreme value.

To clarify how this last level of loyalty is reached, Royce pointed to the person who has already pondered in one's heart the contrast between the non-loyal isolated individual and the lovingly loyal member of the genuine community. Next, on encountering actual instances of loyalty, this person reads their significance[7] for each loyal deed flashes forth "a practical faith that communities, viewed as units, have a value which is superior to all the values and interests of detached individuals" (1:72). But this practical faith can live only if the observer of these loyal deeds believes that the community, to which one is to give one's loyalty, is: 1) a living organic being with a mind of its own, 2) "a very precious and worthy being," and, by implication, 3) a real being of a higher kind than that of a detached individual (1:63, 66). In brief, this person's loyal deeds will express his or her faith in the doctrine of the two levels.

For these reasons a person tends to value the interest of one's community more highly than "every merely individual interest of his own" (1:67-70). In other words, a preference-system of ethical values is emerging in one's consciousness. Furthermore, the *intentionality* at work in the idea of community—the idea central to one's new value system—directs this now loyal member to a whole-hearted service of the universal community. It even opens the loyally dedicated person to the whole of reality and to the divine presence.

But Royce also had to account for the alienation at work in human nature. This alienation impedes people's consciousness from developing the ideal of the universal community in the straightforward way just described. Even if alienation does not pervert the psychological growth processes of human nature, it infects and slows them down (1:58). Alienations unmask how diseased the human race's communal body is. Its swelling abscesses reveal that disordered social group which Royce rightly called "a community of sin" (1:178). This collectivity lures individual sinners powerfully into further sin through its primarily self-preferential attitudes, structures, and collective will. Yet this disordered collectivity, so deeply racked by communal sin, is itself called to healing and transformation through an experience of both the ideal and the saving influence of the Beloved Community.

Thus, by contrast, even alienation shows that the universal community is a value preeminent among all other values and an ideal indispensable if a person is to be transformed from alienation to a new life of basic loyalty to all people. When one knows the conception of the brotherhood of all the loyal, this person is logically led to test how much one's other values promote the better service of the only community that is universal in ideal (1:72-73). By engaging in such a test, one reveals one's faith that genuine loyalty to the universal community serves as humankind's paramount norm of morality. Little wonder, then, why the mature Royce wanted to put loyalty—this love of the individual for the community—where it actually belongs, not only at the heart of the virtues, not only at the summit of the mountains which the human spirit must climb if man is really to be saved, but also (where it equally belongs) at the turning-point of human history,—at the point when the Christian ideal was first defined,—and when the Church Universal,—that still invisible Community of all the faithful, that homeland of the human spirit, "which eager hearts expect," was first introduced as a vision, as a hope, as a conscious longing to mankind. (1:xviii)

SECOND PHASE: SEARCH FOR THE ETHICAL MOTIVES OF THE IDEA AND IDEAL OF THE UNIVERSAL COMMUNITY

Royce's second phase was initiated by the question: Which motives lead an individual to regard one's community, and to behave towards it, not only as a living unit with a mind and will of its own, but also as something so precious that it is worthy of one's most dedicated efforts? For an answer, we follow Royce's order of scrutinizing three aspects of conscious loyalty: its history, its generation of various ideals, and its propelling motives.

History showed Royce many persons who were stimulated to natural loyalty—sometimes by warfare, sometimes by religious practice (1:66–69). Typically a naturally loyal individual or group was gradually prodded beyond the confining thresholds of a consciousness limited to family or clan or tribe into the unlimited range of an essentially different kind of consciousness: universal loyalty towards all individuals and groups (whether actually loyal or only potentially so). Transformed by this highest loyalty to the supra-individual life of the universal community, this person or group now yearns in rational self-consciousness to so help individuals that each becomes a fitting member of this noblest of communities. The desire also arises to live in genuine community in such a way that the universal community becomes worthy of the Spirit-Interpreter who loves it (1:103).

But how are various ideals generated in this development of consciousness into highest loyalty? Royce observed how the conversion process transforms the previously isolated individual into one who loves one's universal community as a person on a higher level. At this point the truest desire of one's heart, far more than the voice of any philosopher, directs that person to relate to one's community as "essentially more worthy than his own form of being" (1:67). Hereupon that person becomes aware of the moral ideal. One also possesses the aesthetic values of the nobler and the more majestic. And just below the surface one glimpses religious values.[8] In making these ideals one's very own, the individual finds one's moral destiny and experiences one's distinctively human fulfillment. As the now genuinely loyal individual begins devotedly to serve the community, this latter begins to pour back into the individual all its wealth of meaningful life (1:67–68). Finding one's ethical home in this universal loyalty, one ceases to be an ethical wanderer. One now knows one's better half, one's truer identity.

Certain motives propel this development toward a genuinely loyal communal consciousness. These motives so closely blend their natural and ethical tones that we here simply present them together. This parallels Royce's procedure of finding a concresence of natural and ethical motives operative as he alternated his research perspectives from the communal to the individual approaches.

In the community, which motives propel this development of consciousness to its mature ethical form? When a genuine community, through its distinctive ambience and through its leading members, exercises a saving presence upon the morally lost individual, its gift of transformative love enters this person who previously had lain captive to habits of self-preference and limited concern. The individual now experiences the community's saving influence as somehow bringing a new kind of unity, a higher life which gives one's own life an unexpected meaning and satisfaction. Meanwhile, the community's ideal of serving all people calls, attracts, and fascinates this individual by its majesty and constancy. Through these motives the community promotes one's continuous ethical conversion and growth.

In the individual, the motives for one's transformation into universal loyalty are the needs one has for a genuine community, for a release from one's moral burden, and for an atoning influence effective enough to offset one's former misdeeds. Now a new kind of love arises in the individual, a love for this community as a person. His new loyalty, glowing with a hope and with a longing for realization of the Beloved Community, integrates one's continuing love for individuals. Meanwhile, a fear of one's clearly remembered former self-enclosure and a repugnance for it provide one with secondary motives. Moreover, the converted individual now experiences the satisfaction of living more meaningfully and committedly than ever before. One finds that genuine loyalty, as the central motive of one's life, effectively integrates all one's other motives—one's needs, love, fear, and satisfaction. All these motives are then further enhanced when the genuinely loyal person clearly apprehends the religious values latent in them (1:70). In this way Royce completed his second phase of searching for the rise of ethical values, ideals, and motives. In his third phase he would test how the individual idea of genuine community dovetailed with both the contemporary mind and with people's basic psychological needs.

RESULTS OF THESE SEARCHES

What had Royce achieved by his serial reinterpretation of consciousness as it develops in individual and group? Common to individual and group consciousness is a pair of ethico-religious experiences that alternate between felt inner conflict and saving presence. Royce demonstrated that a person's ineradicable need for salvation is a fully natural and universal motive. He also showed that this need can be satisfied, but only by the idea of salvation and those satellite ideas linked to it (1:397). In sum, Royce discovered both the human self's common radical need for salvation (with its subordinate triad of needs) and also its dominant idea of salvation (with its subordinate triad of ideas).

How does a person's fundamental need for salvation reveal itself amid the human self's rhythmic experience of inner conflicts and saving presences? Despite one's natural individualism, a person longs to attain unimpeded union with one's highest good rather than to continue one's present futile living for oneself alone. One's deepest spiritual need, then, is for shared life in a community of genuinely loyal persons who somehow embody the Beloved Community. But this need reveals a second need: to be freed from one's enslavement to predominant self-preference, from one's weakness of will. Because a person is caught in original and personal sin, one cannot break out of one's moral chains either by personal efforts or by the help of other individuals similarly enslaved; one cannot escape to freedom. A person's third need, therefore, is to receive the sheer gift of deliverance from some communal reality beyond oneself. Only if a community offers the human self this transforming gift of loving the community as a person can one be saved from self-enclosure and reach one's ethical home. Thus, in the "lost individual"—the person morally separated from a genuine community—these three needs (for union, self-transcendence, and empowerment towards communal love) are three insuppressible signs of the human self's fundamental need for salvation—a salvation the self can sense is seriously endangered.

This leads us to ask about the psychic signs through which the idea of genuine community arises. Royce held that a person becomes aware of the saving idea of "man the spiritual community," or of "man viewed as one conscious spiritual whole of life" (1:406) if one thoughtfully reflects upon three basic human experiences. While musing over the frustration of failing to win one's highest good, a person comes upon the idea of the moral burden which is unavoidably carried by anyone detached from a saving community. If, by contrast, one muses upon the distinctive spirit of loyalty found in a genuine community, one will find that the relationships of loyal persons witness to a higher and unique kind of unified life.

These two reflections taken together suggest a third idea: perhaps somewhere within its distinctive life of loyal service, the saving community can initiate and carry out an atonement process which will heal the lost individual and elevate that healed self to membership. In this way Royce's interpretive musing on positive and negative experiences discovered the basis in human nature for his three Christian ideas. Both the triad of needs and this triad of Christian ideas, rooted in human experience, presuppose that a person's spiritual existence has two levels and that one's ethical transformation can occur if and only if a living mutual bond is established between oneself and one's deeper level of community (1:405).

In sum, then, this chapter invited the reader to enter the musing mind of the mature Royce as he moved through the second stage of his empirico-historical method. The first individual Christian idea he mused upon was that of community. He searched the historical data available for various communities, looking for the natural and ethical motives, needs, and ideals at work in the emergence of communal consciousness. By alternating between communal and individual perspectives, he clarified the idea and the ideal of community. His musement eventually reached close personal touch with the reality of genuine community: that living metaboly of individual selves committed to, and partaking in, a shared life that is oriented universally.

15. Metaphysical Method

At the start of Part Two of the *Problem,* Royce faced the most difficult and critical part of his whole undertaking. He had to subject the Christian doctrine of life to an elaborate truth-test. The doctrine would pass this test if it could be shown consistent with ultimate reality and fruitful for people's practical choices. Royce's overall strategy for developing this two-pronged truth-test was to select judiciously from Charles Peirce's writings certain seedling ideas. These he would graft onto the stem of his own unique purpose. The resultant, novel, hybrid synopsis of epistemology, metaphysics, ethics, and religion would be his mature "philosophy of life."

While mulling over possible strategies, Royce became more convinced of both the limits and the power of metaphysics. To be adequate, his metaphysics had to preserve each individual's uniqueness even as it let each unite freely to what he or she loved most. He saw that his metaphysics could meet this steep challenge *only if* three conditions were met (2:103). First, in the shared life of minded beings he would have to find a metaphysical basis for defining a genuine community.[1] Then he would have to advance evidence that both humankind and indeed the entire universe constitute genuine communities.[2] Finally, finite selves would have to come to love the universal community genuinely. Of course, Royce realized that metaphysics can neither explain the origin of love nor make anyone fall in love with anything—least of all, with the universal community.[3] Despite these limitations, he saw his metaphysical inquiry could open up a perspective larger than that of human history—one suitably rich and broad for investigating the "problem of the religion of loyalty" (2:104). He saw that the metaphysics of interpretation could offer a basis for meaningfulness in human life, for a sense of profound harmony at work in the world, and for the hope "that, in the world's community, our highest love may yet find its warrant and its fulfillment" (2:105).

Towards two favorite metaphysical methods of his day, however, Royce remained critically cautious. Both of these chose narrow initial perspectives. The first method tried to build metaphysics on a simplistic logic of propositions. An example was the traditionalists' proofs for God's existence from nature. Their method created an abstract realm of mere concepts and barren theories. It left the human reasoner alone with his God, untouched by any specific call to serve his community loyally. By contrast, Royce wanted his truth-testing method to remain rooted within communal life and to nurture the genuinely loyal service that promotes "unity in the spirit."

A second defective method was evident in current popular philosophies of religion. They, too, focused primarily on the solitary individual. They led an individual to seek breathtaking intuitions or ineffable feelings of peace (2:104).[4] By contrast, Royce was convinced that any metaphysical method had to be deficient if it left out of account the second and deeper level of human spiritual existence — the level of man the community. He saw that as long as the human mind attends solely to an individual or individuals or Christianity or even humankind itself, it is so preoccupied with a tree or with a cluster of trees or with every tree in the world that it misses the whole of the woods (2:103–104).

Positively, his method would have to be broad and flexible enough to fit the whole processing universe. How could he design a method with the broadest yet deepest reach? Convinced that the universe was "through and through dominated by social categories" (2:280), he gave himself to the idea of a Spirit-led Community of Interpretation as the most fundamental choice in his metaphysical method. This starting point gave his metaphysics its central light and ruling category (2:16, 281) even as it required that his metaphysics generate a "generalized theory of an ideal society" (2:281). Set within the triadic form of interpretive life, such a theory would in general require three members in an ideal society: *idea, reality,* and *spirit of truth* (2:275). Could his methodic interpretation ultimately bring this triad into integral unity and full clarity? Towards this goal he designed a method which would advance through three stages.[5] First, he would take the idea of community and search for its metaphysical basis. Second, he would examine our closest touch with reality: the process of interpretation, viewed as a sign that reality itself is a processing community of interpretation. Lastly, under the lead of the Spirit, he would compare and contrast the ideal of the universal community with the real world of temporal process. In this way he would display the "ground plan of the World of Interpretation" (2:280) and provide an ultimate truth-test of the Christian doctrine of life.

FIRST STAGE OF THE METAPHYSICAL METHOD: SEARCHING FOR THE BASIS OF THE IDEA OF COMMUNITY

His study of Peirce's writings had convinced Royce that our closest contact with life is experienced in the process of genuine interpretation.

Hence, he could no longer accept highly abstract concepts or isolated intuitions as adequate starting points for metaphysics. Rather, he would build upon the sign-process of interpretation that occurs between human selves. He would also devise a new "more precise and restricted" working definition of a community "without going beyond the facts of human life, of human memory, and of human interpretation of the self and of its past" (2:53). With the accurate "spotlight" of this definition he could focus upon the process of interpretation as the real life center of selves and of communities. Its beam would also leave in the shadows those inauthentic forms of community—such as picnickers, passing crowds, mobs, mere organizations, or institutions. Although these groups each behave as a single unit, they lack that kind of history, productivity, and spirit which is proper even to a natural community of interpretation.

Royce's technical definition of community spotlighted a basic pattern in the conscious life of any natural human community. Whenever member-selves concur in their interpretations of idealized common past and future events, the triadic pattern of sign-sender, sign-interpreter, and sign-receiver appears. He adopted this pattern as the basis for his idea of community. Guided by it, he could generalize until his sign-metaphysics referred to the whole universe. When generalizing, however, he had to safeguard the unique individuality of every member-self and the time-flow that moves from irrevocable past into the chancy open future of communally shared hopes (2:52).

His technical definition also enabled him to identify three *conditions* requisite for the kind of communal life and consciousness found in a community of his more precise sense (2:60-78). Furthermore, this definition guided his mapping of the three *degrees* of communal life and awareness which run the gamut from the simply natural to the highest ethico-religious life (2:79-98). In his sign-metaphysics, each of these three degrees would reveal a more profound basis for communal life and consciousness: a) the triadic structure of a community of interpretation, already mentioned (2: 83-86); b) the conscious art of intelligent cooperation and mutual identification of selves in the community (2:88-89); and c) the transforming life of genuine grace-given loyalty, or, in its highest form, Charity (2:91-98). Because Royce attempted so much in this first stage of his metaphysical method, it seems fitting to examine more closely how he moved in the two tasks he there set for himself.

The "problem of community" lies in balancing adequately the uniqueness of its members and the unity of their shared life. Royce sought this needed balance by alternating his approaches to the data available about diverse human social groups. In this way he carried out his first task of gradually honing a technical definition of community sharp enough for his metaphysical purposes. First, then, he insisted on the stubborn fact of individuals' pluralism. He adduced three sets of evidence supporting the common sense conviction that individuals are discrete and separate (2:18-25). Paradoxically, however, his argument closed by finding within each of these diverse individuals that basic structure and process which is both the analogue of any genuine community and the basis for all of these individuals being in the communal life they share.

Next, Royce counterbalanced the fact of pluralism by attending to evidence that the many discrete individuals are somehow really one, that they actually take part in the one life, mind, interest, and will of the community whose members they are. For this alternative approach (2:26-44), the evidence he lined up began with a community generating social products that show a startling unity of agency. For example, a distinctive language, religion, and set of customs are things no single individual can produce. Similarly, he focused on communal deeds, to which individuals contribute, but which are done by the community as a whole. Furthermore, communal consciousness cannot occur without community history or hope—its remembered process of the group's coherent evolution or of its shared expectation. Finally, within each seemingly atomic individual Royce explicated that process and structure of interpretation which is both an analogue of the community itself and reveals the non-atomic nature of each individual. A finite self can be an individual only insofar as, in addition to its uniqueness, it exists both as a community and as a member of a higher community.

Using the data from both these approaches, Royce next identified the structures of consciousness requisite for the communal life shared by uniquely individual members. This allowed him to form his technical definition of a community (2:49-50, 59-60). At the conclusion of his first task, then, he estimated that his progressively refined definition of any real community achieved an adequate balance of every member's unique individuality and of the temporally flowing life of the community. Indeed, he felt that his definition had also cleared the way for generalization beyond human selves and human communities. It could serve as a doorway leading to more intimate knowledge of the entire real world of the spirit (2:53, 57).

But what was the basis in reality for this idea of community and for its ideal? Here was Royce's second task. Applying his new technical definition to various samples, he was to analyze the problem of real human communities. How can distinct individuals actually exist as a real community, really constitute a single entity, and find meaning and value in it both for themselves and for their community? Such was his problem (2:58, 60, 79). So he again went searching for sources—not precisely of religious insight, as he had done a year earlier—but of the existence and values of conscious community life.⁶ What united such life? What produced its human, ethical, and religious worth?

He moved towards an answer to these two questions by both searching for the conditions of his defined kind of communal life and by measuring the degrees in which such a community expresses itself in united deeds.⁷ He developed an in-touch interpretation of such community life by exploring the three conditions required for the minimal functioning of a "conscious community of memory and of hope" (2:60–69). In each of these conditions he found that natural consciousness blends with evaluative consciousness. Take, for example, the first condition—those idealized extensions of the self which converge upon common past and future events. Besides these factual extensions, he discovered the bases both for a life *worth* living, for human *meaning and destiny,* and for the intimation that the latter pair just might fit in with the intent of beings higher than human.

Having identified the conditions for such conscious communal life and its values, Royce shifted his procedure to measure "the degree to which this consciousness of unity can find expression in an effectively united common life" (2:79). He found that deed-doing communities can express themselves in three degrees: first, simply in the conscious extensions of its members to common events, then in its appropriating communal deeds as its own, and finally in arousing a distinctive love for community—a loyalty beyond the love found between individuals. By so calibrating conscious communal expression, he further clarified the sources both of the unity in a community and of that rare intensity of shared awareness found only in the consummate community consciousness (2:79, 92–98).

By two different interpretations, he identified the three conditions for community consciousness and delineated the three degrees of its expression. In this way he gained a doorway for generalization and won a key to a close understanding and an ethical evaluation of the vast variety of communities of minded beings in the universe. This was especially true of those communities whose life and unity have been, are, or will be centered in the religion of genuine loyalty (2:104).

In further review of the whole first stage of Royce's metaphysical method, he was led to the structured process of interpretation within each human self. It became the pattern for his technical definition of community within his sign-metaphysics. Using this pattern of sign-sender, sign-interpreter, and sign-receiver as his basis for generalization, he found the same pattern verified in historically developing, tradition-formed human communities. This pair of triadic structures supplied Royce with grounds for initiating the following metaphysical queries which led him into his second and generalizing stage. Is the interpretive process the root of the individual's significance and worth? Does this process also validate the finite self's sense of harmony with world process? Finally, does this process provide a warranty that in a world of interpretation persons' highest hopes can be realized (2:105)?

SECOND STAGE OF THE METAPHYSICAL METHOD: SEARCHING FOR A NEW WORLD-REVEALING THEORY OF KNOWLEDGE

For Royce, interpretation was a neglected yet fundamental mode of knowing. By understanding it intimately, he would generate his metaphysical perspective for Part Two of the *Problem*. Those who appreciate the fundamental yet too neglected doctrine of the Spirit found in the fourth Gospel will grasp interpretive knowing more easily (2:15-16). To appreciate interpretation, then, mature understanding is needed.

Metaphysical perspectives based upon percepts, concepts, or their combination had to prove inadequate because they were abstract and lacked the needed personal touch with life itself. But interpretation offered a new, deeper, and interpersonal mode of knowing. Its dynamism of free continuing communication kept it alive, fluent, and flexible, even as its Spirit (its Will to create unity among minded beings) inserted a constant direction into this process. Fittingly, then, Royce found the first task in this stage to be a close examination of what an interpretation is.

To begin with, he knew that minded beings rise to self-consciousness and full life only through interpretation. Similarly, through lack of interpretation they die as minded beings (2:111). The individual self's temporal and communal life depends on successive interpretations. Hence, a careful study of interpretation will let one become reflectively aware of the way any member-self grows. It will clarify how every member is gradually individualized as a unique person insofar as he or she takes a cooperative part in the search for that basic unity of interpretation which underlies one's community. Royce's first step had taken him thus far. But could the interpretive process of reading and translating signs also widen his perspective to fit the whole of reality? He thought it worth the effort to investigate. Thus, despite its neglect by many philosophers, Royce inquired whether unity-seeking interpretation might turn out to be the fundamental life-function of any minded being—individual or community—which was reflectively present to itself.

But how could Royce validly transcend human selves in their history and get in touch with a process intrinsic to *all* minded beings and their sign-products (2:104)? Developing his plan of generalizing the idea of a Spirit-led community, Royce found arising a method which he described in the following capital text:

METAPHYSICAL METHOD 237

May we not hope to gain by a method which follows the plan now outlined? This method, first, encourages a man to interpret his own individual self in terms of the largest ideal extension of that self in time which his reasonable will can acknowledge as worthy of the aims of his life. [See Lecture 11.]

Secondly, this method bids a man consider what right he has to interpret the life from which he springs, in the midst of which he now lives, as a life that in any universal sense cooperates with his own and ideally expresses its own meaning so as to meet with his own and to have a history identical with his own. [See Lecture 12.]

Thirdly, this method directs us to inquire how far, in the social order to which we unquestionably belong, there are features such as warrant us in hoping that, in the world's community, our highest love may yet find its warrant and its fulfilment. [See Lecture 13.] (2:104-105)

Situated at the close of Lecture 10, this description of method refers directly to the second stage of Royce's metaphysical endeavor. It presupposes the reader's familiarity with the already completed first stage and his openness to an as yet undescribed, final confirmatory stage. The text is here broken down from Royce's single paragraph into three units to highlight Royce's numeration and thus the three tasks to which he gives clear prominence. (A person is to "interpret," "consider," and "inquire.") Of these functions all three are processes of interpretation, even if a person is to carry them out differently.

The method described here clearly transcends human life and history. Taking my cue from Royce, then, I call it his "metaphysical method" (1:113). His description of this method appears simple enough yet analysis will reveal how Royce's subtle depth pervades it. The series of tasks, the site, and the peculiar terms employed in the text solicit special attention. Accordingly, a textual analysis will precede some general comments on the text.

Royce's "first," "secondly," and "thirdly," emphasize the planned order of serial interpretation that his second stage calls for. It would be disorderly to inquire immediately whether the universe is a community of interpretation before one had discovered the nature of an interpretation and then its work and worth. Royce foreshadows Lonergan's insistence on inserting and maintaining order in philosophizing. One is first to experience, then understand, then judge critically, and finally, decide by embodying the truth in a practical choice.[8]

By situating this description almost two-thirds through the *Problem*, Royce invited his reader to recall several themes presupposed from the ten preceding lectures. First, the human self-interpreter shares in the already discovered basic ethico-religious needs of every human self—needs that are universal and ineradicable.[9] Second, these needs produce the essential ideas which alone can satisfy them. Third, the living metaboly of these needs and ideas has the highest possible significance for ethical and religious life. Last, this living metaboly occurs in communities insofar as the conditions for communal consciousness are fulfilled and insofar as the community attains a certain degree of such consciousness.

Turning to some peculiar terms in the text, one can focus on its three principal verbs: "*encourage* a man to interpret," "*bids* a man consider [or interpret]," and "*directs* us to inquire [interpretively]." These verbs are invitational. They bespeak a distinctive mark of Royce's metaphysical method. Through them Royce *appeals* to the reader to enter into this new mode of knowing. One might paraphrase these verbs by having Royce call to his reader, "Watch my steps and walk after me," or simply, "Would you follow my lead?" By offering his example of pioneering upon this novel metaphysical path, moreover, Royce intends the "strengthening of hearts," not just in the *Problem's* "somewhat extended practical sections" (1:xiv), but also in the steep climbing required to follow his investigation of communities of minded beings who mutually interpret proffered signs.

Next, the text exhibits a number of phrases that may strike toughminded logicians as odd. Royce employs "acknowledge as worthy," "interpret . . . as cooperating with," "to meet with," "identical with," "functions such as warrant us," and "find its warrant and its fulfilment." These phrases do not fit the language of perception or conception. Rather, each of them presupposes the discovery of a suitably mediating idea, a "third" that interprets. Such discovery is indispensable for interpretation. It marks Royce's method. These phrases, then, highlight the distinctive work of interpretation: to discover and/or create "*fittingness*" between either minded beings or their signs or both.

Objectors to classical idealism and to representational theories of knowledge frequently attack the assumed, yet unproven isomorphism between idea and reality. Valid for subject-object epistemologies, this criticism fails to meet the Royce of 1913 who had become an interpretive (triadic) epistemologist. He who uses interpretation to know concretely *need not* presuppose a parallelism between idea and reality. Rather, by experiencing life in its humanly deepest reality, he finds signs which increasingly warrant the position that the central life-process of the universe is interpretation. When Royce tried to deny this basic position, he found himself engaged in a performative contradiction (2:275–276, 325).

What, then, was he doing in this second stage of his metaphysical method? Through his process of interpretation he searched for a larger than human perspective. With that he moved towards a generalization that fitted the whole universe and its Spirit. Interpretation let him get so far beneath the levels of perception and conception that he touched the heart of reality (2:163). By winning such close touch with reality, he could fittingly appreciate many natural, ethical, religious, and aesthetic values.

Certain large tendencies distinguish Royce's metaphysical method from both his empirico-historical method and his general method of interpretation. Three of these tendencies were his search for larger and thus fairer perspectives, his pathfinder's style, and his indispensable intent to generalize.

As mentioned, contemporary metaphysics either relied on propositional linkages of abstract concepts or fed simply upon one's profound experiences (2:104). But such reliances encased metaphysicians within their individualistic perspectives. Their starting choices denied that the human self is involved inescapably in a communal knowing process. In contrast to the narrow perspectives which individual insight and merely *human* history offered, Royce insisted that his method be *communitarian* and thus provide a larger and fairer perspective. So he preferred the process of interpretation because it offered a paradigm of community life and an entryway into the process of the universe.

Royce's pathfinder style surfaced in our earlier chapters on his logic. A similar pathfinder style marks his metaphysical method. He presupposed that the metaphysician is not merely a contemplator of the universe who simply tries to construct its mirror image. Rather, the metaphysician also further creates the universe through his interpretation of it. Since metaphysics involves values as well as beings and events, a philosopher should evaluate whether his next thought-step coheres logically with both remembered and expected ones. *Through conscience* he should also respond sensitively to the ethico-religious signs which emerge through "every temporal happening," psychic as well as physical (2:386). Responding this way converts a metaphysician into a pathfinder. Contemplatively he both evaluates and creates each step he takes. His progress depends on examining the order, rather than the caprice, of his successive modes of action (2:4, 286) and on maintaining that ambience of a dedicated freedom of spirit "which loves both a wide outlook and a well-knit plan of action" (2:6).

A third and most significant tendency in Royce's metaphysical method is its intent to transcend the human, to generalize towards all minded beings and to the whole universe. If such a generalization is well-founded, it will possess universal importance (2:18). What empowered Royce to achieve this desired generalization, however, was paradoxical. He descended into the finite human self, viewing it alternately as an individual and as a community. Then he compared and contrasted the human self with a human community (at the second level of reality), approaching the latter with similar alternation. In this way he found himself directed towards making a generalization about the universe (2:273). Royce entered intimately into the processes of sign-sending, sign-interpreting, and sign-receiving which are familiar to human selves. Hereupon the teleology operant within the human community aligned him towards getting in close touch with the whole process of the universe. For this process, too, was "through and through dominated by social categories" (2:280).

The process of interpretation is so treasure-filled that Royce wanted great freedom in approaching it. To do so, he varied his approaches, using genetic, logical, psychological, teleological, and aesthetic avenues (2:158–161). Genetically, his metaphysical method originated from that series of choices by which he carried out his overall plan (2:104–105). Logically, Royce laid bare the central logical form (an asymmetrical goal-seeking triad) which always underlies sign-communications in community (2:139–142, 158–159). Psychologically, he exhibited the interests and motives ingredient in any human interpretation. Teleologically, he focused on the will to promote unity even while preserving diversity. Aesthetically, Royce sometimes described his method as an effort to employ the medium of signs as adroitly as an artist works his own medium (2:161–163). If an interpreter is artist enough, he easily unveils the ethical and religious signs which emerge in genuine interpretation. By comparing and contrasting the yields of these various approaches, Royce obtained a more nuanced and richer appreciation of how central and powerful interpretation is both in our lives and in a metaphysics of signs which bears upon the real universe and its Interpreter-Spirit (2:11, 13).

Since this second stage of metaphysical method is not directly a musement upon musement, it is distinct from his overall general method of interpretation. Moreover, the just-mentioned three large tendencies distinguish it from his empirico-historical method of Part One. Yet the familiar three-cycle pattern of that earlier method seems to replicate itself within his metaphysical method, at least in its second stage. The movement from experience, through understanding, to judgment of truth is again found in this stage. Royce describes the experience of rudimentary interpretation (Lecture 11), comes to an evaluative understanding of the work and worth of interpretation (Lecture 12), and finally reaches the self-reinstating judgment that any interpretation presupposes that the universe is a Community of Interpretation with its pedagogue Spirit (Lecture 13). What becomes clear, then, is how the second stage of Royce's metaphysical method is both distinct from his general and his empirico-historical methods, even while it is animated by the former and shows resemblances to the latter.

First Task of the Second Stage: Study the Nature of an Interpretation

In Royce's second stage the chief task was to outline a metaphysics of interpretation (2:168). He viewed this, however, as his third task, since preparatory to it, he had to clarify what a process of interpretation is (first task) and had to show the work and worth of interpretation (second task). A bird's-eye view of Royce in his first task, then, shows him proceeding as an interpreter, trying to enter ever closer into the mind of C. S. Peirce. Then he compares and contrasts Peirce's doctrine of knowing by interpretation with the knowledge-theories of conceptualist Plato and perceptualist Bergson. Through such an alternation of comparison and contrast, Royce moves to those mediating "third ideas" which distinguish a process of interpretation from acts of perceiving or conceiving.

Our aim here is to experience the way Royce used his metaphysical method during his first task of uncovering the nature of interpretation. For this, two of Royce's paths help: a) enter Peirce's teaching on interpretation with increasing intimacy (2:113-152), b) search for ethical self-identity by following Royce's own "effort at self-interpretation" (2:104-105).

Royce realized that his search ran counter to that classical dualist tradition in epistemology which builds upon percepts and concepts only. Could he advance solid grounds why he introduced interpretation as a third, fundamental, and irreducible mode of human knowing? At least he could emphasize the uniqueness of interpretation and thus distinguish it clearly from perception and conception.

Starting then with memory, he reviewed with his audience various instances of interpretation which they had already encountered in the previous lectures. In this way he formed a community of memory with them. Next he pointed out the "very definable unity of purpose" at work in each of their interpretations (2:113). For as interpreters, each of them had sought to overcome some spiritual disharmony (some lack of mental fit) since they sought above all to see the particular topic in basically the same way—that is, with unity of minds. Unlike perception and conception, interpretation intends a distinctive cluster of objects—minds, their signs, and their unity—and relates distinctively to these objects in a unity-promoting way.

Next, alternating his approach, Royce invited his audience to follow him into the mind of C. S. Peirce to explore the latter's teaching about interpretations and the logic of signs. However, since Royce here had to fashion a readily intelligible summary of Peirce's doctrine, he had to adopt explicitly the role of an interpreter of Peirce to them. Royce aimed to create a faithful yet unique interpretation of Peirce. In this endeavor, he compared and contrasted Peirce's doctrine of interpretation over against classical theories of knowledge built upon only two basic modes of knowing. By reconsidering the different purposes, objects, and relations of perception, conception, and interpretation, he further revealed the nature of interpretation.

Next, he alternated his musement by entering the pragmatists' highway: their effort to explain knowing and truth by combining concept with percept into a "leading idea." Royce compared and contrasted their attempted synthesis with that novel "third idea" which an interpreter finds and/or creates. In this way he showed that the pragmatists fail logically to coordinate a pair of opposed ideas and that without such coordination no "third or synthetic factor" can be found and/or created (2:126).

Musing still more upon Peirce's mind, Royce identified interpretation's proper object: mind or sign of mind. Here was an "essentially spiritual object," one charged with more life than is a non-minded self. Consequently, human selves, as minded, can win touch with the full richness of life *only* through interpretation (2:136). Entering further into Peirce's mind, Royce next exposed that triadic relation which Peirce found in every interpretive process: "A interprets B to C" (2:142). Unlike perception and conception which depend on a two-term relation (subject-object), an interpretation can occur only if three terms are present and only if they are arranged in a determinate order: A through B to C.

Wanting to clarify the nature of interpretation still more for his audience, Royce proposed various instances to them. In each he indicated the operative triadic pattern distinctive of a process of interpretation. There it was working in each social interchange, in every self-reflection, in the evolution of nature, and even in the cosmic order of time itself. Finally, when concluding his two preparatory first tasks, he shared with them his presentiment. Since interpretation is both targeted on life and is an endless process by itself, it could "throw light" on all the principal issues met thus far in the *Problem* (2:153). All these issues were basically the life-problems of minded-beings communicating through signs.

In sum, then, in his first task, Royce's metaphysical method resembled his overall procedure in interpretation. To win an ever more intimate and clear grasp of interpretation's central structure, he made a series of mental penetrations. In this way he won a basis for generalization.

As one example of an interpretive process, Royce pointed to *self-reflection* (2:143) as opening another path for experiencing how he used his metaphysical method in his first task. At the start of his summary sketch of method (2:104–105), he revealed his own way of describing self-reflection in which he focused on the human self's psychic life. Was it a process of interpretation? If so, did it reveal a pattern of social life upon which he could base his metaphysical generalization about community? More immediately, would his audience grasp the nature of interpretation more easily if with them he explored how one reflects when making "an effort at self-interpretation" (2:159)? More specifically, if one searched reflectively to find one's true identity as an *ethical* self, could one find within that search the process and structure of genuine interpretation?

Pathfinder Royce invited each person "to interpret his own self in terms of the largest ideal extension" that reasonably can be recognized as fitting in with his life aims (2:105). He called the human self to stretch psychically beyond its personally experienced life-course. What are the broadest ranges of *ideal* events, deeds, and relationships which *can fit in* with a human self's life-aims of fullest development?

If the human self is to discover these broadest horizons for its consciousness, it will first need to sift past history for idealized events, deeds, and persons possibly congruent with its own values. The human self will need to ask interpretively which of these past items embodies its own deepest meaning and that of its community. Next, this human self will need to scan the future for certain ideal deeds, events, and selves. Of these, which can steadily call forth the courageous hope required if both this individual and humankind are to grow through an unfolding series of cooperative deeds? By such interpretive siftings of what is worthiest for one's true self, one will come to recognize that the ideal aim of one's life is to reconcile conflicting human selves and, while preserving their diversity, to harmonize them in a universal community. The self will then see that the only thing it can acknowledge as worthy of its own newly discovered ethical self-identity is a series of choices genuinely loyal to this ideal of the universal community.

In brief, if it is to create this "largest ideal extension" of its meaningful self both in time and in interpersonal relationships, a finite human self must produce a series of interpretations. Only in this way can one gain a fitting awareness of one's ethical selfhood and of the authentic meaning of one's life as a human person. By engaging in this process of self-reflection, then, one discovers in the very doing what an interpretive process is. And that was Royce's purpose in the first task of this second stage of his metaphysical method.

In sum, during his first task Royce had gained insights into a process of interpretation through comparing and contrasting it with the acts of perception and conception. He recognized that if he were to discern this third irreducible kind of knowing, he would have to employ percepts and concepts and sift through them. He saw that this sifting and finding and/or creating a mediating idea was the philosopher's mode of knowing *par excellence*. In it one discerned spiritual things spiritually (2:261). As the philosopher's art of interpretation grows, he gets into more intimate touch with community life. Spiritually he senses the "spirit of an idea." He detects the direction of that Will to Interpret which summons selves to unity within a Community of Interpretation. He responds to the felt presence of the Interpreter-Spirit, Royce's Ultimate Ground for human hope and for the right to philosophize (2:221).

Second Task of the Second Stage: Become Better Acquainted with the Work and the Value of Interpretation

Royce knew that this second task, like the first, was wholly subordinate to his overall aim in Stage Two: to investigate the nature and reality of community of minded beings, whether human or superhuman (2:167–168). In his reflective awareness he had planned both his first and second task simply as preparations for his raising the directly metaphysical question: Was the entire universe a community and a process of interpretation?

Since he regarded interpretation as "the sovereign cognitive process" (2:190), Royce wanted to identify several conditions prerequisite for his kind of metaphysical interpretation. To deal with interpretation as a process of knowing that occurs between minded beings and to deal with its values as values was to think metaphysically. Not surprisingly, then, Royce announced that his second task would aim at "becoming better acquainted," with the *work* and the *value* of interpretation (2:167). Clearly, this intent became a condition for the possibility of his doing this metaphysical musement on interpretation.

Considering first "the *work* of interpretation," Royce chose to start with a most rudimentary kind of interpretation: comparison. He focused on its constituent operations, then examined how this very simply cognitive process develops from its incomplete to its completed form. Studying this development in "slow-motion," Royce uncovered a new level of consciousness needed to bring any comparison to completion. This second level of consciousness consists in a reflectively gained insight into that mediating idea in which the initial pair of diverse ideas are similar. Through this discovery Royce won a vital symbol for rational self-clarification and for rational self-mastery which would become indispensable for pointing out the second level of consciousness and of reality found in any Community of Interpretation.

For his second and further entry into the interpretive process, Royce chose to become better acquainted with the values that emerge as interpretive processes become more complicated (2:184–212). He would consider the values found in an individual interpreter and then those found in a community of individuals intent on reaching some communally hoped-for unity of spirit. Gradually he climbed a kind of "value-ladder." It arose from those values found in the simple psychological development of consciousness. It moved through an individual's winning of rational self-consciousness (viewed as the value of attaining an ideal) and up into a community's achieving of shared communal awareness among its members. It climaxed in Royce's final explication of the ethical and religious values latent in the process.

How did Royce shift from considering the "work" of interpretation (those factual operations ingredient within a simple completed comparison) to musing upon the "values" of interpretation? He shifted his focus to the *ideal* which a truth-loving interpreter seeks. He was rightly convinced that values nest in ideals. He approached his hunt for values by raising such questions as "What is the *meaning* of interpretation?" and "What is the *inmost aim* of the Will to Interpret?" Within these queries he was treating the "meaning" of interpretation and "the Will to Interpret" as Signs that pointed to some intended good, to some value. Hence, just as in Part One a symbiosis linked that pair of human needs and Christian ideas, so here in Part Two a similar symbiosis linked the "innermost aim" of interpretation with its valued ideal of "unity in the spirit."

Within the human subject this basic pair lies in that moral life and religious orientation which Royce pre-required in any interpreter who wants to do metaphysics appropriately. To succeed with one true interpretation or with a series of them (and to avoid wrong-headed or simply erroneous misinterpretation), Royce required a distinctive base and quality in the subject interpreter. One had to be morally transformed from individualist attitudes into a life of genuine loyalty. Moreover, one had to be enabled to interpret authentically. For this, one had to possess an openness to the Interpreter-Spirit of the universe—an openness foreclosed in anyone lacking genuine prayerfulness. Such prerequisites for a "truth-loving interpreter" may seem strange to contemporary ears that are far more secularized than were Royce's. His insistence on them is clear (2:221, 309–310), however, and is a simple living out in his mature philosophy of the mystery of his personal prayer-life. He believed that the best way for a process of interpretation to open up to the rich ideals it can reach is through that kind of prayerfulness which the apostle Paul recommends.[10] If an interpreter lacks a genuinely moral base and such prayerfulness, the only kind of community he will build is a "natural" one—one that is exclusivistic and composed of members who are primarily self-preferential because basically still alienated by sin. But with the transformation to genuine loyalty and with a Pauline kind of prayer for empowerment, interpretation builds up a Beloved (authentic) Community. Its hallmark is a universalistic bearing and the Spirit of *caritas* (2:325).

Such preliminary considerations ease entry into Royce's *actual* use of his metaphysical method. In that method, we will focus on three characteristics: guidance (with originality), alternation, and progressive movement.

The interpretive process is *guided* by many influences. Interpretation functions under the habitual guidance which the history and hope of an individual and of his communities exercise by their overall meanings. Then, too, the idea of the truth-seeker—the ideal that one search for an ever more vital, fairer, and fuller grasp of truth—should guide every minded being's whole series of interpretations. In his lecture "The Will to Interpret," Royce made it clear that his musement was also guided by the lines of his overall inquiry into the nature and reality of community (2:167). Moreover, a leader of thought exercises fitting guidance upon interpretation provided his or her influence lies within an area of competence. In the same lecture, Royce chose to have his musement "directed by Charles Peirce's formal definition of the mental functions which are involved in interpretation" (2:169). Royce allowed himself to undergo this guidance by Peirce up to the point where Royce recognized that from here onwards he would have to set out on his own, with the originality of a pathfinder, to explore the *communal* significance of the Will to Interpret (2:204).

A striking occurrence of guidance happens when the interpretive process encounters absolute truth. For instance, an interpreter may discover a logically necessary connection (e.g., if p, *then* q). Or he may confront a morally inviolable principle (e.g., avoid patent unfairness). Or, while attempting to deny some proposition, he may discover the absoluteness of its opposite, by experiencing the psychic pinch of a performative contradiction. The deepest guidance operating upon an interpretation process is the Interpreter-Spirit's doctrine which directs all minded beings. It follows that although the interpretive process is in many ways free, flexible, and endlessly fertile of itself, in its living core it is guided by truth in several absolute forms. Thus within the teleology of this cognitive process a fundamental constancy reveals itself.

Besides guidance, a dynamism of alternation operates within Royce's way of musement, as seen in his lecture "The Will to Interpret." Within the process of interpreting, Royce considered it necessary to alter his approaches to achieve the fuller and fairer view. Had he considered interpretation in the individual (2:193–203)? Then he must move over to consider how it works in the community (2:204–221). Had he started this lecture by identifying the psychological facts occurring in interpretation (2:168–184)? Then he must shift to a consideration of *values* that emerge during a process of interpretation (2:184–212). Similarly, the whole of the second stage of his metaphysical method is a three-step alternation. He focused on the nature of interpretation, then on its work and value, and finally on the metaphysical truth it yields. Perhaps the most obvious form of Royce's use of alternation surfaced when he compared, then contrasted, and finally moved to a synoptic vision of the whole. For example, he compared and contrasted William James's view of an idea (a concept moving as a "leading idea" towards perceptual data) over against Charles Peirce's comparison-contrast of two conflicting ideas. Peirce's interpretation remained primarily within the intelligibilities of the two conflicting ideas even while it recognized as secondary all the perceptual freight, contrasting motives, interests, and conflictive consequences flowing from these concepts themselves.

Sometimes Royce employed alternation not so much with his own ideas as in dialogue with foreseeable objections from his audience. For instance, he forestalled the mistaken idea that Peirce's interpretive triad is a shadow of Hegel's dialectic (2:184). He countered an excessive sense of the fluidity and freedom within interpretation which might lead one to conclude that it cannot know "fixed or absolute truth" (2:194). By alternating from his own processes of thought to enter into possible objections arising in the minds of his audience, he invited them to sense how unlimited is interpretation's dynamic life as it develops both in Royce's mind, in their own, and in the potentially unlimited interactions between the two.

Again, principally for his audience's sake, he frequently alternated between exposition and illustration. In this he explicitly took his cue from Peirce's ideal experiments which used "diagrams and symbols as aids" (2:196). Here he led his audience by alternating from exposition to illustration and back to a fuller exposition. In this way he gradually led them to grasp both the basic triadic pattern of interpretation and the rich complexity of its various kinds.

Besides guidance and alternation, *progressive movement* marks interpretation. As it works with the communication of signs both within and between minded beings, interpretation moves from the simple to the most developed, from the rudimentary to the most precious. As mentioned, the overall design of Lectures 11, 12, and 13 moves from the simply experienced form of interpretation, through its work and value, to the critical question of the truth it presupposes. So, too, within his lecture, "The Will to Interpret," Royce moved progressively from psychological and rational ideals into his eventual uncovering of those ethical and religious ideals which the interpretive process "finds and creates." The entire thrust of the second stage itself thus progresses to the climactic hypothesis: Is the whole universe really a community of interpretation? And with this hypothesis, we find the bridge into the third task of Royce's metaphysical method.

Third Task of the Second Stage

Royce had completed his two preparatory tasks. Now he could outline his metaphysics of interpretation (2:168) in a lecture called "The World of Interpretation." At its start he hinted at his metaphysical method by quoting Professor Minot's maxim that before any researcher's finding can be accepted as a verified scientific discovery, the researcher must submit his new "finding" to the scientific community so they can test, correlate, and confirm or disconfirm it. Royce observed that Minot's maxim of method reminds us of two things. We should try to "read" (interpret) its lesson for philosophy and then so generalize it that we discover that it really is a lesson in metaphysics (2:227-228).

Fortunately for us, however, after Royce had reasoned interpretively in this lecture and reached his metaphysical doctrine, he paused for a reflective review to help his audience recognize the method he had just been using (2:273-276). His review both explained his earlier hint and made the characteristic patterns of his metaphysical method stand out clearly. He started by using a pair of views about the physical world—that of common sense and that of scientific method. Through interpretation he sought to discover some "third idea" that would mediate these different viewpoints. He found that they presuppose our inseparable pair of beliefs in the realities of the physical world and of a community of interpretation. He then sought to further clarify and generalize this underlying pair of beliefs. As his distinctive thought-movement advanced from interpreting physical objects and a scientific maxim to ponder metaphysical signs and our interpretation of the process of interpretation, it both penetrated and expanded according to the helix-like pattern described earlier.

Eventually he arrived at the metaphysical insight that reality itself is so engaged in process and so charged with vital communications that we cannot describe reality exclusively in either perceptual or conceptual terms (2:274). Our attempts to express it must use interpretation, at least in some tentative form. Any attempt to express the real universe presupposes an underlying true belief that there is a real world to be described. Such a belief, however, implies that there exists some "mediator or interpreter, whatever or whoever that interpreter may be" (2:269). This interpreter holds the processing world together as a whole in that unity requisite for a universe.

When Royce attempted to deny this, he found himself caught in a performatory contradiction (2:269). Confirmed by this reverse insight, and impelled by the concrete logic of interpretational reasoning, he was required to infer, "In brief, then, the real world is the Community of Interpretation" which has its fitting mediator (2:269). From this insight he then drew three pointed corollaries and then assisted his audience with a summary review of his doctrine and method.

The foregoing brief conspectus of Royce's metaphysical method raises one's curiosity enough to seek a more detailed examination of the two steps by which he carried out this third and climactic task of his method. In the first he turned to our knowledge of the physical world. In the second he examined our knowledge of the whole universe of all selves, physical and mental.

In his first step, he employed interpretation to show how our human knowledge of any physical object has inescapably a social dimension. He illustrated with the case of two men in a boat with oars and then with the whole physical world. Two or more of us cannot refer to a boat as the *same* boat unless we share in knowing it as a *common* object *and* believe we so share it. Royce showed further that, fictions aside, every human self must believe in the reality of both his own body and other common physical objects which we see and touch together. The same holds true about our having to hold the common sense view that the physical world is real and somehow unified as a whole. Royce then synthesized these two unavoidable psychic facts and proceeded to demonstrate that we cannot have such beliefs in the reality of common physical objects and of the physical world unless we simultaneously believe that there truly exists some community of interpretation *for whom* these physical things are (2:273, 271).

His advance to the second step came when the question was raised, "But how . . . should we know that any community of interpretation exists?" (2:253). Royce judged this question moved the investigation to the "very centre of metaphysics" for it expanded one's viewpoint to regard not merely the physical world, but also the entire realm of minded and non-minded selves. Here he chose to focus on philosophers since they claimed to supply such knowledge of the whole universe. Notorious for their disagreements, philosophers appear the least likely to form a community. Their positions and attitudes towards the real universe differ so radically that anyone searching for some "community of philosophers" would seem to be chasing an illusion. However, Royce penetrated to that root activity in which all metaphysicians share a common life and do so unavoidably. He found a single common intentionality which is inescapably alive within all their diverse, even contradictory judgments about the real world. It is this common intentionality which binds all interpreters of reality into a community. Royce had found that even discordant philosophers cannot philosophize except from some unity of spirit and except by forming a community of interpretation through their common interest in reality.

THIRD STAGE OF THE METAPHYSICAL METHOD: ELABORATELY TESTING THE CHRISTIAN DOCTRINE OF LIFE

Two texts can provide general orientation to the third and final stage of Royce's metaphysical method. In an overall panorama of this method, he had earlier envisioned the final stage as follows:

> Thirdly, this method directs us to inquire how far in the social order to which we unquestionably belong, there are features such as warrant us in hoping that in the world's community, our highest love may yet find its warrant and its fulfillment. (2:105)

How far do our social relationships solidly ground our hope that the future world community will justify and satisfy "our highest love"? The question seems odd. Still more odd is Royce's present maxim for metaphysical method: one should inquire into this question. Yet if the above question and maxim strike one as odd, the experience may be revealing. Are one's habitual associations about philosophical method far more dominant than is one's attunement to Royce's way of doing his metaphysics of interpretation? Most writers on metaphysical method usually regard hope and love as extraneous to their topic. Not so Royce. For him, to philosophize with a heart uplifted by warranted hope and with a will wholeheartedly in love with the universal community is the only way a metaphysician can avoid wasting his time, hurting himself, and hindering community-growth.

In another very general text, Royce described the aim determining his method within the final stage as follows:

> My present interest lies in applying the spirit of my absolute voluntarism to the new problems which our empirical study of the Christian ideas, and our metaphysical theory of interpretation, have presented for our scrutiny. (2:295)

In his final stage, then, the intent of his method will work with four factors: the two outcomes of Part One and Part Two, the "new problems . . . for our scrutiny" and "the spirit of my absolute voluntarism." These four factors are probably among the "threads" that feature in Royce's analogy of weaving. In this third last lecture he stated that finally, "All the threads are in our hands. We have only to weave them into a single knot" (2:312). One thread was the Christian doctrine of life, dominated by the ideal of the universal community—the outcome of Part One. Another thread was the real World itself, regarded in its wholeness as a Community of Interpretation—the outcome thus far of metaphysical Part Two (2:279). A third thread consisted in the string of problems arising from his endeavors to unite the first two strands. His fourth thread was the spirit of his absolute voluntarism—a spirit of profoundest hope, love, and loyalty. He wanted this spirit to mediate between the other threads and to so transform and enliven philosophical reasoning that the latter would contribute distinctively to the authentic humanization of the Great Community (1:13). In this final stage, then, Royce aimed to weave all four strands into one sturdy indissoluble knot. To any truth-seeker the knot would offer a reliable hold on reality. And to anyone following along any line of thought this knot would stand as an unavoidable junction that challenged one's procedure and tested whether one's line of reasoning was leading to error, failure, and folly or to truth, success, and wisdom.

In his introduction to the final stage, then, it is evident that Royce intended "to make clearer" the outline (or "the ground plan") of the World of Interpretation (2:280). He would do this by applying his very general metaphysics of community "to various special problems of life as well as of philosophy" and thus make his metaphysics concrete. The special problems he selected were: a) Which attitude should one take towards the world? b) Is "discerning things of the spirit spiritually" indispensable for life and philosophy? and c) Are we discerning enough both theoretically to appreciate the deep meaning carried by the history of scientific discovery and also practically to cooperate in furthering our common religious interests? These three problems determined the three tasks of his final stage. To them we turn for a more careful scrutiny of the values and choices governing his metaphysical movements.

First Task of the Third Stage:
Find and Prove by Interpretation that the Only Right Attitude of Will towards the Universe is Genuine Loyalty

Royce's Lecture 14, "The Doctrine of Signs," seems the most fundamental in the *Problem*. In it Royce's focus was the will. Its choice of basic attitude towards the universe would direct all one's theory and practice. He knew he was here dealing with a choice at least as radical as that original choice to start from his polyadic O-relation when beginning his pathfinder logic. By noting Royce's mental movements during his first task, then, one can begin to recognize which metaphysical method governs the final stage of the *Problem*.

Royce had set the context for his final stage with its three tasks (2: 279–281). In overview, he began his first task of identifying the right attitude of will towards the world by offering a simple exposition of Peirce's technical formulation of a theory of signs. Royce next moved to illustrate this technical theory by examining a sign-post and its implications (2:286–288). Then synthetically applying both to human experience, he articulated the life-giving ambience presupposed in all his musement: "Our experience as it comes to us, is a realm of Signs" (2:289).[11] His three-step procedure had led him to identify this nurturing matrix. In it he became suitably readied for the question: What is the right attitude of will towards the world?

Some did not accept his "doctrine of signs." What hindered them? He suspected immaturity of moral will and accordingly intensified his procedure of alternation. He applied his just-won interpretation of experience (first step) to the life-problem that human selves encounter in their most profound "realm of Signs" (second step). The problem was whether, of people's three irreducibly basic will-postures towards the universe, only one is right. Guided by his triadic logic of "yes or no or beyond both," he identified three general attitudes of will towards the world (2:298–311).[12] These were "the affirmation of the will to live," "the denial of the will to live," and that loyalty which is the Spirit-gifted wholehearted dedication to the interest of the universal community and the practical acknowledgment thereof (2:305, 309–310). He described these carefully enough to show them as irreducibly basic attitudes and all others as derivative.[13] Beyond description, he discerned between the non-systematized spasmodic spontaneities (which dominate the first two attitudes) and the well-ordered love for community, self, and others (which characterizes the third attitude with its disciplined freedom of the spirit).

A reader can also realize how Royce mused metaphysically by focusing on the human self's primitive awareness of "being with others." For then one can observe Royce exploring how the human self *can* accept *and should* accept this social consciousness that is basic and unavoidable. The exploration gives rise to a burning question for reflection: Is one's own highest priority primarily oneself or the community that embraces oneself?

How did Royce carry out this critical evaluation? Did he *demonstrate* that his third attitude is alone the right one? Without attempting a demonstration — an impossibility when dealing with a *first* principle — he "proved" his adoption of the third attitude. Hence, if someone, forgetful of Royce's interpretive process, expects a deductive demonstration or reads his "proof" from a mere subject-object perspective, one will miss Royce's actual procedure. Since he here adopted his *first* principle — "the principle, at once theoretical and practical, upon which my philosophy must depend" (2:313) — he could not demonstrate it without canceling its firstness. Yet he did not simply assert this principle. He also showed its reasonableness to his audience. In brief, he both asserted his fundamental opinion and also "proved" it.

The human self's moral tie with community is Royce's first principle. The teleological bond translates into metaphysics the ε-relation fundamental to his logic. Through the direction of this relation, his metaphysics would emphasize above all else the human self's *belonging to and appreciating* the universal community and its Spirit. With a religious wisdom, this attitude cries out, "Practically I cannot be saved alone; theoretically speaking, I cannot find or even define the truth in terms of my individual experience, without taking account of my relation to the community of those who know" (2:312). In support of this first principle Royce used four procedures. He employed induction, elimination, analysis of the bases of our ordinary social knowledge, and performative contradiction (2:293-294, 296-313, 315, 323, 325). His procedures of elimination and performative contradiction reveal themselves to an attentive reader. So only his first and third "proofs" need some enlargement.

By inducing the meanings latent in one's successes and failures, Royce clarified that time does not wipe out one's deeds. Rather those deeds remain both irrevocably done—whether well or poorly—and resound on endlessly into the future in that way. But the only thing that can account for this irrevocable bearing within the temporal flow of our deeds is some absolute standard according to which they are right or wrong (2:294). What is this standard? Here Christian philosopher Royce, caught by the time-constraints of his lecture, abruptly identified the absolute standard. With a startling profession of Faith in that norm of final judgment which the Master of Christianity had articulated, Royce asserted, "Each act is to be judged in the light of the principle: 'Inasmuch as ye have done it unto the least of these, [ye have done it to Me])'" (2:294).[14] Any professed devotion to the Head of the body had to be measured by one's treatment of the least members in his body. With stunning accuracy Royce had pinpointed that genuine but demanding human standard which Christians believe is the ultimate measure of whether one's deeds are failures or successes.

As a third "proof" Royce analyzed the bases of our ordinary awareness of our neighbor's reality. Here he was neither doing mere social psychology (as he had done two decades earlier) nor simply showing the solipsistic direction within William James' argument "from analogy." Rather, as Royce's insistent treatment here and elsewhere reveals (2:314-322, 301-303),[15] far more is at stake in correctly identifying the bases of our recognition that our neighbor is real. Here Royce found "a test case deciding the whole attitude towards life and towards truth and towards the universe" (2:315). Thus a more important and critical point in metaphysics could scarcely be imagined. What Royce found faulty in James' view was the presumption that one could know oneself without having first undergone the influence of other selves who in community have already affected one's own self and through contrast-effects brought it to an explicit awareness of itself as an "I." James' position presumed the priority of individualistic thinking. Royce's evidences underlined the priority of community life and influence upon the rise of its members' awareness of others as real. James held that we believe others are real through the likeness of their behavioral expressions to our own previously known psychic acts. In this position Royce spied the poisonous presence of that first basic attitude of will which gives priority to individual self-assertion unrelated to community. By showing its inadequacy, he indirectly supported his fundamental principle that Loyalty is the only right attitude towards one's social environment and the universe. Only an active open recognition of one's neighbor could be a reasonable basis for our awareness of "being with others." Similarly, such a recognition "lies at the basis of my only reasonable view of the universe. As I treat you, so ought I to deal with the universe" (2:323).[16] And with this generalization to the universe, he concluded his first task as well as his foundational lecture, "The Doctrine of Signs."

Second Task of the Third Stage: Discerning Essential from Historical Christianity

The loyal will is the only right attitude towards the world and is indispensable for salvation. On this established basis Royce went on to describe his second task:

> My sole intent is to furnish a test of the degree to which the account of the Christian ideas upon which I have insisted does furnish a just view of the essence of Christianity. (2:343)

His task was "to furnish a test of the degree" of accurate correspondence which his account had with what is vital in Christianity. He wanted to meet this issue as directly as he could (2:333, 343).

If one unites the results of three agenda, he will, I believe, highlight how Royce's mind moved when building that test. In need of synthetic interpretation by the reader, our three agenda are: 1) to examine a central pair operative in his procedure — his "sole intent" and the creative means he devised to reach it, 2) to indicate the fruits he intended to generate by using that means to achieve his intent, and 3) to notice characteristics of his metaphysical method.

By way of orientation, then, he set out with a dialectical contrast of Hegel's philosophy of religion (including David Strauss's inferences therefrom) over against the criticisms of this by Professors William Sanday and H. R. Macintosh. Royce aimed to head between both extremes. He neither wished to give primacy to ideas over experience nor adopt an account that offered no room for intelligent Scriptural hermeneutics. But his mediating approach required that he distinguish duly between essential and historical Christianity even as he showed their vital unity (2:379). For example, he would hold that in its early history the Church needed to believe erroneously that Christ's return was imminent so that Christians could accept the essential belief that salvation was being offered to *all* peoples. Apparently, a shared belief in Christ's imminent second coming alone would have enough psychological shock value both to break down the exclusivism of their habit-bound psychic enclosure within Judaic or Hellenic enclaves and

METAPHYSICAL METHOD   255

to win the essential acceptance of God's salvific will as being actually universal.

For Royce the teasing problem of method was how to facilitate this sifting between the essential and historical. He hit upon a creative fiction. An intelligent Greek who was one of Paul's disciples could provide Royce's audience with both the difference and the likeness needed for discernment. A fiction could convert this Greek into a "modern man" confronted with our problem of discerning between essential Christianity and its historical accompaniments and accretions. Just as this early Christian Greek would distinguish, so should we.

So Royce created the fiction of an unrecorded yet historical and intelligent Pauline disciple whose mind was strengthened by a vigorous Christian faith and a sound training in philosophy. Having died and somehow perdured through the centuries, this Greek stranger was miraculously brought back to life in the twentieth century. Set within a totally a-Christian milieu, he is first educated in today's secular arts, sciences, politics, and history. Only later is he reintroduced to Christianity, but now viewed in the light of what centuries of history have done to it.

Confronted with the contrast between his remembered experience of Christians in Pauline communities and the contemporary sadly divided, institution-bound churches, this Greek stranger must distinguish between the essential and the historical in Christianity. Gradually, he learns to distinguish within Paul's teachings—sifting between what God himself revealed as truth and the symbols and myths Paul used to convey that truth. In this way he distinguished Paul's teachings about the work of Christ and about the nature of the world (2:367). Meanwhile, Royce was scrutinizing how this early Greek Christian was going about his discerning interpretation amid the press of those soul-searing choices involved during this refining of his highest love as a Christian from the impurities in which history had encased that treasure.

Once the Greek had completed his discernment, it was Royce's turn to dialogue with him and to invite him to compare and contrast his statement of the essential faith of Christianity with Royce's philosophy of a World of Interpretation. Were they consistent in the Pauline Greek's eyes? For this phase of the interpretive process, Royce proposed a pair of ideas to be interpreted: a) the feigned problematic situation of the early Greek Christian and b) the general plan of Royce's whole inquiry in the *Problem* (2:370). As an interpreter, Royce discovered a "third idea" which mediated this pair. His idea summarized the results of his whole metaphysical inquiry: the world, *as* the process of the Spirit, is essentially social, historical, and teleological (2:374). Transposing this in terms of the basic triad (B interprets A to C), one sees that Royce's most basic triad appears as follows. A is the temporal process which groans and longs for that from which it is separated, C, its ideal good, the full realization of the Beloved Community. B is "the divine spirit through whom the world is reconciled to itself and to its own purpose" (2:378). Royce's comparison and contrast of the early Greek Christian's central faith assertion with his own metaphysics of a Spirit-led World of Interpretation generated the light he needed for a critical insight. By this light Royce discerned true "Christians" from merely so-called "Christians." The former were found wherever any human group was genuinely loyal to the universal community and was motivated by Pauline Charity. But those who simply claim the name "Christian" while lacking the Spirit are not genuine Christians.

After this survey of Royce's main movements in carrying out his second task, his metaphysical method is better grasped if three results and two qualities of his musement are noticed. In this stage his metaphysical method created the following fruits: a model discerner, a simplified ecclesiology, and a noteworthy distinction between Christian narrative and Christian experience.

First, his fiction of the early Greek Christian effected more than the intermediary step which his process of interpretation then needed. The Greek's discerning activity exemplified a mode of life for twentieth-century Christians. As the Greek solved his problem of Christianity by entering into a discerning interpretation, so must contemporary Christians respond to their problem of Christianity by becoming discerning interpreters. The Greek distinguished the literal truth of essential Christianity from all the symbols, myths, and legends in which this truth was conveyed to him. Twentieth-century Christians, too, must distinguish between Christianity's doctrine of life and all its conveyances. The Greek exemplified how to discern between Christianity's spirit and Paul's documents that preached Christianity. Modern Christians must learn to sift between spirit and letter. Just as the Greek learned to distinguish between the whether and the when of the Lord's coming, so must moderns discern between the kernel and the shell of the Lord's life and work.

The Greek's exemplarity went further. Thanks to his post-resuscitational education in modern physics, he could distinguish between Paul's "heavens and earth" and the twentieth-century view of the same. If a doctrine was inseparably bound to the early cosmology, he recognized it as a symbolic account of the literal truth. Similarly modern people need to see the various formulation of the Christian faith within the various contexts of transient cultures which in part gave rise to them. Such a need is especially urgent in the case of various historical formulations of dogma in contrast to the enduring Christian faith itself. Most importantly, the Greek recognized that what Christians then and now most directly mean by the name "Christ" is that experienced "life-giving Spirit" whose presence in his people operates to save humankind as he leads all through a dying and rising to a new and higher life. It follows that the Christian people's faith-experience takes precedence over the story of the founder's pre-resurrectional life and even over the basic story of the founder's death, resurrection, and appearances. The early Christian community found that its common social religious experience of believing in the saving presence of this "life-giving Spirit" was more vital than the mere narrative—however indispensable the latter was (2:359). In all these ways, then, the Greek early Christian serves as the exemplar of the discernments today's Christians must also make.

A clarified meaning of the Church was a second result Royce foresaw issuing from his metaphysical method (1:xxix; 2:365-369). Unbalanced and even positively distorted views of the Church abound. Only by putting primary emphasis on the Church's mission of ministering salvation to all people can one avoid these misshaped ecclesiologies. When primary emphasis is placed on church organization, for example, or on power-positions or heretic-hunting or man-made church law, no fair description of the Church's essence is possible. Royce found one misinterpretation of the Church particularly serious. This view, "centering all its interests in an effort to perfect its picture of the human personality of the founder believes the Church itself to be a relatively accessory or accidental feature of Christianity" (2:366).

By contrast, Royce's aim was to describe the Church's essence fairly. He would do this only from within the perspective of his *philosophy* of the Christian religion. His successive efforts to clarify the meaning of Church eventually presented it as "the company of all mankind, in so far as mankind actually win the genuine and redeeming life in brotherhood, in loyalty, and in the beloved community" (2:367). Nor did he blanch from a possible, perhaps likely, consequence. Suppose a particular band of Marxists disavowed terror-tactics and strongly promoted human rights. Suppose they showed themselves "most faithful, according to their lights, to the cause of the unity of all mankind." Suppose they did all this better than did tradition-bound Christian churches. Suppose that meanwhile the latter had in a "post-Christian era" become too dominated by concern for power-positions within the churches and too closely tied to interests that aim *primarily* at economic profit. Then, held Royce, *those* Marxists would represent "the true Church" far more than those churches. For the latter would be justifying themselves with the name "Christian" but not be "found full of the spirit and actually furthering the advent of the universal community" (2:368).

A third noteworthy result arose from Royce's metaphysical method.

In the communication of Christian life emphasis currently falls on *story*. But Royce distinguished between narrative and experience in Christian living. His method opened up to him the insight that Christian life lies most essentially in the experience of believing and confessing "that the divine Spirit dwelling in the Church redeems mankind." Admittedly, this experience is only mediated by human beings with their Christian story (about the founder's life and work and about the first disciples and their history). Yet this narrative of the Christian community is so prone to weave symbols, myths, and even legends into the "story" that the transient historical features predominate even over the account of the central belief and confession. It might even distract attention from the lived experience of communally engaging in such belief and confession.

Royce's metaphysical method exhibits two noteworthy qualities: a certain reserve towards ecstatic religious experiences and a reverent yet playful seriousness in his interpretive process. About his reserve, the just-mentioned experience of believing and confessing "that the divine spirit dwelling in the Church redeems mankind" does *not* lie in that communal mystical thrill to the Spirit which both Paul's early Christian communities occasionally felt and charismatic assemblies sometimes feel today. Rather, Royce modestly refrains from requiring a consciously felt presence of the Spirit as such. To be a genuine Christian, one's experience concerning this community-indwelling Spirit need be only a conviction in conscience that such indwelling is true and an urge to translate this faith into deeds. Affective conversion to the Spirit is needed but affectivity is disciplined by the will to serve the community with genuine loyalty.

In the *Problem* Royce's seriousness stands clear. Less noticed is his reverence. One who reads the *Problem* can detect that its author is not dealing with a simple puzzle or with a mere problem to be solved, but with a reality that is mainly paradoxical and even mysterious. It evokes Royce's sense both of the serious reasonableness and reverence due to a life-problem that bears on the destiny of all human beings (2:112-113). Royce was so reverent towards beauty that he preferred not to profane it by talking about it.[17] Expectably, then, such a Royce would deal reverently with the Holy Spirit of the Universal Community (2:14-16).

His sense of reverence flashes forth in many ways. He avoids violating his audience's feelings for "sacred memories and places." He even regards his fictionalized Greek with reverence, regretting to disturb his centuries-old rest with a "seemingly wanton intrusion upon his peace" (2:352). In handling the master's burning norm of judgment, Royce sensitively refrains from completing the then well-known Scriptural verse. Instead, he leaves the direct encounter with its latter half to be handled interiorly according to the freedom of his hearers' hearts (2:294). He refrains from making individual ecclesiastics or princes primarily responsible for the "warts and blemishes" in the historical Church. Such a move shows his reverent respect for all sinful Christians and his conviction that sinful institutional structures and the blindness of original sin have played a far more deadly role throughout the history of the Church (2:366). I find Royce reverent towards the apostle Paul and his communities, but especially reverent towards Christianity's master. In fact, this reverence may play a large part in explaining why Royce generally remains silent about the person Jesus. If the mature Royce felt inarticulate before beauty, how much more did he feel inarticulate before the Logos-Spirit of the Beloved Community (2:214–216)?

Paradoxically, however, playfulness permeated Royce's reverence. His purpose was clearly serious yet he achieved it playfully. Musing with playful freedom he invited his audience into a boat rowed by two men. Again, he invited readers to New Zealand to listen to Maori natives claiming that centuries ago, "I came across in the Tai-Nui canoe." Royce played with ring-strips of paper before his audience and had them puzzle why in Australia it is difficult to discern "the man in the moon." With delightful familiarity he moved from David Strauss to sign-posts, from the ε-relation in logic to that social pressure upon belligerent nations which a system of international insurance would exert. With mildly playful allure he invited his reader to find his meaning of "salvation" in the *Problem*. In the tough game of dialoguing with philosophers and theologians, he proposed himself as an easy target for some of their critical arrows (2:334–336). Playfully his imagination created the fiction of the early Christian Greek and Royce delighted in the fruits this fiction yielded. His proper Oxford audience may have suspected that their quaint Californian lecturer was joshing them when he announced that his approach to Christianity would be that of neither an apologist nor a critic nor even an indifferent, but rather the almost unheard of approach of a second John the Baptist. Sensitive to the possibility of arousing that fear in his audience, Royce used his sense of humor to face it frankly with them (2:383–384). Accordingly, if joy and delight are signs of the Holy Spirit, the playfulness in Royce's musement, particularly in dealing with such a serious topic as the problem of Christianity, bespeaks a union with the Spirit of the Beloved Community.

Third Task of the Third Stage: Confirm the Theory that the World is a Community of Interpretation and Fashion Fitting Maxims for Practice

Royce's metaphysical method achieved the last task of its final stage in Lecture 16, "Summary and Conclusion." Here his method confirmed itself and, facing the future, forged practical guidelines. Here, while retaining disciplined thought, Royce showed himself simpler and more relaxed than elsewhere. Habituated by the fifteen preceding lectures—all of which mused on signs—he now felt at home in his new way of searching for truth.

He concluded his last task in three steps. To form a "summary," he chose to circle back to his apparently unusual starting attitude in order to check its fruitfulness. For his "conclusion," he selected his hearers' interest in natural science in order to lead them to a deeper meaning which their interest and natural science itself presupposed. This deeper meaning confirmed his metaphysical theory that the world is a Spirit-led Community of Interpretation. Finally, he inquired what are the practical consequences if his view about the Church's atoning mission for all is true and if his idealism of Part Two "rightly states the relation of the Christian ideas to the real world" (2:423). For this final step, he redirected his interpretive process to fashion maxims for practical living. In this section, then, our aim is to highlight how he carried out these three steps in his final task.

During his endeavor to discuss the problem of Christianity Royce concentrated on the vital hope of reaching a result. Now he had completed that discussion. Following the lead of his hope, he circled back to inquire why his discussion, despite its paradox, was justified and fruitful (2:385). (Here his move illustrated how interpretation hunts for the more vital rather than for sensible qualities or intelligible forms.) Then with a modesty that increased in his final years, Royce sidestepped the naturally interesting inquiry into what he himself had achieved in the *Problem*. Instead, he preferred to pursue a communally more helpful inquiry: "What would an ideally trustworthy teacher . . . address to the modern man concerning the problem of Christianity?" (2:385). Finding that such a teacher was concretely embodied in John the Baptist as a Sign, Royce mediated John's message: "a religion, long needed, was yet to come." He then witnessed that in its deeper meaning John's message remains true. In its own way every happening prophesies that the Spirit is winning out since every event reveals that, amid our struggling disorderly world, a victorious interpretive Insight is always at hand (2:386).

But this deeper meaning presupposes that "the very being of the time process itself, consists in the progressive realization of the Community in and through the longings, the vicissitudes, the tragedies, and the triumphs of this process of the temporal world" (2:387). So advancing his musement, Royce submitted that this deeper meaning parallels his own thesis concerning "the [social] form in which the life of the community, whether human or non-human finds it conscious expression" (2:387). Hence, the essential Christian doctrine of life and Royce's metaphysics of a processing world of interpretation are in agreement (2:390). He had shown in what way the modern man can consistently be, in creed, a Christian — and had thus answered the first formulation of his problem of Christianity (1:14).

Then with side glances at the other approaches to the problem of Christianity — those of the apologist or assailant or indifferent — he discerned why they reach no solution. The indifferents who know not loyalty refuse to engage themselves in the problem itself. The apologists and assailants so embroil themselves in it that only fruitless controversy results. The inference Royce drew was that his choice of a Baptist-like initial posture enabled him to win touch with the process that apologists and hostile critics equally needed to recognize. Because of his right orientation to the problem of Christianity, then, Royce knew that his inquiry had not been fruitless (2:391).

Since he had completed an evaluation of his own procedure in the *Problem,* he turned directly to his audience "to set our case before you for your judgment" by way of two final endeavors — one theoretical, the other practical (2:391). The living nerve in his audience which Royce chose to contact was their interest in natural science. He knew that if they thoughtfully purified this interest, it would endure and be cherished in the future. Could he find another Sign to relate to this interest of theirs and thus find a confirmation of his philosophical position? His recent experiences with Peirce's writings led his musement to the way he had been impressed by Peirce's article, "A Neglected Argument for the Reality of God," in the *Hibbert Journal* of 1908.[18] In it Peirce had mused upon the conditions required for the improbably frequent, yet continuing successes of advancing science. To use mere chance to explain why scientific hypotheses were successful did not square with reality since these hypotheses were too accurate and their successful confirmations too frequent to result from *mere* chance. For such successes, researchers' minds had somehow to be attuned to nature. Yet such attunement hints at a Spirit-Attuner of human minds.

In order to sketch Peirce's argument to his Oxford audience, Royce first supplied them with the general context of inductive logic which he judged needed for understanding Peirce's argument (2:406). Then he succinctly proposed to them Peirce's argument as a Sign. It revealed an in-depth bond, which most people overlook, between natural science and the mature Royce's transformed idealism, the 1912 revision of his "philosophy of life" (2:422).

As a reflective interlude between his two endeavors, Royce noticed and called attention to the "essentially new aspect of philosophical idealism, as well as to a doctrine of life" which he had just presented (2:422). The interlude allowed him to review Part Two of the *Problem* and to identify the synthesized triad of ideas which govern his entire metaphysical method. These were the ideas of Time, Interpretation, and the Community, along with the idea of the World as a Community which is being brought to unity by the Interpreter-Spirit.

His last endeavor relied on the previous expanding helices of both his empirico-historical and his metaphysical methods to fashion two practical imperatives. The need of heightened discernment in practical matters led him to forge direct commands: "Simplify your traditional Christology, in order thereby to enrich its spirit" (2:424). Then, sensing that the dynamics at work within organized Christian churches are often self-justifying and exclusive of "outsiders," he was led to his final maxim: "Look forward to the human and visible triumph of no form of the Christian Church" (2:430). Instead, invent and apply the social arts of using grace-filled love in order to overcome humankind's original hostilities and thus to draw people to unity because the responsibility of religion is "to aim towards the creation on earth of the Beloved Community" (2:430). In this way the religious interest which had driven Royce into philosophical thinking more than forty years earlier now fulfilled itself, using history and logic, theory of knowledge and ethics as metaphysical signs pointing to this practical outcome of his interpretation of Christianity.

In this chapter, then, we have seen how Royce's commitment to seek the broadest and deepest perspective for his metaphysical testing of the Christian doctrine of life led him on a three-stage search. (For an overall summary of Royce's metaphysical method, see the accompanying outline.) He looked: 1) for the metaphysical basis of the idea of community; 2) for a new theory of knowledge which would reveal the ultimate structure of the universe; and 3) for a lodestone against which to test the truth of the fundamental Christian ideas in a metaphysically elaborated way. He designed and constructed this lodestone according to: a) the only right attitude of will towards the universe; b) the basic spiritual needs of people as they are revealed in the overall history of religions; and c) the confirmation which his metaphysical view received from the real universe, a world of interpretation. In this universe Royce found supports for a person's hope that his or her highest love will be fulfilled in the universal community and in its Interpreter-Spirit.

METAPHYSICAL METHOD

(governing PART TWO of the *Problem:*
"The Real World and the Christian Ideas,"
and indicated by 1:113 and especially by 2:104–105.)

ITS AIM: After winning close touch with the nature and reality of genuine community, *to estimate whether the relation* of the Christian doctrine of life to the life of all minded beings and to the whole universe *is true.*

FIRST STAGE: Search for a metaphysical basis for the idea of community by using a technically carved definition of community to explore whether at the base of every natural human community can be found that firm yet adaptable structure of the interpretive process.

    First Task (Lect. 9): Use the idea of temporal process in minded beings to analyze the problem of community in such a way that the pluralism of member-selves is balanced by the community's unity which is to lie in the members' shared interpretation of past and future events significant to them. Upon the basis of these shared interpretations a technical definition of community can be constructed.

    Second Task (Lect. 10): So analyze the real life of genuine human communities, through the guidance of this definition, that one finds a valid ground for generalizing to the real nature of *any* community that consists of minded beings temporally interpreting signs of mind to each other.

SECOND STAGE: Since interpretation attains closer touch with reality than do all theories of perception and conception, use the results of the First Stage to search for a new theory of human knowledge. This new theory of interpretation is needed to investigate whether, according to a metaphysics of Signs, the universe actually is a Community of Interpretation permeated by its Interpreter-Spirit.

    First Task (Lect. 11): Study the *nature* of an interpretation (2:110).

    Second Task (Lect. 12): Consider the *work* and *value* of interpretation (2:167).

    Third Task (Lect. 13): Inquire whether the *truth* is that the universe is a Community of Interpretation (2:271).

THIRD STAGE: Synthesize the idea of the universal community (taught by the Christian doctrine of life) with the real world viewed as a Community of Interpretation. This synthesis aims at better theory and practice.

    First Task (Lect. 14): Using the pathfinding process of interpretation, investigate whether the only right attitude of will towards the universe is genuine Loyalty, and cumulatively to "prove" this.

    Second Task (Lect. 15): Within the context of Royce's transformed metaphysics of "The World of Interpretation," test whether his account of the Christian doctrine of life furnishes "a just view of the essence of Christianity." Do this both by distinguishing fittingly between historical and essential Christianity and by showing their necessary bonds and unity.

    Third Task (Lect. 16): Confirm the theory that the world is a Community of Interpretation led by its Interpreter-Spirit. Do this by adducing evidence for this theory and by translating it into such practical directives as will further the common religious concerns of humankind.

16. Underlying General Method: Interpretive Musement

Royce's references to an overall method in the *Problem* are less frequent and conspicuous than those to his two subordinate methods. One might even argue, by selecting only certain texts, that the *Problem* is really two books, each with its own method and bereft of any overall unifying method.[1] However, already in his first lecture of the *Problem,* Royce spoke "of *the general method* to be used" (1:13) and, referring to the way he would integrate the two parts "of the present work," he stated, "*Our method* is to consist in an union of an effort to read the lesson of history with an effort to estimate . . . the philosophy of the Christian religion" (1:45).[2] Even more clearly, in his preface of April 1913, his last-penned pages in the *Problem,* he showed clearly that he perceived the *Problem* as one integral study with one purpose, one task, and one overall method. There he spoke of one "closely connected story" that linked its two parts. After surveying how he would study the two parts and, at the conclusion of the whole research, "return . . . to the relation of Christianity to our modern social experience," he stated, "The outcome of this method of dealing with 'The Problem of Christianity' involves . . . a great simplification" (1:xxiii).[3] Royce's direct references to a "general method," "our method," and "this method" for one closely connected work reveal his awareness that one underlying method was to support his entire effort in the *Problem.*

Our foregoing survey of Royce's two special methods has sharpened the need to describe his underlying "general method." As general, this method inspired his two subordinate methods and, in turn, received experiential support and stimulus from them (1:20-21). Hence, to familiarize oneself with his general method is to appreciate the spirit and art with which he created each chapter of *The Problem of Christianity.* If one identifies the powerful pulse at work beneath each chapter, one can contact the musing which characterizes the mature Royce. One can feel the deepest mental rhythm of that philosopher — and feel it most strongly in his critically important preface, introduction, and concluding chapters of synthesis. His general method arose far more from his 1912 scrutiny of Peirce's precise way of philosophizing and his own breakthrough to a new method of lived interpretive musement than from his abstract doctrine on the nature, object, relations, and ends of interpretation (2:109-163). He came to treasure interpretation because, in his view, it "is the great humanizing factor in our cognitive processes and . . . makes the purest forms of love for communities possible" (2:218).

To understand Royce's general method of interpretation as used in the *Problem,* it helps to examine three moments essential to Roycean interpretation. We will, then, briefly survey its logical form, study in more detail the agent-interpreter with his four functions, and finally examine the practical usages of interpretation. One may designate these three as the objective, subjective, and pragmatic moments of interpretation. But to arrange our presentation of these moments in this way risks linking interpretation more with its logical pattern than with the disposition needed in the interpreter. Balance can be maintained, however, if the purpose of interpretation is kept clearly in mind. It aims to bring the "wills" of three or more minded beings (or of their signs) into the creative unity of a determinate order (2:142, 208).

INTERPRETATION IN ITS OBJECTIVE MOMENT: ITS LOGIC

Wherever communication of any type is carried out, there interpretation is at work. The teacher explaining an author to students, the judge construing a statute for litigants, the newscaster informing his audience, the banker instructing his secretary—each instance exemplifies both the process of interpretation and its distinctive central form. Whenever B interprets A to C, the simple logical form of an asymmetrical triad of members "must exist in order to make the interpretation possible" (2:142-143). In this form, the interpreter B must operate between A and C as the center of the process.

Furthermore, the vector-like direction of this logical form is exclusively *from* A *through* B *to* C. In each individual process of interpretation this asymmetrical or irreversible relationship provides the logical basis for that teleology constantly operating within Royce's metaphysical process of interpretation. By being triadic, his interpretation escapes that dual relationship found whenever M *perceives* N or X *conceives* Y. The triadic pattern of interpretation brings three terms into a determinate asymmetrical order. The terms can be member-selves or their signs. Even when a human person interprets oneself, this triadic form predominates. For example, if Betty now interprets her past promise as a guide for what she should next do, her present self B is interpreting her past self A to her future self C (2:142-143). Or in an election year, by their current vote (B) Americans interpret the meaning of their past heritage and experience (A) to future Americans (C) who will inherit it.

INTERPRETATION IN ITS SUBJECTIVE MOMENT: FOUR FUNCTIONS OF THE INTERPRETER

The Interpreter Compares, Contrasts, and Penetrates for Unity

We turn from the objective logical form of interpretation to the interpreting subject and its various functions. If the interpreter B is to complete this distinctive knowing process, he has to do more than consciously compare and contrast A and C—that is, two selves or two ideas or two attitudes. He must also discover or invent that mediating idea which interprets the meaning of one by the meaning of the other and vice versa. Otherwise, he will not have penetrated far enough to "find or create" the distinctive unity of A and C. Hence his comparison will remain implicit and incomplete.

For example, after comparing and contrasting the apologist and the critic of Christianity, Royce found the idea which underlies both these contrary agents and makes them similar: their adoption of an adversary relationship. By failing to maintain sympathy and respect for *all* people (however different such people were from themselves in belief), each allowed a radical hostility to determine his response to the Christian reality (1:13). In this way, by failing in the spirit characteristic of Christianity— love of one's "enemies"—both apologist and hostile critic proved themselves incomplete interpreters. For genuine interpretation Royce required the *completing* insight which goes beyond mere comparison and contrast.

Other examples of this abound. After researching how early Buddhism and Christianity were alike and unlike, Royce did not rest content. To identify their most basic difference, he probed to "self-dedication to community" as the mediating idea which interprets the divergence of these two world religions. Again, Royce did not simply compare and contrast his fictitious Greek Christian and modern man. He also searched for the vital essence of Christianity common to both. By paring aside the fatty tissue of centuries of incidental accrual, he laid bare that nerve of essential identity in life which marks and unites Christians of all ages (2: 341–342). Finally, in his overall procedure throughout the *Problem,* Royce was carrying out serially a continuing comparison-contrast in search of a "third or mediating idea." How should he interpret the differences between experienced facts and estimated values, between history and metaphysics, and between the ideal of the universal community and the reality of a world in process (2:279)? In each of these instances he found that the idea of a Community of Interpretation functioned as the mediating "third idea."

But how did Royce know that such a "third idea" was a genuinely mediating idea and not merely some superficial fancy or illusory unifier? Did his early claim in the *Problem* (that the main principles of his philosophy of loyalty were empirically verifiable) pertain to such testing (1:ix)? Royce's kind of verification, while including the individual's experience, went beyond the Jamesian norm of what fitted a person internally. To be genuinely mediating, an idea had to do more than enable one to say, "Personally, my life is overall richer with this idea than without it." In a more Peircean spirit, Royce's process of verification investigated whether the proposed mediating idea was consistent with those basic "modes of action" required for genuine *communal* life. In other words, did this idea fit the communal moral attitudes and deeds which are respectful of all persons, promotive of community, tentative in their time-bound situation, and chosen in solidarity with all others and in service to them?

Furthermore, a Roycean "third idea" also had to fit in with certain objective judgments requisite for community life. These judgments are known, ordinarily not in an explicit and reflective way, but in a profound, prethematic and prescientific way. For example, a person can know some truths about the human being. He or she can know that reality is neither totally mysterious nor ultimately absurd but, at least to some extent, truly intelligible. In addition to these prethematic judgments, some consensus must exist on the general meaning of their basic terms—terms like "human self," "truth," "reality," and "loyalty." For lacking such consensus, community members cannot share life and values well nor successfully engage in deeds. Royce found that these general meanings possess an absolute constancy which fittingly guides the process of interpretation. Moreover, he found that in turn the process communicates these general meanings to its participants for consensus. So he employed these meanings as indispensable conditions for verifying his "third ideas." He noticed that whenever someone explicitly denied these general meanings, the person's denial actually reinstated them. And with them, it reinstated the objective judgments needed for community life.

In brief, to verify adequately the truth of his mediating ideas, Royce accepted yet went beyond James' individualistic testing of whether the idea "worked" for a person's psychological or physical good. For Royce, the "third idea" also had to fulfill two objective dimensions of communal life. It had to fit the modes of moral action and the meanings basic to life in community for the community confirms whether the meaning of an individual's mediating idea is actually consistent with the meanings and modes of action basic to communal life. When the community does so, one enjoys experiential verification in an eminent way.[4]

Royce exemplified this search for communal confirmation during his actual procedure in the *Problem*. His cross-checks are frequent. To verify the body of his ethical and religious "opinion and teaching" (1:ix), he indefatigably checked whether it was consistent with the deeply felt and inescapable needs of all members of the human community. Did it fit their needs for basic meaningfulness, acceptance, creativity, and union? Again, his highest community of ideas—namely, Community, Time, and Interpretation (2:422)—had led him to his Christian metaphysics. So, against that community of ideas he cross-checked his ethical and religious doctrine.

The Interpreter "Considers" in Order to Unify

As just seen, an interpreter must compare, contrast two initial ideas, and succeed in penetrating to a mediating third idea which requires the further experience of some communal verification. Another function indispensable for Royce's interpretive method is *"considering."* A whole set of tell-tale verbs, which keep echoing throughout the *Problem,* portray this essential function. For Royce, an interpreter is one who "considers," "reconsiders," "meditates," "discusses," "surveys from above," "looks down upon as if from above," "attains a larger unity of consciousness," "reviews," and "ponders."[5] To interpret, then, is in some profound sense, to consider.

As *The American Heritage Dictionary* indicates: "to consider" means "to believe after careful deliberation; to judge . . . [by] holding opinions or views that reflect evaluation of a person or thing. *Consider* suggests objective evaluation based on reflection and reasoning."[6] It connotes simultaneously a recognition of the deeper dimensions of reality and an objective weighing of values in a methodic way.

Because the interpreter considers, he engages in a process. The process of interpretation gets beneath one's grasping of individual sense qualities and universals—the objects of perception and conception. It achieves the union of minded beings and of their intents. Hence, interpretation is a fundamental cognitive process (2:167). To effect this union of minded beings or of their signs, interpretation must interweave many operations into a single dynamic unity. Hence, it must be a temporal process. So, when indicating the central life of interpretation, Royce no longer pointed to a single "act" of perceiving or of conceiving, however needed these may be as ingredients. Nor did he point to the "act" of reasoning—that single insight which grasps the inferential nexus binding premises to a conclusion. Rather, for him interpretation is that fundamental knowing *process* which, through a unity of purpose and wills, goes on weaving together many acts of various cognitions, estimations, and decisions. In this way a serial process of knowing is created which sustains a vital communal consciousness with its blend of practical and theoretical cognitions, of choices and deed.

This process of consideration is inescapably *social*. It achieves its fullest life in richly diversified communities of inquirers. The Harvard faculty and students who met around Royce's table in his famous Seminar on Scientific Methodology can serve as an example. Even when the interpretive method is imitated by an individual thinker, consideration is not done by this person as a solitary self. Royce's meditating alone at the stern of a Caribbean steamer is an instance. There in his "considering," he became a community of mutually communicating selves — his past, present, and future selves or his social, organic, and moral selves all intent on somehow promoting the Great Community.

Granted that consideration has an inescapable social thrust, does considering have one single yet seriated purpose that animates and unifies its stages? To be a genuine interpreter, one must always intend to be sincere and truth-loving. However, one must *also* strive to integrate three selves into a community (2:208). The genuine interpreter — one led by the Will to Interpret — will intend a series of goals that together constitute one's Cause that reveals itself in three stages to human consciousness. An interpreter intends to gain fuller understanding, in order to win more adequate truth, in order to enter profounder unity of life (2:193, 203). Whether his attention focuses within or beyond himself, the interpreter ultimately intends to bring three signs — ideas or selves or intents, for example — into a fuller unity. First, then, by using dialectical clarification, he seeks fuller insight and increased freedom from illusions. Second, believing truth to be in the whole, he pursues a fairer, more comprehensive grasp of the situation. Third, along with other limited selves, he intends to bridge chasms and overcome divisions in order to promote community. These three intents or purposes are integrated within the interpretive process.

First, Royce's characteristic drive towards a dialectical clarification of meaning impresses any reader who studies Royce's major works. To clarify an idea called Royce to sift dialectically the various notions entering the meaning of that idea. In his interpretive process, then, an intrinsically necessitated pattern of logical consistency is required as a minimal condition but this process is guided more profoundly by a quality of creative novelty. A signal of this distinctive novelty is the surprise that joyfully erupts when three individually unique, but freely conspiring initiatives are gathered into a new life freshly shared.

Second, one who considers searches for an ever fair*er* comprehension of some problematic situation. For instance, Royce insisted that Christianity, as an "intensely interesting life-problem of humanity," should be grasped *more* equitably than its apologetes and assailants did (2:12). Again, unlike Spinoza, he refused to rely on only one all-embracing category to integrate his metaphysics of the real universe. Aiming at a *more* adequate grasp of reality, Royce had to find another and more comprehensive way.

The third and synthetic purpose of consideration is to create or promote community (2:208). Thus, in its central thrust, loyalty seems most itself the more fully it promotes and treasures shared life in a genuine community.

In sum, interpretive consideration is a fundamental cognitive process which has a threefold purpose. In addition, the process of consideration is marked by a dynamic unifying order. Royce's general method rests upon his basic belief that, although the real universe is deeply pockmarked by chance and chaos, these latter are not the ultimate reality we can know. Differing with William James on this radical point, Royce held that a great Interpreter-Spirit in the universal community is the ultimate unifier of the chaotic elements of the universe. He also believed that finite selves, as individually unique yet cooperating members of community, can find and fulfill their identity. They do so insofar as they let themselves be directed by the unifying order within the Interpreter-Spirit's process of interpretation.

These beliefs of Royce translated themselves into his evident concern that the consideration which creates and promotes community be *well-ordered* (1:59–60). His stress on this right ordering of consideration stands out clearly in some of his sketches of the *Problem*'s overall procedure. For example, when turning to the Christian ideas, a person has first to grasp the human aspects of these ideas. What do grace, salvation, and loyalty mean for people in their ordinary living? In a person's experience how are the two levels of spiritual existence related to these ideas? Only after answering questions such as these, may one, "go on to the comprehension of what the Christian views about God have been trying, with varied symbolism, to present to the minds of men" (1:410). Only by first deeply appreciating human experience and its levels may the interpreter rightly enlarge his or her community of ideas to the point of harmoniously admitting the divine member into the ideas propelling one's consideration.

Royce again emphasized right order in one's consideration during a yet broader sketch of his procedure in the *Problem*. He pointed out that "each of the three [Christian] ideas . . . had to be interpreted first for itself, and then in its connections with the others," and finally in the relation of these ideas to the real world (2:111). One must expand the scope of one's consideration step by step in an ordered way. Led by the spirit of interpretation, Roycean consideration moves by a dialectical order from musing upon one idea to ordering its relations in a community of ideas to a final recognition of their joint bearing upon the real universe as a whole.

The Interpreter Discerns Things of the Spirit

A third function at work in Royce's interpretive method is a special sensitivity to things of the spirit.[7] He taught that "the values of ideals must be ideally discerned" (1:59). Only that person can remain a Christian in spirit who "learns . . . how not to confer henceforth with flesh and blood, and how to discern spiritually the things of the spirit" (2:361). Genuinely loyal persons possess this special sensitivity towards the ideal of interpretation[8] and towards the values in other ideals that are community-oriented.

Viewed negatively, this spiritual sensitivity is clearly higher than the ordinary sensitiveness of organism, feelings, and mind.[9] It is connected with, but more subtle than, that common psychic sensitivity so dear to Americans. The latter enables a person to direct one's behavioral responses in accord with one's "feel of the group's mind" or one's "sensing of an ebbing interest" or some similar intuition. Finally, Royce's spiritual discernment clearly differs from sensing how to deal shrewdly in one's everyday business world.

Viewed positively, Roycean sensitivity to the spirit presupposes a deeper kind of knowledge which depends on five conditions.[10] To be a discerner of spiritual things, one must: 1) grasp the ideal of an all-inclusive Community of Interpretation; 2) welcome this ideal with a human faith, hope, and love that are both natural and religious; 3) refuse to confer with factors alien to this ideal; 4) become so transformed from one's earlier individualistic ways that through one's deeds one acknowledges the reality of a universal community; and 5) pray for the gift to interpret. These five conditions link one vitally to the second level of human spiritual existence. Their living context gives rise to that more intimate type of knowledge which responds to things of the spirit.

Suppose the idea of a non-exclusive Community of Interpretation has become the ideal towards which one aspires. Then one can "grasp, in ideal, the meaning of the Church Universal, of the Communion of Saints, and of God the Interpreter" (2:221). By hoping in the values which cluster around this overall ideal and by loving them, the aspirant can do more than simply carry out the ordinary psychic interpretations needed for suitable social behavior. Gifted with special sensitivity to this idea, one can test whether the attractions and aversions one undergoes, whether the ideas and attitudes one encounters, are individualistic or collectivistic or actually community-building. Guided by such testing, one can fulfill one's responsibility towards the universal community. Having discerned "the values of ideals" and other "things of the spirit," one can now embody them through one's deeds.

Praying for the gift to interpret is the fifth prerequisite listed above for a discerner. A genuine interpreter fosters openness to things spiritual and to the Interpreter-Spirit by praying for, and thus receiving, the spiritual gift of interpretation which Paul mentioned.[11] Upon a first hearing, this prerequisite may seem odd. Yet the cold strangeness warms to familiarity when one recalls Royce's own prayer life and remembers his admiration for the Paul who advised that one "pray that he may interpret." Remember, too, Royce's avowal that this Pauline advice "in germ contains the whole meaning of the office, both of philosophy and religion" (2:221). Notice that the Royce who made this statement was first driven to philosophy by religious problems. Finally, recall that in his passionate devotion to philosophy during the rest of his life, he reached the mature conviction that "Interpretation is, once for all, the main business of philosophy" (2:168).

If hereupon one senses a wholly new level of life opening before oneself, the impression is well founded. Anyone who moves from a merely natural recognition of the everyday world towards a genuine interpretation of the things of the spirit experiences a deep psychic shift. Royce felt that this shift is quite comparable to the psychic shift experienced by the escapees from Plato's den. Liberated from their prison cave, Plato's former prisoners discerned how differently they now knew the realities outside the cave from the way they had earlier known mere shadows inside the cave. Moreover, once outside that den, these knowers could interpret themselves with far clearer self-identity than they could do during their ascent within the cave when they had only compared and contrasted the figures on the parapet with the shadows on the wall. Now, guided by the vision of the Good, they saw reality as it is in its highest forms.

Similarly, those who want to employ a Roycean method of interpretation need to be converted to a special sensitivity for things of the spirit. Having broken through to a new center, they need to focus away from their previous primary concern for material things so they can be interested *mainly* in minded beings, in their life, attitudes, and spirit. Like Plato's philosopher-kings, they need to reconsider all reality under the light of their new guiding ideal, the universal Community of Interpretation.

The Interpreter Loyally Affirms the Universal Community

The fourth and final function required in Royce's general method of interpretation is the loyal affirmation of the universal community (2: 298–314). For Royce, the community is a reality greater and worthier than any isolated individual. By living out this evaluation which is implicit within loyalty, Royce knew he was also affirming a definite set of metaphysical presuppositions. But these conceptualized presuppositions, however, were not so intimate and vital as the human will's "three distinct modes of appreciating both itself and its realm of actual or of possible deeds" (2:297). Individualistic self-assertion or individualistic self-repression or genuine loyalty to a community are the three, radically different, preferred *estimates* of oneself and of one's field of action which carry with them the three corresponding and radically different, fundamental attitudes that people adopt towards life, truth, and the universe (2:298–311).

The self-assertive Western attitude and the self-repressive Southern Buddhist attitude fail to unite a person with one's highest positive good— community. Both start from "the natural solipsism of the individual will" (2:301). For both, the basic practical posture is: "I am alone in the world and even if there happen to be other wills around, they are not as important in practice as my own will." This only too common practical self-centeredness forces every individualist into self-imprisonment where, sealed within the self, one faces an every-narrowing future (2:312).

By contrast, Royce showed that a fundamental spiritual need for and interest in one's fellows directs each human being to a universal community. Most basically, each person's will is incapable of sincerely willing the ultimate disharmony of all humankind. Consequently, unless a person takes into account one's relation to the universal community, one cannot save oneself in practice. As long as a person imprisons oneself within one's own individual experience, one cannot find or define any truth at all (2:312). Therefore, if anything is real, it is the universal community. And only if rightly related to this community, can the life of any individual self make sense, be really true, and reach salvation. Hence, only a will genuinely related to the universal community can qualify as the "one, right attitude of the will towards the universe," as well as towards truth and life (2:293).

On these grounds Royce recommended that the fundamental choice of one's will be a loving loyalty to the great cause of the universal and divine community. A person should dedicate oneself to this community with the vigor, self-assertion, articulation, and striving of the apostle Paul. If one has already been transformed into a genuinely loyal person, one should imagine and, in practice, acknowledge as real the spiritual realm of a universal and divine community (2:311). If one has experienced that the lack of genuine community life ends in basic frustration, hostility, and meaninglessness, that person will then knock in anguish at the door of genuine communal life, crying: "Let me enter! Let me join! Let me co-create community with you!" (2:325).

This presupposes that the self has undergone a radical conversion to a new and higher way of life—a conversion as deep as that of the apostle Paul, though perhaps less well-known. One's previous self-centered attitude towards reality is now transfigured. Its affirmation is now redirected into an affirmation of something more than the life of one individual. Its thrust to self-annihilation is redirected into a dying to self-preferential individualism. Most importantly, a positive, self-transcending commitment now emerges—a commitment to dedicate oneself wholeheartedly to the service of the Universal Community (2:311-313). And if this third fundamental attitude develops to its highest form, it can be called Pauline "*caritas*" and "life in the Spirit of the Community" (2:325).

But what has all this to do with Royce's method of interpretive musement? Almost everything.[12] For Royce's "metaphysics of interpretation" has its foundations in the meaning of this third attitude of the will (2:309-310). Or to approach an explanation by a different route, suppose there are two persons with very similar mental capacities, with equal education, and with equal commitment to pursue reason as logically and carefully as possible in their solving of the problems of life. Suppose further that the only difference between them is that one is an individualistic self-asserter, while the other is a loyal servant of the universal community. Their eventual interpretation of the basic problems of life will be radically different because the first operates out of self-centered ambition and the second sacrifices himself for the community. Similarly, when considering a basic problem of life, the sophisticated egoist, the pure altruist, and the utilitarian of the exclusively politico-economic type can not reason interpretively to the same conclusion which the loyal servant of community reaches. In brief, the interpreter's loyal affirmation of the universal community is the radical determinant of Royce's overall method in the *Problem*.

To sum up, Roycean interpretive method has at least four indispensable functions: comparing-contrasting-and-penetrating, considering purposefully, discerning sensitively, and making a fundamental preference for loyalty. Loyalty seems the greatest influence and determinant in his interpretive method because the unifying spirit of loyalty animates the other three functions and integrates them into a single process.

INTERPRETATION IN ITS PRAGMATIC MOMENT: OPERATING MOODS AND TACTICS

Through Royce's practical choices in the *Problem*, how did his overall interpretive method express itself? That is, what psychic atmosphere did it generate as its working ambience? Which tactics did it employ? His profound sense of depending on community and of being immersed in real temporal process created a co-pilgrimaging mood in his mature philosophy (1:xv).[13] He felt like Bunyan's Pilgrim loyally climbing up the way of truth alongside other truth-seekers. To them he offered the best observations he could, while inviting and awaiting directional corrections and other enriching aid from his brethren (1:xv, 5-6, 113). This mood animated and directed all the philosophical procedures of the mature Royce.

The psychic atmosphere around his general method is also marked by a felt thrust to ever-expanding breadth. Royce first finds a process of interpretation occurring in his social interactions with others. This leads him to recognize its imitation occurring in his own thinking. So he starts with this kind of process as central to the life of each human self. Soon his method extends to recognize that the life of each community is an interpretive process (1:xliv). He further broadens the scope of this method when he turns to Christianity's master. Here he finds that the life of interpretation unites the level of Jesus' natural spiritual existence with the higher than natural spiritual existence of Jesus' perfect loyalty to the Beloved Community (1:210). And Royce's ever broadening method does not rest until it finds interpretive process as the life of the Universal Community and of its Interpreter-Spirit.

As mentioned, playfulness is a third mark of this method. That Royce's mature mind moved in triads is often asserted. Without gainsaying this, I notice in Royce's late logical notebooks a superabundance of references to transformations of pairs and of tetrads. Playfully the mature Royce muses with pairs or triads or tetrads of ideas that are sometimes closely, sometimes remotely connected. For example, I believe that Royce based his interpretive process in the *Problem* on a pair of tetrads. According to his indications of the ideas most central to the two Parts of the *Problem,* one can arrange the following two columns or pair of tetrads:

A	B
The Four Ideas of PART ONE (1:xxxvi):	The Four Ideas of PART TWO (2:422):
1. The CHURCH, or of Community, graced with Loyalty	1. COMMUNITY
2. LOST INDIVIDUAL, Fallen and Convertible	2. TIME, the temporal process of Salvation
3. ATONEMENT, the saving influence of the Community	3. INTERPRETATION, with will to reconcile into unity
4. The REALM OF GRACE	4. WORLD OF INTERPRETATION

By reviewing Royce's general movements through his lectures in the *Problem,* one can discover how he played there by considering these ideas first singly, then as conjoined into pairs, then triads, and finally tetrads. Such a review can teach one how much play of musement arises here. For one can compare-contrast-and-discover a "third idea" by combining A-1 and A-2, or A-2 and A-3, etc. One can do the same with pairs of metaphysical ideas from column B. Or one can study a pair from both columns, A-1 and B-1, for example. But the major comparison, contrast, and discovery arises when Royce playfully muses with A and B, the two tetrads in their entirety (2:279). Then, recognizing that here he is engaging (with all his affective, executive, and ethical, as well as intellectual, potentials) not just in formal logic, but especially in a philosophy of life, we find him fulfilling his own description, uttered in another context. "The intimate relations between theory and life are nowhere more pronounced than in this case, where reason and sentiment, action and expression, throw light each upon the other" (2:310). In brief, playful musement, expanding breadth, and warm co-pilgrimaging are the "breezes" characteristic of the psychic weather in Royce's general interpretive method.

Tactically, he often employed the counterpoint of a dialectic to sift out and to blend the best of contrary positions. For instance, when Royce endeavored to rescue the idea of atonement from theological encrustations, he identified deeds that might mistakenly be called atonement (1:297-310). Mercifully to withhold due punishment is not to atone. To reassert trust in a former traitor is not to atone. (For his traitorous deed which had undermined the trust basic to community life is not directly utilized and transcended either by some subsequent good deed of his own or by other members' later reassertion of trust.) Having cleared away this thicket of misinterpretations, Royce could now discern atonement accurately. The atoning deed sees in the traitorous act a new opportunity for introducing a greater good into the world. The atoner not only compensates for the evil of the traitorous deed but also renders the overall situation better than would have been possible if the treason had not occurred.

Dialectic becomes a general tactic that in various forms permeates Royce's interpretive method. It finds support in three other subordinate tactics. In these, too, Royce's central intent is to further clarify a chosen idea or viewpoint (2:3).

First of all, he characteristically worked an idea into a series of reformulations which aimed at ever more determinate articulation. Earlier we watched the series of steps he took to clarify his definition of "the problem of Christianity." The whole *Problem* may also be taken as Royce's search for an ever more adequately articulated meaning of Community (2:16-17, 167).[14] In other instances he strove to win an ever more definitive grasp of the ideas of moral burden, atonement, and fuller grace by serially purifying the formulation of each.

Second, in his work of interpretation, Royce sometimes engaged in a spiralling recombination of several ideas. Presupposing his use of serial reformulations, this subordinate tactic added the alternating maneuver of breaking off from work with one idea, beginning to clarify a second idea, then returning to the first idea and reconsidering the second. As each idea was further clarified, it promoted a recognition of its links with the other idea. For instance, having left the idea of community very incompletely stated in his second lecture, Royce, at the start of the third lecture, shifted with seeming abruptness to clarify the idea of the individual's moral burden. Then in the fourth lecture the light just cast by his serial purification of the idea of one's moral burden greatly enhanced his renewed consideration of the idea of community. Next, the idea of moral burden was, in turn, reciprocally strengthened in the fifth lecture by the deeper notion of community just reached in the fourth lecture.[15] In this way Royce demonstrated the interpretive power of his spiralling recombination of ideas.

A final tactic becomes evident when Royce makes a provisional synthesis. A series of his interpretations calls for moments of review or a look forward or a summary. The start and close of many of his lectures demonstrate Royce's mastery of this tactic.[16] In these his intent shifts dialectically from making some principle more precise to so summarizing his results or plan that the general thrust of his whole interpretational reasoning strikes home (1:113).

To sum up, one might borrow the analogy of seeing the forest and not just the trees. Royce's first subordinate tactic (serial formulation) intends to see a single tree more clearly. His second tactic (spiralling recombination) helps one to see the tree within a stand of trees. His third tactic (provisional synthesis) asks one to look at a whole forest to read its meaning.

In review of Royce's underlying method of interpretation, his mature use of it is startlingly simple, unassumingly powerful, smoothly flexible, and deeply probing. Its logical form is simple: B interprets A to C. Its power is its four tightly cooperative functions: compare-contrast-mediate, ponder reflectively with unifying purpose, discern the things of the spirit, and affirm the life of the community as one's cause. Its full flexibility is reached in its mood of pilgrimaging along the way in a companionship of dialogue. Its capacity for deep probing is revealed when its serial reformulations, its spiralling recombination of ideas, and its provisional syntheses reinforce each other for ever-clearer articulation of the deepest principles and ideas of life.

A retrospective survey of our part three may prove helpful. The mature Royce's general method arises principally out of his chosen attitude of a loving loyalty towards the universe. It arises secondarily out of his chosen priority for life and for whatever practically promotes life. Overall, he chose to create a new and philosophically responsible interpretation of the meaning of Christianity and of its earliest textual sources. His choice employed a vision of the human self in community as distinctive as Aquinas', an hermeneutics at least as revolutionary as Bultmann's, and a precursor-like mental stance towards Christianity as startling as Nietzsche's. In this way Royce transcended both the false isolation of philosophic thought from everyday religious life and also the inhibiting mental stances of apologist and critic.

A most powerful aid to this feat was Royce's 1912 insight into the secret of Peirce's forty years of philosophizing. Single-mindedly, the latter had mused interpretively over three very simple ideas. Royce combined his careful analysis of Peirce's method with his own insights and different purpose.

This led Royce to a general method that integrated four functions. It compared, contrasted, and mediated with its freshly discovered "third idea." It considered in order to unify. It actually discerned things of the spirit. (Thus it did not allow the human knowing process to be confined to the admittedly needed, but insufficient, factors of "flesh and blood.") Finally, Royce's general method fittingly arose only out of a will loyally converted to the universal community.

Into his interpretive method he integrated his fundamental Christian ideas, carefully selected according to humankind's universal ethico-religious needs which these ideas alone can satisfy. Earlier these ideas had been explicitly articulated in primitive Christianity's development of the master's Kingdom-message and in that sense of identity which it achieved through its sense of mission to the world. Royce integrated these attitudes, view of man, of hermeneutic policy, interpretive functions, and selected Christian ideas into that "dynamo of the spirit" which was his general method of interpretive musement.

To apply this general method of interpretation to the Christian experience and to the real world, Royce still needed subordinate methods. He had to discover the bases of his three Christian ideas in human nature as experienced. He also had to find in everyday practical religious living the ethico-religious meaning and value of these ideas. As his experiential historical materials for this search, he chose three types of community: that of the earliest Christians, of contemporary Christians, and of any community of loyal selves.

There remained the task of generating a metaphysical context wide enough to test the truth of the "Christian doctrine of life" within these communities. For this he developed the three-step subordinate method of ideal self-extension, valuation of the evolving universe, and inquiry into its warrants for hope. To this end he portrayed the universe as a Community of Interpretation with its Interpreter-Spirit working in each member and in the entire Community-process. At the close of the *Problem,* Royce returned to the essentially practical tone of his masterpiece by both offering some specific directives for loyal people.

It is noteworthy, even deeply challenging, to appreciate how much Royce wanted his philosophy of the Christian religion to be distinctively Christian (2:16). Although his main ideas (community, salvation, lost state, and redemption) are common to many world religions, Royce placed these in a distinctively Christian context. In other words, his method presupposed a transformation to loyalty (a kind of *metanoia* to employ a Christian term) and a new life "in the unity of the spirit" at the second level of humankind's spiritual existence (1: 114, 174). Although applicable to all peoples, these notions derive from distinctively Christian ideas and have specifically Christian forms which Royce sometimes indicated. Finally, he suggested that people use the Christian symbol of the Holy Spirit as the most fruitful approach to God (2:15, 219). Here, indeed, is a challenging way to describe one's method for achieving a genuine and responsible philosophy of religion. But then Royce's last years were a deep challenge to all believers, to all Christians, to all philosophers of religion, and, particularly, to himself (1:xi).

PART FOUR

Royce's Musement Enlivens His Doctrine

17. Loyalty: Center of Christianity and of Human Interests

With a masterful statement on loyalty in his preface, Royce summed up his most central doctrine in the *Problem* (1:xvi). Then, from this viewpoint of loyalty, he announced his "main theses" in the work. Hence, in this chapter our procedure will be to quote serially his four theses (doctrines), then to comment on each doctrine, and finally, to support each with correlative evidence in the *Problem*.[1] Royce himself stated that his work had no positive thesis to maintain regarding the person of the founder of Christianity (1:xxvi). Nor will his mature conception of God be treated here since that study has already been carried out satisfactorily.[2]

That Royce chose to sum up the *Problem* in terms of Loyalty may surprise those who stress this work as primarily metaphysical or logical. But even if others fail to do so, Royce recognized his own kind of pragmatism. He would not allow theoretic contributions to take center stage in the *Problem*. He felt and knew that humankind's crying need is for right action. Fittingly, then, he stressed the practical ethico-religious commitment to live for something more than oneself—that is, for the whole community and for all its members. As a Christian philosopher, he called for a genuine moral life of loyal deeds. Because he viewed his investigation of the *Problem* as chiefly an ethico-religious study,[3] he used his opening doctrinal survey to sound the theme of loyalty like a reveille that was to echo throughout his work.

BOTH ESSENTIALLY AND HISTORICALLY, CHRISTIANITY IS THE RELIGION OF LOYALTY PAR EXCELLENCE

For his opening thesis, Royce proposed:

> First, Christianity is, in its essence, the most typical, and, so far in human history, the most highly developed religion of loyalty. (1:xviii)

The essence of Christianity which Royce sought was the essence of its creed. He recognized that holding the essential creed was indispensable for fully living genuine Christian life. But he did not aim ambitiously to embrace the essence of the entire Christian reality. More modestly and accurately he found the essence of the Christian creed was identified by the Pauline doctrine: "the divine spirit dwells in the Church, and thereby redeems mankind" (2:364). Repeatedly Royce emphasized this central doctrine of the *Problem*.[4] By his analyses of various religious experiences, he verified that unless a person's union with the Deliverer-Spirit is mediated by sharing in the religious experience of a whole genuinely loyal community, the individual risks illusions and impedes his or her salvation (1:xvi).

Clearly at work within this creedal essence are the three fundamental ideas: Community, Lost State, and Atoning Spirit. Royce probed to the self-reinstating truth of these three ideas. In this way he proved that, unless an individual appropriates these ideas, he cannot take part in the salvation-process carried on by a genuine community. Royce discovered that, insofar as the Interpreter-Spirit teaches and guides the Christian community, the latter's inmost life consists in a process of salvation that takes place through redemptive atonement. This is what is most vital in Christianity.

But how deep was he to dig for this treasure and, once found, how should he remove the corrupting elements to extract the pure gold of this essence? Digging beneath the historical deposits of special revelations, theologies, and the dogmas of Christianity, Royce had to reach the level of people's basic spiritual needs and interests. Then he had to clear away four kinds of impurities: superstitions, false hopes, dogmatic constrictions, and the reductionist ways of the liberals.

Among superstitions he included popular traditions, some well-known miracles, "trust in magic," conceiving supernatural powers of good and evil in a physical way, and "leaning on the intervention of such spiritual agencies as the old mythologies conceived."[5] False was every hope that was not founded ultimately on the three fundamental Christian ideas—e.g., hopes based on nothing more than biological generation, or the development of science and technology, or the systemic strength of such institutions as education, media, business, and government, taken simply as such. Describing the mortality of all such visible things, Royce remarked, "In the end, the boat and the human body fail."[6]

Within Christianity Royce found that dogmatic minds often constrict themselves and others within doctrinal theories that derive more from the earlier formulas of dogma than from the master's ideas. He also saw ecclesiastics trapping themselves and many others in jurisdictional debates. Shunning both of these strident groups, Royce also distanced himself from those "liberal Christians" who required no commitment to the true doctrine of Christ—in at least some minimal, commonly held form—and who in this way reduced Christianity to a mere moral imitation of Jesus. Furthermore, these individualistic liberals, by disregarding consciousness of genuine community, also ruled out the possibility that salvation might come through loyalty to a Beloved Community. Hence, because any one of these four misrepresentations would vitiate universal loyalty, which Royce regarded as the indispensable means of salvation, he felt a great urgency to refine most accurately the creedal essence of Christianity.

However, even with these purifications, Royce's first thesis can easily be misunderstood. What, then, did he mean positively when he held that in its essence Christianity is the most typical and most highly developed religion of loyalty? For instance, if one took Royce as holding simply that Christianity is the historically most evolved form of religion, a misinterpretation would have occurred. So, too, if one suspected that Royce thought Christians were generally more loyal than members of other religions.

Royce knew Christianity had played a central role in human history and human salvation. He knew how closely it is tied to humankind's deepest religious needs (1:9–10). But his precise target was the intrinsic development that had occurred within Christianity's essential creed. Here Royce found that the religion of loyalty had achieved its fullest growth thus far and had reached its most characteristic expression. Such was the intent of the main thesis with which he started his summary of the *Problem*'s content.[7]

This thesis, however, carried with it some implications for himself and his work. First of all, the development of doctrine in Christianity gave Royce sound reasons for shifting his approach towards the philosophy of religion. In the *Sources* he had already approached the field generally by examining the structure of anyone's religious experience. Now he wanted to concentrate on that doctrinal milieu wherein the essential creed of the religion of loyalty had reached its fullest development. Although Buddhism and Christianity were both religions of loyalty, the most radical difference between the two lay in the Christian belief that God's love destines individuals to become members of the Kingdom of Heaven (1:342). Hence, Royce had to investigate Christians' *communal* religious experience and the problems contained in such experience.

Second, his shift to a special department of the philosophy of religion revealed Royce's preferred way to philosophize about a specific religion — namely, one should freely and personally adopt its central doctrine as one's own. Therefore, being Christian, he chose to investigate the creed of Christianity, rather than that of Islam or of Judaism. In this way he confessed by deed that if philosophy of religion is to live and grow, it needs to be fed by philosophers' personal confessions of their individual religious beliefs and non-beliefs. Unlike the positive sciences, philosophy of religion cannot survive if it simply gathers data and seeks currently valid generalizations. Rather, in this discipline, objective facts must be correlated with subjective confessions. As Professor James Collins has observed, "Along with the commonly shared method, . . . philosophers of religion must also seek to achieve intersubjective understanding of the realities under discussion."[8] Since this intersubjective kind of knowledge is essential to philosophy of religion, it can only arise by a mutually reverent sharing of the participants' religious affects and beliefs. The focus of their sharing would be the essential doctrine of the particular religion under study insofar as this doctrine leads someone believing in it to meet something higher than oneself.

By sharing with others his professed faith, Royce became a model pilgrim "who speaks to another who is his friend, when the way is long and obscure" (1:xv). Here was a third implication of his starting thesis. Royce's choice of the dialogic method showed his fellow philosophers of religion how each of them could make a positive personal profession of that particular world religion in which he or she was most interested. Philosophers of religion must maintain an objective rigor as well as an interest in the universal features of human religious life and experience wherever found. Nevertheless, they must also express their own personal religious beliefs to each other so that they can generate that intersubjective knowledge likewise required by the peculiar nature of their topic: religion in the entire human family. Through these unique sharings they can enrich each other's grasp of how real and diverse are the lived positions of their colleague philosophers of religion, whether the latter live outside a religion, take part in one, or personally abstain from religious belief altogether. But such sharings make their demands, too. Participants need a broadly held practical belief that their assembly should communicate in accord with the vital fairness and discipline proper to any Community of Interpretation. They should also be open to the possible guidance of an Interpreter-Spirit at work among the philosopher members of this Community. According to Royce, to hold this set of affirmative beliefs is itself a most basic act of religion (2:312–315). And thus to philosophize is to find method and content, action and thought becoming almost one.

LOYALTY IS THE DYNAMIC CENTER OF MAN'S SPIRITUAL LIFE

Royce stated his next main thesis in the *Problem* as follows: "Secondly, loyalty itself is a perfectly concrete form and interest of the spiritual life of mankind" (1:xviii–xix). Here Royce expanded his scope from

Christianity to take in the spiritual life of all people. The heart and pulse of this life is *loyalty*. This life-form alone wholesomely unites the individual and communal levels of conscious life for all humankind (1:164). At the individual level, the person's mental life is torn by the tension between one's inner tendencies: either to follow one's own self-will apart from the group or to comply with the will of the collectivity. So an individual has a deep need to escape this inner tension that expresses self-estrangement. At the communal level, most so-called communities exhibit a similar alienating process in operation. They often simply collectivize human selves by treating them as mere units, or in other words, these communities naturally exist as "communities of sin" (1:178).

The good news is that one communal human being exists as a "realm of grace," namely, the Beloved Community. Only the influence of this community can lift an individual self to that second and higher level of life beyond his former hostilities. The individual's natural loyalties to family, clan, and country are unreflective in their original spontaneity. Beyond these, lies a second, reflective level: the life of *genuine* loyalty. This life empowers an individual member to serve steadily the cause of all minded beings of all time. This universal community, by its communal grace of "life in the unity of the spirit," gives its members such power. Its grace enlivens, or at least can enliven, every member of the human race and even every minded being in the universe. Once elevated to this new life, the now universally loyal person wholeheartedly dedicates one's self to a supreme cause. Furthermore, one is to promote a similar transformation to genuine loyalty and a similar growth of loyalty in all other individuals. Insofar as loyalty to the loyalty of all persons coincides with each person's deepest desire not to miss his or her highest good, it clearly is an "interest of the spiritual life of mankind" (1:xix).

Yet how is this universal loyalty a "perfectly concrete form" of humankind's spiritual life, as Royce held? To begin with, a person's new life of universal (or ideal) loyalty is more concrete than the natural forms of loyalty are—paradoxical as this may seem. Universal, rather than merely natural, loyalty generates a series of genuine moral choices. And what is more concrete than one's moral deeds and growth or decline? Since universal loyalty has an essentially practical intent, it penetrates beneath the distracted level of ordinary social life and actually touches the most concrete being in all reality: the Beloved Community.

Royce's second thesis stated that genuine loyalty is *"perfectly* concrete." To grasp his meaning more clearly, we must brush away some common misconceptions about Christian love, individualism, instant transformation, and personal achievement. First, to characterize Christianity as a religion of love is to say the truth, as far as one goes. But since this characterization omits genuine loyalty, it is an inadequate description of Christianity (1:164). Besides its demand that members love all other individuals genuinely, Christianity also requires them to be committed to communities *as communities* (e.g., to the human race, the Church, and the Trinity). In fact, if a Christian loves nothing but other individuals (human or divine), the very individuality of one's beloveds — especially at the finite fallible level — will only increase one's inner dividedness because individuals, as individual, are not yet healed into the integral life of loyal service to the Beloved Community (1:174). Royce's insight into the distinctive nature of what Paul called "love for the Church," "love for the body of Christ," establishes a complementary contrast with love for individual Christians and with love for the individual Jesus.[9]

Christian love, then, includes loyalty to genuine communities as such. This was the new interpretation that Paul and his early communities arrived at by believing that the Holy Spirit was guiding them. In this way they transformed their founder's doctrine of love, their own understanding of it, and their living out of this doctrine. But by fully accepting this startling yet authentic transformation, they encountered a most profound problem. Much less difficult was the problem of having a family or tribe or nation gradually draw a self-willed individual into a steady *natural* loyalty towards this limited group. These natural loyalties, however, lack both the ideal of the universal community and such a member's commitment to it. Therefore, the boundaries of these merely natural communities keep their members from entering that *whole* of spiritual life which is the homeland of all minded beings. Hence, the most profound problem becomes how to touch the individual's deepest center in such a way that his whole existence is transmuted with a literally new life in the Spirit. The individual human self needs to undergo a "quantum leap" from the captivating level of individualistic life as a morally detached self — whether as an isolated rebel from any community or as a member of a merely natural community — to that distinctive *second level* of humankind's new spiritual life in the universal community. Without undergoing this quantum leap, a person's morality and religion will be restricted to the correspondingly lower level (1:174). Then the whole dawning of a far higher level of ethical and religious ideals and values cannot occur. This is the case even though the deepest interest of all human hearts is for just such a glimpsed dawning of their true homeland of the Spirit.

Moreover, Royce's second thesis points directly to that one quality essential to any genuine social order. He appreciated all the individual good will and naturally loyal endeavors found in so many members of most institutions. Despite this, he asserted that their ultimately individualistic lives must cause their institutions to become sinfully disordered — even intensely destructive of persons (1:178). Hence, the "essential form of any genuine social order" can only be the genuine loyalty of most members towards their community insofar as it is related to the universal community. Moreover, genuine loyalty presupposes that the Beloved Community is itself supporting its every member with a more fundamental practical love. This practical love is as concrete as the everyday acts of friendship whereby this Community enables genuinely loyal selves to express its love for themselves, all members, and all "outsiders."

Third, when speaking of loyalty as a "perfectly concrete form . . . of life," Royce *may* have hinted that a serial process of purifying a meaning had guided this study of loyalty in 1912. In his Gifford Lectures of 1899–1900, he had purified his meaning of Being by working serially through three inadequate conceptions of Being until he arrived at his fourth and final conception. Similarly, in the *Problem,* by his more refined dialectic of interpretive musement, did he gradually purify and clarify the meaning of genuine loyalty? My hypothesis is that Royce scanned his three Christian Ideas and found each of them leading him to a yet fuller grasp of the meaning of loyalty. He followed their attractiveness to the grace-grown synthesis of his fourth and final conception of loyalty. If Royce made these serial purifications, it would be most characteristic of him, even if he did not here make explicit mention of the process. He would be simply pursuing the meaning of loyalty down to its most central, concrete, vital form.

I know of no explicit text proving Royce intended this purification of the meaning of loyalty in 1912 but since it relates to that conversion process so fundamental to Christianity, let me clarify and develop this hypothesis which seems Royce's, at least in germ. First, in the idea of Universal Community he found a call to loyalty, a call to transcend one's individualistic life in dedication to the cause of this universal community.

Second, in the idea of the Lost State of the detached individual, Royce perceived a deeper, more intimate call to a loyalty towards one's truest self. For this idea would lead a person to the difficult, yet constructive, personal confession that one is morally bankrupt and cannot save oneself without the influence of a saving community. Such disillusioning and purifying loyalty inserts the person into that community of people who seek genuine truth about themselves. It counters the tendency to settle into a community of self-deceit and illusion.

Next, Royce put the meaning of loyalty to a third test through contact with the idea of Atonement. A person finds oneself seeking more clarity about loyalty for one is called to foster a greater human community by taking an active part in deeds of atonement. Only such concrete deeds will compensate for one's own and others' disloyal choices. This kind of service brings one finally into the full life of the Realm of Grace. There one cooperates redemptively according to universal loyalty and also clearly grasps the ultimately concrete meaning of this highest type of loyalty.

Fourth, a person recognizes that each of these "liftings" beyond one's own individualistic center is caused by no efforts of one's own. It is done entirely through grace, through the loving action of the Deliverer-Spirit whose presence works redemptively in the community. Within such a Spirit's intentionality and free commitment to the human community and to all minded beings, one discovers experientially what "being loyal" ultimately means in its final concreteness. One gains a glimpse into that level of everyday fidelity which is beyond any human capacity to produce or to clearly comprehend. Yet the grace-filled inner light radiating from within the transformed person enables one to recognize such noble and beautiful loyalty as the most desirable of life-styles. In its most concrete form, then, loyalty is clearly a lived method.

SCHOOLED BY CHRISTIAN COMMUNITY LIVING, THE APOSTLE PAUL TRANSFORMED THE MEANING OF UNIVERSAL LOYALTY

Royce stated his third main thesis:

> This very fact about the meaning and the value of universal loyalty is one which the Apostle Paul learned in and from the social and religious life of the early Christian communities, and then enriched and transformed through his own work as missionary and teacher. (1:xix)

Comment on this thesis has already been offered in chapter 8, as well as in a more detailed study.[10]

AMID EVER-INCREASING CHANGE, MAN WILL BE SAVED ONLY IF THE DOCTRINE OF LOYALTY SURVIVES AND DIRECTS THE COURSE OF RELIGION AND OF MANKIND

Royce explained the sense of this fourth main thesis by offering a seer's insight into what alone can stabilize the future:

> Whatever may hereafter be the fortunes of the Christian institutions, or of Christian traditions, the religion of loyalty, the doctrine of the salvation of the otherwise hopelessly lost individual through devotion to the life of the genuinely real and Universal Community, must survive, and must direct the future both of religion and of mankind, if man is to be saved at all. (1:xix)

As though prophetically describing the last decades of the twentieth century, Royce here clearly faced up to the universal swirl of accelerating changes. This accelerating pace of changes will ever more deeply challenge Christianity's traditions and institutions. He proclaimed that underneath these increasingly rapid currents the doctrine of loyalty will perdure absolutely in its quiet directed flow. In fact — and here Royce's hope shines through — the doctrine of loyalty will provide the fronting wave to lead both religion and humankind into their evolving future.

In connection with this directed flow of the loyal life, we recall the three lessons which Royce read from the history of religions.[11] Religion, a product of human needs, will die if it loses touch with these needs. Second, in human affairs, nothing is so sacred that it is immune from the whirlpools of accelerating change. Last, religion in the modern world has lost its former institutional bases and has been submerged by those life-influences which are more immediately needed: science, education, economics, and government. Amid this sea of changes, Royce recognized that the only absolute constant was the unity of the three ideas. This Christian doctrine of life alone can satisfy people's basic religious needs (1:397) and alone can constitute the dynamic creedal content of every religion of loyalty.

Fortunately, people are not left to themselves to learn the essential ideas which form the saving doctrine of life. Royce's hypothesis that, through the ages, the faithful and loyal Interpreter-Spirit instructs all minded beings with this doctrine offers a potential basis for unlimited hope. On the grounds that the universal community is real and that its Spirit is at work, Royce invites people to expand their hearts with the hope of the Great Community of all humankind.

Near the close of the *Problem,* Royce provides solid evidence for the existence of both the universal community and its directing Spirit (2:225–276, 406–422). But by already uniting these four main theses in his preface, Royce offered his reader a brief preview of the chief doctrines of the *Problem* studied from the viewpoint of loyalty. At the close of the *Problem,* he undertook still another doctrinal survey.

18. Simplification for the Greater Unity of Christians

DOCTRINAL CONTENT SURVEYED FROM THE OUTCOME OF THE *PROBLEM*

The four theses of the *Problem*'s preface offered women and men a potential basis for hope in their lives yet it provided them with no solution to the problem of Christianity. Royce claimed only that his method of dealing with this problem would greatly simplify three areas. If they grasped his meaning, they would discover how far simpler would become "the problems of Christology, of dogma in general, and of the relation between the true interests of philosophy upon the one side, and religion upon the other" (1:xxiii). This chapter aims to explore which simplifications Royce achieved in these three problematic areas. His simplified method of interpretive musement led to certain doctrinal assertions later in the *Problem*. If we examine carefully how these assertions bear upon the three doctrinal areas, we can discover how methodic simplification enriches doctrines.

Simplify Traditional Christology to Enrich Its Spirit

Royce knew that he could not properly conclude the *Problem* unless he referred in some way to the founder of Christianity and to Christians' belief in him. Royce knew that here he had to lead his audience beyond their tradition-bound perspectives concerning the master. Here he knew he was walking a tightrope so he had to be honest, guarded, and ecumenically concerned when he proposed statements about Christ. To provide the needed leadership, he used the following trenchant maxim, cognizant of its implicit doctrinal assertions, especially in its recourse to the religion of loyalty as a norm:

> Simplify your traditional Christology, in order thereby to enrich its spirit. The religion of loyalty has shown us the way to this end. (2:424)[1]

Royce's directive here reveals that he had detected something in traditional Christology that impoverishes people's response to its spirit. Actually, he had found traditional christological dogmas so complex and heavy that they suppressed, rather than stimulated, a growth in the faith of many Christians. Fixed christological formulas often hindered loyal people when they tried to respond freely to the present voice of the risen Shepherd with wholehearted dedication. Relics of past theological controversies, these formulas stifled present Christians' hope of winning an ever deeper personal knowledge of their Christ.

Traditional Christology created another problem. It emphasized Christianity's past to the point of depreciating its present and future. True, in contrast to other world religions, a distinguishing feature of both Christianity and Buddhism was "the conception of a personal savior of mankind" (1:337). But traditional doctrines about Christ the Savior did more than assert that at one moment in the past a unique God-man saved humankind. They also tended to imply that salvation was then so completely achieved that it neither occurs now nor will come in the future (2:423). Formed from largely static perspectives, traditional Christologies failed to include process in their definitions.

How, then, was Royce influenced to recommend the simplification of the problems of traditional Christology? From the account supplied in chapter 1, we infer that, as a boy, Royce probably held the crude Christology suited to his simple me-and-Jesus religion. He knew his Jesus-Savior in a fundamentalistic and largely individualistic way. Gradually, wider educational experiences, scholarship, and attentive reflection on Scripture enabled him to detect that Matthew, Mark, Luke, John, and Paul each presents a different image of Christ, according to the different needs of their diverse audiences. He also found that these New Testament writers lived under diverse socio-cultural conditions and had experienced in themselves and in their audiences different preferences for perceiving Christ. All these factors led them to create and develop different Christologies.[2] Royce noticed, too, how these Christologies of the apostolic age differed from those which early church councils and medieval traditions later fashioned by adopting ontic and Hellenic modes of thought.

As Royce surveyed these "various and perplexing Christologies of the past," he compared "Pauline Christology" with "dogmatic Christology" or "traditional Christology" (2:427). He also came to contrast the "Essential Christ" with the "Historical Christ" — that is, the Christ believed in by the genuine Christian in contrast with the individual Galilean teacher of nineteen hundred years ago.[3]

As seen, the mature Royce was convinced of the reality of the "second level" (of man as community). Accordingly, if Jesus were viewed as merely the individual man of Nazareth, this Jesus was for both Royce and Paul an inadequate center for a Christology. Therefore, Royce shifted his focus to view Christianity's Risen One as a "life-giving Spirit" at work in the Christian community. Here Paul's influence was dominant. Yet Royce's personal images and ideas of the founder led him to a simplified Christology. It was uncluttered with conciliar definitions and open to experiencing the Interpreter-Spirit's movements in the Christian community.

This was Royce's mental set when he began to write the *Problem*. Towards the Christ and a refined Christology, which orientation would Royce adopt? His response arose from his underlying openness to the spirit of loyalty (1:vii) and from a clue he had recently experienced.

In his openness to genuine loyalty, Royce had reservations about using the term "Christ." Too often certain preachers used it as their rhetorical rallying flag to draw uncritical groups to a tenacious holding of some Christology peculiar to some particular denomination. Royce inquired whether it would not promote more unity to delve beneath the term to the reality it symbolized. Beneath all the historically emergent interpretations, perspectives, dogmas, and doctrines about Christ, Royce simply found the redeeming Spirit present in the Church, uniting it, and through it saving humankind (2:426). Let us then follow this Spirit, urged Royce. Let those who claim to be Christians live in and love their present community. But let them also show their practical devotion to the interest of that "perfectly real and divine Universal Community" (2:425).

Moreover, Royce had recently experienced a possible clue for achieving greater simplicity. He had just described in the *Sources* how a person experiences his or her basic religious Ideal or Need or Deliverer. When doing so, one discovers that the transcendence present in oneself makes these three religious objects appear in consciousness with a "mysterious seeming." But the mysterious appearance of these objects occurs in minds that culture, age, and religious training have already differentiated. So, all persons who experience the three objects have room enough, within wide limits, to interpret and formulate them quite differently. But on the subjective side, Royce had found a contrast to this diversification of interpreted religious objects: religion arises only from the subject's desire to be saved. In its prearticulated state, this desire remains simply identical in all human selves.

In the *Problem* Royce's procedure on this point paralleled his way of balancing diversity and unity in the *Sources*. He was again called to explain how Christians' images, ideas, and doctrines about Christ could be so diversified. For an explanation he again turned to cultural differences, apperceptive sets, and stages of communal consciousness — all on the objective side of consciousness. Yet he was again called to explain why all these diverse Christologies nonetheless pointed to a single Christ. In response, Royce boldly employed his own version of the pragmatic maxim.

If one gathers together all the usually experienced effects of a certain X, then the sum of those effects will tell what X is usually doing. By using this version, he could clarify what Christians mean by the term "their Christ." So Royce wrote:

> Now in general, whatever else they held to be true, all the communities of Christian believers have viewed their Christ as the being whose life was a present fact in their community, inspiring its doings, uniting its members, and pointing beyond the little company of the present believers to the ideal communion of all the saints, and to the triumph of the Spirit. (2:425-426)

Royce had discerned that what Christians mean by "their Christ" is that X who now lives, inspires, and unites their community and yet so points beyond it that its members are related both to the larger Universal Community and, amid their pilgrim striving and struggling, to the Spirit who is victorious through it all. This orientation presupposes in each Christian, then, some universal "Christ-symbol" — that is, some commonly recognized, partly identical image of the Christ-figure — for if any human community is to unite and direct its life, it needs some shared perceptible sign and a common focus (2:50-51).[4] So in their community, Christians need to construct together a common perceptible sign and focus. Moreover, the mysterious Spirit, to whom their Christ-image referred, encouraged Royce to identify that unifying dynamism required in any genuine religion: openness to the Transcendent One. As Royce's précis put it:

> The name of Christ has always been, for the Christian believers, the symbol of the Spirit in whom the faithful — that is to say the loyal — always are and have been one. (2:426).[5]

The sum of this and the previous quotation is that for Royce Christians experience and perceive their Christ as the one who inspires and directs them and is the living symbol of the unifying Spirit. On this experience of the Christian community Royce based his Christology.

Like some pilgrim whose "wee light" in the distance beckons him farther along his path, Royce now saw a clear path before him.[6] He could recommend that the faithful simplify their Christology in such a way that they would enrich it. By emphasizing the present experience of Christ which both local and universal communities have, Royce would both widen Christology's perspectives in the present and free from blockage its view of the future. It was far better, held Royce, to focus mainly on the Christ whom Christians believe (or even feel) is currently at work in their community and to face the future which he points to than to focus on a merely historical Jesus or a mere acceptance of past dogma. In this way a person's life of expanding response to the Spirit can be filled with the hope of enhancing that life which circulates within the communion of all the genuinely loyal.

He knew he was not alone in calling for this simplification of Christology. The "redeeming Spirit in the Church" calls all people—Westerners and others, no matter how diverse or latent be their Christology—to "the practical acknowledgment of the Spirit of the Universal and Beloved Community" (2:428). All are to express faith in this Interpreter-Spirit through their simple practical deeds. They are to wash the feet of the "little ones" and to engage in other practical services that build up community (2:431). By such deeds, the genuinely loyal will daily develop a deeper heart-knowledge of the Interpreter-Spirit. They will experience a life far more meaningful, dynamic, and simple than the life experienced by those who, trapped in disagreements about diverse dogmatic formulas are distracted from the Spirit and from practical cooperation in its work of generating and enhancing Beloved Communities.

Simplify Christian Dogma

Royce predicted that his work would simplify the problems both of Christology and of dogma in general (1:xxiii). By "dogma in general" he seems to have meant any system of religious beliefs or statements authoritatively considered to be absolute truth. In the present study we have repeatedly indicated that Royce simultaneously highlighted how relative are creedal formulations and yet how constant are the three central "Christian Ideas." His emphasis on them witnessed to the supreme worth of these Ideas and the futility of bickering about traditionally held formulas.[7] To avoid such bickering, Royce employed his most fundamental doctrine of the two human levels of consciousness, of truth, and of existence (1:405–406). In order to discern between the man-made formula of a dogma and the Spirit's life-giving intent within the formula, the individual person needs an inner light. But this light operates reliably only if the individual has been transformed by the gift of true loyalty to live on the level of "man the community" (1:345). Thus genuine loyalty functions as an indispensable condition for the transformed individual's discerning of the Spirit. Furthermore, such loyalty must also transmit the Beloved Community's light of revelation to the individual, since universal loyalty is the Deliverer-Spirit's indispensable means for revealing the way of salvation to the individual. Consequently, if Royce's inner light is to mediate the genuinely superhuman, it must be fed by both the individual and the communal levels of the human self. Only by living a life of true loyalty, then, can an individual discover which portion of a dogma or other faith-utterance derives from the ever changing human side and which portion derives from the ever constant side of the Interpreter-Spirit. Genuine loyalty is the *sine qua non* basis for the rise of Roycean discernment.

In the *Problem,* then, Royce depicted a process of revelation more naturalized than that portrayed by traditional dogmatic accounts. He carefully consulted the basic religious needs and interests of human nature because these serve each person as one's unavoidable sources of religious insight. Since a religious insight occurs only through the presence of the Interpreter-Spirit, this insight transcends the human and constitutes authentic revelation. However, because people's basic needs and interests impose certain intrinsic limits which a religious insight or revelation must obey, the latter is naturalized.

When naturalizing revelation in this way, Royce did not fall into the opposite extreme of erecting an *a priori* wall of separation against a transcendent Communicator, as some American naturalists have done. According to Royce, neither the human individual nor the human community can, if they act simply on their own, attain a genuine revelation. They must have the additional presence of an immanent yet superhuman Spirit who operates beyond human endeavors and transcends human limits. Through the presence of this Spirit, "man the community" may reveal something transcendent. As Royce said, "the higher of the two levels of human existence may prove to be, not only essentially above our individual level, but endlessly and quite divinely above that level" (1:409). By his doctrine of the two levels, then, Royce discovered and proposed a middle path. He steered between the dogmatists' traditional emphasis upon external revelation received from a transcendent God and the naturalists' equally defensive, *a priori* foreclosure lined up against any approach by the Spirit.

Royce's mature doctrine on revelation was, then, relatively novel. He emphasized that the individual's interior light is a person's indispensable natural source for discerning the Spirit. By this emphasis Royce established a way of personally verifying a revelation through one's own direct experience. Thus he safeguarded the responsible freedom of each person's religious conscience. Yet for genuine revelation, Royce also required that the individual live with a truly loyal dedication to the cause of the universal community. Only if animated by true loyalty could the individual's interpretation of the inner light become trustworthy. The cause of humankind exists as an illuminating and indispensable source of any authentic revelation. Yet in "man the community" a further operative presence is required —that of the universal community's Interpreter-Spirit who creates and sends the saving light. This Spirit becomes, for Royce, the chief Revealer who powerfully yet gently leads and guides the ideal relations of all three members in this interpretive Community of Revelation (2:216). This Spirit calls people to discern between revelation and formulated dogma. If they discern correctly, the problems of dogma become simplified.

Simplify the Relations between the True Interests of Both Philosophy and Religion

Royce called advocates of religion and of philosophy to recognize that their own, and others', truest interests actually converged into a pathway that leads all human beings to a fuller and deeper unity.[8] Hence, he called both groups to simplify the problems in the relations between their true interests. In the *Problem* he did not list these interests explicitly, yet the way he dovetailed the religious interests of its Part One with the philosophical interests of Part Two manifested in deed what he meant by this simplification. His Christian Doctrine of Life (that system of the religious ideas of Community, Lost Individual, and Atonement, integrated by Grace) reflects simply but with breathtaking congruence a parallel with his Doctrine of Signs (that system of the metaphysical ideas of Community, Temporal Process, and Interpretation, united in the World of Interpretation). In the *Problem* Royce has found that the religious interests of the *Sources* (in an Ideal, a Need, and a Saving Deliverer) become congruent with, generalized in, and supported by Part Two's metaphysical interests in the superhuman ideal, process, and Agent (Community, Time, and Spirit). In the *Problem* these religious and philosophical interests involved mutual dependence and support. Religion is disciplined by authentic philosophizing. Philosophy cannot be authentic unless it issues from a person and a community transformed by the religion of loyalty.

The histories of both religion and of philosophy demonstrate how many false paths have misled both. Religion has easily been falsified by allowing its *theos, thea,* or *theion* to become wholly transcendent or wholly immanent or wholly human. Similarly, the history of philosophy shows that philosophy has easily been falsified in several ways regarding religion. Sometimes it has allowed suspicion and hostility towards genuine religion to become philosophy's driving animus. At other times it has yielded to impatience when confronted with the all-too-human stains marring the man-made institutions of religion. Though first reports and appearances might tend toward a different judgment, the genuine interests of religions and philosophy are closer than often realized.

Royce traced three laws which the history of religions has taught concerning the responsibilities of religion (1:385-394). The history of philosophy illustrates three similar laws for philosophy. It also arises from deep human need since people must adopt some "basic wisdom"—some meaning for their lives in their situation as human beings. Philosophy either supplies this need or withers into a technical specialty for the few who speak to ever fewer people. Second, set within a process of ever accelerating change, the history of philosophy jettisons philosophical fads and techniques even more quickly than history sloughs off irrelevant religions. Third, philosophy, like religion, now finds its institutional supports increasingly cut away. Currently people invest far more of their time, talent, and treasure in the more pressing concerns of business, science, government, and communications than in philosophy. Even within academe, the reigning "knowledges" are psychology, sociology, and economics—not philosophy. Accordingly, philosophy will shrivel up much as fossilized religions have unless it finds it own kind of "sword of the spirit" just as the religion of loyalty has. That is, philosophy must adopt the newly explicated mode of knowing: interpretive musing on Community, Time, and the Interpretive Process itself. Only by using such a method, doctrine, and spirit can philosophy ward off the subtle forces threatening it with death. Only thus can it draw deeply upon its authentic life-source.

What, then, are some of philosophy's interests? It longs to purify thought from uncriticized popular beliefs. It seeks to work ideas to clarity and integrate them into a tested synthesis. It wants to discuss issues, not in order to win the upper hand, but to allow the fuller truth to have its rightful place. On the other hand, what are some of the interests of religion? It longs to purify persons from constricting superstitions and in this way to open them to fuller response to the Spirit. Religion wants to promote increased spiritual life by supporting people through the unavoidable dyings and risings of human life. It calls all persons to fuller and fuller practical service of the Spirit, whose life, light, and love leads humankind to fuller pardon, peace, and community. It is these two sets of true interests that Royce sought to keep authentically distinct even as he integrated them and simplified the problems in the relations between them.

The complementarity of Parts One and Two of the *Problem* shows implicitly how these relations are simplified, yet an explicit treatment of some of these relations is called for. We will, then, first trace how these interests converge or coincide in seven ways. Thereupon, by contrasting John Dewey's and Royce's philosophical views of religion, we will illustrate this simplification as found in Royce's profoundly simple yet subtly nuanced philosophy of religion.

In previous chapters we have repeatedly emphasized how Royce chose a third stance of will, universal loyalty, to initiate and carry out his creation of the *Problem* (1:9–13). By this fundamental choice of psychic posture, Royce showed how religion and philosophy debase themselves when their every move originates from defensive mental trenches or flame-throwing hostility or calculatedly cold unconcern. On the contrary, what significantly promotes philosophy and religion is in practical ways to affirm the whole community of minded beings. The true interests of philosophy and religion, then, are promoted only if their practitioners seek artful ways of being respectful, loyal, and sensitive to the whole truth that structures the Universal Community. All can do this even while recognizing that philosophy and religion have vast areas where relativism and pluralism properly operate.

At the conclusion of the *Problem* Royce inquired what results it had achieved. As just mentioned, he had started by adopting a fundamental attitude for doing the philosophy of the Christian religion—the attitude symbolized by John the Baptist. His concluding answer showed that his initial choice contained a universal meaning even deeper than its significance for his method for he also held that each temporal event proclaims the Baptist's announcement: "The Kingdom is at hand, and yet to come." Each finite choice and happening functions as a profound event-and-sign. Each opens up to us an encounter with the Eternal and prophetically directs us towards our future goal, the coming of the Beloved Community (2:384-386).[9]

Moreover, a teleology and an eschatology of minded beings are at work within each Roycean choice and event. This forms another bridge between the true interests of philosophy and religion. The loyal self recognizes that in the "now" it also encounters the Ultimate (the *eschaton*). So, there is a present *eschaton,* more vital for human temporal selves than even an *eschaton* already realized (Christianity's originating events) and an *eschaton* yet to be realized (the Second Coming of Christ). Moreover, because the goal-seeking in each choice and event bears upon the future, each present decision and happening proclaims that the kingdom is to be yet more fully realized in the future. So, by means of this twofold internal structure, every human choice and temporal happening both confirms or disconfirms the rightness of the self's decision in the present and directs or corrects the self towards the future coming of the Beloved Community.

This forward-looking dimension within each choice and each temporal event carries "the essential message of Christianity:

> that the sense of life, the very being of the time process itself, consists in the progressive realization of the Universal Community in and through the longings, the vicissitudes, the tragedies, and the triumphs of this process of the temporal world. (2:387)

Within the events comprising human life, Royce found occurring a natural revelation that strictly parallels the Christian Paschal Mystery. The latter enters into the intent of the Suffering Servant during his dying and rising. This intent and Paschal Mystery embraces the master's individual and communal modes of existence. In other words, the deepest intent which unites events that seem unconnected or even ruptured is that dedication to atonement which gives people life and fills them with hope. Strengthened and directed by such dedication, humankind's most loyal suffering servants constantly struggle to offset alienating forces. By this service they bring the Beloved Community closer to actuality.

In its naturalized embodiment, this atoning intent flashes forth a convincing message. For every question we ask, there is always an answer. For every error we make, there is a corresponding truth to correct us. For every frustration we encounter, there is somewhere a counterbalancing fulfillment. For every alienation, there is somewhere, somehow, a reconciliation. For every failure, there is a kind of greater success. And for every sin, there is a counterbalancing process of redeeming atonement.

If this is the message within each temporal event, then each person is being called through every choice and encounter to enter into the cosmic process of atoning redemption. This assured message along with the loyal response it evokes promotes the Beloved Community. It also reveals one site where the true interests of philosophy and religion converge.

Through this challenging yet life-giving call to atonement the cause of the Beloved Community attracts good but otherwise alienated people. This cause unavoidably draws them into basic commonly shared patterns of meaning, communication, and cooperation since they labor together to foster greater human community. Consequently, the conscious expression of the life people share will always be structured by a definite social form (2:387), the form of a Community of Interpretation. But both philosophy and religion find this form essential to their life. The heart of this form lies in the shared doctrine of life, which Royce took such pains to identify: that living ensemble of the three essential "Christian" ideas suffused with the general idea of Grace. Key supports of the form are Royce's three conditions for the consciousness of genuine community and that third degree of expressing such communal consciousness.

This "social form of communal religious consciousness" can be viewed from the divine side—from the side of the Interpreter-Spirit in its intent and operation. If so viewed, one will recognize this ultimate fact: "In the whole world divine life is expressed in the form of community" (2:388).[10] This form can be viewed from its human side—from the side of the human selves involved, who appreciate taking part in this doctrine of life and in the consequent self-identification. If viewed from this side, the form makes members aware of living together "in the true unity of the spirit." Then people recognize that "we always stand in the presence of the divine interpretation of the whole temporal process, and are members, if we choose, of the truly universal community" (2:388).

Whether practicing religion or philosophy, people who contact this social form find themselves directed along a path leading to their highest possible good. Along this path they come to see wherein this highest good of humankind consists. To the extent that this good is approached, human selves experience salvation progressively occurring not only in themselves but also in their communities. Indeed, at this point it becomes clear that only in and through the Beloved Community can salvation take place. Rather than remaining in, or relapsing into, individualistic self-consciousness, people are saved by committedly devoting themselves to loyal work for the sake of community under the Spirit's guidance. Here the true interests of philosophy and religion coincide.

This assertion by Royce is momentous as well as practical. It requires that each person make strong, constant efforts at ongoing transformation of oneself. Each must further deepen his or her religious commitment in loyalty to the Spirit and to the Community. Only in this way does the Beloved Community's central process of salvation advance through human history. In Royce's opinion, to assert and to live out this many-sided, yet steadfastly loyal response to the Beloved Community is the very core of the Christian experience. By fidelity to this communal process, the relations between the true interests of philosophy and religion are simplified (1:xvi; 2:390).

In sum, the true interests of philosophy and religion allow for a healthy competition, yet they find their life arising from their common taproot: genuine loyalty to the universal community. The foregoing paragraphs highlighted this taproot. They showed genuine philosophy and religion are called to make a similar choice about their fundamental orientation towards the universe. Then, too, in each human action in the present, philosophy and religion share a common work and receive a common gift. They also share a sign-event, a teleology, an eschatology, and a natural revelation in common. Even a common doctrine binds them insofar as philosophy's "doctrine of signs" has its close likeness in religion's Christian Doctrine of Life. If philosophy investigates human life thoroughly, it will discover the human need for commitment to the social form of human life distinctive of any Community of Interpretation and that this commitment orients each loyal person to the divine. Finally, philosophy may emphasize intellectual and affective conversion, while religion may stress moral and religious conversion, yet nonetheless, both philosophy and religion are interested in the integral transformation of human selves and of their communities — that is, in the fullest human conversion attainable.

Another way to clarify what Royce taught in the third area which he mapped out for simplification is to employ his favorite movement of comparison and contrast. For this, we select the doctrines on religion found in John Dewey's *A Common Faith* and in Royce's *The Problem of Chris-*

tianity. During this comparison and contrast, we will focus on three basic questions: Does philosophy have a closed or open relation to the supernatural? Does philosophy challenge individualistic man to admit his moral and religious bankruptcy? Does philosophy find within religious experience a specifiable superhuman referent?

Royce's basic position in the *Sources* and in the *Problem* was that an "interest in the salvation of man . . . [is] the essential feature of religion" (*SRI,* 8). This position implies that human religion has an at least generically knowable central structure and that it is directed towards a superhuman source of salvation. The naturalists advanced a basic counterposition. Dewey held "there is no such thing as religion in general" but only various instances of institutionally organized systems of belief and practice, each of which constitutes "a religion."[11] If I read him correctly, Dewey here views religious phenomena through his nominalism. According to such an epistemology, it is right to assert that there is no reality abroad called "religion in general." Moreover, he also consistently infers that various religions do not share in any real and knowable essential structure. He holds this view despite ordinary folk's meaningful language about world religions.

Furthermore, Dewey felt that every religion, by its belief in a supernatural revelation, siphons off valuable energies from the human enterprise. Consequently, if people cease identifying the fully human values in their this-worldly enterprises with the creeds and cults of a religion, then the religious quality of their experiences will be enhanced. If through their moral choices people actually participate in the "distinctively religious values inherent in natural experience," they will not dissipate these values but find that they release precious energies to enrich human life from within.[12]

For Dewey this religious quality can enhance human experience only if two provisos are fulfilled. As he put it:

> The religious is 'morality touched by emotion' only when the ends of moral conviction arouse emotions that are not only intense but are actuated and supported by ends so inclusive that they unify the self.[13]

A person's experience has a genuinely religious quality only if two things occur. An intense emotion must accompany one's moral conviction. And the values to which one is morally dedicated so embrace all humankind and all nature's processes that one's own self becomes more integrated. Dewey had good reasons for fearing that just those human energies most needed for enriching the quality of human life would be diverted away through the distraction of "a religion." Hence, by conceiving people's natural ends in a very broad and all-inclusive way, he sealed off any openings which might permit escapes to any supposed supernatural. Unfortunately, this move unilaterally locked out the Transcendent, left no opening to receive the initiative of a supernatural Deliverer, and domesticated religious experience totally within the realm of the human.

Suppose, on the other hand, that religion is somewhat different. Suppose it places three demands on people. All must be unswervingly dedicated to promote the integral development of peoples. All must undergo a radical ethico-religious transformation. All must be elevated to take part in a human-and-superhuman salvation. If this is what religion is, then Dewey's generally well-designed strategy has undershot its mark. It has ended up by instilling a poisonous enmity between the true interests of philosophy and religion.

Royce was equally aware of the encumbrances of organized religions upon the human spirit. He concurred with Dewey that both the root and the fruit of religion must be in the human. So, within human nature, Royce used the discernment principle of loyalty as the key to his religious paradox. Further, he required that his religion of loyalty prove its authenticity by steadfast deeds of atonement and service to heal and promote the human community. However, Royce refrained from foreclosing the door to the human-and-superhuman Interpreter-Spirit who saves the lost self and guides humankind to more genuine community. On this point of openness to the Transcendent, then, Royce seems more faithfully to have respected and simplified the relation between the true interests of religion and of philosophy.

Dewey insisted that the religious quality is not present in human experience unless a person's moral convictions embrace values so inclusive that they unify that person. But Dewey's religious quality does not appear to demand as an essential prerequisite that each individual also confess one's own moral bankruptcy and sinfulness. By contrast, Royce had found people's interest in salvation to be the essential feature of religion (*SRI,* 8). Indeed, he discovered that genuine religious experience involves an escape from humankind's greatest evil—the escape in which one finds, to employ William James' phrase, that not all of me has "gone to pieces in the wreck."[14] Put positively, a genuine religious experience must promote human liberation in a person's deepest depths as well as on one's broader dimensions. James' language in the *Varieties* and Royce's in the *Problem* and the *Sources* calls for *something more* in religious experience than Dewey's morality. For them, religion indeed has to include a morality touched by emotions that are made intense by ends inclusive enough to unify the self. Yet for them religious experience also needs help or guidance from a higher being. Although self-integration is an indispensable norm of genuine religion, still acceptance of a saving Community which is both human *and* superhuman seems an even more radical prerequisite.

For Royce, salvation and transformation have to be at work if an experience is to be genuinely religious. This requires more than the radical conversion from amoral to moral consciousness. It further demands that the person be actually elevated to a new life which one can gain only if one personally takes part in a human-and-superhuman saving community. To be truly salvific, genuine religious experience actually requires a cry from the depths of one's helplessness. By calling attention to this demand, Royce has clarified how genuine philosophy and religion can cooperate. They both can mediate and enhance the genuine life of any previously sealed-off individual.

Dewey also held that "the adjective 'religious' denotes nothing in the way of a specifiable entity, either institutional or as a system of beliefs."[15] Contrarily, Royce held that the adjective 'religious' denotes several such "specifiable entities" or referents—namely, the living invisible institution called the Beloved Community and also that minimal system of beliefs called the Christian doctrine of life (the three essential Ideas in unity). In sum, Royce taught that religious experience not only supposed a Deweyan integration of the finite self but additionally requires a transformation and salvation of the self through loyal sharing in the life and beliefs of the Beloved Community. In the future, if both philosophy and religion respect these "specifiable entities," many of the obstacles to the cooperation of these disciplines will be eliminated. This, in turn, will notably simplify the relations between the true interests of philosophy and religion.

The previous sections have outlined Royce's predicted results of his work in the *Problem:* a threefold simplification of Christology, of dogma in general, and of the relations between the true interests of philosophy and religion. This provides an accurate overview of Royce's late doctrinal synthesis concerning his philosophy of the Christian religion. Yet he offered another synopsis shortly before his death. In a letter composed in March 1916, three years after authoring the *Problem,* Royce spoke of the three ideas that had become dominant in his mature period: Community, Spirit, and Process. In so doing, he highlighted the core of his mature doctrine:

> These two ideas, the Community, and the Spirit . . . certainly have assumed, in my own mind, a new vitality, and a very much deeper significance than, for me, they ever had before I wrote my *Problem of Christianity*. . . .
>
> This recent phase, not merely of my thinking but of my experience, . . . may be due to its actual relations to a process which has been going on, in human thought, ever since Heraclitus remarked that the Logos is fluent, and ever since Israel began to realize the life of a little hill town in Judea.
>
> I stand for the importance of this process, which has led Christianity to regard a community, not merely as an aggregate but as a Person, and at the same time, to enrich its ideal memory of a person, until he became transformed into a Community.[16]

PART FIVE

Towards a Critical Appreciation of Royce

19. Evaluation of Strengths and Weaknesses

We can imagine ourselves in 1916 walking in the Harvard yard where we encounter Professor Royce returning home after a lecture in his final course in metaphysics. Suppose we inform him about the gist of the previous chapters. Suppose, too, that in reply he asks us, with a twinkle in his eye, whether we recognize that all his endeavors in philosophy of religion were launched *only* from "the human side." In this way he might ironically let us glimpse vistas yet to be explored in an integral study of religion.

During his professional career, with its evident shortcomings, Royce achieved more and more spiritual penetration and critical poise. Through the decades he reached greater and greater epistemological depth and intellectual breadth. Traces of this development stretch from his transforming religious insight of 1883 to his 1913 masterwork, *The Problem of Christianity*—and beyond. In this chapter, then, we first identify some notable strengths[1] and weaknesses. Second, we limit ourselves to locate both those more central strengths (that grew as his philosophy of religion developed) and his evident weaknesses. Third, we highlight his original verification of deep religious experience as a most valuable, though largely uncredited, contribution. Finally, we zero in upon the new starting points he employed in analyzing this experience.

SOME NOTABLE STRENGTHS AND WEAKNESSES

Royce called attention to the often overlooked Pauline addition to Jesus' doctrine of love (1:75–76, 78, 93–94). That is, Royce highlighted the fact that Paul transformed Jesus' doctrine of loving individuals into a doctrine of *also* loving communities as such. In this important service to Christianity, several contributing factors deserve notice. Even though Royce distinguished, he did not separate the object and subject of Christian love. He taught that God, neighbor, and oneself are all "the objects of Christian love *and* the inspiration of the life of love" (1:105).[2] Moreover, Royce's exegesis of Paul's text, "Christ loved the Church,"[3] uncovers the seed of

Royce's notion of loyalty and instances his prowess as an exegete (1:97–99). Finally, in his ethics of loyalty, Royce chose to emphasize the positive rather than the negative side of the love command. To devise legislation that is clear and workable, it may be more necessary to specify negative prohibitions out of the ethical principle "Do good *and* avoid evil," rather than to exhort to goodness. But when formulating a basic ethics for individual members of a community, Royce rightly placed the weight upon "Promote growth of loving loyalty" rather than upon "Don't harm!" Keenly aware of the downdrag of mere individualism and of bare collectivism, he inserted a spur rather than a bridle. One was to be wholeheartedly committed to serve one's community, guided by "a conscious doctrine regarding what sort of special good one can do to one's neighbor" and to one's community (1:86). The primacy given in many contemporary ethics to the negative imperative ("don't harm") may need a prior distinction. What is more needed to safeguard an institution need not be what is more needed to promote an individual's moral growth.

American philosophy is indebted to Royce for his crucial correction of William James' one-sided approach to religious experience. Counterbalancing James' individualistic tone, Royce insisted on *communal* religious experience and on the form, depth, and potential genuineness of such experience (1:xvi).

Another significant service to religion was Royce's resistance to secularistic "hush-hushers" who would privatize any communal or public exercise of religion. He noticed certain pseudo-leaders who ever so politely yet militantly pressure religious believers to keep their religion a purely private affair. Even William James' selection of only solitary religious geniuses as his examples in the *Varieties* might persuade certain of his readers towards an increasingly non-communal, non-public practice of their religion. Of course, Royce recognized that the way one asserts one's faith-filled commitment to a Beloved Community and its Spirit must show respect and tact towards others with different, even opposed, views. On the other hand, the person who under group pressure retreats defensively into a religion of pure interiority, which lacks verbal and deed-doing professions of one's faith in public, stifles the life of his or her religion. Royce clearly saw this danger. So, he required that every genuinely loyal person both assert and wholeheartedly live out one's faith by acknowledgment and cooperative deeds in community (1:xvi; 2:428).

Realistically Royce blended the positive and negative aspects of human life—community, sin, atoning suffering, and God's gracious love. This mixture kept his philosophy of religion far more balanced than the psychology of religion of those whose chant, "stress the positive," translates practically into "exclude the negative." Their victims turn away from anything negative and detach themselves from reality. For reality is a tattletale grey blend of good *and* evil—a blend that both blesses and challenges to growth. Because Royce emphasized an openness to this balanced blend of reality, he did not stress any "cheap grace." Rather the human spirit, in response to grace, has to climb strenuously upward to the summit of the mountain of morality if salvation is actually to be won (1:xviii).

In the *Problem* Christianity achieves its peak in the "suffering servant" who atones to free the community from the effects of disloyalty (1:xx, 315–317). To unbelievers any atoner looks like a fool. Now Royce could not have read Paul as he did without knowing the Pauline theme of "becoming a fool for Christ." At the heart of Royce's idea of genuine community is the idea of atonement which is "especially foreign to the modern mind, as most of us conceive that mind" (1:44).

However, Royce hardly portrays how shocking the scandal of the cross is for the faithful. Nor does he convey how jarring is the leap from the *seemingly* rational view of the world accepted by "security-wedded one-worlders" to that radically different and broader rational view of the universe held by "suffering-servant two-worlders." What is rational to the latter seems folly to the former. Although Paul conveys this rugged gap between the two rationalities, Royce does not.[4] He contributed to this non-jarring treatment by formulating his problem of Christianity in terms of consistency: "Can the modern man consistently hold a Christian creed" (1:16)? In this way Royce allowed himself to be easily misunderstood for he seems to suggest that a Christian believer can fit well into contemporary trends without experiencing the clash of being regarding as a "fool for Christ."

One can easily perceive other weaknesses in the mature Royce's *Problem*. For instance, he was clearly selective in his reverence. He revered the apostles Paul and John very highly. Strangely however, he did not show reverence towards the other apostles—particularly toward that Peter whom Jesus is reported to have named "the rock upon whom I shall build my church."[5] Royce's selective reverence remains factual, even if understandable in his nineteenth-century American Protestant background.

At times Royce's exegesis leaves something to be desired. For instance, he refers to Paul's teaching the Thessalonians about the resurrection of the Lord and the nearness of his second coming. Then Royce asserts, "Paul had not divided these various teachings one from another" (2:353). Yet in his Second Letter to these Thessalonians Paul reminded them that he had *already* warned them against men deceiving them into believing the Lord's coming was close at hand.[6] Royce may have discountenanced Second Thessalonians as non-Pauline. Or he may have surmised that Paul's text in First Thessalonians was an adequate sample for reading the factual state of faith in all Pauline churches or even in all early Christian churches, including the non-Pauline ones. Whatever the explanation, Royce's exegesis here remains questionable.

Again, Royce's high esteem for Paul led him to overemphasize being a *Pauline* Christian (2:362-363) rather than being a Christian. Paul himself taught the relative insignificance of Christian ministers—whether it be Apollo or Cephas or Paul—because the principal agent of Christian conversion and growth is "God who giveth the increase."[7]

We have identified certain strengths and weaknesses in the mature Royce. Did any noteworthy omissions occur in the development of his philosophy of religion from 1908 to 1913? Christianity as community so preoccupied him that Christianity as institution scarcely received its due. Royce was understandably estranged by many ecclesiastics' mixed motives or primarily self-centered motives. His disaffection, however, hardly justified his omitting an essentially creedal question: What doctrine is essential concerning the institutionalization of the Christian community? Can this community survive unless its members believe that in it certain ministers are entrusted with special coordinating services and are commanded, when dealing with Christian members, to avoid the dominating attitudes of pagan rulers? Royce bypassed this question.

Without Christian virtues the Church cannot be Church. Christian virtues cannot continue to operate, however, unless Christians usually engage in practices that support these virtues. But American economy and politics are fiercely competitive and acquisitive. Their usual practices foster self-preference, aggressive behavior, and manipulation of the weak. Did Royce take a hard look at the kinds of economic and political practices that are needed to support genuine loyalty? He was particularly silent on this question of indispensable practices. He insisted that a religion of loyalty must discover and develop "the social arts" which will overcome people's original hatefulness (2:430) and he proposed in some detail a plan for international insurance against war. But he neither brought forth an ethics for business and politics nor identified the inculturated practices requisite for a civilization of loyalty. Royce need not be faulted too much here. China's passion for moderation took over two millennia to develop.

Royce did not try to rebut his giving center stage to loyalty. For instance, instead of daily finding more depth and life in the ideal of loyalty (1:ix), he might well have held this tendency in check in order to throw the weight of his insight and reasoning into another direction, even if it yielded similar results. If one cultivates such ideals as liberty or truth or justice or beauty, does not he, too, promote human maturation and life? Royce knew that the Platonic Forms intercommunicate and that his own idea of Community is integral to these ideal Forms. He seems not to have sufficiently acknowledged the subjectivity involved when he preferred to give explicit emphasis to the ideal of loyalty rather than to other ideals. Put differently, Royce largely bypassed the medievals' discussion of Being's transcendental attributes: its oneness, truth, goodness, etc.

Current interest in the problem of human death reveals another lacuna in Royce's late philosophy of religion. Though he faced the problem of evil without flinching, he rarely handled the mystery of human death directly. On the other hand, unlike most late twentieth-century thought, he did investigate the question of *human destiny* with fitting intensity and rigor (1:xxii, 384–425; 2:373–379). Today's human pilgrims need philosophical research into human destiny if they are to receive the light they need on their way.

SOME CENTRAL STRENGTHS

During Royce's decades-long development of a philosophy of religion, he revealed certain central strengths: a refinement of method and an increasing respect for the wisdom of "common folk." His greater sensitivity to method gradually inserted more vigor into his philosophy of religion. In it one might start by asking: Which objects should a philosopher regard as religious? Does the Christian God and the Buddhist Nirvana and the impersonal Spinozistic Substance and the Spencerian Unknowable each qualify as religious? One's answer follows upon the approach one selects to the philosophy of religion. In 1885, Royce stipulated that an object was religious whenever veneration and belief marked one's consciousness of the object.[8] Furthermore, one's tenets about such an object constituted religious beliefs. These aprioristic standards revealed Royce's decision to approach the philosophy of religion in 1885 by way of a "least common denominator." At that time he did not engage in the experiential investigations of his later days. Yet only by such empiricism could Royce gain an appreciative understanding of persons' basic need for ultimate meaning or salvation.

Three decades later Royce discerned spiritual things more spiritually (2:361). Now religious belief was genuine only if the believing self practically exercised loyalty to a genuine community and in this way was oriented to the divine. Through his decades of research into religion, Royce had by 1912 developed a general twofold view: 1) that in any discipline, the goal and norm work inside the experiential process being studied; and 2) that fundamentally, values are so interwoven with meaning and facts that "the very recognition of Being is itself an estimate."[9] For example, if one seeks what is distinctive and normative of the human person as such, one concentrates chiefly neither on unachieved human beings like children nor on constricted people like the senile. Rather, one focuses on fully developed men and women. Similarly, Royce found, philosophy of religion needs to investigate the more mature forms of religion, judiciously selected. Otherwise, such philosophy will not clearly comprehend that goal or ideal to which the authentic living impulse of religion is striving to bring humankind.

In sum, Royce gradually corrected certain originally unbalanced attitudes towards philosophy of religion. In 1885 he had concurred with that self-reliant Americanized Pelagianism which asserted that "we want to work out our own salvation by our own efforts."[10] But by 1912 he had found that salvation comes *only* through a human-and-superhuman community and with much dependence upon one's neighbors. In 1885 he had also been convinced that "thinking is for us just the clarifying of our minds."[11] But by 1912 he had recognized that in genuine human knowing the interpretive process achieves a far deeper and broader intimate knowing than comes about through comparing percepts or defining concepts. Finally, by 1912 he had also grown masterful enough to interweave all three of his ways of studying natural religion. He had become explicitly aware of these three ways at least by 1899.[12] At that time, however, he concentrated on his third way: to analyze our human meaning of Being. But he then found that although pursuing this third way best suited his middle-period talents, it also consumed all his available energies. But by 1912 his method of interpretive musement gave him increased strength, subtlety, and ease. As a result of these developments and influenced by the exemplary ways of the Baptizer, C. S. Peirce, and the Holy Spirit, the mature Royce found that the fullness of knowing consists in an interpretive awareness of minded beings and of their meanings, an awareness pulsed by loyal decisions and fully illuminated by the Spirit.[13]

Meanwhile, Royce's respect for the popular mind had grown. He found it simple yet profound. By 1912 he recognized more clearly that this popular mind is "rich and deep" and "means a thousand times more than it explicitly knows."[14] Ordinary folk in America have a vague awareness of God, grace, and salvation. But Royce found that their awareness, while very much alive, is undifferentiated and unarticulated. Thanks to his recent transformation into an interpretive knower, Royce was now able to mediate more sensitively between this popular religious mind and philosophers' refined articulation of God, grace, and salvation into concepts or ideas. In 1912 Royce focused upon this significant gap and its consequences. By doing so, he succeeded in respecting both the concrete unity of communally shared religious life and those abstract concepts or ideas about such life—concepts or ideas that call philosophers of religion to ever further clarification and unending efforts at fuller comprehension of the popular religious mind.

Royce's late concern for prethematic meanings[15] and his growing respect for "simple folk" evidence his maturing preference for the experiential. In the *Sources* he had preferred to investigate people's ordinary encounters with a saving Presence rather than, like James, to select the extraordinary experiences of isolated religious geniuses. In the *Problem* communal religious experience led him to discover that essential form towards which other particular world religions would also be striving insofar as they fulfilled the life of authentic loyalty. Such attention to communally experienced religious life allowed him to identify the logical structure of this essential form as that of a Community of Interpretation. In all these ways, then, Royce had grown strong as a philosopher of religion.

SOME CENTRAL WEAKNESSES

Yet Royce was a victim of religious malnutrition. The *fully* rich nourishment of religion escaped him — whether coming from outside or inside Christianity. Like most of his contemporaries, he lacked direct prolonged encounters with the world religions.[16] His pathway to the banquet table of Christianity was hedged in by the thorny controversies and jealousies of sadly competing denominations and their clergymen. As unchurched during most of his life, he neither took part in the communal celebration of the Eucharist nor chose to listen regularly to the central teachings of those entrusted by the apostles with a special apostolic ministry in the Church. The central weaknesses in his philosophy of the Christian religion stem largely from this malnutrition.

Like many philosophers, he so thoroughly researched one ingredient of religion that he risked unbalancing his overall view of religion. As a first instance, in 1912 Royce so concentrated upon the creedal essence of Christianity that he tended to regard public worship, sacraments, divine law, and the mother of Jesus as unimportant, without supplying his audience with counterbalancing questions or cautions.[17] Again, his focus on the reality of the Kingdom and its partial and deficient embodiment in the Church made him largely silent about the King, the Christ (1:xxiv-xxvi). In early reactions to this, William Ernest Hocking and Mary Whiton Calkins described Royce's "undue subordination of the role of the leader to that of the group, or — historically stated — his underestimation of the fact that passionate loyalty to the person of Christ was the bond of unity in the early Christian church."[18] With Professor John E. Smith, I regard this reading of Royce as too rapid and extreme. Once a reader recognizes that Royce's Interpreter-Spirit in the *Problem* is a Sign of the risen Christ, the latter becomes present throughout the work without any subordination of leader to group. Second, in a crucial passage on the "life" and the "bond linking" the Christian community together, Royce speaks of the need for a "miracle of grace" to initiate this community. He finds just such a miracle in the strange union of a human individual with a Beloved Community (1:185–187). Royce's scarcely veiled reference is clearly to the risen Christ. Third, when contrasting Christianity and Buddhism, Royce opposed Buddhism's Nirvana to Christianity's "realm of absolute loyalty." He described this "realm" as one "where all are one in Christ" (1:191). Finally, given Royce's love and admiration for Paul, it is highly probable that when reporting Paul's faith in Christ as divine, Royce with this Pauline faith also believes in the divine Christ, the "life-giving Spirit" of the Christian community (1:98, 174; 2:426–427).

Since Royce's Christianity is comparable to an ellipse with two foci — the risen Christ as Logos-Spirit and the believing Christian Community — the risen Christ is surely present in the *Problem,* even if not so predominantly as the Community (1:22). Yet several weaknesses mar the Christ of the *Problem.* Royce did not bind the wounded risen Christ inseparably to the human individual mothered by Mary of Nazareth. Nor did he attend sufficiently to that distinction between the Logos and the Holy Spirit to which the writings of the later Paul and of John attest.[19]

As mentioned, the divisions between the Christian churches have kept millions of Americans from experiencing fully the Christian Community in its wholeness. Royce was among these victims. The divided churches fomented bitterness and hypocrisy among their members. In New England's "late autumn," Royce experienced a sickly elderly Christianity rocking away its days.[20] Before World War I and long before the liturgical reform emphasized by the Second Vatican Council, many cultically inclined denominations of Royce's day had stale, routine worship services. This kind of cultic practices confirmed the non-conformists' judgment that the spiritual power of all established churches had declined. Yet within these latter churches, radical critics decried and heavily attacked this clear decline, especially in the second and third decade of this century. But their efforts failed to create liturgical experiences for Royce in which, because of the full, active, conscious, and communal participation by all members present, he personally might have felt the Presence of the Redeeming Spirit in the Assembly of Christians.

Furthermore, Royce generally avoided an encounter with the living voice of those who have been selected and sent to evoke faith in the risen Christ and in his whole Gospel just as the twelve Apostles had first been selected and sent by Jesus.[21] Royce's non-conformist upbringing and his stress in the *Problem* on the mission of the Church as a *whole* community inclined him to neglect the *special* ministries of the apostles and their successors towards other Christians and towards all non-Christians. For example, in a clear allusion to a Petrine text favored by Roman Catholics,[22] Royce interpreted "the rock upon which the true and ideal church is built" as the truth about the reality of the Church's social religious experiences in which all its members unite to share (1:xvi). Thus Royce interpreted the "thou" in the master's reported response to Simon Peter, "Thou are the rock upon which I will build my church," as referring not to Simon as a selected entrusted shepherd, but to "my Community that, in the end, saves me" (1:xvi). For Royce, then, in this text Jesus intends neither the person of Simon Peter (whether viewed as a human individual or as the visible head of the Christian community) nor that temporally extended community of those entrusted with the Petrine office.

In sum, Royce's priority for clergymen was that they simply be men of evident faith, courageous rather than hesitant shipmasters.[23] It was far less important for him that they be entrusted by the Christian People and its Head with special responsibilities for the overall good of the Church.

Rather than harken discerningly to bishops charged to serve as "ambassadors of Christ," Royce read the Scriptures. His Protestant upbringing moved him in this direction. For Protestantism generally, and particularly non-conformist churches, have developed a certain liturgical celebration in Scripture reading. Individually or in a group they read Scripture reflectively and prayerfully. Their Scripture services can create a deep and intense religious experience — with even a vivid sense of taking part in a community of believers that transcends time and space.

Royce's individual reflective reading of Scriptures during his life shows that such reading can invoke a strong sense of mystical union with the transcendently spiritual yet concrete Entity.[24] On some Sunday mornings he shared religious ideas with a few fellow academicians. Little wonder, then, that when Royce read his Bible privately as best he could or heard it read in an elite group, two results followed amid the press of his heavy professional responsibilities at highly academic Harvard. The scholarly atmosphere inclined him to reduce Holy Writ to "traditional reports." He also failed to experience the human support and the challenge to his charity that comes from taking an active part in a widely diversified Christian Community — including uneducated Irish maids and smelly dockhands — all gathered to listen in Faith to the living Word of God. In sum, although lacking the nourishment that comes through Eucharist, the living voice of the apostles' successors, and enriching contact with a wide spectrum of believers, Royce drew deep draughts of Christian life from his prayer life, his reading of Scripture, and his undergoing "the religious mission of sorrow," especially in his final years.

Ironically, despite his isolation and intellectualism, Royce developed a profound and prophetic contribution to the philosophy of religion. He demanded that Christian churches exercise a discerning openness to the widest pluralism of life-giving religious factors. This gave a powerful thrust to the whole ecumenical movement. It also offered a new freedom of thought and action to all believers.

ROYCE'S SOUNDING OF RELIGIOUS EXPERIENCE TO VERIFY ITS DEEPEST PULSES

How does Royce compare in methods and findings with current investigators of religious experience? To enter into such a comparison and contrast would require another book — one exceeding the present author's competence.[25] More modestly, the comments that follow aim mainly to underscore Royce's contributions within the investigation of religious experience.

Unlike many idealists, the mature Royce placed primary emphasis on experience. The mid-century disputes over verifiability had not yet begun when he claimed that the main outlines of his philosophy of loyalty were experientially verifiable (1:ix). So, this statement calls for clarification. By it he did not mean that the standards of objective scientific procedure could measure and test either the *Problem*'s principal findings or his two factual bases for the religious interest (*SRI,* 38). Instead, by "verifiable in terms of human experience," the Royce of 1913 meant to assert three things about our basic experiential judgments concerning religion. 1) These judgments can be grasped interiorly as congruent with one's own fundamental needs, interests, and ideals. 2) These judgments can be felt as carrying the inner press of authenticity. 3) Interpersonal sharings about these inner congruencies can confirm the truth of these judgments. However, Royce had built a proviso into this kind of verifiability. The person validating his or her own experiences must have undergone at least an initial ethico-religious transformation. Only by undergoing this transformation could one discover what being committed means personally. Lived commitment to community is the basic value operative at the center of Royce's validating process. And only by way of this commitment can the ideals and values proper to the second level of existence arise to consciousness in order to guide one's authentication of the religious facts experienced.

Already this late Roycean approach to religious experience will have divided philosophers of religion in two ways. First, Royce implied that initial experiential judgments, concretely lived, cannot be value-free for they inescapably involve some evaluative response to the universe. Royce's implication holds true whether one's basic response is to dominate the universe, withdraw from it, or affirm it in loyal love (2:298-325).

Second, by limiting himself simply to the human side of religious experience—to people's fundamental religious needs and interests—Royce operated as if he could distinguish experientially between the divine side and the human side. Yet, if the Interpreter-Spirit of Royce's community is subtle like a fox, can Royce detect all its graceful ways and mysterious movements? Can Royce successfully remove all divine graces to "the other side" in his attempt to be concerned exclusively with "the human side"? Moreover, by choosing the imagery of light to convey his reading of religious experience, he only complicates this difficulty. When he uses the basic myth of "increasing light" and "insight" to describe religious experience, who will say where human light leaves off and divine light begins in religious experience?

Yet these two difficulties suggest that Royce is entering deeply into the vital pulse of religious experience where discernment is difficult. Phenomenologists will tend to agree with Royce's precision from the divine side. Others will find his neat distinction pretentious. They will call for the less neat and unscientific admission that in human religious experiences the divine presence may be at work unknown to us. Still others will take a position of explicit faith and hold that divine grace is certainly at work in human experiences even if our religious sensitivity is usually too gross to detect this Presence and its operation.

Royce also contributes in other ways to current discussions among philosophical theologians. We saw that Royce answers affirmatively to the question whether religious experience includes genuine cognitive elements. Another current question is whether religious experience is a distinct kind of human experience—parallel to the aesthetic and moral kinds of experience—or simply a dimension of every human experience. Royce would seem to side with the latter view for within every human experience he finds human judgment and within every human judgment he discovers the presence of the all-Knower. As Royce said, "We are always seeking to know even as we are known."[26]

Another current question is whether the religious dimension in human experience is explained adequately by previously learned socio-cultural forms. (These latter would include the conceptual and affective meanings of language.) Gordon Kaufmann gives an unqualified "yes" to this question.[27] But Royce had some qualifications. He employed the social psychology of Wundt and Tarde and the ethnology of Bastian (1:64; 2:26-29,

86). Admittedly, their disciplines lacked the subtleties of today's updated social sciences. These latter take into account the constructive element which the sociology of knowledge etches so clearly. Royce would, of course, concede that religious experience is not simply given but is in some way constructed by us. An analogy between the human self and a baseball player may help. A person depends continuously upon his or her community for the peculiar linguistic and cultural meanings it supplies. A baseball player depends upon the gradually developed peculiar "feel" of his glove in order to catch the ball accurately.

To this admitted subjectivity, however, Royce inserted a significant counterpoise. He emphasized the objective meaning of his three essential ideas. He stated, "Such Christian ideas as I have tried to interpret, I certainly did not invent. They found me. I did not devise them" (2:335). Royce here indicated that when an idea encounters a human minded being, the mind's constructive activity is different and far less than when the mind either interprets the same idea or uses it to devise a new idea. Here the human stomach may provide an analogue. It finds and does not invent the proteins, carbohydrates, and vitamins which it derives from materials other than itself. Meanwhile, it immerses and modifies all of these elements in its distinctive digestive process for the good of the whole organism. Similarly, Royce held that not all the content in cognitive religious experience derives from the subject's constructive activity. He conceded, however, that the constructive activity of the person undergoing a religious experience works upon all the ingredients in that experience.

It follows that Royce's language about religious experience and interpretation of it reflect a vital "in-touchness." For him religious experience is richly diversified yet rhythmically coherent.[28] It resembles an organism with its "distinguishable interpenetrating factors."[29] For Royce religious experience is more individual on some occasions, more communal at others. It is sometimes extraordinary but usually ordinary. At times it needs the felt absences of the Deliverer while at other times it requires his felt presences. Royce is both an investigator of the essential form of religious experience and a discerner of the Spirit's coming "from above." In his descriptions of religious experiences, then, he blends the structural and the charismatic. He also carefully calibrates the levels of increasing insight (*SRI,* 100–102). He cumulatively assembles the sources feeding one's "inner light." Moreover, he suggests the harm that self-preference, social insensitivity, and lack of prayerfulness inflict upon the normal patterns of religious development in the individual and the community. Through such soundings of religious experience, Royce contributes as significantly to the philosophy of religion in our day as he did in 1912.

DEEPER STARTING POINTS

Ever since his days as an Instructor at Berkeley, Royce had committed himself to philosophize earnestly, independently, and reverently.[30] Furthermore, at Harvard he gradually became convinced that the center of everyone's personality is a continually creative initiative.[31] Expectably, then, the mature Royce raised fresh inquiries and generated novel starting points. The following questions and initiatives illustrate how Royce creatively rephrased traditional problems and deepened philosophical discussions in his overall effort to promote the unity of humankind.

Some of the demonstrative procedures he had used earlier were called into question by the choices of method he made in the *Sources* and *Problem*. Yet these later choices suggested procedures more needed and helpful for today. He shifted from his earlier approach that relied chiefly on a logic of propositions to demonstrate the existence of an all-Knower to an approach that raised questions about the presence or absence of a Holy Spirit. This more mature approach is more human and helpful than attempting a formally logical demonstration of God's existence. Royce's new procedure reflected both the tone of Peirce's "Neglected Argument" and this American logician's concern that only finite beings are properly said to "exist." Interestingly, Gabriel Marcel, who as a youth had carefully studied Royce's metaphysics, came to a similar belief. He held that the more pressing question for most people today is not whether God's existence can be formally demonstrated but whether the Holy One is felt to be present or absent and what such feelings mean.[32]

Again, one might ask, "Is it knowledge *or* faith that you have — about God, religion, and human destiny?" This question is tightly tied into a subject-object theory of knowing and fares poorly when transposed into the triadic interpretive process of communal knowing. Royce suggested that since human beings must be embodied amid temporal process, any true human cognition must combine both faith and knowledge. Accordingly, Royce's every act in the interpretive process unites belief and knowledge. He dismissed any presumed kind of "pure knowledge" as a dream. It follows that by starting with interpretation, Royce revealed a hugh shift from the Platonic tradition of the line that divides knowledge from faith.

Again, Royce was familiar with self-styled Christian metaphysicians whose approaches were to talk about Being or about God. Instead, he recommended a distinctively Christian approach to the divine by way of the "Holy Spirit." He judged that this approach both suggests a more appropriate understanding of the divine and tends to produce the same. Talk about God is neither philosophic nor distinctively Christian but properly religious. Talk about Being tends to evoke a type of objective thought which is often impersonal. Furthermore, it does not promptly suggest the holy as a principal characteristic of the divine. However, the term "Holy Spirit" indicates something holy, hidden, subtle, and intimate to human persons in community. Applied to the divine, the term "Spirit" suggests mystery for it refers to Someone personal who both labors yet also plays lovingly with human beings. This Spirit surprises people even as it remains faithful in its commitment to their greater good. Moreover, this Spirit's loving fidelity can neither be manipulated to support the mere whim of people nor can the concrete manifestations of its movements be certainly predicted. In this usage, then, the term "Spirit" refers to a Reality higher than the human and to its personal response-evoking activities within human communities and within their every member.[33]

Hence, Royce's shift from God-talk and Being-talk to Spirit-talk seems to meet contemporary requirements for disciplined language in the philosophy of religion. Such language should be ontological and existential.[34] Furthermore, the term "Spirit," if used without an article, neither categorizes nor particularizes the divine. Though derived from the Judaeo-Christian tradition, the term "Spirit" fits in with other religious traditions more smoothly than Jesus' unique term "Abba," which seems too immediately trinitarian and patriarchal in connotation

Royce found in each ethical choice the essentially Eternal (his *eschaton*) (2:386). He defined Loyalty as "the Will to Believe in something eternal . . . the will to manifest . . . the Eternal."[35] By such centering on the Eternal in the present choice Royce shifted the usual focus of the Christian doctrine of "the last things" (of eschatology). Instead of seeking "the ultimate" (or *eschaton*) in the temporal close or start of cosmic process, Royce asked whether the finite self, in its present temporal choice, encounters and recognizes the Eternal. On the other hand, Royce did not limit his eschatology to the present moment. He also looked forward to "that final union of temporal sequence, of the goal that is never attained in time, and of the divine spirit through whom the world is reconciled to itself" (2:378). By interpreting the apostle Paul's talk about "the end of the world" as merely symbolic (2:376), Royce found no inconsistency between the essential Christian creed and the temporal endlessness of the cosmos.

For our final instance of the way Royce suggested deeper starting questions, we turn to the relation between ethics and religion. Here, by penetrating to the central human intentionality that unites ethics and religion, he avoided compartmentalizing the two. From his study of loyalty he showed that the dynamic seedling of the moral life finds its true development by blossoming into religious interest.[36]

In the foregoing instances, then, Royce moved a familiar issue to a new and deeper level. His doing so leads us to inquire how he achieved this result so regularly. This inquiry, in turn suggests an appraisal of his methods, especially an appraisal of his underlying interpretive musement.

20. Contribution to Method for Philosophy of Religion

ROYCE'S GENERAL METHOD OF INTERPRETIVE MUSEMENT

Royce's will to interpret was strengthened by steady sighting on the ideal goals of his method: to know with breadth of range, with coherent unity of view, and with closeness of personal touch (2:186-193, 208).[1] Keeping this triadic norm in mind, we can proceed to examine, one by one, how these ideals steadily influenced the development of his overall method of interpretive musement.

First Methodic Ideal: Breadth of Range

Royce's pursuit of comprehensive vision through breadth of range made him a passionate anti-reductionist. Whatever the topic, he wanted a "fair comprehension" of it. To gain this he strove to escape limiting viewpoints so he could enjoy a Peircean "free play" of mind at the start and thereafter balance a broad range of perspectives. Meanwhile, his two other ideals of unified view and close personal touch continuously urged him to seek more genuine and fuller unity and life.

More specifically, Royce's anti-reductionism saved him from equating religion simply with a certain affective and imaginative response to the ideal. For him religion was also more than the loftiest symbols and myths which human selves create — even more than projections from one's subconscious. Each of these interpenetrating ingredients may play an indispensable role in the life of religion but that life also needs several other realities: the processes of history, of interpretation, of salvation, of community, and of Spirit.

When applied to the communal traditions of religion, Royce's antireductionism became his gift to the dialogue between world religions. By 1912 he no longer approached world religions on the basis of their "least common denominator." In this way Royce showed today's philosophers of religion how to promote their discipline. To begin, they can clearly specify why they think their usual "least common denominator" approach to world religions is more reasonable than Royce's carefully chosen way. Many contemporary philosophers of religion seem to say under their breath: "You, O Buddhist, scratch my Christian back, and you, O Taoist, scratch our Buddhist's back, while I will scratch your back, dear Taoist." The underlying assumption is that religion is not primarily a discipleship under the Holy Spirit but basically a set of knowable doctrines and objective structures.

In response, Royce might well ask: Does this insistence on a guarded politeness, on equality in all things, and on a pure impersonal objectivity promote a stronger philosophy of religion? Or does it deprive the dialogue partners of authentic witnessings to personal religious life and faith? And does it thereby tend to miniaturize, even trivialize, religion? Apparently the assumption is widely accepted that having or not having a personal religious life is irrelevant to the experiential bases from which philosophers of religion make their assertions about religion. Admittedly, to handle the challenges of these various personal witnessings would call for respect and understanding, patient courtesy, and not a little humor. But if in this way philosophers of religion shared their personal faiths in public statement and discussion, they would powerfully promote a saving dialogue among themselves and an increase of unity among the world religions — one of Royce's most prized values (1:13, 17).[2]

Finally, when intending to fashion a "fair comprehension" of Christianity itself, Royce sought such breadth of range that he refused to focus on the founder alone or on the community alone. Such reductionism, he felt, would hinder a full experience of the problem of Christianity. He also felt that both the defenders and the critics of Christianity, by oversimplifying this problem, failed in one indispensable requisite for any genuine Community of Interpretation: namely, a profound respect for *all* human selves, especially those who hold positions different from one's own and with whom one interacts.

Paradoxically, however, during Royce's interpretation of Christianity, his two other ideals for method — more coherence and more vitality — led him simultaneously to adopt a "least common denominator" approach towards the *most essential creed* of Christianity. These latter two ideals directed Royce's "will to interpret" into discernment. He would sift through Christianity's many life-giving essential doctrines so he could eliminate all but the *most* vital and the *most* essential.[3] These two ideals so disciplined his mind "to discern spiritually the things of the spirit" (2:361) that he was freed from two entrapments. In the fascinating history of how Christian doctrine developed, the highly significant accidentals did not preoccupy his attention. Nor was it preoccupied by those many essential doctrines which simply *derive* from that most salvific and vital "sending of Signs" which the Interpreter-Spirit of Christianity is always initiating.

Second Methodic Ideal: Coherent Unity of View

As his second methodic ideal, Royce sought coherence and unity of view through his interpretive musement. He strove to form a synoptic interpretation not only of Christianity, of ethics, and of cosmic history, but even of the whole universe of minded beings and their signs. He could have stopped striving for an ever saner and growing meaningfulness in human life and for an ever more correct series of world views. However, that would have meant giving up his arduous search for wisdom and settling instead for a highly refined understanding of a few pieces in the puzzle of life. More profoundly, he would have faltered in two of his basic beliefs: that the Holy Spirit endeavors to lead all finite minded beings to a full*er* vision of the truth, and that the same Spirit calls each philosopher to a particularly earnest and reverent search for this fuller vision.

Royce's boldness and breadth may amaze certain readers today. They may wonder how he could be so confident in the dialectical workings of interpretation when many of its participants are alienated and self-centered. Contrariwise, however, such readers might ask themselves whether anyone *could lack* such confidence if he or she were as passionately convinced as Royce that the Holy Spirit is actually working liberation within the minds and hearts of all those who seek truth loyally. As Royce asserted, "Here, then, in this [fourth Gospel's] doctrine of the Spirit, lies the really central idea of any distinctively Christian metaphysic" (2:16).

At the dawning of "the age of analysis," then, Royce stands like a prophet calling for constructive synthesis (as well as for exact rational analysis). Is the analytic mind sometimes marred by a vicious inclination? Indeed, at times, it tends to launch missile-like questions and to lay down a barrage of devastating critiques, yet it fails to accept the correlative responsibility to reconstruct overarching patterns of meaningfulness. To balance our passion for analysis, we need, as John Roth expressed it, "the effort and the ability to construct new styles of thought and action or to transform old ones so that they give life instead of thwarting it."[4] With his balanced pursuit of both analysis and synthesis, Royce provides leadership in our currently needed quest for philosophical coherence and unity of view. He did more than rely on a transformative process guided by the Interpreter-Spirit to synthesize human reason, will, affect, and heart into a philosophical anthropology of the genuinely loyal ("Christian") person. He also succeeded in coherently wedding Part One, the Christian doctrine of life, with Part Two, his universal "Doctrine of Signs." The *Problem*'s unity and breadth of view may not be deductively derivable from System Σ yet they clearly depend on Σ's basic elements (the individual, ε-relation, class, modes of action, and temporal series). They receive illumination from Σ's principles when these latter are paired with his metaphysical Signs.

Third Methodic Ideal: Closeness of Personal Touch

Closeness of personal touch was the third methodic ideal sought by Royce's interpretive musement. His method approached that ideal by burrowing beneath the abstractions characteristic of percepts and concepts and by entering into the intimate appreciative presence of one mind to other minds. One can experience vicariously what this closeness of personal touch meant in practice, thanks to the record of Royce's 1913-1914 seminar.[5] Through the detailed interaction described in this record, one sees Royce serving as a most sensitive mediator between highly gifted minds like those of T. S. Eliot, Harry T. Costello, and members of the Harvard faculty. A sympathetic participant begins to breathe that air of respect, independence, intellectual challenge, and team creativity which characterize the interpretive musement of the seminar group. In it Royce's method emphasizes the individual members' diverse freedoms even as it effects a counterbalance through the felt expectation that their choices and deeds promote intelligent cooperation. Each member's unique communication and cooperation help build the "lifeblood" of this Community of Interpretation. Its "cause" inspires each member to create his or her series of loyal choices. And each recognizes truly loyal dedication to the "cause" of the seminar as here the only way to grow personally in genuine freedom.

By imaginatively taking part in this seminar, a person can come to appreciate how powerfully Royce's interpretive musement promotes close interpersonal meeting of minds. This is indispensable in situations such as ecumenical exchanges in which participants need respectfully to affirm other persons' dignity and different opinions, and equally need to discern ideas critically. But in relationships far wider and more frequent than ecumenical ones, people need to apply the art of "fair interpretation." If the nuclear danger permits it, world civilization will become ever more technological and scientific. The trend will only increase that counterbalancing demand for the close personal touches which channel interpersonal understanding and reverent respect for the further fostering of life. Already in his day, Royce foresaw the accelerating demand that the art of interpretation be refined ever more seduously (2:109-113, 133-137; 2:430-431).

Some Problems Concerning Royce's Overall Method

However, even if the three ideals just considered effectively oriented Royce's method of interpretive musement, some problems still have to be faced. First, did his musement actually result in a balanced view of Christianity's doctrine and history? He certainly sent out signals to his audience to forestall an unbalanced interpretation. Still, when reading the *Problem,* even a careful thinker can get the impression that the historical is relatively unimportant when compared with the essential. Royce put so much emphasis on the essential creed, the essential Christ, and the essential form of community life, that a reader may feel justified in giving only passing consideration to the historical creed, the historical Christ, and the historical form of community life. To do so would violate Royce's intent. But his stress and tone can tempt the unwary into this superficial interpretation.

Royce's "essential Christ" — the one alive in the heart of the believing Christian — may push the historical Christ offstage. To the extent that Royce's essential Christian creed bypasses the life of the pre-Calvary Jesus, Jesus is absent in Royce's Christianity. On the positive side, if this emphasis counters a mere "me and Jesus" spirituality by inserting the needed ecclesial dimension, Royce deserves more credit. Amid today's accelerating world civilization, this Roycean approach to the Christ-Spirit (radically transfigured from the pre-Calvary Jesus) may help a person go beyond the merely pious cries of "Lord! Lord!" in order to dedicate oneself strongly and steadily to the ecumenical building of the universal human community. If this be the case, then Royce deserves still more credit. Furthermore, besides the latent presence of the Christ-Spirit throughout the *Problem,* Royce's Christ has other significant advantages. His Interpreter-Spirit is the fourth Gospel's Logos-Spirit and Paul's *pneuma zoopoioun* ("life-giving Spirit"). Christians believe this Spirit is God's anointed suffering servant resurrected into glory as Lord of all. This Spirit fits in well with Paul's cosmic Christ[6] and with Teilhard de Chardin's Point Omega. Moreover, since the pre-resurrectional Jesus lived within one limited past culture and era, Royce wisely put primary emphasis on the Christ as the "life-giving Spirit." This emphasis effectively promotes the gradual recognition of the deep level of unity both in world religions and among Christian churches and communions. Meanwhile, it respects their irreducible differences and avoids conformism.

Nevertheless, Royce's Christ remains a problem. Royce finds Christians believing that Christ is the being whose life is a present fact in their community, the being who unites and inspires all the genuinely loyal, the being who points them in hope towards the Beloved Community (2:426,

428). He is indeed Paul's "life-giving Spirit." But is this Christ-Spirit no longer that unique individual Jesus of Nazareth who now enjoys a psychic and bodily history still clearly marked with its Galilean origins? Is Royce's Logos-Spirit one from whom Jesus of Nazareth has evaporated? If so, then Royce seems to have accepted as an *adequate* Christian faith in the Incarnation, a slight development of Eckhart's doctrine that the enfleshment of God occurs essentially when any believer becomes consciously aware of his or her own spirit's essential relation to God.

By 1912 Royce had developed his 1909 position on incarnation. In the *Problem* he honored Jesus as the one who *started* this conversion-process by first uniting the two levels of individuality and perfect loyalty. Nonetheless, if the "Word made flesh arises," he is "only a symbol," so that Jesus' resurrected humanity seems to cease to be real and serves *only* as a Sign (1:210–211). This 1912 view would fall far short of the belief that the divine Word became the actual person uniquely embodied in the human individuality of Jesus. To put it differently, if Royce's redeeming Spirit in the Church is so spiritual that it lacks human feelings, human sympathy, and human companionship with the members of its Christian Community, then Royce would seem to have become blind to the mystery of the Incarnation and to have lost the heart of Christianity. I suspect that such is the case with Royce and if so, then, through this progressive blindness, Royce would have become yet another victim of divided Christianity.

In fact, another problem arises in the Christianity of the Royce who paradoxically was so historically minded. Granted, he studied closely the development of doctrine in Christians of the first century. Still, his omission of the following eighteen centuries seems to generate an imbalance in his historical understanding of Christianity. Or did Royce's overall strategy force him to bypass the last eighteen hundred years of Christianity? Hegel, one of Royce's early mentors, provides a significant contrast. He scrutinized Christianity's development from 100 to 1800 A.D. He came to a deep human appreciation of the historical Christian Community through his dialectic of its failures and successes, of its excesses and plainness.

I suspect that, largely because of a latent conviction, Royce omitted the last eighteen centuries of Christianity's history when writing the *Problem*. He believed that since the Spirit had not been manifestly present after Christianity's first century (1:105–106), the intervening centuries did not need to be examined. He also seems to have believed that the deviant trends of those subsequent centuries had generally warped the original Good News. Meanwhile, the accumulating crimes of Christians had generally expelled the Spirit from the Church. Thus, if asked whether a genuine Christian community had survived through those dark centuries, Royce would have been forced, I suspect, to point only to a thin series of "saving remnant" communities through which the communal basis for creed and life had been transmitted to the present.

My suspicion may seem harsh when directed at such a devotee of history and of the Spirit as the mature Royce. Yet I think he would find it difficult to believe that the redeeming Spirit was intimately and operatively present in the Christian People of the Dark Ages, of the Crusades, of the Inquisition, and of the Religious Wars. Even more so would he doubt that during those times this same Spirit was saving humankind through Christ's Bride, the Church, who despite her missteps in practice and quirks in discipline, despite her wrinkles and blood-stained dress, always remained this Spirit's *beloved*.

Amid these shadowy suspicions, the bright side of Royce's method needs further appraisal. The values of his empirical research into religious experience, of his pioneering in philosophy of hermeneutics, and of his use of loyalty to integrate morality and religion have already been highlighted. In attending to these achievements, we perhaps have overlooked what may be Royce's greatest achievement. Long before today's methodologists reached their reflective articulations, Royce was demonstrating by his choices a new methodology for philosophy of religion. For example, long before Bernard Lonergan rendered explicit the eight "functional specialities" of theology,[8] Royce postponed any more labors invested in polishing special doctrines or in elaborating further theological syntheses. Lonergan situates these tasks among his *terminal* specialties. Instead, Royce saw that research, interpretation, historical study, and the use of dialectic—precisely Longergan's four *initial* special functions in theology—were the tasks which were then far more urgently needed. Only through these would the absolute foundations of the philosophy of religion be eventually discovered in the intentionality of human consciousness. In agreement, Lonergan would add that today these remain the very fields of endeavor in which philosophical theologians must first toil.

Royce tilled these fields with his method of interpretation and garnered a rich harvest. He identified the essential forms of individual and social religious experiences. He discovered the inevitable need for communal union at the second level of human conscious existence. He showed that this union can be achieved only if the individual undergoes transformation. He laid bare some of the deepest realities of the salvation process, the Interpreter-Spirit's gracious forming and increasing of the Beloved Community. To put it all briefly (and to change the metaphor), on behalf of today's philosophers of religion, Royce blazed a new trail, a determinate order of new questions to be examined serially according to his interpretive musement with its two interrelated special methods.

HIS DEVELOPMENT OF SPECIAL METHODS

As seen in our part three, Royce applied his interpretive musement in three ways in the *Problem*. With it he selected and investigated the leading ideas essential to the Christian creed. With it he probed human nature for the bases of the three Christian ideas and for the values found in these bases. With it he developed a truth-test for these ideas: a metaphysics of community carefully constructed out of these valuable experiential bases. In these three applications, Royce's musement created a series of insights, endlessly rich in themselves. More than that, his musement generated a pair of subordinate methods and molded them to fit the materials being interpreted. The question arises, what made Royce's interpretive musement so fertile? If from among his many revealing paragraphs on method, we select just one passage for study, it may reveal some of the secret of his method.

When concluding his fourth Lecture entitled "The Realm of Grace," Royce stated what he had already accomplished and what he had not yet achieved:

> In all this I have meant to say, and have said, nothing whatever about the truth, or about the metaphysical bases of Christian dogma.
> I have been characterizing the human motives that lie at the basis of the doctrine of the realm of grace, and have been pointing out the ethical and religious value of these motives. (1:213)

In the first sentence Royce acknowledged that he had neither broadened the perspective enough to raise metaphysical questions nor broached the critical issue of truth. In his second sentence Royce reported that he had been characterizing certain experiential motives. These are the hidden springs for our set of ideas about the realm of grace: that is, about the superhuman communion of life lying beyond the natural reach of human beings. He had also been "pointing out the ethical and religious value of these motives."

In this way Royce showed himself aware that his first task was to find the distinguishing mark, or the characteristic form, of these human motives. In this he clearly resembled those later phenomenologists whose first painstaking effort is simply to identify and to describe with care the central features of our experience.

Yet no *epoché* confined Royce within this operation. For him "to have a world is to estimate it either spasmodically or systematically. . . . [For] the very recognition of Being is itself an estimate," as he would soon teach explicitly in his final lecture on metaphysics.[9] That is, since embodied minded beings inevitably seek goals (and thus are teleological selves), they cannot experience the world without also, consciously or subconsciously, making valuations about it. Ingredient in their primary experiences, such judgments as the following operate: easy or hard to know, helpful or harmful to oneself, deserving one's attention or not, inherently worthwhile or not. Hence arose Royce's second task: to point out to his audience the ethical and religious values (the lures and demands, the goods and goals) present within these experienced motives (one's felt needs, interests, ideals, etc.).

Yet amid all this experiential richness, Royce reveals a far-sighted *plan* which amazes at least one reader. From the outset he is fully aware of his major goals, of the required series of steps to these goals, and of the major obstacles to be surmounted. During his investigation he is mindful of the steps already taken and those still to be taken. He reveals his conviction that a deep philosophical investigation must proceed according to one general order of persistent questioning. He maintains such an order throughout the *Problem*. Royce's mastery, then, arises positively out of the conspicuous fruits produced by such orderly investigation. Negatively, it arises from his experience that premature raising of questions or spasmodic straying from the main line of questioning is disastrous for the pursuit of truth.

In general, then, the mature Royce disciplined himself to follow *in non-violable series* the four following, principal, philosophical procedures. First, he would experience the realities of which he was becoming conscious and carefully describe what he was experiencing. Second, sensitive to the values and disvalues within his experience, he would seek, through valuational questioning, an appreciative understanding of his experience. That is, he would estimate the human and esthetic, the ethical and religious meaning and worth of his experience. Third, he would test the truth of this rich, integrally human appreciative understanding by checking whether it was consistent with his own and his genuine community's overall grasp of reality. And fourth, if he thus found his understanding to be true, he would further dedicate himself to the whole processing community of reality through his newly found truth-value. His overall aim throughout these four procedures was to grow both more free and more dedicated to promote in practice the coming of humankind's Great Community.[10]

With this background, one can glance briefly at the way Royce applied his interpretive musement to the three areas indicated at the start of the present section. This glance may detect something of Royce's special contributions to philosophical method and uncover the source of his two special methods.

The first area was his encounter with and selection of the three most essential "Christian" ideas. Here Royce's musement serially pursued many diverse but interrelated paths in personal and historical experience. As a result, any thinker loyally accompanying Royce on this process of serial musement finally experiences contact with what Bernard Lonergan calls the "virtually unconditioned." That is, the serial experience of such varied evidences gradually creates a mounting confirmation in one's mind. Eventually, one comes to feel and know that any further doubting about Royce's selection of these three ideas—as most essential for his adopted purposes—is certainly an arbitrary and useless activity.

The second area was to search for the nature and value of the experiential bases of these three ideas. In his musement Royce first noted and carefully described various types of communal religious experience which varied in subject, situation, and affect. Next, he appraised the values within the human experiential bases of these ideas and integrated these values into an overall description. If a transformed loyal researcher repeats Royce's investigation, he or she finds Royce's appraisals unavoidable, for this appreciative understanding takes the triadic form of hope for an ultimate good, fear of losing it, and a cry for superhuman help. To test the truth of this structure, Royce persistently penetrated through a great variety of religious experiences. Yet he kept uncovering the now familiar, self-reinstating three-fold structure: one's ultimate good, one's endangered interest in it, and the super-individual help needed to attain that good.

The third area was the development of a metaphysics of community to serve as a test of Royce's identification of the Christian doctrine of life. As he applied his musement to this area, Royce revealed much free play of thought with his purposeful movement. He also revealed much of what he would soon call "fecundity of aggregation" despite the diversity and dispersion of the individual elements he explored.[11] Thus a participant who faithfully follows Royce's mental movements in Part Two of the *Problem* discovers that Royce's triadic theory of knowing and of reality attractively yet insistently authenticates itself. One finds it undeniably preferable to dyadic theories for finding fuller truth.

Another approach to this third application may prove helpful. Pedagogically, Royce showed through his free musement that he could start his metaphysics either from an individual or a community. He could start from within an historical individual self. Such a self cannot long hide its historically dynamic essence as a Community of Interpretation. This Community within the individual thus becomes both a Sign to all similar individual selves of each one's nature as a processing community and a Sign of each one's core identity. It also becomes a Sign that illuminates the universe as a whole and a Sign of the communal nature of the processing universe.

On the other hand, Royce showed that metaphysics could also start from within any human group that shares belief in the reality of the physical world. His musement showed that this communal belief is inseparable from a second belief that a community of minded beings is interpreting nature. But these two beliefs lead investigative musement to a third inseparable belief that the universe itself is a Community of Interpretation, "whose central member is the spirit of the community" (2:272–273).

Hence, to live through Royce's musement as it generates this metaphysics of community is to be delivered from a primary reliance on percepts, concepts, and their propositional combinations. It is to enter into a new communitarian context for philosophizing. This community is a process of interpretation directed both by minded beings seeking truth and by the central Interpreter-Spirit of the Community.[12] In this way Royce's interpretive musement generated his metaphysical method as the second armature in his subordinate procedure.

Little wonder, then, that by deploying his general method and two subordinate methods, Royce could effectively interpret persons, problems, language, Scripture, and other ingredients of human experience. He could do all this in spite of his lack of formal training in hermeneutics and exegesis. So Royce's stature as an interpreter first dawns when one correctly reads his entire work in the *Problem*. Such a reading calls a person to identify with Royce's persistent effort therein to interpret what the master meant by "the kingdom of heaven." One's estimate of Royce's stature as an interpreter grows when he or she surveys Royce's many scholarly attempts to locate the major turning points in the early Christian Community's developing interpretations of love, sin, and redemption, for on these topics Royce adeptly identified the few new critical interpretations and their sources.[13] In his skillful scriptural interpretations, one strong dynamic was his insistence that one "discern spiritually the things of the spirit" (2:361). Such discernment empowered him to distinguish regularly between the symbolic and literal meanings of Scripture.[14] This methodic thrust for discerning insight was distinctive and daring. For decades before Rudolph Bultmann and C. H. Dodd, Royce engaged in demythologizing as a central activity in exegesis.[15] Thereafter he incorporated the remaining essential structure into his novel philosophy of religion.

Yet a single dynamic attitude towards all reality drove Royce's powerful general method of interpretive musement and its two special methods. A change in this attitude would have sent Royce's philosophy veering off down a quite different road. It is time that we evaluated this crucial attitude.

21. The "Christian" Future of the Universe

Royce pointed out clearly that a person's fundamental choice controls one's basic attitude towards reality. This indication served ethics, religion, and metaphysics well. A person either harms the world by his self-centered aggressiveness or withdraws from it by his self-serving defensiveness or serves it committedly by his community-centered loyalty (2:298–315).

The world in which a person lives is partially constituted by community. This was a favorite theme of Royce. For example, we have often mentioned that during his final class in metaphysics, when sharing perhaps his most mature wisdom, Royce taught: "The very recognition of Being is itself an estimate. The categories of metaphysics are from the first teleological."[1] These statements alerted his students to something fundamental. The basic estimates of reality that people make are surely diverse yet Royce taught that people fashion these estimates more by direct action in reality than by subsequent reflection upon it. For instance, directly and immediately we trust or distrust reality. Either we enter it—perhaps dominatively, perhaps cooperatively—or we hesitate and withdraw before it. Either we overcome reality for our use and pleasure or we are overcome either by its pain and seeming illusion or by its mysterious call and challenge. And if we hear its challenging call, we respond cooperatively or resist stubbornly. Through these diverse dealings we express towards reality basic attitudes, expectations, and resolves which are most diverse. Through these different responses, we indicate our radically different estimates of the universe and of Being. At the same time, each of us also reveals that beloved object (or value or goal) which each has actually made supreme in one's own life. These, too, are most diverse for none of us can avoid setting some life-goal and seeking it, even if that goal be to have no goal.

In his encounter with Christianity, Royce himself exemplified one aspect of this radical choice of beloved object (or value). After critical reflection, he decided to point primarily to the Christian reality not allowing either defensiveness about Christianity or hostility towards it to become his principal attitude. His model in this was, as we have seen, the affirming loyal attitude of John the Baptist.

Again, Royce found that whenever one interacts realistically with one's neighbor, he or she can estimate the neighbor as a complement to one's own needs. If one then adopts this same faithful affirmative attitude, it further fathers one's own spiritual sensitivity and one's postulate and resolve towards the neighbor (2:314-315). Furthermore, insofar as any nascent community creates and develops a genuine spiritual unity of life, it touches each participant in one's depths where one freely responds to the community's call for genuine loyalty. Consequently, Royce widened this same affirmative attitude of radical loyalty to include modern people, life in all its forms (2:312), truth, and, most importantly, the whole universe (2:315).

As mentioned, this basic attitude of loyal love for humankind and for the Universal Community presupposes at least the beginnings of an ethical transformation. Yet Royce taught that such loving loyalty to Being ultimately lies beyond our wit and effort to generate. "Love, when it comes, comes as from above" (2:102). So, when a person gifted with this loyal love is seized by the problem of evil but nevertheless persists in faithful affirmation of the universe, the trust one thus exhibits towards the universe is supremely religious.

It may even be that this person—perhaps quite implicitly but nonetheless really—accepts the vocation of a suffering servant. Then the person's call is to create atoning deeds which more than counterbalance one's own and others' disloyal choices. By such deeds of redemptively loyal love for the whole human community, one strongly advances the coming of the Beloved Community. Such redemptive love, with its loyal affirmation of the Universe, contrasts sharply with other fundamental attitudes advocated today. How different it is from the popularly promoted, passionate pursuit of pleasure or of at least a secure painless life! Roycean redemptive loyalty is miles away from certain attitudes occasionally advocated by some self-styled intelligentsia: sophisticated boredom, sceptical distrust, studied disdain, Sartrean nausea, or revolutionary rage. Genuinely loyal persons stand in solidarity with all those human selves who are involved in their present striving out of historical failures and successes and towards their future hopes and fears. They shun any self-righteous searching for others' faults. They especially flee that superficially polite yet passionate preference for a comfortable life defensively withdrawn from humankind's real problems.[2]

It follows that Royce's loyal affirmation of the universe can profoundly change the study of contemporary ethics, religion, and metaphysics. Moreover, his philosophy of the religion of loyalty can deeply affect religious practice. To evaluate this fecund philosophy of religion adequately would require another volume.[3] Let it suffice here to review how Royce's final philosophy of the religion of loyalty arose out of his persistent and passionate desire to help unify the Christian reality.

SUMMARY REVIEW: ROYCE'S PASSION FOR UNIFIYING CHRISTIANITY PRODUCES HIS UNIFIED PHILOSOPHY OF RELIGION

Although simple sounding, Royce's late descriptions of religious experience are actually as nuanced and intricate as life. With insight and fidelity, they record the constant rhythms that fluently structure such experience. The *Sources* and *Problem* record Royce's discoveries of the essential triadic forms of both individual and communal religious experience.[4] Hence, they mark historical turning points for American philosophy of religion and, more importantly, offer a basis for the unification of that philosophy.

Through interpretive musement, Royce became increasingly convinced that his 1912 mode of considering minds and the signs of minds provided the basis for unifying the community of philosophers. He strove to release traditional philosophy of religion from the constructions and divisions promoted by its many dualistic habits of thought. He even invited his colleagues personally to experience this liberation. In his seminar or in the *Problem* they could find how a triadic communitarian process of interpretation deepens, differentiates, and yet unifies philosophy of religion by its novel suggestions and inventive methods (1:13; 2:391).

In the *Problem* he allowed his interpretive process to generate and differentiate two subordinate methods. From the start they were eminently experiential, yet coherent with each other and integrated into a living whole by his overall goals. His general method began opening up insightful perspectives — first upon the Christian reality, then upon the evolving universe, and, finally, upon the whole realm of metaphysics. Eventually these sightings bore fruit for practical life. First, they revealed specifically needed long-range goals, together with the shared expectations suited for pursuing these goals. Second, they produced practical directives, as in Royce's maxims.[5] Third, they suggested policies and plans — for instance, the kind he offered tentatively in his final years to counteract world war. During his lifetime, he became increasingly dedicated to movements promoting unity — whether among nations and cultures, among world religions, or among sadly divided Christian churches. His passionate dedication to such movements led him to that religion of loyalty in which both humankind and its Spirit sustain and increase the unifying life of reconciliation.

The common faith of this unifying religion anchors in the single essential "Christian doctrine of life" — that grace-permeated union of the three most vital Ideas: Community, the detached individual's Lost State, and a Spirit-led process of Saving Atonement. By identifying this most essential doctrine of life, Royce offered a profound basis for Christian unity.

At present, however, Royce's doctrine of life is a largely untapped reservoir of leading ideas, of powerful dynamisms, of built-in methods and balances, and of practical directives for the future. This inadvertence to Royce's thought, amid the violence of divided contemporary society, is baffling. His philosophy is designed to promote unity of life in the Spirit within any Community of Interpretation; for example, the community within an individual's historical self-consciousness, or between individuals, or of various groups, or between communities on diverse levels. Royce's thought is a resource which all those concerned with healing alienations and with promoting human unity should study intensely.

On this score, Royce's pioneering discoveries in hermeneutics warrant special notice. They led him to distinguish methodically between religious symbols and reality. In this way he cut through to that central dynamic of human life, resolute fidelity. Nourished by the interpretive process, this dynamic draws its life from a people's history and hope and thus naturally fashions the human religion of loyalty. With synoptic insight Royce increasingly comprehended how vital was this process of responding loyally to the Universal Community and to its Interpreter-Spirit. Hence, he gained close personal touch with the basic meaning and purpose that underlie the Scripture and unite all Christian groups and even all humankind. With the apostle Paul, he chose insightfully to discern spiritually the things of the spirit and to know Christ mainly after the spirit rather than after the flesh. This choice illumined and warmed his hermeneutics and exegesis. His bold accuracy here strikes professional Scripture-scholars as a breathtaking feat by a "frontiersman unschooled in biblical hermeneutics" — even though they may later concur with Royce.[6] Long before demythologizing became a familiar term, Royce had grasped its hermeneutical principles, as we saw. By adroitly applying them to the Bible, he had already substantially carried out his task: to discover the communally shared life-response essential to all religions of loyalty. By this discovery, Royce's philosophic genius identified a profound basis for Christian unity in human subjectivity. Fittingly, it complemented his objective basis, the Christian doctrine of life.

Still, for this writer, the most profound contribution of Royce to philosophy of religion is his recommendation that the most fundamental choice of every person be to affirm his or her loyal love of the whole universe. Thus, by way of antecedent reflection and a touch of grace, he simplified a life-problem familiar to every adult. Moreover, he critically tested this recommendation for he discovered that whenever one tries to deny it, the value judgment present within a person's loyal affirmation of the universe always reinstates itself. Meanwhile, the two other basic choices (of aggressiveness and of withdrawal) fail to reinstate themselves (2:325). By simplifying a basic problem in ethics, Royce offered remarkable unity both for the life of individuals and of their communities as well as for that of the community of philosophers of religion.

In the foregoing ways, Royce offered some noteworthy services to the philosophy of religion and to humanity in general. He also established a basis for the hope that, through Christianity's essential creed and through loyal interpretive musement, humankind may yet form one Great Community. So, a unified philosophy of religions sprang from his passionate loyalty to Christianity and to the universe.

CONCLUSION: THE FUTURE OF "CHRISTIANITY"

We saw that Royce proved to be a pioneer along many paths in the philosophy of religion. He was also a prophet. Unlike Teilhard de Chardin, he did not see the evidence which trends emerging from 1916 to 1950 would add. Shortly before his death in 1955, Teilhard clearly predicted that an enormous tidal wave of cultural change would rush in upon peoples during the latter half of the twentieth century.[7] Yet already in 1912, Royce recognized that Western civilization was entering vast conflicts which would threaten the unity and community the world then had (1:421). He did not pretend to see distinctly the outcome of these conflicts yet from the accelerating rate of scientific and cultural change and from the human forces thus made increasingly conflictive, Royce foresaw one result. This torrent of change simply had to transform those European institutions which for centuries had expressed the human ideal of loyalty (1:420–421). It also had to transform the single foundation of all those institutions: the correlative ideas of the natural and the supernatural.

Despite such a forecast, Royce recognized that Christianity possessed in its creeds and legends a generally wholesome "mythology," by which it had continuously alerted people to the persistent need for love, loyalty, and redeeming deeds. He foresaw that the ever swifter and vaster changes permeating civilization would make it increasingly difficult for future generations to accept this "mythology" literally (1:422). Religious history convinced him that the life or death of Christianity depended on its maintaining vital contact with the ever more rapidly changing expressions of people's fundamental religious needs. Accordingly, he prophesied that, along with other world religions, Christianity had to undergo profound crises in this ever swifter and more profound change of civilization (1: 421-424).

According to Royce, the crises of Christianity would pivot around her adherents' ability to distinguish the essential unifying center of the Christian faith (its core creed) from its derivative elements and its historical accidents (1:422). If they failed in this basic discernment, these Christians would experience disorienting crises at different levels. Lacking a grasp of Christianity's inmost essence, these Christians would feel uneasy about their self-identity, about their membership in the visible organizational structure of Christianity, and about their expectations of the kind of Christian community they should belong to. For instance, would this kind of person leave a self-styled Christian community that was bent mainly on winning others' approval and not on offering clear prophetic witness? Or, would such a person leave a genuine Christian community that was intent on fulfilling its suffering servant mission to all people in need? The recent history of the Roman Catholic Church since 1960 is one instance of how accurately Royce prophesied the future of Christianity.

His prophecy had its hopeful tone, too. In his eyes, science was "already one of the principal organs of religion" (2:431). So, he foresaw that the increasing rate of technological and scientific advance would promote people's loyalty to communal insights rather than to merely individualistic views (1:423). Further, the method of science would increase people's passion for pursuit of knowledge. It would not allow them to rest satisfied in unquestioned "established positions," which were divisive because closed to further experiential testings and to critical review of assumptions (1: 423). Royce did foresee that, as a result of the advancing technological-scientific front, civilization would become ever more complex and its social changes ever more swift and vast (1:388). Yet, his final seminars in the comparative methodology of the sciences reveal that he was also aware of the unifying power of science.[8] He knew the living tensions of healthy scientific intelligence. It needs to draw its life-giving nurture both from an attentive openness to experience and from the refined humanistic arts. It needs both to diversify itself into its ever-more specialized disciplines and to drive constantly for the all-encompassing hypothesis. Its drive for the latter demands single-minded cooperation among people and nations. Only by aggregating the various methods and perspectives of the different disciplines can a tentative yet ever more integral and unifying insight or hypothesis be reached.

Royce foresaw that the advance of technology would lead people to discard traditional structures. He foresaw that the new and greater potentials made available by science would serve either good or evil. So he also foresaw the heightened ambivalence of power—whether technological, scientific, or political. Hence, the spiritual unity of Christianity's central life, sustained by the virtues of love and loyalty, would become more urgently needed than ever (1:422-424). He likewise foresaw that the demand would be increased for that calm stern conscience and resolute will towards life which Christianity's three essential ideas define and recommend (1:423). Finally, amid growing tendencies towards every kind of alienation, he foresaw that the greatest need would be for those atoning deeds that are Christianity's noblest expression (1:xix-xx). Only by a redeeming deed can each disloyalty be effectively neutralized and rendered indirectly unitive.

Several future trends within Christianity, foreseen by Royce, deserve special notice. First of all, he predicted that everyone would benefit if Christianity were regarded, not as something to be defended or opposed, but as a profound and perduring problem.[9] This last attitude opens a person to the two experiences which allow the saving idea of community to dawn. So equipped, one will find first that one is morally impotent by oneself. Second, upon experiencing some dedicated loyal life or deed, one will thereupon recognize that salvation comes through an essentially higher and super-individual kind of reality (1:407).

If people follow this experiential problematic approach to Christianity, Royce predicted, they will share more readily in a valuation urgently needed for genuine communal life. Then, as a community, they will together appreciate their commonly felt basic religious needs and life-interests (1:xv). Royce's sound hope was that, by the sharing of such valuations, dedicated people of all nations would increasingly recognize three basic truths.[10] First, how essential for human progress are the realities of human love, loyalty, and that gift of life in the unity of the Spirit. Second, how great is people's need today for that calm stern conscience which makes decisions by regarding the interests of the whole human community without favoring or excluding certain people. Third, how deep is humankind's dependence on the Spirit who battles divisive disloyalty by creating atoning deeds (1:424). Since the Second Vatican Council, this sharing of faith, of religious experiences, and of commonly held human and religious needs and values has become the standard for all ecumenical and human dialogue. Royce's recommended approach is much preferred to that trite and frustrating insistence upon starting from postures of combat.

As a second definite trend in Christianity's future, Royce foresaw a profound revision in Christology. From its origins in the early Christian community, Christology had gradually stiffened into a single dogmatically imposed interpretation: Jesus is the God-Man (1:414). But now that Christianity was heading towards its third millennium, Royce knew in advance that a new Christology had eventually to emerge from the transformative process that is permeating civilizations, institutions, and dogmatic formulas (1:422). He also knew that the growing habit of differentiating consciously between religious symbol and reality would demand a revision of Christology. Moreover, since Christians differ in their images, affective movements, and overall perspectives concerning Christ, these unique individuals will offer different responses to Christ. Their differences are intensified by the different cultures in which these Christians live. So, like others, Royce recognized that these deep differences will necessarily generate a rich pluralism which will promote an in-depth evolution of people's minds regarding Christianity. In turn, Christians will become increasingly sensitive to the fact that the history of the early Christian community holds priority over later dogmatic formulas. This will make educated Christians aware that any absolute interpretation of dogmatic formulas about Christ has to be an exaggeration. In other words, the experiences of Christians amid all these changes will school them back to the Pauline faith and its Christology: the divine redeeming Spirit always dwells in the living Church and thereby redeems humankind (2:362-364). In sum, Royce predicted that the galloping rate of change would lead people to simplify their complex problematic Christologies and thus unify Christianity.

The new Christology, Royce foresaw, would arise from people's experience of living in a genuine community wherein they actually find the healing of alienations and the promotion of more unity. These people would come to know that their living Center is the redeeming Spirit who operates in and through their community. In its simplicity, then, this new unifying Christology will be somewhat implicit and thus open and flexible to ever new happenings in the process that transforms the world.

Just such a Christology as Royce predicted seems actually to be in formation during the last decades of the twentieth century. The strategic distinction between faith and any formula of the faith has become familiar. Educated Christians have come to see a legitimate relativity in "all the various and perplexing Christologies of the past" (2:427). (These may be found in different New Testament writers or in the various councils and theologians or in the variety of spiritualities.) Beneath such variously emphasized teachings, people have discovered the unifying Center of their Christian Community and recognized that, in Royce's words:

> The name of Christ has always been, for the Christian believers, the symbol for the Spirit in whom the faithful—that is to say the loyal—always are and have been one. (2:426)[11]

What we find today, then, is that alert Christian minds are far less dogmatic in their Christology and far more attentively docile when challenged by new voices. Such minds await the advances of the social sciences, literature, and other disciplines to discover which new facets of "the whole Christ" will be presented for assimilation. Similarly, such minds are turning to the new Christologies being created by the developing peoples of Latin America, Africa, and Asia. These views reveal the rich variety of ways in which the redeeming life-giving Spirit is present in his Church and is saving humankind.[12]

A third and final trend which Royce foresaw in the future of Christianity is a move towards a humbler, more responsible understanding of the Church itself. This would be an ecumenical ecclesiology, marked by three traits. It would be more sensitive to the whole human race. It would be more inventive of the unifying "social arts." It would better promote humankind's genuine progress. Royce recommended that Christian communions stop competing for the triumph of some particular denomination and start emphasizing the creation of those "social arts" whereby all these Christian communions can cooperatively serve a world in need.[13] The thrust of Royce's recommendation has been incorporated in the ecumenical decree of the Second Vatican Council. Triumphalism in any form — whether resting on past achievements, boasting of present deeds, or competing for future "first places in the kingdom" — ill befits a people missioned to lead the human race by serving the latter's needs ever more effectively and tellingly.

Today the Christian Church as a whole sees that the attitude and spirit exemplified by John Bunyan and John Henry Newman are far more in touch with authentic Christian life and mission. In the eyes of these two Englishmen, all Christians form a Pilgrim People called up a narrow path towards a wicket gate leading to salvation. Each Christian Pilgrim has to pray from the depths for that kindly light to lead him or her on to take the next step in loyalty, even though the distant scene still be wrapped in mystery (2:388). Today, crisis-scarred but faithful Christians are aware of their basic union in the life-giving redeeming Spirit yet they are also ashamed of their past disloyalties and continuing dividedness. So, proceeding as pilgrims, more humbly and tentatively than before, they also pray more deeply for the saving Light which dawns through the Saving Community.

In these three special ways — approach to Christianity, Christology, and ecclesiology — and in many other ways, Royce stands before us as an exceptionally accurate prophet. In 1913 he deftly characterized what would be the religious situation at the dawn of the third Christian millennium. With his passionate loyalty to the universe and with his unifying philosophy of religious loyalty, he also pointed to the ultimate basis for forming that Great Community which is humanity's hope.

Epilogue

Seven great religions of the world are Christianity, Judaism, Islam, Zoroastrian Mazdaism, Hinduism, Buddhism, and Taoism. At the base of all of these and despite their great differences, philosophy of religion has unearthed one common basic religious doctrine.[1] Through this shared doctrine, billions of human beings hold the following creed:

> Immanent in human hearts, there is a transcendent reality, who is supreme beauty, truth, righteousness, and goodness, as well as love, mercy and compassion; and the way to him is repentance, self-denial and prayer through both the love of one's neighbor, even of one's enemies and the love of God, so that bliss is conceived as knowledge of God, union with him or dissolution into him.[2]

For human beings this basic doctrine of life is indeed solid meat. Yet does it need something *more* to keep it from being interpreted as the creed of mere individuals in relation to God? Does this solid meat taste flat to philosophers of religion as long as it lacks the salt of Royce's "Christian doctrine of life"? Does it not also need three further beliefs: In the Beloved Community? In our Lost State—both as mere individuals and as merely natural communities? In the Atoning Deeds through which the Spirit-led Beloved Community communicates to us that Graced-life indispensable for salvation? In the *Problem* Royce stated straightforwardly, "In fact, the most significant choice for the modern man, in dealing with Christianity, lies between accepting and rejecting the Christian doctrine of life" (1:404). Royce's appraisal still strikes home accurately today.

With the approach of the third millennium, psychological, economic, and political pressures intensify in our world. Over everyone the shadow of the nuclear mushroom spreads a pall. It also symbolizes all those lethal tendencies working towards an eventual nuclear holocaust—those other death-dealings at work in human hearts, families, businesses, and nations. In our situation of accelerating danger, then, a sorely burdened, pilgrim-aging human family urgently needs a person who, like John the Baptist, raises a herald's voice crying in our wilderness. People need a pioneer to point out the true path, a prophet to foresee the real future, and a professor to witness reliable doctrine. In our deep unrest we need a sage who accurately identifies the basic and ineradicable religious needs of people. We need a teacher who designates the central truths which alone can satisfy these needs. We need a person of prayer whose life exemplifies what it is to discern spiritually things of the spirit. We need a mature philosopher of religion who shows us how to wield the purifying and protective "sword of the spirit" (1:396). Inescapably we are involved in a spiritual warfare against those alienating spirits which isolate human selves by suavely yet militantly advocating a secularism which is exclusively human, even if communitarian. In this way these spirits disrupt the balance of human selves' relations to the whole universe. Thus they impede the Interpreter-Spirit's wise guidance of the progress of genuine secularization and so of integral human development.[3]

Almost three centuries ago, the human race was gifted with that genius in physics and mathematics, Sir Isaac Newton. When he neared the end of his work on optics, he started to muse interpretively along larger lines of thought concerning the mysteries of our physical universe. As he sat wondering about nature in probing ways, he began to jot down some of his "queries." Could it be, he pondered, that natural light travels like a wave? Or even like a particle? Could it be that light and its apparent opposite, matter, are actually interrelated? Or even continuous? His musings continued to heap up his "Could it be's" until his jottings formed a stockpile fecund with powerfully suggestive new ideas. In fact, until at least Einstein's day, physical theorists regarded Newton's famous "Queries" at the close of his *Opticks* as their most teeming source of hints for fruitful hypotheses and of suggestions for new theories.

The physicists who followed Newton scrutinized his "Queries" diligently. With similar care, philosophers of religion can probe into Royce's *Problem* and *Sources*. If they do, the present writer predicts that they will discover another "dynamo of ideas" that will generate hints even more fecund for further clarifying the true nature of religion. They will find in Royce's mature philosophy of religion suggestions even more fertile for discovering new ways of studying religious problems. Forty years earlier, these "first drove the author [Royce] to philosophy, and . . . they of all human interests, deserve our best efforts and our utmost devotion."[4]

Abbreviations and Short Titles

WRITINGS BY ROYCE

Basic Writings	*The Basic Writings of Josiah Royce,* ed. John J. McDermott, 2 vols. (Chicago: University of Chicago Press, 1969), with an excellent bibliography of Royce's writings by Ignas Skrupskelis, 2:1167–1226.
Essays	*William James and Other Essays on the Philosophy of Life* (New York: Macmillan, 1911).
HARP	Harvard University Archives, Royce Papers.
HGC	*The Hope of the Great Community* (New York: Macmillan, 1916).
Last Lectures on Metaphysics	Last Lectures on Metaphysics, 1915–1916 (Richard C. Cabot Papers, Harvard Archives).
Letters	*The Letters of Josiah Royce,* ed. John Clendenning (Chicago: University of Chicago Press, 1970).
Loyalty	*The Philosophy of Loyalty* (New York: Macmillan, 1913).
"Mind"	"Mind," in *Encyclopaedia of Religion and Ethics,* ed. James Hastings (New York: Charles Scribner's Sons, 1916), 8: 649–657. Reprinted in *RLE,* 146–178.
Outlines of Psychology	*Outlines of Psychology: An Elementary Treatise with Some Practical Applications* (New York: Macmillan, 1913).
PC	*The Problem of Christianity,* 2 vols. (New York: Macmillan, 1913). Also, ed. John E. Smith (Chicago: University of Chicago Press, 1968).
"Principles"	"The Principles of Logic," Royce's contribution to *Logic* (London: Macmillan, 1913), 67–135, vol. 1 of the *Encyclopaedia of the Philosophical Sciences,* ed. Arnold Ruge. Reprinted in *RLE,* 310–378, and by Philosophical Library, 1961.
RAP	*The Religious Aspect of Philosophy* (Boston: Houghton Mifflin, 1885). In the Harper Torchbook edition (1958), pagination differs only in the preface.
RLE	*Royce's Logical Essays,* ed. Daniel S. Robinson (Dubuque, Iowa: William C. Brown, 1951).
SRI	*The Sources of Religious Insight* (New York: Charles Scribner's Sons, 1912).
WI	*The World and the Individual,* 2 vols. (New York: Macmillan, 1899–1901).

WRITINGS BY OTHERS

"Analyst"	James Collins, "Josiah Royce: Analyst of Religion as Community," in *American Philosophy and the Future,* ed. Michael Novak (New York: Charles Scribner's Sons, 1968).
CPP	*Collected Papers of Charles Sanders Peirce,* ed. Charles Hartshorne, Paul Weiss, and Arthur W. Burks, 8 vols. (Cambridge, Mass.: Harvard University Press, 1931–1958).
Encyclopaedia	*Encyclopaedia of Religion and Ethics,* ed. James Hastings (New York: Charles Scribner's Sons, 1916).
"Graced Communities"	Frank M. Oppenheim, "Graced Communities: A Problem in Loving," *Theological Studies* 44 (December 1983): 604–624, and reprinted in *A Reasoning Heart: Towards a North American Theology* (Washington: D.C.: Georgetown University Press, 1986), 97–117.
"Hypothesis"	Frank M. Oppenheim, "Josiah Royce's Intellectual Development: An Hypothesis," *Idealistic Studies* 6 (January 1976): 85–104.
Life	John Clendenning, *The Life and Thought of Josiah Royce* (Madison, Wisc.: University of Wisconsin Press, 1985).
Seminar	*Josiah Royce's Seminar, 1913–1914, as Recorded in the Notebooks of Harry T. Costello,* ed. Grover Smith (New Brunswick, N. J.: Rutgers University Press, 1963).
Voyage	Frank M. Oppenheim, *Royce's Voyage Down Under: A Journey of the Mind* (Lexington, Kentucky: University Press of Kentucky, 1980).

Notes

PREFACE

1. Josiah Royce to Professor Warner Fite, September 5, 1912, in John Clendenning's edition of *The Letters of Josiah Royce* (Chicago: University of Chicago Press, 1970), 580 (hereafter cited as *Letters*).
2. Milton R. Konvitz, review of *The Basic Writings of Josiah Royce,* ed. John J. McDermott (Chicago: University of Chicago, 1969), in *Saturday Review,* January 24, 1970, p. 29.
3. Royce identified these marks of "insight" in his *The Sources of Religious Insight* (New York: Charles Scribner's Sons, 1912), 6.
4. John Clendenning, *The Life and Thought of Josiah Royce* (Madison, Wisc.: University of Wisconsin Press, 1985).
5. Royce to Alfred Deakin, April 17, 1912, in *Letters,* 570.
6. For instance, see Josiah Royce, *The Problem of Christianity,* 2 vols. (New York: Macmillan, 1913), 1:xi–xii; 2:185–186.
7. Gabriel Marcel, *Royce's Metaphysics,* trans. by Virginia and Gordon Ringer from the original French edition of 1918–1919 (Chicago: Regnery, 1956), 147.
8. For a reassertion of these stereotypes and caricatures, see Herbert W. Schneider, *A History of American Philosophy,* 2d. ed. (New York: Columbia University Press, 1963), 415–424.
9. For a survey and discussion of these critical editions, see John J. McDermott, "The Renascence of Classical American Philosophy," *American Studies International* 16 (Spring 1978): 5–17.
10. Royce to Mary Whiton Calkins, March 20, 1916, in *Letters,* 645.
11. Josiah Royce, *The Spirit of Modern Philosophy* (Boston: Houghton Mifflin, 1892), chap. 12, pp. 381–434. As still captive to a dyadic epistemology, this distinction of 1892 lacked the transformation which Royce's "Peircean insight" of 1912 would give it.
12. Josiah Royce, *The Religious Aspect of Philosophy* (Boston: Houghton Mifflin, 1885), v; (New York: Harper Torchbook edition, 1958), x.

1. GROWING THROUGH PHILOSOPHY, PAIN, AND PRAYER

1. Josiah Royce, *The Spirit of Modern Philosophy* (Boston: Houghton Mifflin, 1892), 342–344.

2. Royce to Mary Whiton Calkins, March 20, 1916, in *The Letters of Josiah Royce*, ed. John Clendenning (Chicago: University of Chicago Press, 1970), 645 (hereafter cited as *Letters*).

3. Royce's Last Lectures in Metaphysics, Lecture of January 11, 1916, 130. (Harvard Archives: Richard Clarke Cabot Papers); cited with permission.

4. Ibid. See also Royce's *The World and the Individual,* 2 vols. (New York: Macmillan, 1899, 1901), 2:vii, where Royce published his account of leaving "my earlier skeptical position" (hereafter cited as *WI*).

5. Royce's "First Berkeley Lecture, 1914," in the Harvard Archives, Royce Papers, Folio 84, #3, pp. 8-15, esp. 11-13 (hereafter cited as HARP). On Royce's overall intellectual development, his transforming insights, and the grounds for so dating his periods and subperiods, see either Frank Oppenheim's "Josiah Royce's Intellectual Development: An Hypothesis," *Idealistic Studies* 6 (January 1976): 85-104, esp. 89-90 or his *Royce's Voyage Down Under* (Lexington, Ky.: University Press of Kentucky, 1980), viii-xv.

6. The most careful and thorough biography and intellectual history of Royce is John Clendenning's *The Life and Thought of Josiah Royce* (Madison, Wisc.: University of Wisconsin Press, 1985). For a more compact general sketch of Royce's life, see Clendenning's introduction to *Letters,* 9-40, and his special introductions to the five sections of that work. See also Bruce Kuklick, *Josiah Royce: An Intellectual Biography* (Indianapolis, Ind.: Bobbs-Merrill, 1972). Ralph Barton Perry's account in *Dictionary of American Biography* (New York: Charles Scribner's Sons, 1935), 16:205-211, merits notice.

7. The present and subsequent paragraphs derive largely from Royce's "Autobiographical Sketch," *The Hope of the Great Community* (New York: Macmillan, 1916), 122-136, esp. 123-127 (hereafter cited as *HGC*). For his parents' sense of the immediacy of the divine presence and their immersion in the evangelical spirit of New York State's "Burned-over District," see Clendenning, *Life,* 8-12.

8. Josiah Royce, *The Religious Aspect of Philosophy* (Boston: Houghton Mifflin, 1885), v; (New York: Harper Torchbook edition, 1958), ix (hereafter cited as *RAP*).

9. *HGC,* 124.

10. See Sarah Eleanor Royce, *A Frontier Lady: Recollections of the Gold Rush and Early California,* ed. R. H. Gabriel (New Haven, Conn.: Yale University Press, 1932), 103-104, and Guy C. Earl's "Memorabilia," August 10, 1931 (MS in Rowell Papers, Bancroft Library, University of California, Berkeley).

11. For his 1886 indications of some values in organized religion, see Josiah Royce, *California from the Conquest in 1846 to the Second Vigilance Committee in San Francisco: A Study of American Character* (Boston: Houghton Mifflin, 1886), 403.

12. *HGC,* 126-127.

13. *HGC,* 127, and Josiah Royce, *The Problem of Christianity,* 2 vols. (New York: Macmillan, 1913), 1:129-132 (hereafter cited as *PC*). Also available in a 1 vol. cloth edition (Chicago: University of Chicago Press, 1968) and paperback reprints (Archon, 1967; Regnery, 1968). See Appendix for paginal correlation of these various editions and reprints.

14. Royce to George Buchanan Coale, December 5, 1881, in *Letters,* 104.
15. Ibid. and *WI* 2:xiv–xv. In sharp contrast with the traditional piety that Royce had expressed in his earlier student composition "The Miner's Grave" (HARP 53, #1), his meditation on death made by a tomb near Webster Street in May or June 1872 is agnostic (HARP 53, #4).
16. Royce to George Buchanan Coale, December 5, 1881, in *Letters,* 104. This letter to Coale significantly portrays Royce's own perception of his intellectual development before 1881. In it Royce sketched "a certain circle of thought," spiraling through many years—a circle which "we students of today run through," from traditional belief, through first doubts, back to purified beliefs, and so on.
17. *PC* 1:8–9. Royce also encountered these anti-Christian attitudes shortly before, as well as after, his year in Germany. He recalled that his undergraduate readings of the British thinkers Mansel and Mill had been "epoch-marking events" in his education. He specified Dean Mansel's *Limits of Religious Thought* and especially John Stuart Mill's pointed critiques of the theological conclusions of Mansel and of Sir William Hamilton. His reading at Berkeley seems to have included Mill's three skeptical *Essays on Religion* (1874) (HARP 96, "Confession of Educational Influence"). Royce continued to encounter these unsympathetic attitudes at the Hopkins. See R. H. Gabriel's account in *A Frontier Lady,* xi–xii.
18. *PC* 1:9–13.
19. See Clendenning, *Life,* 73, 77.
20. In *RAP,* the title of his famous chapter 11, "The Possibility of Error," seems elliptical for "The Possibility of Our Meaning of Error." Somewhat similarly, William James confessed having mistitled his famous essay "The Will to Believe," which he later, perhaps more accurately, wanted to call "The Right to Believe."
21. *RAP,* 425. Defending the foundation of this argument (but not its conclusion), William James informed Charles Renouvier, Royce's French reviewer, of the reason why thinkers easily misunderstood Royce's point in this argument; namely, Royce was concerned solely with the constitution of error and truth, but not with their verification. Royce's own failure to express his argument clearly is partly responsible for this easy misunderstanding, added James, who then appended his own endeavor to express Royce's argument accurately. See Ralph Barton Perry, *The Thought and Character of William James,* 2 vols. (Boston: Little, Brown, 1935), 1:703–704.

A similarly aimed endeavor, a century later, might put Royce's argument this way. He recognized that our experienced doubts are implicit affirmations that error is really possible. But we cannot mean that error is really possible unless we imply that the contradictory of this error is really different (i.e., is true) and yet is intending that one identical object which the error intends. The actual knowledge of these three factors and of their distinct relations must lie beyond the finite erring knower; otherwise he could not err. Unless this relational set is actually known by someone, the true judgment could not stand up as different from the erroneous one, nor could determinate meaning exist. Thus total relativism would inevitably possess this proposition. Hence for error to be possible, the one identical object and the two contradictory intents have to be present together within some actual knower whose rational decision about this object constitutes the error false and its contradictory true.

22. See *RAP,* 424–430, esp. 427, and Clendenning, *Life,* 139–144, esp. 143.

23. Royce's preface to *RAP,* vi, dated January 11, 1885; Harper ed., x.

24. I do not know whether the young couple came to this decision by diverse paths or whether one led the other to it.

25. For Royce's childhood view see HARP 72, #5; for the Father view, see *RAP,* 271.

26. Royce to William James, May 21, 1888, in *Letters,* 215–216 and *WI* 1:xv–xvi. For a fuller account of Royce's intellectual development during 1888, see Oppenheim, *Voyage,* 16–79, 98–106.

27. For Royce's review, see *Nation* 57 (September 28, 1893): 231–233.

28. The most notable benchmarks in this clarification are his 1896 Augustus Graham Lectures on Theism (HARP, 67–68); his published Supplementary Essay to *The Conception of God,* rev. ed. (New York: Macmillan, 1897) — an often overlooked highpoint in American metaphysics of God — and his "Browning's Theism," *New World* 5 (1896): 401–422. Royce's serial redrafting of "Browning's Theism" reveals Royce's growing conception of God as a God of love.

29. Royce's "Monotheism," in *Encyclopedia of Religion and Ethics,* ed. James Hastings (New York: Charles Scribner's Sons, 1916), 8:817–882.

30. Royce to Richard Clarke Cabot, June 25, 1912, in *Letters,* 577–578.

31. *WI* 1:4–5.

32. *PC* 1:xiv.

33. In Royce's 1903 "Summary of Philosophical Conference," HARP 73, #4, pp. 11–15, he thus appraised the Gifford Lectures of William James, published as *The Varieties of Religious Experience* (New York and London: Longmans, Green, 1902), cited here through the Collier edition, 1961. In other critiques Royce seems to have had James, or at least his popularizers, in mind; see Josiah Royce, *William James and Other Essays* (New York: Macmillan, 1911), 164–165 (hereafter cited as *Essays*).

34. This entire paragraph with quotation is derived from Royce's 1903 "Summary of Philosophical Conference," HARP 73, #4, pp. 16–17.

35. For Royce's mature articulation of this *something more* in terms of "Spirit," see *PC* 2:14–16.

36. *PC* 1:viii–ix. During his final decade, some highwater marks in the swelling tide of Royce's mature philosophy of religion were his *The Philosophy of Loyalty* (New York: Macmillan, 1908) (hereafter cited as *Loyalty*); then his 1910 "Loyalty and Insight" (*Essays,* 49–95); his 1911 Philadelphia Lectures on Loyalty (HARP 83, 85); his fifth lecture "The Religion of Loyalty," in *The Sources of Religious Insight* (New York: Charles Scribner's Sons, 1912), 161–213 (hereafter cited as *SRI*); the whole of *PC;* and his 1915–1916 Extension Course in Ethics (HARP 94).

37. *The Hibbert Journal* 7 (October 1908): 90–112; republished in the *Collected Papers of Charles Sanders Peirce,* ed. Charles Hartshorne, Paul Weiss, and Arthur W. Burks, 8 vols. (Cambridge, Mass.: Harvard University Press, 1931–1958), 6.458ff (hereafter cited as *CPP*).

38. See William James to C. S. Peirce, November 7, 1908 (William James Papers, Houghton Library, Harvard University). Royce described this article by Peirce as "extremely interesting" (*PC* 2:395). Also see *Josiah Royce's Seminar, 1913-1914, as Recorded in the Notebooks of Harry T. Costello,* ed. Grover Smith (New Brunswick, N.J.: Rutgers University Press, 1963), 41-42.

39. *CPP* 6.458.

40. See, for example, *PC* 2:408-420, esp. 410, and Royce to Richard Clarke Cabot, June 25, 1912, in *Letters,* 577-578.

41. For this insight I am indebted to the late Professor James Collins of St. Louis University.

42. HARP 78, #2b, pp. 20-21. Royce addressed this first of six lectures on "The Sources of Religious Insight" to "Gentlemen of the Theological Club" at Yale on May 14, 1910.

This interior preadaptation to recognize the divine voice had shown itself much earlier in Royce's life and writing. In 1879 he wrote of feeling that he was under a "command of the World Spirit"; see his meditation of February 12, 1879, published in *Fugitive Essays of Josiah Royce,* ed. J. Loewenberg (Cambridge, Mass.: Harvard University Press, 1920), 6. In 1893 he wrote of sensing how solid was Paul's criterion for "spiritual gifts" because of its "appeal to the test of the spiritual utility to the brethren"; see his review of Br. Azarias' *Phases of Thought and Criticism* in the *Atlantic* 71 (January 1893): 126-129, esp. 129. In 1899 he wrote of discerning that the coming of the Spirit of Truth never seems dreary to any heart (*WI* 1:8).

43. Royce to Mary Whiton Calkins, March 20, 1916, in *Letters,* 645. Here Royce recounted, "These two ideas, the Community and the Spirit, have been growing ever since [the *Problem*]. . . . They certainly have assumed, in my own mind, a new vitality, and a very much deeper significance than, for me, they ever had before I wrote my *Problem of Christianity,*" On this, see Frank Oppenheim, "The Idea of Spirit in the Mature Royce," *Transactions of the Charles Sanders Peirce Society* 19 (Fall 1983): 381-395.

44. Royce set down this account in his first Berkeley Lecture of Summer, 1914 (HARP 84, #3, pp. 13-14). Published excerpts of this account are available in Clendenning, *Life,* 361-362, and Oppenheim, "Hypothesis," 85-86.

45. Royce's marginal note, published in *The Basic Writings of Josiah Royce,* ed. John J. McDermott (Chicago: University of Chicago Press, 1969), 2:1214.

46. Royce to George Herbert Palmer, August 15, 1912, in *Letters,* 579.

47. *PC* 1:12.

48. *WI* 2:415-452.

49. See *Loyalty,* 390-391, and *SRI,* esp. 37-75.

50. Royce to his Australian friend Alfred Deakin, April 17, 1912, in *Letters,* 570.

51. *RAP,* v; Harper ed., ix.

52. *HGC,* 123.

53. *HGC,* 124.

54. Henry Hart Milman, *History of Latin Christianity: Including that of*

the Popes to the Pontificate of Nicholas the Fifth, 6 vols. (London: John Murray, 1854-1856), 1:13. Milman's work was thrice reedited and often reissued from London and New York until 1903. From it Royce culled several pages of excerpts, including Milman's quotations in praise of the works of Renan and Strauss.

55. Royce's Student Notebook, "A. 1., General & Misc.," HARP Box A, pp. 11-12.

56. *PC* 1:8-9.

57. See Royce's 1878 draft of "Spinoza's Religious Liberty in the State," HARP 55, #3, pp. 43-47.

58. Royce's Notebook, "Hegel's *Phaenomenologia.* Lecture Course of 1889-90. Book of General Notes," HARP Box E, #15, at the close of the notebook. Derived by Royce from *Aus Schellings Leben in Briefen,* vol. 1, 1775-1803, ed. G. L. Plitt (Leipzig: Hirzel, 1869), 1:285.

59. *PC* 2:221.

60. In the year of his death Royce identified his seminar at Harvard as his "best concrete instance of the life of a community [of interpretation]." In firm possession of the living logic of the interpretive process, he presided as servant-interpreter of these memorable sessions; see *HGC,* 131, and G. Smith, *Seminar.*

61. *HGC,* 122-123; see also his composition "A Miner's Grave," HARP 52, #1.

62. See *HGC,* 126-127, and Clendenning, *Life,* 39.

63. HARP 53, #2.

64. Guy C. Earl's "Memorabilia," August 10, 1931, 1-2. Even when a professor at Harvard, Royce held only modest resources which were reduced by the tragic illness of his son Christopher; see Clendenning, *Life,* 317-318, 343-344, 398.

65. See *Spirit of Modern Philosophy,* 465-467, and Clendenning, *Life,* 114. In 1892 Royce recalled this lesson of the "tusks" and linked it with Sill's authentically religious poem, "The Fool's Prayer."

66. Royce to G. H. Howison, August 31, 1896, in *Letters,* 347. In the 1897 edition of *Conception of God,* Royce published a "Supplementary Essay" (pp. 135-354) of a quality far higher than that of his 1895 address.

67. For Royce's doctrine of atonement, see "The Problem of Job," in Royce's *Studies of Good and Evil* (New York: D. Appleton & Co., 1898), 1-28; "The Struggle with Evil," *WI* 2:405-411; and especially "Atonement," *PC* 1:271-323 and 365-374.

68. *SRI,* 215-254. For the tragic aspects of Royce's late years, see Clendenning, *Life,* 343-344, 378-379, 387-396.

69. For these impassioned addresses, see *HGC.*

70. In "God's Grandeur"; see *The Poems of Gerard Manley Hopkins,* 4th ed. (New York: Oxford University Press, 1970), 66.

71. Royce developed his description of these three potentials in his *Outlines of Psychology: An Elementary Treatise with Some Practical Applications* (New York: Macmillan, 1903), see esp. vii-ix.

72. *Loyalty,* x-xi.

73. *PC* 1:315-318, where Royce's personal tone seems to veil thinly a reference to C. S. Peirce, then using enforced isolation while shivering from cold and poverty to create ideas both insightful and fertile.

74. Royce's strange union of the self's incapacity to be saved without a superhuman community's effecting the "utter transformation of the primal core of the social self" (*PC* 1:344) *and* this self's capacity to discern a genuine from non-genuine saving influence constitutes Royce's "religious paradox," basic to *SRI;* see 19-25, esp. 23.

75. *PC* 1:134.
76. *PC* 2:373.
77. James, *Varieties,* 393 (Collier edition).
78. Royce's contributions to these discussions could scarcely have sustained the peak shown in *Letters,* 536-537. With the present author Richard Hocking shared his recollection of hearing his father, William Ernest Hocking, narrate how he had first met his future wife by coming early to one of these 11 a.m. "Roycean oratories." For a published reference to these mutually edificatory gatherings, see Leroy S. Rouner, *Within Human Experience: The Philosophy of William Ernest Hocking* (Cambridge, Mass.: Harvard University Press, 1969), 26.
79. *PC* 1:xv.
80. Royce, "Impressions of Australia," *Scribner's Magazine* 9 (1891): 79.
81. *PC* 1:xv-xvi.
82. *HGC,* 123-124.
83. *PC* 1:368-369; 2:338. See also his 1909 "What is Vital in Christianity" (*Essays,* 159), where he instructs young men that the Gospel's "miraculous reports are best understood when we indeed first dwell upon them lovingly and meditatively, but thereupon learn to view them as symbols." To recommend a way as "best" usually implies prior personal experience.
84. *Essays,* 68.
85. CF. 1 Cor. 14:13 with *PC* 2:221.
86. Loewenberg, *Fugitive Essays,* 6-7.
87. *RAP,* 439-440.
88. Cf. *Spirit of Modern Philosophy,* xiii with 465-466.
89. *PC* 1:399; see also Ronald Albert Wells, "A Portrait of Josiah Royce," Ph.D. diss., Boston University, 1967.
90. *SRI,* 228-229. He recognized that this *de profundis* "sort of prayer was an essentially religious act" (*SRI,* 132-133).
91. *PC* 1:xvi. Royce clarified, "As incorporate in the community, . . . the Christian life expresses the postulate, *the prayer,* the world-conquering will, whose word is: Let the spirit triumph" (*PC* 1:379-380, emphasis added).
92. Rom. 8:15, emphasis added to highlight communal experience.
93. See *CPP* 6.458ff.
94. Traces of his engaging in this "cult of the dead" can be found throughout Royce's writings—for instance, *HGC,* 94. It included communing with great philosophers of the past as well as with his departed family members and friends. Just before he died, Royce left on his desk a sample of this cult of the dead, pos-

sibly his final MS, published in James Harry Cotton, *Royce on the Human Self* (Cambridge, Mass.: Harvard University Press, 1954), 7.

95. The late Col. William F. Kernan, who was Royce's assistant and attended him in his final weeks, offered the author his reminiscences of Royce's last days and years.

2. DEVELOPING A MATURE PHILOSOPHY OF RELIGION

1. That is, *The Problem of Christianity,* vol. 1, p. ix. Subsequent references to *PC* will be inserted directly into the text.
2. See HARP 53, ##1 and 4, or above, n. 15 of chap. 1.
3. This expansion was largely due to Royce's restoration to health during his trip to Australia in 1888 and to his reading of F. H. Bradley in 1893. See Oppenheim, *Voyage,* xii, 22.
4. See *Conception of God,* 133-354, especially the footnotes by Howison.
5. Ibid., 223-245.
6. Ibid., 259, 266-268.
7. See *WI* 1:3-6. For a comparison of his methods in *World and Individual* and the *Problem,* see the close of the present section.
8. See *Essays,* 187-254, or McDermott, *Basic Writings* 2:681-709.
9. "The Principles of Logic" was Royce's contribution to *Logic* (London: Macmillan, 1913), 63-135, vol. 1 of the *Encyclopaedia of the Philosophical Sciences,* ed. Arnold Ruge, translated from the original German of 1912 (hereafter cited as "Principles"); reprinted in Josiah Royce, *Principles of Logic* (New York: Philosophical Library, 1968) and in *Royce's Logical Essays,* ed. Daniel S. Robinson (Dubuque, Iowa: William C. Brown Co., 1951), 310-378 (hereafter cited as *RLE*).
10. *RLE,* 122.
11. *SRI,* 17-18.
12. See Royce to George Herbert Palmer, August 15, 1912, in *Letters,* 579.
13. See Royce's "First Berkeley Lecture, 1914," HARP 84, #3, pp. 5-14. Pertinent excerpts are published in Clendenning's *Life,* 361-362, and in Oppenheim, "Hypothesis," 85-86, 99. Cf. this with Royce to R. C. Robbins, November 8, 1914, in *Letters,* 618-619.
14. See Royce to Mary Whiton Calkins, March 20, 1916, in *Letters,* 645-646. He here further informed Professor Calkins that this 1912-1913 experience and reflection were as novel to him as his great insight of 1883 and yet that these later happenings were basically consistent with his earlier position.
15. *WI* 1:11.
16. See *Letters,* 645.
17. For Royce's reticence on the role of his 1910 "Principles of Logic" in *PC,* see chap. 3.
18. *Essays,* v-vi.
19. Ibid., 124-125.
20. Ibid.

21. In *Essays* the two addresses relevant to our purposes are "Loyalty and Insight," 49-95, and "What is Vital in Christianity?" 99-183.
22. *SRI,* 8-13, 28-29.
23. *WI* 2:417, 426-427.
24. This emphasis is even more pronounced in *Sources* than in the *Problem.*
25. *Loyalty,* 282-284, 396-397; *Essays,* 158-159; *SRI,* 8-13; *PC* 1:348-349.
26. *Loyalty,* 390-391.
27. *PC* 1:405-406; 2:99-102; see also 1:62-63, 92-93, and Lecture 4, esp. 173-174, 194, 203.
28. *Loyalty,* 282-287.
29. *RLE,* ##19-20, pp. 348-362; (Philosophical Library ed., 48-61).
30. *Essays,* 71-74.
31. *SRI,* 28-29, 32-33.
32. For this insight I am indebted to the late Professor James Collins of St. Louis University.
33. *SRI,* 38.
34. *Loyalty,* 17, 22, 72-77; *PC* 1:35, 64-66, 111, 304-305, 374-375; 2:53.
35. See Royce to R. C. Cabot, June 25, 1912, in *Letters,* 577-578, and *PC* 2:50; cf. *HGC,* 94-95, with Cotton, *Royce on Human Self,* 7.
36. *SRI,* 18.
37. Long before the feminist movement of the 1960s, Royce used the term "man" in its generic sense. In what follows we usually transpose his "man" to "human person."
38. Derived from the close of Royce's masterly article, "Mind," in James Hastings, *Encyclopedia* 8:649-658, esp. 655-656; reprinted in *RLE,* 146-178, esp. 175.
39. On May 27, 1902, C. S. Peirce wrote in response to vol. 2 of Royce's *World and Individual,* "Perhaps the most suggestive phrase in your book is your 'dynamo of ideas'." See *CPP* 8.122 n. 19.
40. See *Outlines of Psychology,* viii-ix. For a more detailed treatment of Royce's phenomenological "pathway of increasing interiority," see the final third of Oppenheim, "Royce's Community: A Dimension Missing in Freud and James?" *Journal of the History of the Behavioral Sciences* 13 (1977): 182-187.
41. For Royce's middle-period view of the self, see *WI* 2:276 and Cotton, *Royce on the Human Self,* 13-106. A similar kind of panpsychism is found in the mental pole of each of Whitehead's actual entities. This pole possesses the sign-sending proper to each event. Teilhard de Chardin advanced a generally similar doctrine.
42. "Mind," 655-656; reprinted in *RLE,* 175.
43. Concerning Royce's use of the term "person," he recognized two usages of the term — one for the "morally detached individual man," the other for "a live unity of knowledge and will, of love and of deed" (*PC* 1:352). In this latter sense Royce used the term "person" to refer both to a loyal self morally alive by reason of commitment to a genuine community *and* to a loyal community itself.
44. Hence, Royce's meaning of "man the mere individual" is more profound

and contrasts strikingly with that popular sense of "man the individual unit (or cipher)," in which a person is taken simply as one factor in a mere collectivity. The quest for efficiency has led large organizations to use "individual" frequently in this latter mechanical and quantified sense. They seem carelessly oblivious to Royce's sense of "man the mere individual" with its awesome relevance for the people who deal with or are members of organizations.

45. "Mind," 656, or *RLE,* 175.

46. *Essays,* 164-165; see also *PC* 2:3-4. For Royce's 1911 exploration of religious experience as a contrast-effect and as a serial cumulation of insights, see chap. 8.

47. *Essays,* 165.

48. *Essays,* 89-90, see also 124-125. When specifying this practical relation to *Christian* religious experience, Royce was sure that it lay in "the relation of the real individual human person to the real God" (*Essays,* 165).

49. *Essays,* 89.

50. Ibid., 108-109.

51. Ibid., 117-118.

52. Ibid., 118-121.

53. See *PC* 1:xiii-xvi, and especially Royce to A. O. Lovejoy, December 30, 1912, in *Letters,* 586-587.

54. *Loyalty,* 380-381, and *SRI,* 287-289. With these, cf. James Collins' essay, "Josiah Royce: Analyst of Religion as Community," in *American Philosophy and the Future,* ed. Michael Novak (New York: Charles Scribner's Sons, 1968), 199-200.

55. Since C. S. Peirce increasingly influenced Royce's thought from 1908 to 1913, Royce's mature conviction about religion can be expressed in Peircean terms: the meaning of religion requires not only its logical interpretants but its emotive and dynamic interpretants as well.

56. *SRI,* 220. For religion's union with the "eternal," see n. 60.

57. *Loyalty,* 377; see also *SRI,* 7-8.

58. *SRI,* 8-9.

59. For Royce's meaning of salvation and the way to it, see *PC* 1:344 and *SRI,* 9-17. His reference here to the superhuman world as an "it" conveys the humanly transpersonal aspect of the Community of Interpretation, which also needs to be viewed complementarily as the Interpreter. For in all our intents and relationships with the superhuman world "we are consciously met, from the other side, by a superhuman and yet strictly personal conscious life" (*Loyalty,* 391).

60. Royce's "essentially eternal" is *not* to be imagined as some fixed preexistent plan according to which our life in time is to pattern itself exactly and painstakingly. Instead, Royce's eternal is a "whole of life" embraced in a synoptic knowing. It is called "eternal" simply "because it is the conspectus of the totality of life, past, present, and future" (*Loyalty,* 394-395).

61. *Loyalty,* 377.

62. Ibid., Royce's emphasis.

63. Ibid. and *Essays,* 89.

64. *SRI,* 4, 8, Royce's emphasis.

65. Ibid., 19.
66. See, for instance, a provisional draft of Royce's first lecture for the *Problem* in HARP 39, #2, pp. 36–37, 45.
67. *SRI,* 278, 293. Royce stressed the teleological priority of the whole to its parts in any human community. His teaching antedates by fifty years the Second Vatican Council's explicit emphasis on the Church's servant relationship towards the modern world.
68. As a living and self-transforming process, however, revelation can never be adequately caught within a dogmatic definition. For the growing process of interpretation affects human consciousness and a revealed doctrine contains endless potentials for deeper insights. Royce held, "There is no one way of defining in dogmatic formulas the view of . . . revelation to which they will always require us to adhere" (*PC* 1:408).
69. *SRI,* 20–26.
70. Collins, "Analyst," 213–214.
71. *SRI,* 26.
72. Collins, "Analyst," 213–214.
73. *SRI,* 24.
74. Ibid., 51–52; see also 28–29.

3. CREATING A PURE LOGIC AND METHODOLOGY

1. Cf. *PC* 2:117 with *Letters,* 436–438 and n. 44. Peirce's similar entreaty to William James to study logic brought forth no sustained efforts in this direction from James. See Perry, *Thought and Character of James* 2:437, 439, 680; also 419–420, 432.

By late 1903 the relationship of teacher and student of logic between Peirce and Royce showed strain. See Carolyn Eisele, *New Elements of Mathematics by Charles S. Peirce* (The Hague: Mouton, 1976) III/2, pp. 958–962). Two years later, Royce published his memoir, "The Relation of the Principles of Logic to the Foundations of Geometry" (*RLE,* 379–441). In August–September 1905, when Peirce prepared a response for the National Academy of Sciences on Royce's memoir, a "flurry of correspondence" arose between them; (see *Letters,* 428 n. 129). Its progress revealed more and more how difficult it is to achieve exact mutual understanding on the starting points of pure logic. In the midst of this exchange, Peirce turned to William James' "anti-mathematical" mind, as he styled it, and "fire-hosed" him with a lengthy letter on logic that even in printed form runs to 27 pages (Eisele, *Elements,* III/2, pp. 809–835). In this letter Peirce leaned heavily on James' patient ear in order to work out one approach for his upcoming paper for the National Academy. In it he criticized Royce's O-collections, especially because Peirce thought Royce was trying to derive asymmetrical relations exclusively from symmetrical ones. In replies which started modestly but ended tartly, Royce disclaimed ever attempting such an absurd move (*Letters,* 488–492). Peirce's critical but unpublished paper, "The Relation of Betweenness and Royce's O-collections," was read before the Academy at its November 14–15, 1905 meeting (*CPP,* vol. 8, p.

298, in General Bibliography, under G-1905, #4). In a partial draft of this paper, Peirce wrote that Royce's "memoir is unquestionably of very considerable value" before scoring Royce for insufficient perspicacity (Peirce Edition Project, Indianapolis, MS 816[a], 1-2). Thereafter, the flurry of correspondence ceased but, assembled together and including Peirce's August 1905 logical effusion to James, it clearly testifies how exceptionally diverse were the minds of these three American philosophers and how easily too many words and too little tact hinder efforts at genuine dialogue.

2. For the eleven logical studies Royce published from 1902 to 1913, see McDermott, *Basic Writings* 2:1205-1216. For his unpublished logical researches after 1901, see HARP folio vols., 73, #6; 75, #3; 86-87 entire, along with the six HARP boxes that contain more than forty of Royce's notebooks on symbolic logic. Roycean scholars await the much needed research results to be published by logician Robert Burch of Texas A & M University, who is fittingly integrating and interpreting these mazes of Royce's logicalia.

3. See, e.g., *RLE,* 378. Ruge gathered contributions from internationally recognized logicians, Windelband, Couturat, Croce, Enriquez, Losskij, and Royce, into *Logik,* the first and only published volume of the projected *Encyclopaedia der philosophischen Wissenschaften.* First published in German in 1912, *Logik* appeared in English in 1913.

4. In McDermott, *Basic Writings* 2:1214, Ignas Skrupskelis published this marginal note with Royce's emphasis and the needed references. Even with the pioneering done by C. I. Lewis, Bruce Kuklick, and others, we still do not know how much of that "future possible Logic" lies *un*recognized in Royce's logical remains in the Harvard Archives. Whatever results this programme for a possible pure logic may yield in the future, in late 1913 Royce planned a never-completed book of seven articles on the "relations between logic and geometry"; see *Basic Writings* 2:1215.

5. See *Letters,* 604.

6. Kuklick, *Intellectual Biography,* 214-217. Just how well Royce disguised the influence of his "Principles of Logic" upon the *Problem* can be inferred from the index to the *Problem.* When referring to his debt to Peirce, Royce used the term "logic" repeatedly in the *Problem.* Soon he regarded J. Loewenberg, who as Royce's assistant from 1908-1915 was aware of Royce's interest and work in logic, as "the only person besides myself who could properly make the index [to the *Problem*]" (*Letters,* 589). Yet when Loewenberg prepared this index, he included neither the title, "Principles of Logic," nor even the term "Logic"; see *PC* 2:438, 440, along with 114-117, 158-159.

7. Kuklick, *Intellectual Biography,* 217.

8. In addition to the leading influences of Peirce, Kempe, and Russell, many other logicians entered into Royce's logical researches during 1901-1912. Simply sampling some whom Royce studied attentively and recalled accurately, we find Klein, de Morgan, and Whitehead from England; Couturat, Bergson, and Poincare from France; Schroeder, Frege, and Dedekind from Germany; Peano, Croce, and Enriquez from Italy; and Ladd-Franklin, John Dewey, and C. I. Lewis from

the United States. As a self-styled "student of logic," Royce familiarized himself with the diverse approaches of these and other logicians.

9. C. I. Lewis, J. Harry Cotton, and others have reaffirmed this estimate; see *Letters,* 488 n. 129. During the first half of Royce's 1902-1913 studies of logic, his articles "The Sciences of the Ideal" (1904) and "The Present State of the Question Regarding the First Principle of Theoretical Science" (1906) signaled genuine advances in his logical researches, even if less outstanding than those shown in his 1905 "Memoir."

10. See *RLE,* 379-441 for the text and McDermott, *Basic Writings* 2:1208 for details.

11. *RLE,* 373, where Royce in 1910 summarized his 1905 "Memoir." Interestingly, C. S. Peirce was walking when he perused Royce's "Memoir." As a result, even Peirce overlooked *assertion* as a mode of logical action and temporarily misinterpreted Royce's principles. With a sting perhaps deserved, Royce replied to Peirce, "You are attacking, then, a position which I have nowhere taken" (*Letters,* 491). See also *Letters,* 488-492 and notes. Evidently, after Peirce had in 1901 unforgettably jolted him into studying logic, Royce judged that his subsequent four years of self-schooling in logical research had enabled him to grasp with certainty at least the distinctive elements of his own System.

12. *RLE,* 373.

13. See *PC* 2:395 n. 1, and the letter of William James to C. S. Peirce, November 7, 1908 (James Papers, Houghton Library). Peirce's article is found in *CPP* 6.452-485; the "brief passage" may be 6.474-477.

14. *RLE,* 377; Royce emphasized all these words at the conclusion of his "Principles."

15. See the close of Royce's article "Error and Truth" in Hastings, *Encyclopedia* 5:366-373, esp. 371-373, or *RLE,* 122-124.

16. *RLE,* 123-124, Requirement #7.

17. Ibid.

18. Ibid., 258.

19. Ibid. Here Royce echoed the "three marks of insight" which he had just published in *SRI,* 6.

20. In *PC* 1, cf. p. 203 n. 1 with pp. 405-406.

21. See John E. Smith's introduction to *Problem,* p. 21.

22. Royce found that the early Christian communities, confronted with the problem of consistently formulating their Faith both in God *and* in their human master, could be loyal to their Faith *only* by expressing it in the doctrines of Christ's "two natures" and of God as triune. See *PC* 1:195 and esp. 202-205; 2:425-428.

23. *Letters,* 604-609.

24. See n. 20.

25. "Principles," *RLE,* 312, #2. We use the term "Methodology" and "method" in the present section and later in part three according to Royce's predominant usages. Thus "Methodology" means a survey of the methods used in the various arts and sciences and a systematization of those methods in accord with the norms of "Pure Logic" taken in the sense of a "Theory of the Forms of any Orderly Realm

of Objects, real or ideal." By contrast, the term "method" indicates a general plan of procedure which directs the scientific process within a particular discipline. Thus in part three we will speak of Royce's interpretive musement as the overall method (*not* Methodology) of his mature philosophy of religion and speak of his "empirico-historical" and "metaphysical" methods which directed the main subordinate movements in Parts One and Two of the *Problem*.

26. "Principles," *RLE,* 321, #8, with *RLE,* 326, #9.
27. *RAP,* v.
28. For the classification of structures in religious experience, see *SRI* and chap. 8 of this text. For hints of Royce's use of statistics to find structure, notice how he relies on inductions by Peirce and Henderson (*PC* 2:394-422).
29. G. Smith, *Seminar,* 38.
30. *HGC,* 131.
31. Royce took unusual care to introduce his reader to the *Problem*'s overall plan that employed a main and two subordinate methods. He wanted to offer many guides to his reader. First, Royce retained the many retrospects, prospects, and summaries of his lecture format — even though the book format would render some of these superfluous. Then, to his new table of contents, he added the Programme used by his Oxford audience, since it provided far more details about the content of these lectures. Finally, to his entirely preparatory first lecture, he created a new, more recently devised preface to orient his reader yet more accurately into the logic underlying the *Problem*.
32. In spring 1912 Royce reported doing "much planning" for his Christianity book. An extant set of five early plans verifies this statement. About four months later, he reported having "fairly worked out" his plan for Part Two of the *Problem*. See HARP, Logic Box 4, #4, for these plans, along with *Letters,* 579, 582.
33. HARP, Logic Box 4, #4, pp. 3-4. For the remaining quotations in this paragraph, see pp. 5, 12, 15 of the same. In a redraft of his plan, Royce dropped his first general title "Intuition and Action," but inserted a new second lecture to be called "Logic, Intuition and Action" (pp. 1, 12), a title suggesting his logical concern with freely chosen "modes of action."
34. Ibid., 21-22.
35. See ibid., 21-23, and *PC* 1:271-323, and esp. 365-374.

4. A GENERAL SCIENCE OF ORDER, SYSTEM Σ

1. C. I. Lewis, "Types of Order and System Σ," *Philosophical Review* 26 (1916): 407-419, esp. 408.
2. Ibid., 408, 419.
3. By contrast Russell held the opposition between symmetrical and asymmetrical relations was absolute. Meanwhile Peirce at first thought Royce was deriving asymmetry from symmetry alone; see *Letters,* 409 n. 133, and *RLE,* 384.
4. This reference is to Royce's "Principles of Logic" as reprinted on p. 371 of *RLE,* which, in other printings, occurs in Section 23. Subsequent references from *RLE* will be inserted into the text.

5. As a start towards such scrutiny, see Lewis, "Types of Order," and above all Kuklick, *Intellectual Biography,* chaps. 9-10, with his references, esp. pp. 197-200.

6. So C. I. Lewis styled Royce's method in *A Survey of Symbolic Logic* (Berkeley, Calif.: University of California, 1918), 362-372, esp. 370.

7. See A. B. Kempe, "On the Relation between the Logical Theory of Classes and the Geometrical Theory of Points," *Proceedings of the London Mathematical Society* 21 (1890): 147-182.

8. Royce, "The Relation of the Principles of Logic to the Foundations of Geometry," *Transactions of the American Mathematical Society* 24 (1905): 354-415, esp. 381; also in *RLE,* 379-441, esp. 407. The $p \prec_y q$ notation is derived from Peirce.

9. Ibid., 382, or *RLE,* 407.

10. See Lewis, *Survey,* 367.

11. Ibid. and *RLE,* 407-408.

12. Lewis, *Survey,* 367.

13. *RLE,* 385, Royce's emphasis. His inclusion of "would," as well as of "exhaustive" and "in their entirety, inconsistent" seems crucial for grasping the pluralism and infinity of infinite subsets contained within System Σ. The fact that Royce's O-relation is an infinitely polyadic base for infinitely variable modes of free action undercuts any anti-Roycean charge of "block universe." This trite charge misses the mature Royce's logic, intent, and expressions. *PC* 2:17, 270, and *SRI,* 131-161, esp. 142-147, show that James' charge of "block universe" is irrelevant to Royce's late thought.

14. *PC* 1:343, where Royce asserts that the whole Christian doctrine of life is due to the exposition and practical application of the "sacred pair" of terms and of ideas: "the individual *and* the Community."

15. See *PC* 2:361 for this indispensable learning "how to discern spiritually the things of the spirit."

16. *PC* 1:343, Royce's emphases.

17. Royce's emphasis.

18. In 1911, Royce linked "system" and "theory" revealingly when he wrote, "a theory is the portrayal of some coherent system of ideas and of relations of ideas, — a portrayal such that some of the properties of the system in question can be deduced, by logical processes, from the other properties" (Philadelphia Lecture #2, "Theoretical and Practical Truth," HARP 85, #4, p. 10).

19. See *PC* 2:282. When writing his 1910 "Principles," Royce had not yet come to his Peircean insight. The term "sign" did not then function in a pivotal way as it did in the *Problem* (1913) and in "Mind" (1916).

20. Royce's emphasis.

21. Royce had the entire quotation italicized in the original.

22. See *Letters,* 605 n. 7, for Clendenning's helpful clarification of Royce's failure to distinguish and of his misleading example.

23. See *PC* 1:164-167, 207, 405-406; 2:294.

24. See *PC* 2:135, 138, 147-148; John Smith's introduction to *PC,* 27; Lewis, *Survey,* 363.

25. Lewis, *Survey*, 368 n. 31. Royce himself offered a basis for this comparison in *PC* 2:198.

26. Royce's emphases, which seem accidentally omitted in item (4).

27. Royce emphasized almost all of this text.

28. Kuklick, *Intellectual Biography*, 195. Royce's own procedure in his 1916 article "Mind" confirms Kuklick's view. For there Royce regarded mind as "equally definable" in terms *either* of the idea of self *or* of the idea of community; that is, logically as individual or as set. Both approaches are needed to achieve close personal touch with minded being; see *RLE*, 176.

29. *Letters*, 609.

30. See also the conclusion of Royce's article "Mind," *RLE*, 375–378.

31. Cf. this with Royce's 1916 statement: "The very recognition of Being is itself an estimate" (Last Lectures on Metaphysics, 462).

32. Here Royce contrasted James' and Peirce's understandings of "leading idea" yet, according to John Smith (Introduction, 27 n. 23), Royce here selected only one of James' two senses of "idea."

33. Cf. *RLE*, 321; #19 with *PC* 2:279.

34. See *Outlines of Psychology*, vii, 299–375.

35. See also *RLE*, 384.

36. *RLE*, 407–408. C. I. Lewis stressed this advantage of System Σ in *Survey*, 367.

37. Compare and contrast Lectures 2, 4, and 9 of the *Problem* to find how Royce progressively generalized the idea of community.

38. Lewis, "Types of Order," 418.

39. William James, *Pragmatism* (Cambridge, Mass.: Harvard University Press, 1975), 32.

40. Cf. *PC* 2:167–217 with 217–221.

41. *PC* 2:186 and 196 suggest how impressed Royce was with Peirce's method of combining empirical and logical elements.

42. When Kuklick states that Royce's O-relation "defines the structure of the divine mind" (*Intellectual Biography*, 204) would the compound verb "defines and symbolizes" provide a yet "fairer understanding" of Royce's intent?

43. According to Royce, the process of atonement has its own logical structure.

5. GENESIS OF Σ AND ITS APPLICATION

1. This third section is "the most enigmatic of all the Roycean texts," according to Kuklick, *Intellectual Biography*, 203.

2. For a different interpretation, see Murray Murphey's view in E. Flower and M. Murphey, *A History of Philosophy in America*, 2 vols. (New York: Putnam's Sons, 1977), 2:742–745.

3. Along with well-ordered series, Royce emphasized "dense series" more in his 1910 "Principles" than he had done in his 1899 "Supplementary Essay" to *World and Individual*. It seems fair to say, then, that the 1910 System of his "Prin-

ciples" is richer and more flexible than his 1899 self-representative system. If so, it deserves proportionately more investigation.

4. *RLE,* 375; #24, Royce's emphases. With his fellow logicians he knew that for human selves the "very conception of an absolutely unlimited universe of discourse would involve manifold logical contradictions" and that for human selves values can be found only in a limited universe of discourse; see *RLE,* 198.

5. Kuklick questions the consistency that Royce claimed; see *Intellectual Biography,* 208–211.

6. Emphasis added.

7. That is, *Sources,* pp. 9–10. Subsequent references to *Sources* will be inserted within the text. Writing to G. P. Brett, January 7, 1912, Royce underlined "apply" in his letter, "I propose, erelong, to write *another* book, intended to *apply* my philosophy to the special case of Christianity" (*Letters,* 562).

8. See *SRI,* 22 and 293 as instances. The focus here is on the way the mature Royce used the phrase "applying the principles" rather than his usages of it in his early or middle period, e.g., in his preface to *RAP,* v; Harper ed., ix.

9. When Kuklick asserts that Royce did not succeed in making the *Problem* an analogue to the "harmonic construction," he is speaking of the fulfillment of an architectonic design rather than of Royce's "application of principles" to Christianity (*Intellectual Biography,* 211).

10. See *PC* 1:xxxix, and *SRI,* 204–207.

11. Also see *SRI,* 10.

12. See *PC* 2:279–280, and *RLE,* 321; #8.

13. Cf. *PC* 1:247–248 with 2:314–315 and 1:363.

14. Emphasis added.

15. Foreshadowed in Σ's infinite rational agent, the Spirit of the *Problem* directs the basically rational process of the universe by communicating its doctrine of signs and its Christian doctrine of life to finite fallible human selves through their mediating communities. Σ's traces are also discernible in the "rational modes of action" shown by Royce's fictitious primitive Christian and learned Greek (2:315, 322), in the historical education of the human race and in the present generation's distillation of wisdom from the past to provide yet wiser signs for future ages (1:xvii–xix, 19, 21; 2:374–375). For other traces of Σ in the *Problem,* see 1:137, 161–162, 409–410, 412–413.

16. *Letters,* 604, Royce's emphasis. To grasp fully the role that he assigned to the ε-relation in the *Problem,* see his entire letter to Professor Fite, including the postscript in *Letters,* 604–609.

17. *PC* 1:xvi, 344–345; *Letters,* 609.

18. For other ways in which the *Problem's* doctrine of loyalty mediates Σ, see *PC* 1:186–187 along with 71, 74, 77–78.

19. *SRI,* 254; *PC* 1:xix–xx.

20. Lewis, "Types of Order," 419.

21. In subsequent chapters, occasional usage of this phrase is accordingly present as a shorthand reference back to the light that the present section has cast upon Royce's style of thought and expression.

6. THE SEVEN SOURCES OF ELEMENTARY RELIGIOUS EXPERIENCE

1. A fairly accurate tracing of the development of these investigations can be inferred from Royce correspondence from late 1909 to early 1912—that is, from *Letters*, 537–538, 561–562, 569–570, and from his unpublished letters of November 6 and December 3, 1911 to E. S. Bristol (in the Gilman Family Papers, Sterling Library, Yale University)—and from his 1910–1911 lectures at Yale, Smith, and Simmons; (see HARP 77, #4; 78, ##1, 2a, 2b).

2. See *PC* 1:viii where the "principles" he speaks of applying seem to be the common psychic structures which are experientially discoverable (and thus "laid down" in the *Sources* rather than in his "Principles of Logic") and which determine religious consciousness from its human side.

3. Royce to Alfred Deakin, April 17, 1912, in *Letters*, 570.

4. *Loyalty*, 377; Royce emphasized each of these words. For an even fuller description of "religion, in its higher sense," see *Essays*, 89–90.

5. See *PC* 1:343 and *Letters*, 645.

6. *HGC*, 35. In this text of 1916 Royce reached even fuller clarification of his meaning of "salvation" than he had reached in *PC* 1:344, a meaning he had invited his readers to discover (*PC* 1:xix); see also *SRI*, 9–17, 272.

7. Royce's emphasis.

8. The "religious paradox, . . . one of the deepest facts in all religious history and experience" (*SRI*, 21) controls the *Sources* and is described in pp. 20–26. Royce did not mention this paradox explicitly in the *Problem*. Nevertheless, it underlies one of his main concerns there: What are the fit (proportionate) sources in human selves for the "Christian doctrine of life"? If the "essence of Christianity . . . [is] empirically verifiable within the limits of our experience," only by the inner light of a genuinely loyal person can it become thus verifiable (*PC* 1:xxvi).

9. Royce was not alone in regarding this paradox as a "stupendous question" and "a fact upon which all that is most vital in the religious consciousness has in every age depended" (*SRI*, 23). A sixteenth-century Spanish theologian, Francisco Suarez, S.J., saw the absolute necessity that human nature have some intrinsic capacity whereby it could be raised by God to share in the life of divine grace. This element in human nature he called its "obediential potency," its capacity to receive divine agency for transforming it beyond its natural limits. A twentieth-century German theologian, Karl Rahner, S.J., wanting both to preserve the gratuity of grace and to employ the categories of nature and supernature, holds that a "supernatural existential" is indispensable within the human person's rational intentionality. Royce faced up to the human self's similar "need for equipment" if it is to relate salvifically to the divine. Yet he did not ontologize this equipment nor describe it only generally. Thus he seems to have surpassed Suarez by both avoiding ontic categories and by locating this natural endowment in the human self's most intimate rational life. And he seems to have surpassed Rahner by here avoiding nature-supernature categories and by specifying this endowment as a *discernment principle* sensitive to the divine presence and activity.

10. Of course, sources of religious insight are in many ways diverse. Some

are perennial, others intermittent; some genuine, others dubious; some fundamental, others accretive. For Royce's purposes, however, all these differences were not so important as that between sources unstructured by a creed communally shared and those so structured. For upon this difference he distinguished between elementary religious experience and complex religious experience, respectively. He studied the former in the *Sources* and the latter in the *Problem.*

11. So Royce wrote in "The Master, the Religion, and the Modern Spirit," a preliminary draft of the first lecture of *PC;* see HARP 39, pp. 8-10.

12. For Royce's main intent in *SRI* the term "sources" seems even more central than "elements" because "sources" focuses attention on the channels through which human selves receive a divine communication. Furthermore, he tailors the term "sources" to fit the religious paradox, the central focus of his 1911 research; see *SRI,* 26. Finally, "sources" fits in better with the image of "taking soundings," an image which Royce employed explicitly when he later spoke of the activity and the limits of fathoming by soundings not merely individual but especially social psychology for the origins of Christian experience; see *PC* 1:419.

13. Concerning Royce's reserve about talking of beauty, see his "Sciences of the Ideal," *Science* 20 (1904): 462, along with *Loyalty,* 289-290, and *Letters,* 577-578. Concerning the natural cult of the dead, see above, chap. 1, n. 94, where it was presented as one form of his communing type of prayer. Throughout his life, Royce carefully fostered this cult of the dead, a powerful influence for religion in both primitive and those higher civilizations which have not become totally secularized. See his suggestions in Lowenberg, *Fugitive Essays,* 276-279, esp. 279; *PC* 2:50; *HGC,* 94-95; and Cotton, *Royce on Human Self,* 7.

14. See *RAP,* chap. 9, "The Possibility of Error," esp. 428-432.

15. Instead of the terms, "all-knowing Seer" or "Deliverer," Royce would within a year substitute "Interpreter" or "the Spirit of Interpretation," thanks to the Peircean insight soon to dawn on him.

16. Royce analyzed these three basic interpretations of the universe in *PC,* Lecture 14, "The Doctrines of Signs."

17. *PC* 1:406. Royce's doctrines of the second level of humankind's spiritual existence and of this unique kind of love for community as community are significantly absent from the teachings of William James but most characteristic of the mature Royce. See, for instance, the close of his letter to Warner Fite, July 20 [1913?] in *Letters,* 608-609, and "Mind" in Hastings, *Encyclopedia,* 656-657 or in *RLE,* 176-178.

18. See also *PC* 1:67-68, 189-193.

19. Royce had encountered presentations of sorrow as a source of religious insight in the course of his literary readings which included, for instance, Goethe and Carlyle. In *Wilhelm Meister,* Goethe had spoken of the "Sanctuary of Sorrow" which was to reveal the "divine depth of sorrow," and Thomas Carlyle had echoed this theme in his *Sartor Resartus;* see "The Everlasting Yes," in the Norton Anthology of English Literature, 3d ed. (New York: W. W. Norton, 1974), 2:942. For the mature Royce's personal encounters with sorrows, see Clendenning, *Life,* 340-344, 357-358.

7. THE MOST BASIC STRUCTURE OF ELEMENTARY RELIGIOUS EXPERIENCE

1. Royce's explicit usage and application of the term "Community of Interpretation" to the individual self would occur a year later in *PC* 2:213-214.

2. Royce's more exact meaning of "structure" formed the progressively clarified target of an exchange between John E. Smith and Charles Courtney published in *Logos* (Santa Clara) 2 (1981): 5-20, 73-82 (Courtney's critique), and 83-84 (Smith's acceptance of the criticism). The correction occurred in presenting Royce's structure as phenomenological, not ontological. Hence, Royce's "Deliverer" must be taken in his linguistic usage as a *philosopher* of religion, and not in that of a religious person. "Deliverance" rather than "Deliverer" better connotes Royce's openness to the divine as also impersonal and quite Other than common Christian tradition usually presents God to be. From Remy Kwant I develop the theme that operative in Royce's investigation of communal religious experience is a "socially activated orderly field of SACRAL meaning"—often found in so-called primitive cultures like the Masai (Africa) or Sioux.

Concerning Royce's relation to phenomenology, he appraised Husserl's "wise program of the now so much needed 'Theory of Forms'." See Royce's notes and marginalia in his copies of Edmund Husserl's *Logische Untersuchungen* (1900) which are reserved in the Robbins Library, Harvard.

3. Contrast-effect plays a central role for Royce in the development of not only the cognitive potential, but also the socialization and individualization of the human self. In both the self and its surrounding universe contrast-effects are produced by the principle of alternation—a principle William Ernest Hocking derived from Royce, his teacher, and made more explicit.

Here Royce employs contrast-effect between narrowness of view and an occasional broader view to explain the rise of an interest in religion. Professor Jacquelyn Ann Kegley called my attention to this correlation. See *SRI,* 259-272, for Royce's contrast between the natural limitation of our conscious span and our striving to transcend instantaneous glimpses whenever "we are trying to know or to do anything significant."

4. This "myth" of enlightenment, operative in all major world religions, is fundamental to "insight," as Royce's object of inquiry, and is ubiquitous in *SRI;* e.g., 4, 11, 24-26, 29, 50, 53-54.

5. If this transformed religious consciousness is to remain genuine, however, it must maintain a bearing upon the whole human community, a bearing first inserted affectively and effectively by genuine loyalty, the fifth source of religious insight.

6. The mature Royce repeatedly expressed his view that the "philosopher's endless task is to find out what this deep [popular] mind means, and to tell what it means"; see *Letters,* 586-587, and *Essays,* 157-158.

7. James, *Varieties,* 393; James' emphasis. Concerning religious experience, Royce differed from William James in many ways. Yet in regards to its individual dimension, Royce acknowledged that he depended most on James and here came closest to agreeing with him (*SRI,* 27-28). But he scored James' omission of the

social dimension in religious experience as a "profound and momentous error"; see *SRI,* 61-65, and *PC* 1:xvi.

8. Emphasis added.

9. These "unless" clauses represent additional tests for the genuineness of a religious insight. In 1911, Royce's growing awareness of man the community (the second level of human existence) seems to have fostered and strengthened this development of his early moral insight of 1883; see *RAP,* 131-170.

10. Logically, this consideration reflects the ε-relation which binds an element to a higher level. Metaphysically, it clearly foreshadows Royce's radical position that the community is the human self's indispensable second level of spiritual existence. See *PC* 1:409, and also 203 n. 1, and 405-406.

11. Royce clearly presents this transformation and recognition in his story of Peter Lannithorne (*SRI,* 247-250). The second source of religious insight, our ordinary social experience, is clearly fundamental with its own kind of importance. Although closely related to Royce's fifth source, genuine loyalty, it is as distinct from it as the ordinary is distinct from the rare.

8. THE SOCIAL FORM OF COMPLEX RELIGIOUS EXPERIENCE

1. The term "experience" will recur frequently in this chapter because suggested substitutes lack the same essential meaning. For Royce, human experience is a socio-temporal "realm of Signs" being interpreted (*PC* 2:289-290).

2. The contemporary bearing of this challenge upon the Roman Catholic Church is clearly stated by Karl Rahner: "This, then, is the situation: either the Church sees and recognizes these essential differences of the other cultures, into which is has to enter as world-Church, and accepts with a Pauline boldness the necessary consequences of this recognition or it remains a western Church and thus in the last resort betrays the meaning of Vatican II." Karl Rahner, *Theological Investigations,* vol. 20 (New York: Crossroads, 1981), 86. See also Collins, "Analyst," 203, 214.

3. *SRI,* 38; see also *PC* 1:xx, xxvii.

4. According to Royce, if religion is to be true to this life and mission during this age of ever-accelerating change, it will move away from the point where the most conservative powers of today's society are massed. To be true, religion must respond to, rather than repress, newly growing interests, once it discerns them to be authentically human. Thus true religion may no longer depend primarily upon conservative institutions and similar "worldly weapons" to preserve and propagate itself. Instead, it must rely less upon human institutions and far more upon its "leading and essential ideas" — its "sword of the Spirit," as Royce, using Paul's phrase, called them. See *PC* 1:xxxv, 396.

5. Royce's central task of identifying Christianity's "leading and essential ideas" becomes increasingly urgent. According to Karl Rahner, if Roman Catholicism is to become a world-Church rather than a church narrowly tied to Western culture,

it will be necessary to have recourse . . . to the *basic substance of the Christian message* and from that point, in spontaneous creativity corresponding to the particular historical situation [then current in the world], to formulate again the Church's faith as a whole.

This reduction of the Christian message to its *ultimate basic substance* as a first step to a fresh statement of the whole content of faith is not easy; it will be necessary in this connection to take advantage of the efforts made in recent years to find basic formularies of faith; but it will also be necessary to raise the question hitherto scarcely considered as to whether there is a formal criterion in the light of which it can be decided what might and what might not be part originally of a supernatural revelation strictly so-called. (*Theological Investigations,* vol. 20, 87-88; emphasis added.)

6. For one description of the early Christian communities, see *PC* 1:415-416.

7. Royce emphasized each of these words in his text.

8. For this observation, I am indebted in part to Professor Georgi of Harvard Divinity School and in part to Percy Gardner, to whose *Religious Experience of the Apostle Paul* Royce owed much when composing the *Problem;* see *PC* 1:196. In the first chapter of this work, Professor Gardner had graded the Pauline epistles into three chronological groups and on the earliest of these groups Royce relied most heavily.

9. For Royce's own interpretation, see *PC* 1:74-106, 163-205 and 2:69-78.

10. Notice how the origin of this belief is attributed to the master himself in John 14:26.

11. A description of Royce's "interpretive musement" occurs in Oppenheim, "Graced Communities: A Problem in Loving," *Theological Studies* 44 (December 1983): 604-624, and reprinted in *A Reasoning Heart: Towards a North American Theology* (Washington, D.C.: Georgetown University Press, 1986), 97-117.

12. To readers this concluding "Him" may rouse feelings of ambiguity but Royce interprets that for Paul the Risen Lord is the Spirit.

13. See Rom. 16:1-16.

14. In my earlier study, "A Roycean Road to Community," *International Philosophical Quarterly* 10 (September 1970): 341-377, I failed to distinguish, as Royce does, between conditions and degrees of communal consciousness — an error corrected in this work.

15. See *PC* 1:166 and also the close of "Mind" in Hastings, *Encyclopedia* 8:656-657, or as reprinted in *RLE,* 177.

16. Emphasis added; see also *PC* 2:86.

17. See "the moral insight" in *RAP,* 144, 148-149, 168-170.

18. See *HGC,* 42-43 and *PC* 2:102-103.

19. See *PC* 2:83, 89, and Oppenheim, "A Roycean Road," 363, from which the quotations are taken.

20. Emphasis added.

21. See also *SRI,* 276, 280. Against Royce's careful exploration of the social form of religious experience with its doctrine of life and its many identified ingredients, it seems instructive to compare and constrast the concluding lines of

John Dewey's *Human Nature and Conduct* with their use of community as a symbol of religion:

> Within the flickering inconsequential acts of separate selves dwells a sense of the whole which claims and dignifies them. In its presence we put off mortality and live in the universal. The life of the community in which we live and have our being is the fit symbol of this relationship. The acts in which we express our perception of the ties which bind us to others are its only rites and ceremonies. (Modern Library Edition, 1929, 302)

Here Dewey communicates a "sense of the whole" that claims and dignifies the otherwise inconsequential acts of separate selves. In the life of the community he finds, without distinguishing, a "fit symbol" of how selves "live in the universal." Yet Royce's rich synoptic insight into community is missing here. For Royce, community is more than a symbol; it is to be treated as reality. Furthermore, he is open to a basic ecclesiology in which cultural rites and ceremonies are indigenous, not imposed from the outside, and in which there is a vital openness (rather than an *a priori* negative foreclosure) to the initiatives of a transcendently free Deliverer-Spirit.

22. See Collins, "Analyst," 215.
23. Ibid.

9. ORIENTATION TO *THE PROBLEM OF CHRISTIANITY*

1. *CPP* 5.505–508, 547–548.
2. By not focusing exactly on Royce's 1912 musings, Bruce Kuklick seems to have settled for the general statement that Royce's final decade was marked by an increasing interest in logic, accompanied by correspondingly growing but derivative interests in religion and ethics. This overlooks the fact that Royce went to great lengths to show how his own thought, thanks to Peirce, had undergone a maximal transformation about 1912. On this, see Kuklick, *Intellectual Biography,* 217; Clendenning, *Life,* 361–362, and Oppenheim, "Hypothesis," 85–102, esp. 99 with n. 37.
3. *Essays,* 99–183.
4. *Essays,* 146.
5. In *SRI,* esp. chaps. 2, 4, and 6.
6. Because the phrase "The Christian doctrine of life" identified Royce's major concern in the first volume of the *Problem,* he used it as the title fit for that volume.
7. Matt. 13:47–48. For an earlier account of the good and bad in Christianity, see *SRI,* 277–279 and 282–285.
8. See 1 Tim. 6:20 and John 15:3.
9. John 18:38.
10. *HGC,* 123–124. Royce's Bible-quoting father came from a strong Baptist tradition and his mother insisted on total immersion; see Clendenning, *Life,* 8–9, 27.

11. John 1:29-34; Matt. 3:11-17.

12. Royce saw the Church as a community of people engaged in the process of *so* proclaiming the Word that sinners are called out of their lost state and transformed into members of a saving, reconciling community. Royce's view of the Church as *herald* antedated that of Karl Barth (at least during one period of his development) and of Hans Küng; see Avery Dulles, *Models of the Church* (New York: Doubleday, 1974), 72.

Yet since Royce was reared in his mother's denomination of Disciples of Christ he was influenced in his mature period to give even more predominance to that other model of the Church as *"a community of disciples"* (*PC* 1:37). This latter model clearly emphasizes the teaching role of the Community's Spirit-Interpreter as well as all disciples' loyal observance of that Spirit's doctrine.

13. As the originating choice of any rational agent determined a particular order-system from Σ, so this initial rational choice of a particular mode of action towards Christianity (that of designative witnessing) determined Royce's style of philosophizing about the Christian religion.

14. Echoes of the traditional assumption of a divine pedagogy can be heard among scriptural writings in the Psalms, Wisdom, Paul, and John, among the Fathers in Augustine, and among post-Reformation writers in Boussuet. In the twentieth century Rudolph Bultmann traced variations on this theme in his *The Presence of Eternity* (Westport, Conn.: Greenwood Press, 1975), 58–64. See also "The Church and the Modern World," #53, in *The Documents of Vatican II,* ed. W. M. Abbott, S.J. (New York: America Press, 1966), 259.

15. For a fuller and deservedly well-known explanation of such a community, see John E. Smith, *Royce's Social Infinite* (New York: Liberal Arts, 1950), 64–108.

16. Accordingly, temporal process, understood in Royce's principal sense of "time" as a process of successive signaling between minded beings, becomes an indispensable root of Royce's theory of community and thus of his problem of Christianity; see *PC* 2:11, 37, 40, 52.

17. *PC* 1:14, emphasis added for the reader's easier reference later on.

18. As instances of Royce's explicit awareness of preferring traditional terms, of having reasons for such a choice, and of meeting the consequent responsibilities, see *SRI,* 258 and *Letters,* 586–587. On the need of liberating Christian ideas from dogmatic molds, see *PC* 1:45, 353. Harvard theologian Dieter Georgi portrays Royce as a predecessor of Rudolph Bultmann and as frequently a more skilled expert in hermeneutics and demythologizing; (see Foreword).

19. See also *Essays,* 150–151.

20. This description of modern man as "present minister" is closely linked with Royce's forthcoming descriptions of him as "interpreter" and "suffering servant."

21. Royce tested the truth of this postulate when concluding his study; see *PC* 2:392–394.

22. Such bonding not only made evident evolving Christianity's function of a signal-sender to the nations, but also empowered the receiving nations (terrestrial or even extraterrestrial communities of minded beings) to exercise a natural selection upon sign-sending Christianity. This interaction would require Chris-

tianity to sift out of its message all those over-beliefs not essential to its mission of promoting the coming of the Great Community of humankind.

23. This contribution was needed because, although familiar, these fundamental ideas were "still almost wholly misunderstood" by both sides (*PC* 1:44–45). Christian apologists, trapped within their dogmatic mindsets, missed the real significance of these ideas. Meanwhile the opponents of Christianity, unable to discern spiritual things spiritually, assailed the letter of Christian dogmas and thus missed the spirit of these central life-giving ideas. Hence, he felt some justification for discussing and clarifying these ideas in the *Problem*.

24. His discussion and clarification of the Christian ideas in the first half of the *Problem* would divide as follows: Lectures 2 and 4 for the idea of Community; 3 and 5 for that of Lost State; 6 and a section of 7 for that of Atonement; and the rest of 7 and all of 8 for an interpretation of them as a set linked by Grace and as related to the "modern mind."

25. As a pedagogue, Royce chose to introduce these ideas to his readers in an order of "increasing foreignness to the modern mind" (*PC* 1:44). The idea of a unifying spiritual community is attractive. The idea that each individual by himself is lost is far less attractive. But that each individual's saving entry into the spiritual community can be achieved only by the sacrificial atoning deeds of the community and of its suffering-servant members is an idea so problematic and even abhorrent to the contemporary mind that it must be, in Paul's words, a "stumbling block" and "foolishness" (1 Cor. 1:17–25). Yet unless a person keeps open to all three ideas, however apparently foreign, that person impedes any genuine understanding of a saving community, stays mired in a lost state, and never breaks through to divine the essential meaning of Jesus' teachings of the Kingdom.

10. OVERVIEW OF *THE PROBLEM OF CHRISTIANITY*

1. *Letters,* 646–647.

2. For Royce's meaning of a "doctrine of life" and the ethical and religious elements comprising it, see *PC* 1:328–329.

3. Royce recognized how the internal differentiation of Christianity into its various traditions had entangled metaphysics, epistemology, and above all, technical theology. Yet he searched like a detective for the one "doctrine of life" amid the ruins of strikingly diverse Christian world-views and the often discordant formulas of faith.

4. See, e.g., *RLE,* 95–97.

5. Preparation for this insight followed Royce's 1909 musings upon Peirce's "Neglected Argument for the Reality of God" and his 1912 insight into Peirce's method. Thereupon Royce could reasonably interpret the loyal communal labors of the scientific community as an approach to the Object of their ultimate common consensus, the Great Reality beloved above all. Genuine scientific life became an organ promoting authentic religion; see *PC* 2:431.

6. See *PC* 2:431 and Teilhard de Chardin's *The Phenomenon of Man* (New York: Harper & Brothers, 1959), 276–285.

7. Royce's philosophy of nature made him regard atomic, organic, or brute "selves" far more hypothetically than he regarded "minds"; see, for example, *WI* 2:10, 204.
8. See *PC,* Lectures 14-16.
9. For these promises, see *PC* 1:19-21 and 383.
10. *CPP* 6.452-458.
11. For a similar ordering of materials to the better, see B. J. F. Lonergan, *Insight* (New York: Philosophical Library, 1957), 115-128, where he describes how manifold moves to higher and higher organization.
12. Note the remarks of Ludwig Wittgenstein to this effect, in Anthony Kenny, *Wittgenstein* (Cambridge: Harvard University Press, 1973), 173-174. Royce's focus upon the human mind's ordination towards real signs knowable in nature here contacted that fundamental principle of a basic, even if never fully comprehensible, isomorphism between the intentionality of the human mind and nature. This principle underlies the phenomenological method, Aquinas' correlation of the human person's specific powers to formal objects, and the transcendental Thomism's direction towards Being within the pure desire to know (as seen for example in Lonergan, *Insight,* 315, 483).

11. INTRODUCTION TO ROYCE'S METHOD

1. G. Smith, *Seminar,* 38.
2. An interesting study, not pursued here, would examine how Royce drew his audience to his ideas, let them share in his search, and kept persuading them to accompany him, both during his lectures and through the chapters of his books.
3. Royce's free use of various techniques would provide another fascinating topic as well as document his stature as a mature philosopher. For instance, he sometimes analyzes linguistic usages or human affections or classical texts. At other times he almost becomes a phenomenologist of socialized behavior or of moral choice. At still other times he almost seems an existentialist in the way he postulates ideals, interprets values, and insists on the primacy of each agent's "modes of action." During his middle period, Royce developed a new approach to philosophy, one he called the "morphology of concepts." (See his "The Sciences of the Ideal," *Science* 20 [1904]: 449-462.) Later in the *Problem,* he frequently enough employed a form of linguistic analysis which was disciplined, even if rudimentary. Throughout his philosophical career, perhaps the most evident technical procedure was his dominant practice of the serial clarification of a concept and of the term expressing it.
4. See also *RLE,* 188, 198, 200-201, 230-231, 253. Royce stated how clearly indispensable limitation (negation) is in all vital human activities—logic, ethics, science, art—when he asserted, "Moreover, all that is valuable to us takes place in, and is subject to the *limitation* of, the universe of discourse of our present human life" (*RLE,* 198, emphasis added). See also chap. 5, n. 4.
5. *HGC,* 131.
6. Hastings, *Encyclopaedia* 8:817-821.

7. See *Essays,* 99–183.
8. Royce to George Herbert Palmer, August 15, 1913, in *Letters,* 579; see also *PC* 1:xxiv, xxxi, 196.
9. James, *Varieties,* 58 (Lecture 2, near close).
10. Ibid., 389 (Lecture 20, middle).
11. Ibid., 41–42, 47, 55–56, 68 (Lecture 2).
12. See John Dewey's rightly renowned *Logic: The Theory of Inquiry* (New York: Henry Holt & Co., 1938), along with his *A Common Faith* (New Haven, Conn.: Yale University Press, 1934).
13. Dewey, *Common Faith,* 38.

12. EMPIRICO-HISTORICAL METHOD: FIRST STAGE

1. Arnold Toynbee provides an illuminating comparison and contrast to Royce's aim and methodic steps. See Toynbee's chapter entitled "The Task of Disengaging the Essence from the non-Essentials in Mankind's Religious Heritage" in his *An Historian's Approach to Religion* (New York: Oxford University Press, 1957), 97–108.
2. See also *PC* 2:390–391.
3. Some refer to this form today as Christianity's "I-Thou" dimension.
4. See Royce's 1909 address "What is Vital to Christianity?" *Essays,* 146, 164–166, and also *PC* 1:32–33; 2:372.
5. Royce clearly distinguished his inquiry into the Christian community's inmost creedal structure from two related questions which he chose *not* to investigate: *how* the communal Christian consciousness of being Church had originated; and, from a theological viewpoint, *how* the Holy Spirit had formed the beliefs, desires, and commitments which the members of the earliest Christian communities shared. See *PC* 1:xxviii.
6. See Royce's "Religious Paradox" in *SRI,* 19–25, which called Royce in the *Problem* to investigate the Christian reality "from the human side."
7. See *RAP,* "The Moral Insight," 131–170.
8. John 12:24.
9. See Clendenning's *Life,* 361–362 (derived from Royce's "First Berkeley Lecture, 1914," HARP 84, #3, pp. 8–15), or pertinent excerpts published in Oppenheim's "Hypothesis," 85–86, 98–99. In *PC* 1:xi; 2:115, 395, Royce published hints of the way his late readings in Peirce had transformed his own mind into its mature stage.
10. Cf. *PC* 2:281 and 422 with *Letters,* 645–646. When Royce applies his kind of interpretive musement to this trio of categories, they, too, would "work themselves out." By employing the alternation implicit in his "yes-no" pair, Royce would view the idea of Individual as infinite or finite, as member or detached. He would view the idea of Spirit-Interpreter as human or superhuman, as intending loyalty or fostering treason, and so on.
11. For hints of this attraction, see *PC* 1:39, 212, 354; 2:221, 362, 428; and see esp. *Letters,* 645.

12. For a report on six major philosophical senses of "Spirit" in the late Royce, see Oppenheim, "The Idea of Spirit in the Mature Royce," *Transactions of the Charles S. Peirce Society* 19 (Fall 1983): 381-395.

13. John 6:45; 1:9.

14. For his middle period understanding of idea, see *WI* 1:19-26.

15. Yet John Smith finds Royce omitting one of James's senses of idea: see Smith's introduction to *PC,* 27 n. 23.

16. For example, see *CPP* 6.452.

17. As early as 1878, in his "Lectures Introductory to Philosophy," Royce had used the organism metaphor to inquire about one form of idea, the proposition: "Can I find the heart and brain, the soul and purpose of the typical proposition, that which makes it a proposition and not anything else?" (HARP 58, Lect. II, p. 5). The middle Royce's deliberate choice of "singing a melody" as his admittedly paradoxical illustration of an idea parallels his organism metaphor; see *WI* 1:34-36. For correlations between the mature Royce and John Henry Newman on their ideas of "idea," see the latter's *An Essay on the Development of Christian Doctrine* (1845) and his *Idea of a University* (1852, 1859).

18. See *PC* 1:394-397. Although familiar with the Greeks' more intellectualistic sense of idea (*logos*), Royce approached the biblical sense of idea (*dabar*) with its emphasis on spirit, will, embodiment, and action (*PC* 2:16). Taken in the latter sense and then shaped into the everlasting "sword of the Spirit," his set of leading ideas meant far more to Royce than various worldly weapons. In support of his view he could cite strong Scriptural precedent: "Not on bread alone is man to live, but on every word [*dabar,* "idea"] that comes from the mouth of God" (Matt. 4:4).

19. Royce borrowed the last three quoted materials, without credit, from John Henry Newman's popular hymn "Lead, Kindly Light."

20. Cf. *PC* 1:392 and 2:388 with 1:5-6, 2:14-16, and with *Letters,* 645-647.

21. See *SRI,* 38.

22. On Paul's requirement of love for community within Christian *caritas,* see *PC* 1:91-98 and the central section of Oppenheim's "Graced Communities," 610-615.

23. *Essays,* 99-183, esp. 142-183.

24. See *Essays,* 146, 154.

25. Ibid., 155-183.

26. According to John 1:3, 9-12.

27. *Essays,* 181-183.

28. *Essays,* 155-166, esp. 166. The history of Royce's pre-1912 approaches to Christianity and his earlier exposition of an Eckhart-like interpretation of the Incarnation (*Essays,* 164-166) may illumine Royce's position on the Incarnation before and during the *Problem.* This position is interpreted differently by two eminent Roycean scholars. See William E. Hocking's review of the *Problem* in *Harvard Theological Review* 7 (1914): 107-112, esp. 112 and John Smith's *Royce's Social Infinite,* 118-123 along with his introduction to the *Problem,* 19-21 with nn. 17 and 18.

29. Royce to Mary Whiton Calkins, March 20, 1916, in *Letters,* 647.

30. Royce to Warner Fite, July 20, 1913(?), in *Letters,* 604–609. See also p. 607 n. 9, and G. Smith, *Seminar,* 169, 172 for the importance Royce assigned to the ε-relation. In the text the two subsequent quotes from Royce to Fite are from *Letters,* 608–609. Royce judged this logical foundation lay beyond the ken of most of his Oxford audience in 1913.

31. A set is freely interpretable as either a community or as an invididual member of another set.

32. See *PC* 2:102. Royce wrote, "My book [*PC*] deals with a *special* case of the ε-relation" (*Letters,* 608, emphasis added). A partial clarification of his meaning may be won by recalling that just as in logic the ε-relation links individual elements to a set, so in Royce's philosophy of the Christian religion, his third idea of interpretive Atonement (or of reconciling Spirit) mediates between humankind's two levels of spiritual existence, and as functioning in the "realm of grace," directs man-the-individual into vital union with man-the-community. In this sense, the ε-relation, as graced, transforms the ideas of Individual and Community into a *"sacred pair"* (*PC* 1:343).

33. See *PC* 2:291–297, 309–311; cf. also B. J. F. Lonergan's *Insight,* chaps. 6–7, 18.

34. See *PC* 2:91–105, 168, 217–221, 311–315.

35. See also *PC* 2:11–12, 58.

36. In his work, *The Moral Philosophy of Josiah Royce* (Cambridge, Mass.: Harvard University Press, 1965), not even Peter Fuss gives a central role to transformation. Neither it nor any equivalent is mentioned in his index. By contrast, Bruce Kuklick in his *The Rise of American Philosophy* (New Haven, Conn.: Yale University Press, 1977) detects the importance of transformation (pp. 390–391) but then does not mention it in his sketch of Royce's early and later ethics (pp. 497–504).

13. EMPIRICO-HISTORICAL METHOD: SECOND AND THIRD STAGES

1. For other explicit indications of this overall strategy, see *PC* 1:xx–xxiii, xxxviii–xxxix, 175, 213, 331; 2:111–112, 334, 422.

2. At first Royce's penetrating search for the fullest meaning in each of his Christian ideas might seem like the drive central to C. S. Peirce's essay "How to Make our Ideas Clear" (*CPP* 5.388–410). There Peirce provided his "pragmatic maxim" for attaining a "third grade of clearness in our apprehensions." Both Peirce and Royce shared a passionate thirst to achieve higher grades of clearness. It might be, however, that both thinkers would classify the clearness of the "essential Christian ideas" on a "fourth grade" because the notion of God has this super-clarity and the set of these Christian ideas is the doctrine of the divine Spirit. Accordingly, the Christian ideas would lie beyond the scope of Peirce's pragmatic maxim. Furthermore, the kind of conception that Peirce admitted for refinement into a third grade of clearness seems to differ markedly from these self-like "ideas" which Royce strove to clarify. Finally, Royce's three-phased strategy of tracing an idea's experiential sources, normative significance, and truth-value in order to reach its

ultimate meaning strikes the present writer as a move distinctively different from Peirce's procedure of gathering together all the conceivable effects of a conception.

3. In this advance, Royce will, with his newly discovered insights, often return to some only partially examined idea in order to submit it to yet further scrutiny. For example, in his fourth, fifth, and seventh lectures, he intends to return and does return to clarify and further interpret the Christian ideas of community, moral burden, and atonement, respectively.

4. See above, chap. 5, pp. 75–78.

5. Emphasis added.

6. See also *Letters,* 645–647.

7. This communal side of Royce's "basis in human nature" needs special attention because of the heavily individualistic presupposition in contemporary Western culture.

8. The mature Royce was familiar with this central theme in the thought of his former student and recent colleague George Santayana and published in the latter's *The Life of Reason,* 5 vols. (New York: Charles Scribner's Sons, 1905). For example, see *PC* 1:113; 2:188.

9. Last Lectures on Metaphysics, p. 462, emphasis added. Royce delivered his final lecture in metaphysics on May 27, 1916.

10. Royce's idea of saving grace has genuine loyalty as its human face and the free and freeing gift of charity as its divine face.

11. See also *Letters,* 645.

14. AN INSTANCE OF THE SECOND STAGE: ROYCE MUSES ON THE IDEA OF COMMUNITY

1. Royce found the psychological origin of his mature ethics in this union of two shared interpretations: the members' common awareness that their community has a life, mind, and interest of its own, and their mutually maintained consciousness of the natural history of, and hope for, their community's mind. He found the vital moral origin of his mature ethics could only be the love of many individual members for their community. For only this unique love majestically calls them by its higher level of demands and motives (which transcends those of detached individualists who merely interact). Only this love unites them by its common interest and relates them ultimately to the universal community of humankind (*PC* 1:69–70).

2. An extended description of these three periods is found in Oppenheim's "Graced Communities," 610–615.

3. Royce's dynamic idea of the true (genuine) Church projects itself as an ideal future hope which evokes longings in the consciousness of each Christian and of his Christian community. By calling to all people "Create me!" this idea works as an ideal persistently challenging all people within the natural histories of individual and community minds. When interpretive musement brings the past, present, and future of these minds into interaction, this idea of the true Church with its universal aim generates the ideal of the universal community (*PC* 1:54).

4. Royce repeatedly returned to this connection. See *PC* 1:157–158, 407–408; 2:48–60, 104–105.

5. Royce preferred to stay strictly within those human relations which disclose the spirit of loyalty within firsthand encounters. The experience of these relationships may also open up, for further inquiry, endless vistas of the super-individual, perhaps even of the divine. But first, one has to delve into the common human experience of discovering a spirit of loyalty within some human relationships. Then one can simultaneously recognize how different this spirit is from the spirit of a predominantly self-interested individualism. See *PC* 1:408–409; 2:361.

6. Royce indicates this shift at *PC* 1:63, 66–74, 136–137, 188–191, 349, 410–412; 2:52–53, 217, 271.

7. See, for instance, *PC* 1:69, 73–74, 91–99. The potential for such interpretive reading is intimately connected with that "interior light" whereby Royce solved his religious paradox. See *SRI,* 22–26.

8. In his method of proceeding, Royce was not eager to get to the religious aspects of this ideal of the universal community. From history he knew that wherever this ideal has functioned in its ethical and aesthetic roles, it has led through loyalty to religious interpretations of itself (*PC* 1:69). Hence he felt that in the latter half of his lecture series (Part Two), he could properly raise the related question of whether our human contact with reality, established by these true ideas, also has divine reverberations calling for a religious response. Following Royce's pace, we treat the religious aspect of this ideal at the close of this chapter and in the next.

15. METAPHYSICAL METHOD

1. See *PC* 2:59–60.
2. See *PC* 2:225–276.
3. The universal community can be loved only through genuine loyalty—a gift from the universal community itself. Loyalty is genuine only when it simultaneously requires the ever more wholehearted cooperation of member-selves and by this means the further individualization of each member.
4. See *PC* 2:xvi, 3.
5. For a chart of these stages, see pp. 262–263.
6. See *PC* 2:57–105. Instructive contrasts to Royce's pioneer method of analyzing structures within community consciousness can be set up by consulting subsequent, more detailed, phenomenological approaches; e.g., Alfred Schutz, *Collected Papers,* vol. 2 of *Studies in Social Theory* (The Hague: Nijhoff, 1964) or Maurice Nedoncelle, *Love and the Person* (New York: Sheet & Ward, 1966).
7. See above, chap. 8, pp. 132–141 concerning these three conditions and three degrees of expressing communal consciousness. The present version more faithfully revises my earlier 1970 effort, "A Roycean Road to Community," to gather within five conditions what Royce had more wisely distinguished as three conditions and three degrees.
8. See Lonergan, *Insight,* xviii.
9. The human self's direct, universal, and irremovable religious need to

win a highest good (salvation) also includes certain subsidiary needs: to win insight into the way of salvation, to undergo transformation for entry into that way, and to be empowered steadily to achieve salvation.

10. See 1 Cor. 14:13.

11. Royce's kind of physical and mental empiricism is primary for him. Here that empiricism is so couched in terms of a sign-processing community that it avoids the necessary abstractness of precepts and concepts.

12. Since for the mature Royce "the very recognition of Being is itself an estimate" (Last Lectures on Metaphysics, 462), these three attitudes of will are ways of valuing oneself and one's realm of deeds—both actual and possible—through which one relates to and further creates the world process.

13. Royce did not, for example, treat explicitly of the option of preferring another individual self above oneself and all other things. Presumably, this reduces to a particular mode of the atomistic individual's will of self-assertion, the first option.

14. See Matt. 25:40, 45.

15. See *RLE,* 162-164, 168.

16. Royce underlined this entire quotation.

17. See Royce to R. C. Cabot, June 25, 1912, in *Letters,* 577-578.

18. Both Royce and William James were much interested in this article; see Wm. James to C. S. Peirce, November 7, 1908, Houghton Library MS.

16. UNDERLYING GENERAL METHOD: INTERPRETIVE MUSEMENT

1. For example, see Royce to G. P. Brett, January 7, 1912, and September 6, 1912, in *Letters,* 561, 581.

2. Emphasis added.

3. Emphasis added. Similarly, after contrasting the distinct subordinate methods of Parts One and Two of the *Problem,* he added, "The two parts, however, are closely connected in their purpose" (*PC* 1:xxxvi). For indirect evidence of this close connection that expresses Royce's one overall purpose, task, and method, see *PC* 1:xxiii, xxvi, xxix.

4. For any theory of truth to be adequate, Royce required that it synthesize the three distinctive motives of the instrumentalist, the individualist, and the objectivist. See his pivotal essay "The Problem of Truth in the Light of Recent Discussion," *Essays,* 187-254 (or *RLE,* 63-97). See also Daniel S. Robinson's study "Royce's Concept of Modes of Action," *Philosophy and Phenomenological Research* 14 (June 1954): 553-559.

5. The term "ponder" may approach Peirce's term "musement" most closely.

6. *The American Heritage Dictionary,* ed. William Morris, New College Edition (Boston: Houghton Mifflin Co., 1975), p. 284, col. 1.

7. See *PC* 1:5-6, 71-72, 356; 2:15-16, 361; see also *SRI,* 286.

8. For Royce, the ideal of interpretation arises psychologically. If a person succeeds in completing a comparison of two of her own ideas, she experiences a luminous self-possession along with her grasp of the "third idea" which brings the

two initial ideas into an objective unity. This momentary experience of luminous self-possession becomes a model for all her following interpretations and thus gives rise to the ideal of successful interpretation. If one hypothetically extends this experience to include all minded beings within a mutual understanding that is complete but distant and hoped-for, she comes to grasp the ideal of the truth-seeking interpreter. See *PC* 2:205, 220, 187.

9. Royce described this ordinary sensitivity in *Outlines of Psychology,* chaps. 5-7.

10. These conditions are assembled from *PC* 2:220-221, 311, 361.

11. Cf. 1 Cor. 14:13 with Luke 11:13. As an instance of Royce's interest in the subject of "spiritual gifts" in Paul, see Royce to G. H. Palmer, October 28, 1910, in *Letters,* 547.

12. For instance, amid Royce's lengthy description of his 1912 Peircean insight, why did he become most specific about the fact that, through this insight, he discovered the *vital bond* between interpretation and loyalty and between the philosophies of both? See HARP 84, #3, 5-14, or Oppenheim, "Hypothesis," 86.

13. John Bunyan's *Pilgrim's Progress,* a favorite classic of the evangelical tradition, became a theme to which Royce kept returning throughout his life. See, for example, *Studies of Good and Evil,* 29-75, and, from his final year, that authentic but unpublished Section Five of his *The Hope of the Great Community,* in HARP 51, #2. In this section, Royce makes a detailed application of its opening sentence: "We stand, like Bunyan's Pilgrim, at the wicket gate which leads towards the New World that will gradually come to human vision after this war [World War I] is over."

14. This Roycean intent becomes conspicuous if one compares Lectures 2, 4, and 9 of the *Problem.*

15. In the *Problem,* compare Lectures 2 and 4 on community with Lectures 3 and 5 on moral burden.

16. See, for example, *PC* 2:4-6, summarizing Part One; or 2:279, summarizing Parts One and Two.

17. LOYALTY: CENTER OF CHRISTIANITY AND OF HUMAN INTERESTS

1. For Royce's listing of these four theses, see *PC* 1:xviii-xix.

2. See Edward A. Jarvis, S. J., *The Conception of God in the Later Royce* (The Hague: Nijhoff, 1975).

3. In his preface to the *Problem,* dated April 13, 1913, Royce chose to summarize this work from the ethico-religious viewpoint of loyalty. Those who tend to regard the *Problem* as primarily a work in either logic or metaphysics or theory of knowledge need to examine this Roycean choice and its implications. See *PC* 1:xviii-xix.

4. For example, see *PC* 1:xvi, xxvi; 2:312, 325, 390.

5. See *Essays,* 64-71.

6. *Essays,* 65.

7. This first thesis of Royce was closely paralleled recently when Karl Rah-

ner, shortly before his death in 1984, uttered the following counterbalanced statement: "One can maintain Christianity's claim to be the culmination of the graced relationship of humanity to God both verbally and institutionally without in any way denying the teaching that anyone who does not lock God out by real, personal, deadly guilt is safe in God's love and in His salvation." Karl Rahner, *I Remember* (New York: Crossroad, 1985), 78.

8. Collins, "Analyst," 212.

9. See Oppenheim, "Graced Communities," 610–615.

10. See above, pp. 127–131 of chap. 8, and Oppenheim, "Graced Communities," 610–618.

11. See *PC* 1:383–395.

18. SIMPLIFICATION FOR THE GREATER UNITY OF CHRISTIANS

1. Royce emphasized each of these quoted words. His recommendation that Christology be simplified rested on the conviction that Christology could reach its integral development only if consciousness reached a transcultural state. In this, Royce pioneered a position which resembles the one described and documented by William M. Thompson in his "Risen Christ and World Religions," *Theological Studies* 37 (September 1976): 381–409.

2. His reading of Percy Gardner's *The Religious Experience of the Apostle Paul* (see *PC* 1:196) inclined Royce to go further and to differentiate three Christologies in the early, middle, and late Paul.

3. *Essays,* 166.

4. Already in 1887 such shared perceptible signs and common focus were implicitly present in Royce's description of the formation of communities among California's miners of 1849. See Oppenheim, "Josiah Royce as Teacher," *Educational Theory* 25 (Spring 1975): 177.

5. Royce emphasized each of these words.

6. One of Royce's favorite readings in his youth and final decades was John Bunyan's *Pilgrim's Progress.* Royce often alluded to Christian the Pilgrim, the central figure in this work.

7. Such bickering usually mistakes the point at issue and hence provokes disputes between Christians.

8. A half a century later, Pope Paul VI invited all people to engage in salvific dialogue in order to follow this same pathway to unify the human family. See Part Three ("Dialogue") of his first encyclical letter, "The Paths of the Church," (*Ecclesium Suam*) in the official edition *Acta Apostolica Sedis* 56 (1964): 609ff. or in the English edition (New York: America Press, 1964), 35–59.

9. For his supreme instance of community, why did Royce favor the title "Beloved Community"? Its members are "beloved of such a Spirit" (*PC* 1:351), having received the saving gift which allows them to share in this loyal life (*PC* 1:410). Reciprocally, the loyal selves have a beloved distinct from the individual selves they love. They regard as "the apple of their eye," as their "Beloved," the

superhuman reality of the universal community which orients them through their loyal deeds towards the divine (*PC* 1:357). In sum, within this community, the Spirit unites its beloveds and, in turn, they make both this community and its Spirit their beloveds.

    10. The Second Vatican Council struck this same note fifty years later. See the close of the paragraphs #12 and #32 of "The Church in the Modern World," *The Documents of Vatican II,* 211, 231.

    11. Dewey, *A Common Faith,* 9.
    12. Ibid., 28.
    13. Ibid., 22.
    14. James, *Varieties,* 394.
    15. Dewey, *A Common Faith,* 9.
    16. Royce to Mary Whiton Calkins, March 20, 1916, in *Letters,* 645–646.

19. EVALUATION OF STRENGTHS AND WEAKNESSES

    1. Limitations of space preclude evaluation of other strengths, such as Royce's conception of God, his psychology of the religious life, his investigations into the various sources of religious insight, and his studies of mysticism, of immortality, and of the Christian scholastics.

    2. Emphasis added.
    3. Eph. 5:25.
    4. Cf. *PC* 1:vii with Romans, chaps. 3 and 8 or with 1 Cor., chaps. 2–3 and 15.
    5. Matt. 16:18.
    6. 2 Thess. 2:2–5.
    7. 1 Cor. 3:5–7.
    8. See *RAP,* 2, 6.
    9. See Royce's Final Lecture, May 27, 1916, Last Lectures on Metaphysics, 462.
    10. *RAP,* 6.
    11. *RAP,* 4.
    12. See *WI* 1:3–5.
    13. See Royce's article "Mind," esp. 656–657 (or *RLE,* 175).
    14. Royce to A. O. Lovejoy, December 30, 1912, in *Letters,* 586.
    15. See *SRI,* 100–102.
    16. Yet more widely than most, Royce read the literature of world religions and deeply appreciated occasional encounters with their various believers. See *PC* 2:341–342.
    17. If one considers Royce's dominantly Protestant milieu and his religious background in non-conformism, it becomes clearer why he would feel aversion for cultic practices and sacraments and why he would not mention Mary, the mother of Jesus. The substance, or at least the clearer articulation, of this and of the following four paragraphs derive from the observations of Professor Dieter Georgi.

18. Mary Whiton Calkins in *Philosophical Review* 25 (1916): 293. For William Ernest Hocking's critique, see *Harvard Theological Review* 7 (1914): 107-112, esp. 112. John E. Smith's replies occur in his *Royce's Social Infinite,* 118-123 and in his introduction, *PC,* 19-20.

19. See John, chaps. 14-16.

20. This theme pervades Van Wyck Brooks' *New England's Indian Summer: 1865-1915* (New York: E. P. Dutton, 1940).

21. Mark 3:13-14.

22. Matt. 16:18.

23. See Royce's "Andover Address on the Relation of Philosophy to the Clergyman's Profession" (June 7, 1904), in HARP 75, #1, pp. 12-13, 27-31.

24. The reader can detect how Royce often read the Scriptures by inquiring which kind of mental process is presupposed for his statements in *Hope of the Great Community,* 124; *WI* 1:156-158, 175-182; *PC* 1:368-369; and in *Letters,* 547, 580.

25. Any qualified comparison and contrast would seem to need familiarity with a vast field of literature, including such works as John Cobbs, *Christianity in a Pluralistic Age* (Philadelphia: Westminster, 1975); Bernard Lonergan, *Method in Theology,* 2d ed. (New York: Herder and Herder, 1973); Richard R. Niebuhr, *Experiential Religion* (New York: Harper & Row, 1972); Karl Rahner, *Schriften zur Theologie 12: Theologie aus Erfahrung des Geistes* (Zurich: Benzinger, 1975); and David Tracy, *Blessed Rage for Order* (New York: Seabury, 1975).

26. *SRI,* 115, where Royce echoes 1 Cor. 13:12, the apostle Paul's allusion to God's knowledge of us.

27. See Gordon Kaufmann, *Essay in Theological Method* (Missoula, Mont.: Scholars Press, 1975), 5.

28. Earlier in part two, for the sake of clarity, our exposition stressed Royce's differentiations within religious experience—elementary and complex, primitive and acculturated, essential form and experiential whole. Here in part five, however, emphasis should be put on Royce's descriptions of the coherence, seriation, and rhythmic flow found in religious experience taken integrally.

29. For this phrase and the suggestions behind it, I am indebted to Professor Robert Evans of McCormick Theological School.

30. Loewenberg, *Fugitive Essays,* 7.

31. *Outlines of Psychology,* 299-332.

32. See Gabriel Marcel, *L'homme problématique* (Paris: Aubier, 1955), 68. One naturally wonders whether Marcel derived this priority from his attentive investigation of Royce during World War I. See Marcel's insightful study, *Royce's Metaphysics* (Chicago: Regnery, 1965).

33. See the sixth sense of this term in Oppenheim, "The Idea of Spirit in the Mature Royce," 381-395, esp. 391-392.

34. See John Macquarrie, *Principles of Christian Theology* (New York: Charles Scribner's Sons, 1966), 170.

35. *Loyalty,* 357.

36. Ibid., 381-383.

20. CONTRIBUTION TO METHOD FOR PHILOSOPHY OF RELIGION

1. See also *PC* 1:20-21 and especially *SRI,* 6.

2. The reader can discern how a similarly respectful confessional sharing of personal faith would promote dialogue within that narrower field of the various Christian churches and communions. See 1 Pet. 3:15-16.

3. Royce thus preceded Karl Rahner by half a century in underscoring how significant for theology and ecumenism is the *de facto* saving faith of what Rahner calls "*dritte Konfession*" Christians. Such Christians believe in Christianity's most vital essentials but are not concerned with the controversial questions separating the various churches and maintain a loose connection with their respective official churches. See Harvey Egan's Review of Karl Rahner's *Schriften zur Theologie 12* in *Theological Studies* 37 (1976): 692.

4. John K. Roth, *Problems in the Philosophy of Religion* (Scranton: Chandler, 1971), 2.

5. See G. Smith, *Seminar.*

6. Col. 1:15-20.

7. Cf. Royce's views of the incarnation in his 1909 *Essays,* 163-181 and his 1912 *PC* 1:209-213. Although Royce grew beyond a pure Eckhartian view of the "Essential Christ," his risen Christ seems to lack the body Mary gave Jesus and the power to touch persons today through that body. For Royce, even in 1912, the incarnation of the divine Word in Jesus was not necessarily a transcendentally unique instance of incarnation. It was not radically different in kind from many essential incarnations of the Word in human believers—that is, Eckhart's "Essential Christ." As a corollary, Royce relegated to the status of over-belief, not vital to Christianity, the doctrine that the individual Jesus will come to judge all human persons. See *Essays,* 149.

8. See B. J. F. Lonergan, *Method in Theology,* 125-148. He delineates each functional speciality in Part 2, 149-368.

9. Delivered on May 27, 1916; see Last Lectures on Metaphysics, 462-463.

10. During much of my reading of Royce, Lonergan's four levels of human questioning were in my mind. See B. J. F. Lonergan, *Insight.* This fourfold pattern also appears frequently in Royce's late writings. In Royce, the second step (understanding) apparently includes more spontaneous valuations than Lonergan described in his relatively early work *Insight.* On the other hand, Royce's independent fulfillment of this fourfold pattern provides yet another confirmation of the general accuracy of Lonergan's analysis of human intentionality.

11. *RLE,* 60.

12. Royce pioneered in this interpersonal communitarian approach long before John MacMurray presented it in his 1954 Gifford Lectures as an urgently needed matrix for philosophizing. See MacMurray's *Persons in Relation* (London: Faber and Faber, 1961), along with his preceding Gifford Series of 1953, *The Self as Agent* (London: Faber and Faber, 1957).

13. See *PC* 1:78, 91-93, 231-233, 289, 320-321.

14. See, for example, *PC,* chap. 15.

15. In the *Problem,* Royce's interpretation of the New Testament clearly foreshadows the main thesis expressed by C. H. Dodd in *The Apostolic Preaching and its Development* (New York: Harper & Row, 1936), esp. p. 3. Like Royce, Dodd presents Paul and John as grasping the living center of the original apostolic *kerygma* with greater accuracy and with fewer distracting emphases than did the remaining authors of the New Testament. Hence, like Royce, Dodd relies more heavily upon Paul and John.

21. THE "CHRISTIAN" FUTURE OF THE UNIVERSE

1. Lecture of May 27, 1916, in Last Lectures on Metaphysics, 462.

2. Those who adopt this final attitude rarely reflect that its accompanying politico-economic life-style and captivating sense of superiority over "less fortunate nations" first promotes spiritual poverty and then foments wars internationally. For in our actual human community, precisely this attitude, life-style, and hubris is what daily widens the gap and deepens the alienations between the affluent few and the impoverished multitudes.

3. Such an evaluation would explore how fruitful was Royce's method of centering on Ideas. It would compare and contrast this method with those of other philosophers. It would thoroughly test his recommendation that the problems of traditional Christology be simplified in order to enrich its spirit. It would probe to see whether his late insights are powerful enough to transform ecclesiology. As one norm for such evaluation, we have already pointed to Royce's concluding maxims (*PC* 2:424, 430).

4. Royce found that the individual's religious experience always undertakes to reveal a triad of objects: the individual's Ideal, Need, and Deliverer. See *SRI,* 29. Then in the *Problem* Royce found the triad of objects that form the communal creed: the ideas of Ideal Community, Lost State of the detached individual, and the Redeeming Spirit.

5. See *PC* 2:424, 430.

6. Some contemporary Scripture scholars now concur with the main lines of Royce's interpretation of Scripture. For instance, in his *The Apostolic Church in the New Testament* (Westminster, Md.: Newman, 1966), xi, Professor David Stanley, S.J., states that certain facets of the Church's character were either unknown or only half-consciously realized by the Christian community at the beginning of the formative apostolic age. But these facets, he contends, became more consciously recognized about two decades later during the time of Paul's preaching. They became still more fully conscious several decades later with the writings of John. Professor Stanley thus enunciates the hermeneutical viewpoint fundamental to Royce.

7. See Pierre Teilhard de Chardin, *The Phenomena of Man,* 214.

8. See, for example, *Seminar,* especially the introduction by its editor, Grover Smith, pp. 1-4.

9. Christianity has perdured as a problem from 1913 to the present. Anyone doubting this need only read Leslie Dewart, *The Future of Belief* (New York:

Herder and Herder, 1966), Harvey Cox, *The Secular City* (New York, Macmillan, 1966), and more recently, Karl Rahner, *Christian at the Crossroads* (New York: Seabury, 1975).

10. This experience of loyalty, along with its presupposed sense of the individual moral impotence, provides the experiential verifiability for the mainlines of Royce's religion of loyalty. He considers Christianity the prime instance of this kind of religion, the religion of "The Beloved Community." See *PC* 1:ix, xxv; 2:6.

11. Royce emphasized this entire sentence.

12. As an instance, see Jon Sobrino, S.J., *Christology at the Crossroads: A Latin American Approach* (Maryknoll, N.Y.: Orbis, 1978).

13. In his deservedly acclaimed work, *The Coming of the Third Church* (Maryknoll, N.Y.: Orbis, 1977), Walbert Bühlmann makes a similar recommendation. He corroborates the trend Royce predicted and calls for ecumenical cooperation so that a creative response may be made to the outstanding opportunity which the developing Third World offers the Church.

EPILOGUE

1. See Friedrich Heiler, "The History of Religions as a Preparation for the Cooperation of Religions," *The History of Religions,* ed. M. Eliade and J. Kitagawa (Chicago: University of Chicago Press, 1959), 142–153. In his *Method in Theology,* Bernard Lonergan integrated "these seven common features of the world religions" by finding them "implicit in the experience of being in love in an unrestricted manner" (p. 109). *Such* love seems very close to Roycean loyalty.

2. Paraphrase of Heiler's list as presented by Lonergan in *Method,* 109.

3. I borrow the distinction between "secularism" and "secularization process" that is found in David J. Hassel, *City of Wisdom* (Chicago: Loyola University Press, 1983), 217–218.

4. *RAP,* v; Harper ed., ix.

Appendix

CORRELATION OF PAGES IN VARIOUS EDITIONS OF JOSIAH ROYCE'S *THE PROBLEM OF CHRISTIANITY*

	MACMILLAN, 1913, 2 vols. Archon, reprint, 1967 *Regnery (Gateway) edition, 1968	UNIVERSITY OF CHICAGO edition 1968, 1 vol.
Vol. I: The Christian Doctrine of Life		
(Foreword:	Regnery: Jesse A. Mann, vii–xiii*	John E. Smith, 1–36)
Preface:		
Introduction	vii–viii	37
Section I	viii–ix	37–38
II	ix–xii	38–39
III	xiii–xvi	39–41
IV	xvii–xix	41–42
V	xix–xxiii	42–44
VI	xxiv–xxix	44–46
VII	xxix–xxxii	46–48
Table of Contents	xxxiii	5
Author's Introduction-Preliminary Notes	xxxv–xxxix	49–51
Topics	xxxix–xlvi	51–54
Lecture 1		
Section I	3–6	58
II	6–9	59–60
III	9–13	60–61
IV	13–22	61–65
V	22–30	65–68
VI	30–36	68–70
VII	36–44	70–73
VIII	44–45	74

*Although the overall *arabic* numeral pagination in the Regnery edition corresponds perfectly with that of the original Macmillan edition, and of the Archon reprint, to find the corresponding locus in the *Preface of the Regnery edition, ADD 8 pp.;* e.g. a footnote reference in the present work to p. xix (Macmillan) would be verified in the Regnery Preface on its p. xxvii.

	MacMillan, 1913, 2 vols. Archon, reprint, 1967 Regnery (Gateway) edition, 1968	University of Chicago edition 1968, 1 vol.
Lecture 2		
Section I	49–53	75–77
II	53–56	77–78
III	56–59	78–79
IV	59–61	79–80
V	61–65	80–82
VI	66–74	82–85
VII	74–78	85–87
VIII	79–83	87–89
IX	83–91	89–92
X	91–96	92–94
XI	96–106	94–98
Lecture 3		
Introduction	109	
Section I	110–111	99–100
II	111–116	100–102
III	116–121	102–104
IV	121–127	104–106
V	127–135	106–109
VI	135–137	109–110
VII	137–140	110–111
VIII	140–148	112–114
IX	148–155	115–118
X	156–159	118–119
Lecture 4		
Introduction	163	121
Section I	164–169	122–124
II	169–172	124–125
III	173–175	125–126
IV	175–179	126–128
V	180–185	128–130
VI	185–187	130–131
VII	187–192	131–133
VIII	193–196	133–135
IX	196–205	135–139
X	206–213	139–142
Lecture 5		
Introduction	217	143
Section I	217–221	143–145
II	221–224	145–146
III	224–227	146–147
IV	227–235	147–151

APPENDIX 391

	MacMillan, 1913, 2 vols. Archon, reprint, 1967 Regnery (Gateway) edition, 1968	University of Chicago edition 1968, 1 vol.
V	236–242	151–153
VI	242–245	153–155
VII	246–254	155–158
VIII	254–258	158–160
IX	259–267	160–165
Lecture 6		
Introduction	271	165
Section I	272–278	165–168
II	278–282	168–170
III	283–288	170–172
IV	288–289	172–173
V	290–293	173–174
VI	293–302	174–178
VII	302–304	178–179
VIII	304–310	179–181
IX	311–318	181–184
X	318–323	184–186
Lecture 7		
Introduction	327–329	187–188
Section I	330–331	188–192
II	331–339	189–192
III	339–342	192–193
IV	343–349	193–196
V	349–354	196–198
VI	354–357	198–199
VII	357–360	199–201
VIII	361–364	201–202
IX	365–374	202–206
X	374–380	206–208
Lecture 8		
Introduction	383–384	209–210
Section I	385–387	210–211
II	387–390	211–212
III	390–394	212–214
IV	394–397	214–215
V	398–402	215–217
VI	402–409	217–220
VII	409–412	220–221
VIII	412–415	221–222
IX	415–419	222–224
X	420–425	224–226

APPENDIX

	MACMILLAN, 1913, 2 vols. Archon, reprint, 1967 Regnery (Gateway) edition, 1968	UNIVERSITY OF CHICAGO edition 1968, 1 vol.
Vol. II: The Real World and the Christian Ideas		
Part II Table of Contents	v–vi	
Lecture 9		
Introduction	3–4	229–230
Section I	4–7	230–231
II	7–10	231–232
III	10–12	232–233
IV	12–13	233
V	14–16	234–235
VI	17–18	235
VII	18–25	235–238
VIII	26–35	238–242
IX	35–39	242–244
X	39–44	244–246
XI	44–49	246–248
XII	49–53	248–249
Lecture 10		
Introduction	57–58	251–252
Section I	58–60	252–253
II	60–67	253–255
III	67–69	255–256
IV	69–72	256–257
V	72–78	257–260
VI	79–80	260
VII	80–82	260–261
VIII	83–85	262–263
IX	85–91	263–265
X	91–95	265–266
XI	95–98	266–268
XII	99–103	268–270
XIII	103–105	270–271
Lecture 11		
Introduction	109–110	273
Section I	110	274
II	110–113	274–275
III	113–117	275–277
IV	117–120	277–278
V	121–123	278–279
VI	124–127	279–281
VII	127–129	281–282
VIII	129–133	282–283
IX	133–136	283–284

APPENDIX 393

	MACMILLAN, 1913, 2 vols. Archon, reprint, 1967 Regnery (Gateway) edition, 1968	UNIVERSITY OF CHICAGO edition 1968, 1 vol.
X	136–139	284–286
XI	139–144	286–288
XII	144–148	288–289
XIII	148–152	289–291
XIV	152–154	291–292
XV	154–158	292–293
XVI	158–163	293–295
Lecture 12		
Introduction	167	297
Section I	167–168	297–298
II	168–170	298
III	170–175	299–301
IV	176–180	301–302
V	180–184	303–304
VI	184–193	304–308
VII	193–198	308–310
VIII	199–203	310–312
IX	204–208	312–314
X	208–214	314–316
XI	214–217	316–317
XII	217–221	317–319
Lecture 13		
Introduction	225–227	321–322
Section I	227–228	322–323
II	229–232	323–324
III	232–234	324–325
IV	234–240	325–327
V	240–245	327–329
VI	245–247	329–330
VII	247–249	330–331
VIII	249–252	331–332
IX	253–255	332–333
X	255–260	333–335
XI	260–264	335–337
XII	264–270	337–339
XIII	270–271	339–340
XIV	271–273	340–341
XV	273–276	341–342
Lecture 14		
Introduction	279	343
Section I	279–281	343–344
II	281–286	344–346
III	286–291	346–348
IV	291–296	348–350

394 APPENDIX

	MacMillan, 1913, 2 vols. Archon, reprint, 1967 Regnery (Gateway) edition, 1968	University of Chicago edition 1968, 1 vol.
V	296–297	350–351
VI	298–300	351–352
VII	300–305	352–354
VIII	305–308	354–355
IX	309–311	355–356
X	311–314	356–357
XI	314–315	357–358
XII	315–319	358–360
XIII	319–322	360–361
XIV	322–325	361–362
Lecture 15		
Introduction	329	363
Section I	329–333	363–365
II	333–336	365–366
III	336–340	366–368
IV	341–344	368–369
V	344–351	369–372
VI	351–355	372–374
VII	355–361	374–376
VIII	361–365	376–378
IX	365–369	378–380
X	369–373	380–381
XI	373–379	381–384
Lecture 16		
Introduction	383	385
Section I	383–386	385–387
II	387–388	387
III	388–391	387–388
IV	391–394	388–390
V	394–399	390–392
VI	399–403	392–393
VII	403–406	393–395
VIII	406–408	395
IX	408–411	396–397
X	411–414	397–398
XI	415–417	398–399
XII	417–418	399–400
XIII	419–420	400
XIV	421–432	401–405
Index	433–442	407–412

Index of Names

Aquinas, Thomas, 21

Barth, Karl, 372 n 12
Bergson, Henri, 66, 146, 241
Bradley, F. H., 356 n 3
Broad, C. D., 43
Bultmann, Rudolf, 372 n 14
Bunyan, John (Pilgrim), 275, 343, 381 n 13, 382 n 6
Burch, Robert, 360 n 2

Cabot, Richard and Ella, 16
Caird, Edward, 7, 9
Calkins, Mary Whiton, 315, 356 n 14
Carlyle, Thomas, 367 n 19
Clendenning, John, xii, xiv, 363 n 22
Collins, James, 142, 286, 358 n 54
Courtney, Charles, 368 n 2

Dewey, John, 27, 49, 178, 181-182, *302-305*, 370 n 21
Dodd, C. H., 386 n 15

Eckhart, Master, 329, 376 n 28

Fuss, Peter, 377 n 36

Gardner, Percy, 370 n 8, 382 n 2
Georgi, Dieter, 372 n 18
Goethe, Johann, 367 n 19

Head, Katharine, 7
Hegel, G. W. F., 45, 247, 254, 329
Henderson, L. J., 168, 201

Hocking, William E., 16, 204, 315, 355 n 78, 368 n 3, 376 n 28
Howison, G. H., 13, 21
Husserl, Edmund, 368 n 2

James, William, 6, 8, 14-17, 49, 65-68, 72, 93, 109, 111-112, 118, 146, 152, 178-181, 190, 253, 267, 270, 310, 351 n 21, 368 n 7
John the Baptist, 150, 260, 300

Kaufmann, Gordon, 319
Kempe, A. B., 44, 56, 73
Kuklick, Bruce, 44, 63, 364 n 28, 365 n 5 n 9, 371 n 2
Kung, Hans, 372 n12

LeConte, Joseph, 11
Lewis, C. I., 54, 62, 67, 87
Locke, John, his idea of substance, 213
Lonergan, B. J. F., 237, 330, 333, 374 n 11, 385 n 10

McDermott, John J., xiv
MacMurray, John, 385 n 12
Marcel, Gabriel, xiii, 321, 384 n 32
Miller, Dickinson S., 8
Mill, John Stuart, 351 n 17
Munsterberg, Hugo, 14
Murphey, Murray, 364 n 2

Newman, John Henry, 343, 376 n 17

Paul, the Apostle, 11, 23, 92, 129-131, 188-189, 195, 223, 272, 309, 311, 322, 328-329

Peirce, C. S., 4, 8-9, 12, 14, 23, *31-32,* 38, 43-46, 50, 60, 65, 68, 144-145, 168, 188, 190, 241-242, 246, 251, 261, 321, 359 n 1, 361 n 11, 377 n 2
Plato, 9, 241, 312, 321

Rahner, Karl, 29, 366 n 9, 369 n 5, 381 n 7, 385 n 3
Renouvier, Charles, 351 n 21
Royce, Josiah: authors read by, 60, 178, 360 n 8; early life, 3-7, 11, 13; family of, 4-5, 7, 11-13; letters of, 349 n 5 n 10, 352 n 26, 354 n 66, 368 n 6, 381 n 11
Russell, Bertrand, 54-55, 66, 73

Santayana, George, 8, 378 n 8
Schelling, Friedrich, 12

Schopenhauer, Arthur, 66
Scotus, Duns, 21
Sill, Edward Rowland, 7, 13, 18
Skrupskelis, Ignas, xiv, 360 n 4
Smith, John E., 315-316, 368 n 2, 372 n 15
Spinoza, Baruch, 12, 66
Stanley, David, 386 n 6
Strauss, David, 254
Suarez, Francisco, 366 n 9

Teilhard de Chardin, Pierre, 165, 328, 339
Thompson, William M., 382 n 1
Toynbee, Arnold, 375 n 1

Whitehead, Alfred North, 54-55, 204
Wittgenstein, Ludwig, 374 n 12
Wundt, Wilhelm, 213, 319

Index of Topics

Absolute all-Knower, argument to, 7, 21, 351 n 21
Affective life, role in philosophy of religion, 26, 38, 93, 117, 120, 141, 180
Alienation, 226-27. *See also* Lost State
Alternation: in comparison-contrast, 224-226, 233-234, 375 n 10
  requisite for religious insight, 108-110
Analogy, strict, 168
Appreciation: nexus with interpretive knowing and values, 214-215
  with primitive knowing of Being, 215, 331-332
Approach, Royce's, to the *Problem*, 144-148
Atonement, 13-15, 51-52, 82, 158-159, 197, 199, 289, 298, 311
Attitudes of will, Three. *See* Will

Beauty, Royce's reticence about, 367 n 13
Being, recognition of, 215, 331-332
Bible, 189, 293, 311-312, 384 n 24, 386 n 151 n 6
  Fourth Gospel, 128-129
  Pauline letters, 128-129, 370 n 8
  Royce's interpretation of Petrine text, 317
  Royce's reading of, 11-12, 17-18, 27
Boys' High School, 3
Buddhism, compared to Christianity, 27, 177, 208, 266, 273, 316

Caritas, 134, 140, 194, 274
Christ, 46, 189, 195, 257, 293-296, 315, 328-329
  Essential and Historical, 195, 293, 328-329
  Royce's dominant images of, 189, 293, 342

"Christian," Royce's meaning of term, 153
Christian doctrine of life, 24, 48, 66, 81, 86, 156-159, 193, *249-263,* 298, 338, 345
  testing of, 250-251
Christian, fictive Athenian, 154, 167, 201, *255-259,* 266, 365 n 15
"Christian idea," Royce's meaning of, 212
Christianity, 29, 61, 94, 118, *124-127,* 144, *146-149, 157-159, 184-188,* 270, 283-286, 300, 316, 325-326, 341
  approach to, 148-149, 185-186
  challenge to, 123-124
  characteristics of, 154-156
  destiny of, 290-291
  forms of, 51
  future trends of, 341-343
  institutionalized, 16, 118
  master of, 315-316
  reduced to love only, 118
  religion of loyalty, 283-286
  Royce's discerning of Essential from Historical, 254-256
  Royce's grasp of history of, 10-11
  Royce's meaning of, 10, 22, *29*
  Royce's problem of, 87, 147-148, 152-159, 275-276
  superhuman dimension, 119-120, 303-304, 358 n 59
Christians: contemporary, 124-131, 162
  Liberal, 51, 126, 284-285
  Orthodox, 126, 284
  Pauline, 127-131, 157, 162, 258
Christology, 170, *292-296,* 341-342
  future revision of, 342-343, 382 n 1
Church, 127-131, 155-156, 191, 221, 312, 315
  future understanding of, 343
  Pauline, 164
  Royce's meaning of idea of, 4, 5, 221-222, 257, 372 n 12, 378 n 3, 381 n 7

398   INDEX OF TOPICS

Church (cont.)
  Universal, 80, 221, 227, 343
Class (set) in logic, 59–60, 62–64
Common Faith (Dewey's), 27, 181
Community, *29–31,* 132
  Beloved, 28, 82, 122, 124, 130, 135, 201, 245, *287–289,* 327, 382 n 9
  consciousness of, 132–141, 233, 235
  Dewey's presentation of, 370 n 21
  early Christian, 223
  genuine, 30
  Great, 14, *30,* 37, 169
  Idea of, 158–159, 199, 212, 220–223, 227–228, *232–236,* 305
  Investigation of, 236–247
  love for, 288–289
  "Man the Community," 26, 34–35
  natural, 30, 222
  of Interpretation, 11, *30–31,* 37, 58, 70, 106, 232, 325, 327, 338
  Royce's experiences of, 11–12
  Universal, 30, 70–71, 77, 79, 85, 227–228
  World as, 260–262
Comparison-contrast, an alternation, 244, 303–305, 368 n 3. *See also* Interpretation
Conception, 31, 236, 239, 241–243
Consciousness of others (social), 252–254
Consistency, in Royce's thought, 301–302
Conversion. *See* Transformation
Creedal aspect of religion, 26, 153
Cult of the dead, 18, 355 n 94, 367 n 13

Deliverance. *See* Salvation
Development: of ethical consciousness, 224–227; (maturation) of Royce's thought, 3–10, 314–315, 321, 350 n 5, 352 n 28 n 36; in logic, 43–44, 45–46; in philosophy of religion, 20–24, 145–147
  Royce's personal, 4–19
Discernment, 97, 98, 120, 179, *271–274,* 296–297, 325, 340, 353 n 42
Disciples of Christ, 5, 11
Doctrine: Christian, of life, 24, 48, 66, 81, 86, 193, *249–263,* 298, 338, 345, 373 n 2 n 3; of love, as transformed by Paul, 290

Doctrine (cont.)
  of evolution, 151–152
  Royce's mature, 283–305
  of Signs, 66, 72, 74, 167, 201, *251–254,* 298, 301
  of Two Levels, 26, 126, 142, 156, 197–199
Dogma, simplifying Christian, 296–298, 361 n 22

E-relation, 63, 64, 79, 83
Ecumenism, 16, 17, 292–305, 315–317, 320–323, 337–339, 385 n 2 n 3, 387 n 13
Empirico-Historical Method, 183–218
Episcopal Church, 16, 80
Epistemology, 200–201, 374 n 12
Epsilon relation, 44, 46, *52,* 57–58, 70–71, 79–80, 83, 122, *197–199,* 377 n 30 n 32
Eternal, the essentially, 38–39, 322, 358 n 60
Ethics, psychological origin of Royce's mature, 378 n 1
Eucharist, 17, 315, 317
Evaluation. *See* Appreciation
Evangelicalism, 4–5, 17, 27–28, 381 n 13
Events, as signs, 300–301
Evolution, 151–152, 162–166
Evolution of Religion (Edward Caird's), 7–8
Experience: as a process of Signs, 31
  Royce's mature meaning of, *31–32,* 318–320
Experience, Religious, 35–37, 93
  complex, 91–93, *122–143*
  elementary, 91–121, esp. 91–93
  related to "story (narrative) theology," 258
  Royce's critique of James on, 8
  Royce's openness to further, 27
  social approach to elementary, 118–121
  social form of complex, 122–143
  sources of, 96–105, 107–113, 367 n 12
  structure of individual, 118–121
  superhuman dimension of, 119–120, 303–304, 358 n 59

Index of Topics

F-relation, 56, 83
Family, Royce's, 4-7, 11-13
Formulations, serial of "the problem of Christianity," 152-155

Generality, 144-145
Generalization, 200-201, 235
Germany, 6, 12, 14
Gifford Lectures, 8, 22
God, 37, 141, 278. *See also* Spirit-Interpreter
  as all-Knower, 7, 15, 18, 21, 33, 100-101, 319
  as Deliverer, 106, 110-111, 114-117, 196, 290, 294
  as Father, 18, 146, 313
  as Holy One, 16
Grace: idea of Saving, 171, 193, 196, 200, 205, 208, 216
  in relation to Loyalty, 36
  Realm of, 85, 196, 287, 331
  response to, 310-311
Grass Valley, California, 3-4, 11, 13

Harvard University, 7-9, 309, 327
Hermeneutics of Royce, 310, 338, 372 n 18, 386 n 6
History of Latin Christianity, (Milman's), 11, 353 n 1
"Human nature," Royce's meaning of, 213-214

Ideas: leading, 192-193
  Royce's focus on in 1909, 146-147, 195
  Royce's mature meaning of, 190-193, 386 n 3
  as sources of morality and religion, 192-197
  "third" or mediating, 266-267
  three metaphysical, 268, 275
  three most essential Christian, 26, 156-159, 183-204, 206-207, 284, 320; criteria for discerning, 127, 157, 187-188; meaning of, 160; meaning of term, "Christian idea," 212; metaphysics of, 201; Royce's intrinsic reasons for selecting, 190-197;

Ideas *(cont.)*
  Royce's orientation for finding and selecting, 183-190; social and teleological approach to, 176, 195; tests of consistency of, 197-201
Incarnation, 44, 46, 376, 385 n 7
Individualism, as fallen state, 130, 159
Individuality, Royce's "American theory of," 21
Insight, 7, 94-95
Interests (or needs): basic human, 186, 202-203
  in salvation, 94, 113-114
  root of religious insight, 82, 94-95, 97
Interpretation, *231-263*
  comparison-contrast, required in, 108-110, 241-242
  effect of upon philosophical method, 203-204
  as expanding and generalizing, 161-162, 207
  as forming community, 269
  four functions indispensable in, 266-274
  guided by leading ideas, 65-66, 145
  ideal of, its psychological origin, 380 n 8
  moods and tactics operative within, 274-277
  as musement, 219-220, 275-276
  negativity (or self-limitation) and, 175-176
  objects known by, listed, 64-65
  results arising from, 66-67
  as Royce's mature theory of knowing, 141-142, 233
  scriptural, 129-131
  Signs, their mutually illuminating role in, 77-87
  subordinate methods of, 337-338
  text wherein Royce describes, 237

Jesus of Nazareth, 275, 283, 311, 328
Johns Hopkins University, 6, 12

Kingdom of heaven, 196-197, 221
  master's message about, 155, 194, 221, 278, 334

Kingdom of heaven (*cont.*)
  membership in, 77, 159

Levels. *See* Doctrine of Two
Liberalism, 51, 126
Lincoln Grammar School, 5, 13, 15
Life: divine expressed in form of community, 196
  as source of religious insight, 105
  in Unity of the Spirit, 102, 186
Life-problems, Royce's interest in, 22
Limitation (Negation), 27, *174–176*, 374 n 4
Logic, *43–87*. *See also* System *Sigma* and *Epsilon* relation
  as General Science of Order, 54–87
  of interpretation, 265
  relation to *Problem,* 43–44, 50–52, 53, 64–67
  Royce's development in, 43–44, 45–46, 48–52, 54–55, 359–361 n 1–n 11
  of Royce's pragmatic Modes of Action, 51–52
Logic, the Theory of Inquiry (Dewey's), 181
Logos, 376
Logos-Spirit, 94, 189, 192, 195, 203, 316, 328, 342
Lord's Supper, 16
Lost State of morally detached individual, 156–159, 199, 229, 289
Love: destructive, 224
  Paul's transformation of Jesus' doctrine on, 290
  Christian, 193–194
Loyalty: essential form of any genuine social order, 289
  genuine, 139–141, 227–228, 251–254, 379 n 5
  in human religious life, 286–290
  natural, 227
  and *PC's* organization, 283–291
  purification of Royce's 1912 meaning of, 289–290
  religion of, and Christianity, 283–286
  source of religious insight, 102–103
  Third Attitude of will, 177–178, 251–254, 272–274

Man-the-community, 26, *34–35*
Man-the-individual, 26, *34*
Man, "modern," 35, 154
Mary of Nazareth, 316, 383 n 17
Metanoia, 193, 202. *See also* Transformation
Metaphysics: and Being, 215
  of Community life, 333–334
  Royce's mature idea of, 22, 24, 231–232, 334
  Royce's metaphysical method, 231–263
Method: Critique of defective metaphysical methods, 231–232
  Distinctive tendencies in Royce's, 239–240, 258–259
  Interpretive Musement, 161, 264–280, 324–334; effect on philosophical method, 203–204; fecundity of, 331; four procedures in, 331–334; ideals (three methodic) of, 324–327; objective moment of (its logic), 264–266; pragmatic moment of (its moods and tactics), 274–277, 283; problems with, 328–330; subjective moment of (its four functions), 266–274
  Empirico-historical: First Stage, 183–204; Second and Third Stages, 205–218; outlines of, 202, 217
  Metaphysical: First Stage, 232–236; Second Stage, 236–249; Third Stage, 249–262; outline of, 262–263
  Royce's mature philosophical, 174–180, 206–218; analyzed through Royce's major text on, 206–218; compared with James and Dewey, 178–180; linked with loyal love of universe, 176–178; viewed as process of self-limitation, 174–176
Methodology, Royce's Applied Logic, 43–53, esp. 47–48, 361 n 25
Mind or "minded being," *33–34,* 300, 364 n 28
Misrepresentations of Royce, xiii
Modes of action, 62–63, 73–75, 82
Musement, interpretive, 8–9, 23–24, 58. *See also* Interpretation in empirico-historical method, 205

Musement (cont.)
  Royce's musement on idea of community, 219–228
Mysticism, 117, 125

Needs, basic human. See Interests
Negation. See Limitation

O-relation, 54–58, 62–64, 67, 72–73, 364 n 34
Order, General Science of. See also Logic and System *Sigma*
  need for in philosophy, 237
  objective, in *Sigma*, 56–67
  other types of, 72–73
  requisites for, 58–62
  subjective, in Will to Interpret, 67–70
Orthodoxy, 126

Paradox, the Religious, 9, 41, 95, 116, 355 n 74, 366 n 8
Pedagogy, universal, viii, 151–154, 372 n 14
Peircean insight, Royce's, xiii, 9–10, 23
Peirce's article, "A Neglected Argument," 8–9, 45, 168, 321
Pelagianism, American, 314
Perception, 31, 236
Performative contradiction, 238, 248, 253
Person, the human (self), *32–35*, 235–236, 357 n 43
  ethical, metaphysical, psychological views of, 33–34, 112
  structured by bond between needs and Christian ideas, 203
Phenomenology, 33, 368 n 2, 379 n 6
Philosophy: and religion, 298–302
  Royce's mature conception of, 231–263, *331–332*
  Royce's mature method of, 264–279, 324–334
  and Third Attitude of Will, 273–274
  three laws of its life, illustrated, 299
Philosophy of Life, 24
Philosophy of religion, 7–8
  Royce's contributions to, 324–334, esp. 330

Philosophy of religion (cont.)
  Royce's development in, *20–24*, 313–316, 366 n 1, 371 n 2
Philosophy of the Christian religion, 149–150
  Royce's emphasis on *distinctively* Christian, 202–203
  Royce's mode of practicing, 285–286
  truth-test of, 166–170
Platonic Forms, 312
Positivism, Royce's methodological, 27, 111–112, 379 n 5
Pragmatic Maxim, 377 n 2
Praxis, teleological priority over theory, 162
Prayer, 12, 16–17
Problem, meaning of term for Royce, 31
Problem of Christianity, 24. See Writings of Royce
  application of System *Sigma* to, 75–81
  compared with other works, 24–28, 106–107
  experiencing "the problem of Christianity," 147–148
  Introduction, Preface and Lecture 1 of, 144–159
  Lects. II–VIII, 160–170, 205–218
  Lects. IX–XIII, 163–170
  Lects. XIV–XVI, 231–263, esp. 249–263
  orientation to, 144–159
  overview of, 24, 160–173
  title selected by Royce, 149
Process: accelerating rate of, 290–291
  idea of, 163–170
  temporal (time), viii, *160–161,* 163–166, 260–261, 322
Protestantism, 317

Realism, Royce's moderate, 169
Reason, 100, 120
Relation (in logic), 58–59
Religion, 35–40, *37–40,* 93–94
  Dewey's doctrine on, 302–305
  of loyalty, 283–286
  and philosophy, 298–302
Religions, World, 345
Religious objects, 97–98, 114–116
Repentance, idea of. See Transformation

402 INDEX OF TOPICS

Revelation, *40–42,* 297–298, 359 n 68
Roman Catholic Church, 317, 340, 369 n 2 n 5, 382 n 8, 383 n 10

Salvation (Deliverance), 14–16, 38, 93–94, 108–110, 114, 304–305
  need of, 108–110, 229–230
  way of, 111
Scriptures. *See* Bible
Science: and religion, 11, 165, 340–341, 373 n 5
  why continuously successful, 261
Science of Order, 54–71, esp. 58
Secularization, 387
Self: Royce's wide sense of, 33
  the human. *See* Person
Self-identification, 20–21
Self-identity, Royce's philosophical, 3–4
Seminar of 1913–1914, 49–50, 52, 173, 269
Series (in logic), 60–61
Signs, 31, 76–78, 81–82, 85–86, 151–152
  doctrine of, 252, 298
  each event as, 300–301
  fittingness of, 168
  function of, 77–87
Simplification, 292–306
  of Christology, 291–296
  of dogma, 296–298
  of relations between religion and philosophy, 298–302
Sin, Royce's meaning of "original sin," 5, 136
Social consciousness, 252–254
Sorrow, religious mission of, 104
Source, Royce's idea of, 95–96
Sources of Religious Insight. See Writings of Royce
  aim in, 96–99
  basic terms in, 93–96
Spirit, 9, 39, 52, 135, 142, 150, 189–190, 192–193, 196, 212, 279, 288, 296–298, 316, 320–321, 322, 342
  of *any* Community of Interpretation, 265, 268–270
  how to gain effective touch with, 108
  idea of, 3, 305, 321–322
  Interpreter-Spirit of Universe, 301, 365 n 15
  as model interpreter, 189–190

Story (or narrative) theology, 257–258
Strengths of Royce's mature thought, 309–311, *311–315, 318–323*
Structure, in elementary religious experience, 106–121, esp. 110–116
Suffering, 13–14
Supernatural, 303–304, 358 n 59
Superstitions, 284
"Sword of the Spirit," 192, 369 n 4
Symbolism in philosophy of religion, 26, 37–38
System *Sigma,* 54–71, 72–83
  objective order in, *56–67*

Techniques, Royce's philosophical, 374 n 3
Temperament, "essential," 3, 16, 18–19
Terminology, Royce's, 28–42, 56–64, 93–96, 152–154
Theology, Royce's parallel emphases in methodology of, 330
Time and temporal process. *See* Process
Transformation of any self (individual and communal), 123, 193, 202–203, 274, 304–305, 369 n 11, 377 n 36
Trinity, the divine, 44, 46
Truth, 161, 216, 218, 380 n 4

Ultimate (the *eschaton*), 300
Unity of Spirit, 79–80, 82, 85, 98, 102–103, 186
Universal Community. *See* Community
Universe, as Spirit-guided, 151–152, 160–161, 165–166, 275, 278–279
Universe of Discourse, 60
University of California, 6–7

Varieties of Religious Experience (James'), 8, 112, 114, 118, 127, *178–181,* 310
Vatican Council II, 316, 341, 343, 359 n 67, 383 n 10
Voluntarism, 55

Weaknesses of Royce's mature thought, 311–313, *315–318*
Will: in community, 138
  to interpret, 46, 56–71, 66, 68, 212, *243–245,* 322

INDEX OF TOPICS   403

Will (*cont.*)
   in Loyalty, 251–253, 287–289
   in pure logic, 55
   in religious insight, 100–101
   three basic Attitudes of, 74–75, 135, 177–178, 250–254, 273–274, 335–337
Writings of Royce:
   articles: "Error and Truth," 22, 45; "Meditation before the Gate," 18; "Monotheism," 175; "Note," 51–52; "The Holy Grail," 21; "The Relation of the Principles of Logic to the Foundations of Geometry," 44–45; "What is Vital in Christianity," 28
   books: *Conception of God,* 13; *Philosophy of Loyalty,* 25–28, 38, 42;

Writings of Royce: books (*cont.*)
   Principles of Logic, 9, 22, 26, 43–88; *Problem of Christianity,* 9, 10, 15, 19, 20, 22–23, 25–28, 42, 43–44, 50–51, 61, 160–170, *173–305; Religious Aspect of Philosophy,* 7, 21; *Sources of Religious Insight,* 10, 25–28, 42, 44, 48, 75–85, 91–121, 122, 285, 298, 337; *William James and Other Essays,* 25–28, 42, 48; *World and the Individual,* 8, 21, 23–24, 43, 51
World, as Community of Interpretation, 160, 259–260
World religions, 343, 387

'Yes-no' relation, 55, 57–58, 62, 85